THE ROUTLEDGE INTRODUCTION TO AMERICAN WOMEN WRITERS

The Routledge Introduction to American Women Writers considers the important literary, historical, cultural, and intellectual contexts of American women authors from the seventeenth century to the present and provides readers with an analysis of current literary trends and debates in women's literature. This accessible and engaging guide covers a variety of essential topics, such as:

- the transatlantic and transnational origins of American women's literary traditions
- the colonial period and the Puritans
- the early national period and the rhetoric of independence
- the nineteenth century and the Civil War
- the twentieth century, including modernism, the Harlem Renaissance, and the Civil Rights era
- trends in twenty-first century American women's writing
- feminism, gender and sexuality, regionalism, domesticity, ethnicity, and multiculturalism.

The volume examines the ways in which women writers from diverse racial, social, and cultural backgrounds have shaped American literary traditions, giving particular attention to the ways writers worked inside, outside, and around the strictures of their cultural and historical moments to create space for women's voices and experiences as a vital part of American life. Addressing key contemporary and theoretical debates, this comprehensive overview presents a highly readable narrative of the development of literature by American women and offers a crucial range of perspectives on American literary history.

Wendy Martin is Professor of American Literature and American Studies at Claremont Graduate University, USA.

Sharone Williams has a PhD in American Literature and is the Managing Editor of *Women's Studies: An Interdisciplinary Journal.*

ROUTLEDGE INTRODUCTIONS TO AMERICAN LITERATURE

Series Editors: D. Quentin Miller and Wendy Martin

Routledge Introductions to American Literature provide a comprehensive overview of the most important topics in American Literature in its historical, cultural, and intellectual contexts. They present the most up-to-date trends, debates, and exciting new directions in the field, opening the way for further study.

The volumes in the series examine the ways in which both canonical and lesser known writers from diverse cultural backgrounds have shaped American literary traditions. In addition to providing insight into contemporary and theoretical debates and giving attention to a range of voices and experiences as a vital part of American life, these comprehensive volumes offer clear, cohesive narratives of the development of American Literature.

The American literary tradition has always been flexible and mutable. Every attempt to define American Literature as a static body has been thwarted by the nature of its subject, which is—like its nation's ideals—pluralistic, diverse, democratic, and inventive. Our goal in this series is to provide fresh perspectives on many dimensions of the American literary tradition while offering a solid overview for readers encountering it for the first time.

Available in this series:

The Routledge Introduction to African American Literature
D. Quentin Miller and Wendy Martin

The Routledge Introduction to American Modernism
Linda Wagner-Martin

The Routledge Introduction to American Women Writers
Wendy Martin and Sharone Williams

"With *The Routledge Introduction to American Women Writers*, Wendy Martin and Sharone Williams have contributed an authoritative, yet succinct, volume that presents the rich contributions of American women to the literatures of the United States from the seventeenth century to the twenty-first. The accessible prose and impeccable scholarship combine to make this an important study and reference text for both beginning students and seasoned teachers. Martin and Williams place the complex history, literary production, and cultural achievement of women writers seamlessly into the multifaceted fabric of American writing. Informative and engaging, it is one of the best books to guide readers through a gendered understanding of literary and cultural history. What further distinguishes the meticulously contextualized and judiciously focused analytical narrative is the thoughtful inclusion of a broad range of writers from multiple ethnic, racial, social, and political groups. African American, Asian American, Native American, Chicana, and Latina writers are situated, along with American women of British and European descent, as integral to the evolving periods, movements, poetics, and practices characterizing an American literature."

—Thadious M. Davis, University of Pennsylvania

"This book does all it promises and more, presenting a dazzling range and variety of American women's literary expression—and along the way giving a crash course in close to four centuries of American history and culture. Its broad coverage and brisk lucid prose belie literary readings that are consistently subtle and complete. That rare creature, a study of both breadth and depth, *The Routledge Introduction to American Women Writers* is an invaluable resource and scholarly model for students and teachers alike."

—Cathryn Halverson, University of Copenhagen, Denmark

"*The Routledge Introduction to American Women Writers* is a clear, comprehensive, and compact guide to American women's writing from the colonial period to the present. Martin and Williams skillfully locate the literature of American women in the multiple contexts of American history, transnational literary movements, and American cultural movements. They provide an astute analysis of the controversies and trends in American literary studies, and take note of the current important developments in digital technology, ePublishing, social media, graphic fiction, popular genres, and young adult writing. This is an indispensable overview for students and scholars of the American women's literary tradition."

—Elaine Showalter, Princeton University

"In this remarkably concise and deeply informed survey of America's women writers, Wendy Martin and Sharone Williams beautifully expand our awareness of America's literary history. Moving deftly from Anne Bradstreet to Adrienne Rich, from Harriet Jacobs to Marilynne Robinson, the authors have shown that for the past four hundred years woman authors have triumphed in every literary genre. For students and teachers of world literature, this book is a required text."

—Donald Stone, Peking University

THE ROUTLEDGE INTRODUCTION TO AMERICAN WOMEN WRITERS

Wendy Martin and Sharone Williams

Routledge
Taylor & Francis Group

LONDON AND NEW YORK

First published 2016
by Routledge
2 Park Square, Milton Park, Abingdon, Oxon OX14 4RN

and by Routledge
711 Third Avenue, New York, NY 10017

Routledge is an imprint of the Taylor & Francis Group, an informa business

British Library Cataloguing-in-Publication Data
A catalogue record for this book is available from the British Library

Library of Congress Cataloging-in-Publication Data
Names: Martin, Wendy, 1940– author. | Williams, Sharone, author.
Title: The Routledge introduction to American women writers /
Wendy Martin and Sharone Williams.
Description: Milton Park, Abingdon, Oxon ; New York: Routledge, 2016. |
Series: Routledge introductions to American literature | Includes
bibliographical references and index.
Identifiers: LCCN 2015035835 | ISBN 9781138016231 (hardback: alk. paper) |
ISBN 9781138016248 (pbk.: alk. paper) | ISBN 9781315779133 (e-book)
Subjects: LCSH: American literature—Women authors—History and criticism. |
Women and literature—United States.
Classification: LCC PS147 .M36 2016 | DDC 810.9/9287—dc23
LC record available at http://lccn.loc.gov/2015035835

ISBN: 978-1-138-01623-1 (hbk)
ISBN: 978-1-138-01624-8 (pbk)
ISBN: 978-1-315-77913-3 (ebk)

Typeset in Bembo
by Book Now Ltd, London

CONTENTS

ACKNOWLEDGMENTS

As with any project of this magnitude, we have had the help of many people along the way. We would first like to thank series coeditor Quentin Miller, as well as Ruth Hilsdon, Polly Dodson, and the rest of the editorial team at Routledge, who have been wonderfully patient and helpful through this process. We are also grateful for the research assistance of several PhD students from Claremont Graduate University over the last two years, including Daniel Lanza Rivers, Alex Lalama, Laura Bauer, Jeanne-Arli Crocker Hammer, Brian McCabe, and Juliette De Soto; we particularly want to thank Lauren Morrison, who worked with us through the entire research period and whose hard work, enthusiasm, and thoughtful engagement with the material have greatly contributed to this project's success. In addition, we have been fortunate to work with the excellent librarians and staff at the libraries of the Claremont Colleges. We would especially like to thank the Special Collections staff at the Ella Strong Denison Library at Scripps College and Michelle Levers and the ILLiad staff at Honnold/Mudd Library for their assistance with the location of many rare and hard-to-find materials. Many thanks also go to Lesley Rankin, whose editorial services and wisdom have been invaluable, and to the community of writers, readers, and colleagues who have offered insights, advice, and support throughout this project, including Stefani Okonyan, Jan Andres, Rachel Tie Morrison, Emma Álvarez Gibson, and Matthew White. And finally, we would like to acknowledge the many women writers, scholars, and activists who have come before us, and to whom we are deeply grateful. Without their creativity, dedication, and perseverance, this book would not have been possible.

Credit

Chapter 3 of this book includes quotations from "The Contrast" (p. 118) and "On leaving my children John and Jane at school" (p. 142) in Jane Johnston Schoolcraft.

The Sound the Stars Make Rushing Through the Sky: The Writings of Jane Johnston Schoolcraft. Ed. Robert Dale Parker. Philadelphia: University of Pennsylvania Press, 2007. Reprinted with permission of the University of Pennsylvania Press.

INTRODUCTION

Writing has been a countercultural act for women throughout most of the history of the United States, a mark of resistance to the prevalent idea that the world of literature and letters belongs properly to men. This attitude was inherited from the European cultures responsible for colonizing North America and has continued throughout American history, leading to the general suppression of women's writing and the establishment of conceptions of American literature that have largely excluded women's contributions. While the sustained efforts of feminist scholars in the last several decades have significantly reshaped literary canons around the world, in many places this perspective remarkably (and often unconsciously) persists—so much so that a Canadian literature professor made headlines in 2013 when he said in an interview that he didn't teach women's writing because "I don't love women writers enough to teach them, if you want women writers go down the hall. What I teach is guys. Serious heterosexual guys" (Keeler n. pag.). Another easily demonstrable result of this longstanding cultural attitude is the general public's apparent near-total ignorance of the subject. When asked to name famous American writers, most people outside of the halls of college-level English departments who can reel off the names of Mark Twain, Nathaniel Hawthorne, Herman Melville, Jack London, John Steinbeck, and Ernest Hemingway have difficulty coming up with more than one or two women to go along with them; Emily Dickinson might make the cut, but she's lucky if she is joined by Harriet Beecher Stowe or Edith Wharton. And a shockingly low number of the people we've surveyed informally over the course of this project have heard of Nobel laureate Toni Morrison, who has been publishing bestselling and critically acclaimed novels for more than four decades. In spite of the strides of the last forty or fifty years, for many people, American women writers essentially do not exist.

And yet the truth is that American women from across a range of racial, ethnic, and social groups have been writing and sharing their writing with others in significant numbers for nearly four hundred years. Though they faced stiff cultural opposition, women in the seventeenth and eighteenth centuries wrote in secret, circulated texts among friends and family, published under pseudonyms, or presented elaborate justifications for writing as women in order to get their works into print, offering from the beginning their own versions of the most often-told tale in American literature, that of the individual confronting the wilderness or finding her place in a hostile or bewildering society. As the restrictions on women's writing shifted and eroded with changing cultural conceptions of femininity in the nineteenth century, women wrote, published—and sold—in even greater numbers, in spite of the condemnation of writing women as unfeminine or the growing depiction of their texts as silly, sentimental, and decidedly unliterary. And throughout the twentieth century and into the twenty-first, as women have fought for full participation in every aspect of American life, they have continued to write and publish in numbers that their seventeenth-century ancestresses could scarcely have conceived, and to challenge those who still maintain that they don't belong.

From the beginning, women have written every kind of text and in every genre imaginable: poetry, religious treatises, drama, political and polemical essays, textbooks, domestic manuals, newspaper and magazine articles, short stories and novels, philosophies, histories, memoirs and autobiographies, and more. They have been part of and in many cases at the vanguard of every major literary movement and every major protest and reform movement in the United States. While women have written some of the bestselling and most popular books in literary history, their work has often been denigrated, minimized, erased, and suppressed; up until perhaps forty years ago the American literary canon was entirely dominated by the works of white men, and it has taken the work of many feminist scholars to recover women's texts, recuperate their critical reputations, and otherwise rehabilitate the canon to more closely reflect the multiethnic, multiracial, and gender-diverse realities of American literary history. What they have helped to reveal is that from the earliest days of colonization through the present day, women have found ways to act as vital participants in the arenas of American letters and ideas, offering their own experiences and points of view and challenging others, shaping and reshaping aesthetic considerations and literary forms, and lending their voices to the long traditions of declaration, exploration, protest, and dissent that are so important to American cultural mythologies.

While there are many scholarly texts that address much narrower segments of American women's writing in much greater detail, or essay collections that look broadly at women's writing across all of American history (the 2012 *Cambridge History of American Women's Literature*, edited by Dale M. Bauer, is an excellent recent example), there has not yet been anything like what we have hoped to accomplish with this book: that is, to provide a concise but fairly comprehensive overview of women's participation in American literary history. In a time when most people take for granted that women can and should be able to write, and when women's texts are readily available in bookstores, libraries, and other places, many people have asked whether such a history is necessary, whether it makes a difference who writes a book as long as it is good, or interesting, or meets some other subjective criteria. But the richness of this literary heritage and the persistence of the cultural, social, and political structures that have conspired to obscure it suggest that such a history is in fact deeply important, not because the history of American men's writing should be supplanted but because it can help to restore an important part of the larger picture of American literature that has long been missing. This book can help to fill in some of those gaps.

Toril Moi has famously observed that feminist criticism is built on the principle that "no account can ever be neutral" (xiii), and this account certainly isn't. It originates from two scholars with deeply feminist viewpoints; it has as its foundation key assumptions about structural and social inequalities based primarily on race and gender that have been built into the fabric of the United States from its earliest colonial history and continue to affect the study of literature and the formation of American literary canons; and its development has been guided by a set of priorities related to ours and others scholars' efforts to address these historical injustices. Thus, for example, while we deal with women writers and texts that have become canonical in the decades since feminist scholars began to recuperate women's literary history, we place them alongside writers and texts that are less known or studied but offer equally important perspectives. While we celebrate the historical movements that have worked to advance the rights and opportunities of women, we also recognize the ways that the women in these movements have consciously or otherwise reproduced the white supremacist and heteropatriarchal values of larger U.S. culture, to the detriment and even the active harm of women of color and queer women; and while we generally move chronologically in our discussions of literary and cultural movements, we also work to foreground the experiences, texts, and when possible the scholarly perspectives of those most nearly concerned when addressing subjects such as Indian removal, slavery and abolition, and the representation of various marginalized groups. And we know that the term feminism wasn't coined until 1912, but we identify works from across U.S. history as having feminist qualities based on the belief that women who have staked claims for themselves as able and deserving participants in cultural, political, and intellectual discourse have something in common with those of us who subscribe to the broadest present-day definition of feminism, the belief that people are equally deserving of rights and opportunities regardless of gender or other categories of identification.

We also recognize that American myths about the North American continent and the origins of the United States are tied heavily to the idea of brave white European colonists subduing a howling wilderness in the name of religious and political freedom. But the truth is that regardless of the various philosophical justifications for the actions taken, the geopolitical entity now known as the United States was built through the colonization of already inhabited lands, and through a series of genocidal campaigns against the sovereign Native nations who occupied them. Similarly, the popular perception of the United States as a nation whose gleaming cities, agricultural bounty, and material prosperity are the natural result of its exceptional national character is belied by another ugly truth: that the economic foundation of the United States was built on the forced labor of millions of enslaved African Americans over nearly three centuries. While chattel slavery is no longer the law of the land, the economic and cultural hierarchies of race created by this system are entrenched in all levels of American society, and the wounds it inflicted have not healed. And there are many other marginalized groups in the U.S.—immigrants from Asia, Latin America, Africa, and the Middle East, lesbian, gay, bisexual, trans, and queer or questioning (LGBTQ) individuals, and of course women from every ethnic, racial, and social group—who have been excluded from full participation in American life in more or less overt ways. Millions of Americans have complicated relationships with the United States and find it difficult to reconcile the sacred American rhetoric of freedom, democracy, and equal opportunity for all with their lived experiences as Americans. These considerations make it clear that the ways we talk about and define American literature and its traditions have political, cultural, and deeply personal implications as well as scholarly ones.

While some reductiveness is inherent in the creation of this kind of historical narrative, we have also tried to resist the temptation to read the literature of the past through its relationship to the present. We do trace the progress of women's participation in the literary marketplace, but we try to avoid relying on an evolutionary model of the literature itself, which by its definition tends to overemphasize linear development and exclude writers and works that don't fit into the idea of progress toward ever-greater feminist awareness. Instead, we do our best to embrace what Angela Vietto has called the "discontinuity" of women's literary history (12); we examine the ways that women throughout American history have played roles in the exploration of ideas that are central to American culture and consciousness, attempting to hold in tension the ways texts and their authors were understood in their own time with the shifting and often contradictory ways those texts have been interpreted in the years since. We have undoubtedly made some missteps along the way, but all of our choices have been motivated by the desire to present American women's literary history as honestly and justly as possible.

Many of the central assumptions upon which this book is based have to do with the ways we define American literature and women's participation within its traditions. This is a knotty task complicated by numerous factors, including the nature of the United States' founding, its continually shifting geographical borders, the many peoples who have been pulled into its compass as a result, and the terms of acceptable literary production. Each of these factors has a bearing on the questions that go into the shaping of a definition of American literature: Who counts as an American, and when does American literature begin? Where are the borders of this literature, and how do they shift over time? And what kinds of texts are considered as literary production? These are the basic questions that need to be answered in order for the claim of a broad study of American women writers to cohere.

These questions of definition might seem separate from one another, but they are not. We can't get very far in asking who counts as an American before we are confronted by questions of what, when, and why. It seems somewhat clear that women who immigrated to the areas that were or would become the United States would fall into the category of American writers, even as they maintained links to the cultural and literary traditions from which they came, but what of those women who have been unwilling participants in the American experiment? Do the oral and textual cultural transmissions of indigenous American peoples count as American literature? What about the contributions of enslaved African Americans? If so, when do these cultural transmissions become "American," and what are the political implications of these choices? Who has the right to make them? Native American literary traditions have been co-opted into American literature, but each Native nation has a history and cultural traditions that extend back far before Europeans first reached North American shores, and which have continued irrespective of, independent of, and in many cases in spite of Euroamerican efforts at overwriting and erasure. Enslaved Africans likewise carried preexisting traditions with them when they were brought forcibly into contact with Euroamerican ways of life, traditions which are imbricated within the earliest African American cultural productions.

Each of these cultural traditions deserves its own careful consideration. They are not in and of themselves a common American heritage to be celebrated without respectful understanding of the repeated traumas to which they are so intimately connected. Nor can Native American traditions of cultural transmission simply be grafted into American literature now that scholars have begun to recognize their value. Attempts to do so in effect perpetuate the cultural violence against Native cultures that Euroamerican institutions have enacted along with the physical violence. As Native scholar Robert Allen Warrior (Osage) has noted, to treat Native American literature as "belong[ing] first to the national literature of the United States and only secondarily to itself and to the literature of other colonized people ... smacks of assimilationism" and a perhaps willful ignorance of the fact that Native nations are sovereign political entities with the right of self-determination ("Marginal" 30). Even using the term "American" to describe this literature involves political assumptions that privilege a Euroamerican-centered interpretation of the events that have transpired on the North American continent in the last five hundred years.

At the same time, we cannot pretend that the Euroamerican, Native, and African American cultures existed in vacuums independently of one another. There were complex relationships between Euroamerican colonizers and the Native colonized that involved cooperation and friendship as well as exploitation, resistance, and enmity, and mutual fear, hatred, and desire, intermingled; complex, but marked by an imbalance of power and a will to dominate on the part of the colonizers, and a paternalistic justification for this imbalance based on notions of cultural and racial superiority.[1] The relationships between Euroamericans and enslaved African Americans were just as complex, and more imbalanced. Such intimate contact between cultures makes exchange and influence on one another inescapable, but the nature of the exchange and influence is always inflected by the unequal power dynamic. Theft, appropriation, and exploitation are the most common results, but there is a broader spectrum, and it is this aspect that needs to be delineated as much as possible.

How, then, should such cultural traditions be treated in the context of a history like this one? It seems grotesque to identify as American the literary productions of Native Americans, enslaved African Americans, and others long denied even the basic protections of American citizenship—and yet it seems only slightly less bizarre to exclude them as if they did not exist in the same physical and cultural space as the literary productions of Euroamerican writers. Instead, it is our goal to pick out a careful path between the two. We are reluctant to claim Native writings as specifically "American," given the colonialist implications of such a choice, and we want to acknowledge the sovereignty of Native nations and their right to define their own literatures; we also want to acknowledge the cultural violence that stripped enslaved Africans of their languages, histories, and communities. However, we recognize that for better or worse, since the initial contact between indigenous and European cultures and the introduction of African slavery in North America, the cultures and histories of these peoples have been bound up with the cultures and history of the United States; that writers from dominant and marginalized groups have participated in and commented on the same historical events and the same literary and cultural traditions; that the traditions of these groups have overlapped and changed each other, reacting to and incorporating parts of each other in a continuous process of adaptation; and that the perspectives of writers from outside the dominant group in many cases offer a much needed corrective, helping to de-center the accepted Euroamerican understandings of these events and traditions. Thus, we include in our discussions the works of Native American and African women that interact with, respond to, and resist Euroamerican literatures and traditions alongside those of Euroamerican women and immigrant women with Asian, Latin, and South American ethnic and racial heritages, but we also note the complexities involved in these choices where possible.

The when and where questions of American literature have been no less subject to debate than the questions of who. Arguments over when literature became definitively American (as opposed to British or otherwise) have carried on since the beginning of North American literary productions, and some scholars have as a result moved toward transatlantic considerations of colonial literature that acknowledge the middle ground it occupies. But since the work of the earliest colonial women writers is profoundly affected by the North American environments within which it was created, we see no reason not to begin our examinations of American literature with them. In addition, the rise of transnational studies in literature in recent years has called attention to the artificiality of national and even geographical barriers when it comes to examining the influences that act upon various literatures, especially in the Internet age.[2] It has also raised not insignificant questions about terminology related to the United States' arrogation of a term, American, which should properly apply to all of North, Central, and South America. How does the use of national boundaries in the study of literature limit our ability to understand it? And is it appropriate to have a discussion of "American" literature that examines only work produced in the United States? In response to these and similar questions, many scholars have expanded their research across borders, hemispheres, and oceans in order to better reflect the historical realities of literary and cultural transmission; others have sought new terminology to describe the literary productions of the United States while continuing to examine the influence of the conceptual United States, "imagined community" though it may be, on these texts.[3] While we continue to use American as one of multiple designations for the literature we discuss, and while we have limited our discussions to the literatures produced within the areas that are or would eventually become the United States, we also work to consider the broader contexts of these writers and texts and the conditions in which they were produced.

And the question of what constitutes American literature has found increasing salience in recent years, especially in considerations of the lives of colonial and early American women. Literary study in general has expanded to include letters, journals and diaries, manuscripts, both circulated and uncirculated, and other materials that were unpublished at the time of their creation; because of the limited publication options historically available to women, these unpublished materials have become an important resource for scholars studying women's literature, especially scholars examining women's movements between and access to public and private spaces. While we cannot look at every text in this vein, we consider both published and unpublished materials within this study as part of the body of women's written expression. But some scholars look to broaden our understandings of women's texts even further. For example, Carla Mulford has recently argued that the study of early American women's culture should be expanded to consider women's oratory, as well as "all forms of women's symbolic expression," including painting, decorative stencil work, and quilt- and clothing-making, noting that most women in this period had little of the technical skill or leisure time that writing requires; in looking only at women's written work, she suggests, we may be wrongly limiting our view of "women's attitudes about and their participation in" social and political conversations ("Writing" 114).

It is a tantalizing idea. How might the concept of women's "symbolic expression" be transformed if we thought about quilting and other expressive household activities as part of the same networks of cultural transmission that encompass poetry, drama, and various narratives, as being equally expressive of ideas about love, friendship, progress and justice, faith, the American experience, and the human condition? Such analyses will undoubtedly enhance our understandings of women's lives across the early colonial period, but they are largely outside the scope of this book. We do consider some oratory and several dictated texts, but our primary focus is on written expression. We recognize that this emphasis can give an inappropriate weight to wealthy and educated women at the expense of nearly everyone else, and we aim to combat this minimization and erasure by acknowledging and addressing these sites of oppression where we find them. We do not claim that by primarily studying written expression we are addressing the totality of the cultural contributions women have made in the United States. But we also recognize that for most of European and American history, even white, wealthy women writers have largely been seen as trespassers in the domain of educated white men, and women writers of color exponentially more so. One of the main objectives of this book is to examine the ways in which women with varying levels of social, racial, and economic privilege have intervened and participated in these literary traditions, and the ways in which through their participation, the traditions have themselves been changed. Written expression may offer only a partial view of women's participation in American culture, especially in the colonial years, but that partial view is still rich and important.

The defining qualities of American literature are continually subject to revisions as literary and cultural scholars reevaluate existing material, make new discoveries, and reconceptualize interpretive frameworks. But while these questions cannot be answered once and for all, we can answer them for this book, in 2015, considering the broader currents of the study of American literature as well as the narrower constraints of this particular project. Thus, while we recognize the many directions in which the definition of American women's writing could be broadened, for the purposes of this study we are considering texts written, dictated, or in the case of some speeches and songs orally transmitted and transcribed; by women from a range of racial and ethnic backgrounds who saw themselves as working within, against, or otherwise in relation to Euroamerican traditions of letters, primarily in English; published, circulated in manuscript form, or otherwise intended for sharing, distribution, or recordkeeping; bounded geographically by the limits of the Euroamerican-occupied lands that were or would become part of the United States at the time of composition; beginning with the colonization of the North American mainland and ending with the present day.

In terms of organization, we have generally followed the common chronological divisions used to discuss American literature, although we have divided the colonial period into separate chapters on the seventeenth and eighteenth centuries to better address the cultural and social shifts that occurred as colonial activity expanded. Subsequent chapters address the nineteenth century through the conclusion of the American Civil War, the postbellum and fin de siècle years, the interwar period, and the second half of the twentieth century, finishing with a coda on literature in the twenty-first century. While the book moves chronologically, there may be some overlap from chapter to chapter because we have chosen to follow literary movements and themes rather than strict periodization. We have also allowed these considerations to dictate chapter length to some degree; it should be noted that Chapter 6 is particularly long because we believed it was more important to address the interrelated literary and cultural movements of the late twentieth century and the lengthy careers of many of the writers involved than to impose a chronological break. Each chapter provides historical, social, and cultural contexts for the major movements and writers of the period it addresses, and while several writers are mentioned and discussed in each chapter, we have also given deeper focus to a few writers and their works in each chapter as representatives of particular movements or ideas. With considerations of length in mind, we have given the major sections and subsections in each chapter clear headings to allow for quicker reference and greater ease of reading.

We do however want to emphasize that this book does not represent an attempt at imposing coherence on what is in fact an incredibly diverse group of women involved in the creation of texts that vary infinitely in terms of genre, form, subject matter, perspective, style, and a number of other categories. Nor is it (or could it be) a detailed examination of every woman writer who falls within the frameworks outlined above. Each woman in this book deserves to be and in most cases already is the subject of her own book or books, and there are many more deserving women writers even than those we are able to address in this relatively narrow volume. Our aim is not to create a definitive narrative of the history of women writers in the United States, but to provide a reasonably comprehensive overview that traces major themes and developments, one that provokes questions in our readers and points them in directions for further exploration. We are telling only one of many possible versions of this story, a version which of necessity gives more attention to some writers and less to others—and determining which writers and texts to include and which, for sheer lack of space, to leave out has been one of this project's greatest challenges. While we can only give each writer a fraction of the full attention she deserves in this book, it is our hope that this narrative will prompt readers to dig deeper, to question—even to hotly disagree!—and in so doing develop their own versions and understandings of the long, beautiful, and diverse history of American women writers.

Notes

1 For more on the development of justifications for slavery in the early colonial period, see Chaplin.
2 For one example of the ways scholarship is moving in this direction, see Marlene Daut's review essay "Daring to Be Free / Dying to Be Free: Toward a Dialogic Haitian-US Studies."
3 The term "imagined community" is taken from Benedict Anderson's landmark text on the rise of nationalism by the same name; see Anderson for more.

1

ACROSS THE ATLANTIC

Women in British North America

When eighteen-year-old poet Anne Bradstreet boarded the *Arbella* in April of 1630, she left nearly everything she knew behind her on the shore: a home filled with cultured friends, ample food, the best books, and all the comforts of wealth afforded her as the daughter and wife of genteel and high-ranking managers on the estate of the Earl of Lincoln. Ahead of her lay the blue-black expanses of the Atlantic Ocean, her home for the next three months, and then what? She had no way of knowing.

Bradstreet sailed with several family members, including her husband, Simon Bradstreet, and her father, Thomas Dudley. Along with John Winthrop and other colonial investors, they had founded the New England Company (later renamed the Massachusetts Bay Company) and recruited several hundred of their fellow dissatisfied Puritans to join them in settling the New England shores, believing at the other end of their voyage they would find the makings of a Promised Land for true believers. But Anne Bradstreet's devotion was less to a religious cause than to her father, the man who facilitated her education in history, literature, philosophy, and languages, and to her husband, her love for whom was the source of her most enduring poetry. Simultaneously part of and outside this cultural movement, Bradstreet was on a ship bound for a world about which she could have known almost nothing. No drawings or paintings of Bradstreet survive, so we do not know what she looked like; we have only her clear, slanting handwriting to show us the lines and life of a Puritan woman in seventeenth-century New England.

Many of us think of the Puritans when imagining early American colonial history: brave people in buckled shoes crossing storm-tossed seas in the quest for religious freedom. We picture their arrival on the rocky shores of a New World, a vast and empty wilderness peopled by a handful of peaceful, generous

Native Americans who were largely content to remain in the background of the more important story being told. The narrative of the Puritans in New England has taken a powerful hold in the American imagination, largely due to the Puritans' fusion of sacred and secular history and their conviction that they were establishing a New Jerusalem blessed by God to be an example and inspiration to the world (Bercovitch *Puritan* x). While some of the religious elements have faded since the *Mayflower* first crossed the Atlantic, this belief in the American project as exceptional remains, and the Puritans still loom large in Americans' conceptions of themselves and their national origins, and in the writing of many American women. For this reason, it's important to understand the origins of this view—but it's just as important to acknowledge how much this view of the colonial period misrepresents and excludes.

North America was not quite what the Puritan settlers were led to believe it would be. For more than a century, European imperial powers—including France, Spain, Portugal, the Netherlands, and England—had been attempting to lure colonists across the Atlantic with reports of plenteous lands, unpopulated except for some primitive, heathen people with a childlike simplicity who saw Europeans as gods or powerful sorcerers because of their weaponry and apparent ability to fell their enemies with disease.[1] But North America was frequently a deadly place for Europeans in the early seventeenth century. The hot, humid summers of the mid-Atlantic region killed as many people as the fierce winters of the Northeast, food was often hard to come by, and the labor required to carve out even the loosest approximations of European civilization was backbreaking. What's more, the land was far from empty or free for the taking. Native North Americans numbered in the millions, thousands of distinct groups with unique languages, traditions, and cultural practices who had inhabited every region of the continent for millennia (Thornton 69). These Native cultures were sophisticated and well-established, and many had experience with European explorers and traders; European goods had made their way through long-established Native trading networks, reaching much farther than Europeans themselves had explored, prior to full-scale settlement of North America (Kicza 38).

European colonists came to North America for various reasons. The majority of the colonies were founded by commercial charter or imperial edict, based on promises of gold, agricultural riches, slaves, land, and empire; even on the *Mayflower*, the majority sailed in search of economic opportunity.[2] But European settlers were also inspired by imperial rivalries born of religious, economic, and political concerns. The tensions between Protestant and Catholic powers that led to the Thirty Years' War across most of continental Europe naturally spilled into North America, and colonial fervor was fed by Protestant and Catholic empires' desires to save this new world, its resources, and its inhabitants from each other (Pestana 72–3; Lepore 9). The Algonquian-speaking woman known as Pocahontas, who converted to Christianity, married an English man, took an English name, and traveled Europe in the attire of a perfect English gentlewoman, served as a useful representative of the "transformative power of English money and religion"

(K. Brown 43), inspiring investors and potential colonists alike as a symbol in the European struggle for world dominance.

Pocahontas and John Smith, the *Mayflower* Pilgrims celebrating the first Thanksgiving, and the quest for religious freedom all make appearances in the texts we frequently study from early American literature. Notably, these texts are all in English, written by English explorers and settlers. Despite the polyglot diversity of the early colonial period, English literature by English settlers has historically received the most attention from scholars of American literary history. Only in the last half-century has the canon expanded to include Spanish, French, and Dutch writers, and the inclusion of Native American texts, complicated as that is, has been more recent still.[3] But when it comes to women writing in the early colonial period, the range is still fairly narrow: of the handful of women writers from the seventeenth century discovered thus far, almost all are Puritans, which shifts any discussion of women writers in the early colonial period toward New England almost as a matter of course. One obvious reason is that the English came to dominate the part of North America that would become the United States, and thus English colonists' perspectives and cultural productions have dominated the narrative of how American literature came to be. While scholars have made significant efforts in the last fifty years to expand our understanding of early American literature outside this narrow scope, there is still much work to be done.[4]

The Puritan narrative is both powerful and seductive in the way it fuses a religious sense of covenant and promise with commercial and imperial enterprise. Convinced they were leaving behind the corruption and religious tyranny of the Old World and making something new and sacred, the Puritans laid the foundation for an American national identity based on the denial of the heterogeneity of its origins and a profound sense of the rightness of their endeavor; they are the first "rebel-icons" in the "heroic lineage of dissent" that features so prominently in American cultural mythologies (Bercovitch *Jeremiad* xvii). The power of this narrative in the American imagination has far outlasted the Puritans themselves; its pervasiveness suggests another reason scholars have spent so much energy on the Puritans, but they were in fact only one of many groups with a stake in colonial ventures.

Beyond the Puritans' cultural legacy, there are practical reasons studies of early American women writers have tended to focus on white women in the Northeast. New England boasted the first printing press in the U.S. colonies, set up in 1638 by Elizabeth Harris Glover at the newly established Harvard College (Hudak 9–19), as well as the first volume of poetry by any colonist, from Bradstreet, printed in London, in 1650.[5] Demographically, there were more and wealthier white women in New England than in other mainland colonies, where most white women were servants, and they had higher rates of literacy than other colonial regions because Puritan women were generally encouraged to read the Bible, keep spiritual journals, and prepare testimonies as required for church membership (Innes 156) in what little leisure time they might have. On the other hand, even if Native American or African women had the education or leisure time for literary endeavors, their cultures had no alphabetic literacy. Most slave owners prevented enslaved Africans from learning to read or write because literacy was thought to precipitate rebellion, and while some Native American women were encouraged to attend missionary schools, many considered writing as the tool "through which their identity was most forcefully erased" (Wyss 123). Thus, whether by lack of opportunity, choice, or other circumstances, writing was not a primary form of cultural expression for Native American and African women in the seventeenth century.[6]

The kinds of texts scholars look at have also tended to limit the range of studied literature by women in the early colonial period to Puritans. In this volume we focus largely on circulated and printed texts written in English, but writing was not the primary form of cultural expression for most women in this period. While outside of Puritan communities only the wealthiest colonial women would have had the resources to produce written texts, Carla Mulford notes women of "all relevant races and classes" participated in oral and visual cultural practices, including storytelling, painting and home decor, and quilt- and clothing-making—all significant forms of "symbolic expression" potentially rendered invisible as cultural work in a discussion that only addresses writing ("Writing" 114). Although these cultural productions are outside the scope of this book, it's important to acknowledge that the small number of written texts by women is no indication of the volume of women's cultural expression; similarly, though we talk primarily about New England women writers because they wrote the majority of the available texts, we recognize they represent only a fragment of women's experience in the early colonial period.

Although there were only a handful of women writing in the seventeenth century, between them they generated what would become the major modes of written expression for a much wider variety of colonial women over the next hundred years. Kirstin Wilcox identifies three broad and overlapping categories for early American women's writing: "poetry, life-writing, and testimony" (56). In the early colonial period, these categories appeared as the poetry of Anne Bradstreet, the spiritual autobiographies and writings of Sarah Symmes Fiske, Bathsheba Bowers, and others, and the captivity narrative of Mary Rowlandson. These women engaged with literary, spiritual, and intellectual traditions in texts that reached beyond colonial boundaries to the wider world. Bradstreet's poetry engaged her male contemporaries in debates about philosophy, medicine, history, and gender and provided frank, vulnerable explorations of the difficulties and joys of her domestic life in New England, but always made a case for feminine subjectivity. And while it might be difficult for twenty-first century readers to think of the spiritual autobiographies and religious tracts written by Fiske and Bowers as radical or feminist texts, their religious practice and "religious sensibilities" gave them a sense of specifically female worth and authority (Schweitzer "Body" 406). Finally, Mary Rowlandson's captivity narrative engages intimately with issues of Native–settler relations, gender, and faith, offering a critique of the patriarchal religious and social structure and more nuanced portraits of Native Americans than most of her peers. The work of these women writers is integral to the intellectual and cultural fabric of the seventeenth century, and their writing places them at the genesis of the tradition of dissent, protest, and reform that would shape the American cultural and political landscape.

Anne Bradstreet, poetry, and colonial life

Anne Dudley Bradstreet was born in 1612 in Northampton, England, to parents of considerable means and position. She was steeped in Puritanism from birth—taught to examine her thoughts and actions to detect sinfulness, repent, and present herself to God with a clean conscience (*Works* 4)—but her father also gave her a deep appreciation for learning and the arts. She read widely in poetry, history, philosophy, and science, as well as Puritan staple texts such as the Geneva Bible and Foxe's *Actes and Monumentes*. Her father also taught her French, Latin, Greek, and Hebrew and encouraged her to write poetry. Bradstreet's education was highly unusual for the women of her time, but it was consistent with earlier Elizabethan traditions that placed value on women's intelligence.[7]

At age sixteen, Anne married Simon Bradstreet, and when she was eighteen, they emigrated to New England with a group of family and friends. They would relocate several times in their first fifteen years in New England; each relocation brought them closer to the shifting frontiers of English settlement and likely threatened Bradstreet's health, already weakened by childhood illnesses, the difficulties of colonial life, and the births of six children between 1633 and 1645 (two more children would follow in 1648 and 1652). Simon was often called away from home by his political responsibilities, leaving Anne to care for their household and eight children. His success meant the Bradstreets were more well-off than many of their fellow colonists, and Anne had indentured English, Native American, and possibly enslaved African servants to help care for their large home and family.[8] Undoubtedly, their comfortable financial situation and the help of servants helped make Anne's poetry possible.

Bradstreet's career as a poet is all the more unusual because of the closely intertwined religious and social structures that governed the behavior of New England Puritan women. Christianity in the Puritan colonies was a dissenting form of Protestantism that rejected the hierarchical structure of the Church of England in favor of the decentralized religious authority of the church congregation.[9] They believed in a "radically unmediated" relationship between the individual and God (Fitzpatrick 6), in which God could make individual believers more like Christ as each individual carefully examined and repented of their sinful thoughts and actions. Like John Calvin, they believed God had separated people into the saved, or "elect," and the damned, but New England Puritans took election even farther, believing they were responsible for establishing God's true church to usher in the Second Coming of Christ (Bercovitch *Puritan* xiii). To be successful in their sacred task, they had to create a cohesive Christian community that valued the physical, social, and spiritual needs of the group over the needs of any individual (Fitzpatrick 4). If each individual was faithful to God and to the community, God would bless and protect them, but hardship and struggle were signs of God's displeasure, requiring individual and community soul-searching.

Religious and social relationships in the English colonies were structured around a patriarchal social system under which male heads of household controlled labor, property, and sexual access to the women of their households, while women were expected to be quiet, respectful, and obedient to first fathers and then husbands. To this, Puritans added the expectation of Christian modesty, appropriately subdued dress, and chastity (K. Brown 32). In England and in the colonies, a woman was all but invisible outside the home, with no legal records or public presence unsanctioned by a husband or father—and she was supposed to be content to be that way. Women who stepped outside their prescribed roles were called into court to account for their unruliness and tried for scolding their husbands and neighbors, sexual immorality, including premarital sex and adultery, and witchcraft (K. Brown 30). In New England, women were prosecuted for membership in radical sects such as the Quakers, who encouraged women's public speaking and interpretation of scripture—activities seen as a threat to both state and church authority (K. Brown 141–3). In this way, religious dissent was translated as a failure to adhere to proper gender roles; feminizing dissent as merely the work of uncontrollable women was a way of containing it and shoring up the existing order.

The consequences of unruly womanhood were well known to Bradstreet: her husband was one of the magistrates that evicted Anne Hutchinson from the Massachusetts Bay Colony in 1638 for preaching and questioning Puritan doctrine, and Bradstreet's own sister, Sarah Keayne, was subject to public censure and disinheritance after returning from a visit to England in 1647 with "a bad case of unfettered self-expression" (Schweitzer "Body" 406). Thus, it is not surprising that Bradstreet's poetry is occupied with questions of gender and a woman's proper place in the world, full of defensive maneuvers designed to protect her reputation as a modest Christian gentlewoman whose activities are sanctioned by the appropriate men, and to carefully circumvent the many restrictions on female speech.

Based on the span of her publication and revision history, we know poetry was a personal and intellectual practice that spanned Bradstreet's adult life. Her first volume of poetry, *The Tenth Muse, Lately Sprung Up in America, by a Gentlewoman of those Parts*, was published in London in 1650. The subjects of the poems were largely historical and philosophical, addressing topics in medicine, philosophy, nature, ancient history, and contemporary British political and social events; they also included elegies to Queen Elizabeth, Sidney, and du Bartas. It sold well and was praised by Cotton Mather and other eminent Puritans (Martin *Triptych* 28–9). Bradstreet would continue to write new poetry and revise her earlier poems until her death in 1672, but her work was not published again in her lifetime. In 1678, a second edition of *The Tenth Muse* was published with revised versions of the poems from the first edition as well as several previously unpublished works, including epitaphs to her mother and father, personal poems to her husband and children, and the longer "Contemplations," exploring questions of religious faith. Although Bradstreet never intended their publication, these personal poems are some of Bradstreet's most frequently read today. While Bradstreet was regarded mainly as a historical curiosity for nearly three hundred years, in the late twentieth century feminist scholars brought attention to the artistry and literary merit of her work, and she is now widely acknowledged as a poet of great intellectual accomplishment and emotional force.

During her lifetime and since, many groups have wanted to claim Bradstreet as one of their own: a submissive Puritan daughter, wife, and mother, a symbol of the cultural sophistication of New England, and a covert feminist operative in a deeply patriarchal culture, among other things. But Bradstreet was more complex than any one label allows. She was invested in the social structures that dictated filial and wifely obedience, but her probing of her Puritan faith and experiences and of history, philosophy, and gender in her poetry reveal her as someone who loved her earthly life and questioned the religious, social, and political systems that told her how she ought to experience it. Bradstreet likely would never have identified herself as a radical, but her deep involvement in the world of ideas in her public poetry and her exploration of the emotional depth and validity of the female experience in her later, private work reveal her as a poet with feminist concerns.

The Tenth Muse (1650) opens with careful delineations of Bradstreet's limited authority and ambition, including reassurances from her brother-in-law that Bradstreet has not neglected her familial duties to compose poetry. In spite of modest disclaimers of the "obscure" merits of her poetry (*Works* 6–8), Bradstreet's work is scholarly, intellectual, and philosophical, following established male poetic forms and traditions. In observing these dictated forms and writing on such impersonal subjects as history, medicine, and philosophy, Bradstreet is in a sense obeying masculine poetic models that privilege the great deeds of men and public life over the more quotidian details of life in the home and family. The poems included in the first edition have been criticized for this very reason by feminist scholars writing at the time of Bradstreet's scholarly rediscovery; they found the earlier public poetry imitative and often clumsy, suggesting Bradstreet's lack of confidence in her poetic ability, particularly compared to her later, private poetry, which is more assured and emotionally compelling.[10] Bradstreet herself felt the insufficiency of her early work, and she continued to revise her public poems over the rest of her life. But scholars have recently begun to reevaluate her early public poetry, not just for purported quality but for what it might reveal about Bradstreet and her intentions. Ivy Schweitzer and others have linked Bradstreet's strategies to a kind of mimicry in the style of Luce Irigaray, in which a dominant discourse designed to exclude women's voices is repeated in ways that parody, ironize, and perhaps even subvert that discourse (Schweitzer "Anne" 293; Wright 243); Alice Henton has found a "preponderance of feminine content and feminine strategies" (304); Carrie Galloway Blackstock has described Bradstreet's quaternions in particular as evidence of her ability to perform several self-constructed identities (222); and Rosamond Rosenmeier, Tamara Harvey, Timothy Sweet, and others have explored the ways in which Bradstreet practices a kind of doubleness, writing poetry that appears to conform to a particular standard but can be read in potentially subversive ways.

The introductory letter and prefatory poems of *The Tenth Muse* hasten to assure readers that in spite of her unfeminine habit of writing poetry, Anne Bradstreet still knows her place. Even the conditions of the publication—the omission of Bradstreet's name, and a title implying Bradstreet is the muse to greater men rather than an artist in her own right—reinforce this narrative. The male-authored prefatory poems are careful to remind readers of the preeminence of men in the world of poetry: for all her surprising talent, Bradstreet is only borrowing "Chaucers Boots, and Homers Furrs" (Ward 15), a reference to the Aristotelian argument that men's bodies were warmer, more fully developed, and therefore superior to women's bodies (Harvey 3). Bradstreet's poetry appears to affirm this point of view. She hews closely to traditional poetic forms, obeying the conventions of the quaternion and the elegy and demonstrating an almost slavish devotion to the heroic couplet, as if to confirm her determination to adhere to the bounds of poetry dictated by men. Her avowals of modesty and lavish praise for the male poets who precede her signal Bradstreet's understanding that she is beneath them in the poetic (and gender) hierarchy. Yet Bradstreet's poetry reveals a deep knowledge of subject matter and traditional forms that allows her to take advantage of poetic conventions, make knowing allusions, and revise her source material in ways that undercut her pose of inferiority and would have resonated with careful, similarly knowledgeable readers (Schweitzer "Anne" 294; Wright 244). In other cases, Bradstreet uses established traditions as an excuse to make still veiled but more specifically feminist claims. As several scholars have pointed out, the explicitly misogynistic matter in Nathaniel Ward's prefatory poem and Bradstreet's demure responses were not merely territorial posturing and self-defense, but were part of the poetic and philosophical tradition of the *querelle des femmes*, or battle of the sexes, a humorous but sharply barbed series of unofficial exchanges in which poets and philosophers debated the virtues of men and the vices of women, or vice versa.[11] This may reduce the male poets' participation to something on the level of an old joke newly rehearsed, but it also allows Bradstreet to respond in a way that is considerably more "invested in the actual status of women," even if it requires readers "attuned to [the] irony" of her position (Harvey 23, 32).

In spite of her declarations of feminine modesty in her prologue, Bradstreet also takes on traditionally masculine subjects throughout her poetry, critiquing specific political events and masculine hierarchies and expressing her desire for a different kind of rule, particularly in the figure of Queen Elizabeth I. In her elegy, Bradstreet praises Elizabeth for having "wiped off th' aspersion of her Sex, / That women wisdome lack to play the Rex" (*Works* 156, ll. 29–30)[12] by bringing prosperity and peace to England while still being mighty and fearsome in war, superior not only to female rulers such as Dido, Cleopatra, and Zenobia, but to most kings as well. But Bradstreet is also more pointedly political, suggesting France would quickly abolish laws preventing women from inheriting the throne if Elizabeth were in their royal line, and reminding readers that misogyny was not always the culturally accepted position:

Now say, have women worth, or have they none?
Or had they some but with our Queen ist gone?
...

Let such, as say our sex is void of reason,
Know 'tis a slander now, but once was treason.
(*Works* 157, ll. 105–10)

Bradstreet observes that during Elizabeth's rule, the derogation of women's reason and value would have been tantamount to a capital offense. In suggesting that restrictive laws can be abolished and calling attention to the ways perceptions of gender have changed, Bradstreet emphasizes their impermanence, highlights the arbitrariness of rigid gender distinctions, and exposes the underlying power structures these distinctions uphold. But this emphasis on mutability also points to a quiet hope for future change. The immediate prospects might seem dim, but the battle of the sexes is far from decided.

If Bradstreet's earlier, public poetry grappled with intellectual and philosophical subjects in distinctly feminist ways, her private poems and other writings show her more personal struggles. These writings have garnered Bradstreet significant praise, and rightfully so; they are clearly written, expressive, and emotionally powerful. For example, poet Adrienne Rich lauds Bradstreet's writing while raising eight children, suffering from recurring, debilitating illnesses, and managing a household on the "edge of the wilderness" as "an act of great self-assertion and vitality" ("Tensions" 32); literary scholar Elaine Showalter also praises Bradstreet's later writings for their humor, wit, originality, emotion, and the way they emphasize the place of domestic subjects in the field of serious literature (*Jury* 5–6). Bradstreet writes candidly of her love for her husband and children, her fears related to death and her visions of heaven, the beauty of nature, the deaths of her grandchildren, and the burning of her beloved house, and through it all runs a single thread: her deep ambivalence about her faith. Entrenched in a Puritan orthodoxy that treats the world as a temporary home of bodily temptations and emphasizes trials as a form of spiritual preparation for the return of Christ, Bradstreet struggles to reconcile the joy found in her earthly attachments and her suffering from sickness, grief, and loss with the expectations of her faith community. Ultimately, these writings reveal her faith to be an act of willed determination that sometimes contradicts her experience, as much or more the result of personal resolve than religious conviction.

In the letter to her children that contains her spiritual autobiography, Bradstreet describes working to obey Puritan strictures on behavior from an early age and her efforts to understand her bouts of illness as "correction ... the Lord sent to huble [*sic*] and try me & doe me Good" (*Works* 216). But Bradstreet also wrestles with serious doubt about Puritanism as the only true faith practice, the disappointments of her own experience, and the existence of God and the holy trinity (*Works* 217–18). Her spiritual struggle is evident in the poems written after the deaths of her grandchildren, which express faith that it is "his hand alone that guides nature and fate" (*Works* 187, l. 14), but which nevertheless can scarcely contain her grief and anger: "Three flours, ... / Cropt by th' Almighties hand; yet is he good," she writes; though she wants to "dispute" the reason why, instead she will bow down with her mouth "put in the dust" and "say he's merciful as well as just" (*Works* 188, ll. 3–4, 6–8). In this case, declaring God's goodness is an act of faith, will, and bitter resignation.

Bradstreet's questioning of her faith is not just tied to hardships. As a dutiful Puritan, she was supposed to focus on the higher things of the spirit and the afterlife rather than the lower, sinful body and earthly existence—but her poetry shows how keenly she feels the struggle between flesh and spirit. Lines written to her husband show the great happiness he brings her, particularly in what is perhaps her most well-known poem, "To my Dear and loving Husband," in which she depicts her marriage as a true union characterized by abiding love and contentment (*Works* 180). Elsewhere Simon is "My head, my heart, mine Eyes, my life, nay more, / My joy, my Magazine of earthly store," the "Sun" whose "warmth" can resuscitate "chilled limbs now nummed," while she is "Flesh of thy flesh, bone of thy bone," the "welcome house" and "glowing breast" in which he resides (*Works* 181, ll. 1–2, 8, 10–11, 21–2, 25). These lines paint a picture of mutual dependence and emotional and physical longing. Love and fidelity were demanded of Puritan wives as a "proof of piety"—but if such love was "selfish" or "carnal" it became proof of idolatry, of loving one's spouse more than God, and of having too much attachment to the temporal world (Martin *Triptych* 68). Bradstreet must have wrestled with the question of whether she loved her husband too much by Puritan standards, but her poetry focuses not on guilt but on her "desire and longing" for him (Martin *Triptych* 68), the sun who warms her cold limbs and heart.

Bradstreet's poetry about nature and her children similarly reflect this tension between her deep attachments and the expectations of her faith culture. In "Contemplations," which many critics believe is Bradstreet's most artistically accomplished poem, she appears in places to endorse Puritan orthodoxy, but her senses are nonetheless enraptured by the natural world around her. Looking on the sun, she confesses something verging on idolatry: "No wonder, some made thee a Deity," she marvels, "Had I not better known, (alas) the same had I" (*Works* 168, ll. 27–8); she also rhapsodizes about trees, the renewal of nature each year, and the music of insects. She acknowledges the "great Creator" responsible for nature's grandeur and the deceptiveness of temporary earthly joys, but her pleasure in the sensory richness of the natural world lingers (*Works* 169, l. 54). Other poems emphasize her fear of loss. In "Before the Birth of one of her Children," a very pregnant Bradstreet reflects on the possibility of her death in childbirth, and rather than contemplating the eternal glory that may await her in heaven, she focuses on those she would leave behind. She beseeches her beloved husband to "Yet love thy dead, who long lay in thine arms," to "protect" their children from "step Dames injury," and to "kiss this paper" and honor her with "sad sighs" (*Works* 180, ll. 20, 24, 27, 26). Bradstreet knows such attachments are vain because they represent the investment of hope in an empty and unfulfilling world, but this does not make her pleasure or fear easier to shake. In contemplating her life, Bradstreet finds herself in some ways helplessly and not always unwillingly earthbound by the people and places that have brought her so much joy.

Bradstreet frequently pulls in multiple directions in her poetry, exploring and exulting in her earthly attachments while still affirming her commitment to Puritan values. Even as she obeys Puritanism's call to accept pain and loss with a thankful heart, she allows herself to question and experience fully joy, sorrow, anger, and doubt. She makes sophisticated critiques of the philosophical and cultural orthodoxies upon which patriarchal power structures are built, and she treats her experiences as a woman as valid subjects for poetic consideration—but she also demonstrates her considerable emotional and spiritual investment in a Puritan culture that frequently devalues women and their contributions. Bradstreet may not be an outspoken rebel like Anne Hutchinson, or even her own sister, Sarah Keayne, but she is also no demure Puritan poetess. Her work is complex, rendering visible the struggle between artistic and intellectual expression and the expectations of cultural and religious conformity in ways that speak not only to her moment, but also to our own.

Fraught texts: Women's religious writing in seventeenth-century North America

Like Bradstreet, many colonial women wrote out their stories of spiritual experiences and beliefs and shared them with others. Most spiritual autobiographies were intended not for publication but for the edification of a small group, usually a family or church community. The faithful of all Protestant denominations were expected to be able to demonstrate their awareness of their own sinfulness, their misguided attempts to live without God, their moment of conversion, and their knowledge of God's saving grace. Occasionally, these texts were published in the hopes of drawing readers to booksellers and converts to Christ—and a small number of those published accounts were written by women. But spiritual autobiography was not the only form of religious writing allowed to women. Although forbidden by most denominations to speak or teach in church, mothers were considered the first instructors of their children in the faith, particularly in Puritan communities, and some women in Europe and the North American colonies published catechisms and instructional texts designed for this task.[13] The ability to articulate principles of faith and to relate personal spiritual experience was thus paradoxically entwined with motherhood, the most sacred of feminine responsibilities. Within a fairly rigid set of boundaries, then, both privately circulated and published religious writing was an arena in which seventeenth-century women were able to find their voices.

While in contemporary American culture, some feminist critics might be tempted to dismiss most religions as institutions which support patriarchal, heteronormative practices, to do so is to fail to understand religious faith as a source of self-empowerment and strength for many women. While Puritan views of appropriate gender behavior limited women in significant ways, their religious practices and expectation of women's personal and intellectual engagement with spiritual ideas allowed women to take ownership of their spiritual experiences through various written texts. Quakerism gave women an even greater degree of ownership because it encouraged women to speak and interpret scripture publicly and acknowledged women as equal members of the religious community. Women who embraced Quakerism were not always accepted by a culture with deeply ingrained views about women's silence and submission in church, but they were given an unprecedented degree of freedom to pursue religious callings. As Ivy Schweitzer argues, European colonial women relied on their spiritual practices for strength and personal solace, and for many the Bible offered "what they would consider feminism or female empowerment, and … an argument for their worth, authority, and position as speakers and writers" ("My Body" 406). Women writing religious texts could buttress their arguments with scriptural imagery and language, as Sarah Symmes Fiske did in *A Confession of Faith: or, A Summary of Divinity* (1704), or claim to be acting as instruments of the Holy Spirit, as Bathsheba Bowers did in her spiritual autobiography, *An Alarm Sounded to Prepare the Inhabitants of the World to Meet the Lord in the Way of His Judgments* (1709). Not surprisingly, such accounts were frequently prefaced by male publishers' avowals of the writers' humility and lack of desire for worldly fame and fortune, but this practice of authorization does not negate the fact of women's authorship. Religious writing gave early colonial women the opportunity to lend their voices to "broader currents of religious debate" (Wilcox 68) that shaped life on the North American continent.

Sarah Symmes Fiske's *A Confession of Faith* offers an excellent illustration of the tensions between orthodoxy and radicalism in women's religious writing. While few details about Fiske's life have survived, we know she was, like Bradstreet, a member of New England's elite. The granddaughter of a prominent Puritan minister, Fiske was born in 1652 in Charlestown, the same town where Bradstreet and her family made their first North American home. At age nineteen she married Moses Fiske, the popular minister of the Congregational Church in Braintree, Massachusetts—the same church from which Anne Hutchinson was so dramatically ejected forty years earlier—and she went on to bear fourteen children in seventeen years, only eight of whom are believed to have survived infancy (McQuade 115 n.1). In the early years of her marriage, Fiske wrote a clear, concise, and intellectually sophisticated account of her rather orthodox Puritan beliefs as part of her application for membership in her husband's church. In 1704, more than a decade after her death, Benjamin Eliot of Boston published this text as *A Confession of Faith*. Although the text was not addressed to children, Eliot's title page proclaims Fiske's book is "published for the Benefit of ALL, and more especially YOUNG persons"; it was, as Paula McQuade notes, an attempt to authorize Fiske's "entry into a largely masculine Colonialist print culture" by tapping into the growing popularity of domestic teaching texts for mothers (110).

The designation of *Confession* as a children's text makes clear that certain kinds of religious speech were permissible for women, but they were largely concentrated within the home. Puritan women were expected to speak privately in the cause of salvation; Cotton Mather encouraged wives to use their "Ingenious Perswasions" to coax backslidden husbands to return to church, even up to "humbly" repeating the words of the minister's sermons to their husbands in appropriate situations (qtd. in S. Brown 190–1). More importantly, they were expected to ensure their children had a firm foundation in Puritan doctrine. Fiske's *Confession*, with its "pithy but intellectually rigorous discussions of the faith," its traditional Puritan theological forms of classification and argumentation, and its "interweav[ing of] scriptural words and phrases" (McQuade 110–11), was amply suited to this task, and so was conscripted into domestic service by an eager publisher. Fiske's text might be clearly and persuasively written, but in order to be acceptable it had to work toward the social and political goals of Puritan leadership, and its usefulness for children had to be delineated to neutralize any threat to a social cohesion predicated on men and women occupying their proper places.

Fiske is one of the more obscure women writers of the seventeenth century; she is not typically anthologized, and she is rarely included in discussions of early American literature. McQuade speculates she has received so little scholarly attention because beyond her thorough grasp of complex theological matters and her lack of a disclaimer related to her gender, she does not seem to challenge the "traditionally masculine forms of religion or government" in any way (114). But Fiske's religious conservatism should not preclude the study of her work, which tells us as much about the conditions under which seventeenth-century New England women spoke, wrote, and were published as the work and lives of more radical women (114). What's more, to dismiss Fiske as insufficiently radical is to miss the broader religious contexts of the time: within Puritanism she might have been orthodox, but Puritanism was itself a direct challenge to the religious and political majority in England. Making so clear a declaration of Puritan faith during the period of fiercest debate was a radical act, the reproduction of "words of orthodoxy, which were also words of activism and dissent" (S. Brown 195). While it is easy to fixate on the women who, like Anne Hutchinson, dared to flout Pauline injunctions for women to keep silent in church, further study of women like Fiske shows that the relationship between women's speech and writing, religious orthodoxy, and radicalism was much more complex than a simple orthodox–heretic binary allows.

If Fiske's *Confession* suggests how the publication of a religious text was a double-bind for even the most conservative women, Bathsheba Bowers' *An Alarm Sounded* reveals the difficulties experienced by women who took up more radical positions. Bowers lived an entirely unorthodox life by Puritan standards. She too was born in Charlestown, Massachusetts, in 1671 or 1672, one of twelve children of Quaker parents who had emigrated from England. Massachusetts was not a welcoming place for Quakers. Quaker founder George Fox believed inequality of the sexes was a product of the fall of mankind and should be rejected by Christians who had "found the divine light" (Shea 123); and although the apostle Paul might have forbidden women to speak in church, Quaker Margaret Fell argued in a 1666 tract that this prohibition did not preclude the Holy Spirit from speaking through women (Barbour 62), a view that was heretical to most other Christian sects. After experiencing religious persecution in Massachusetts (Potts 112), the Bowers family sent Bathsheba and three of her sisters to the much larger Quaker community in Philadelphia, where Bowers would live for most of her life. She never married but was an avid reader and writer whose strong mind and zest for intellectual debate drew "the *elite* of the city" to her home, which was known to her friends as Bathsheba's Bower ("Heroic Women" 2). She eventually felt called to preach and traveled throughout South Carolina to help its growing Quaker community. To Bowers, the Quaker commitment to equality between men and women was more than a piece of controversial doctrine; it was the principle around which she organized her life.

Most of what is known about Bowers outside of her text comes from the diary of her niece, Ann Curtis Clay Bolton, who writes with disapproval of Bowers' rather singular life.[14] Bolton describes Bowers as never having married because she was "crossed in love" at eighteen; she suggests Bowers retreated alone to her house (pointedly noting it was also known as "Bathsheba's Folly") because she wanted "something to bear up her Name, and ... could not expect fame and favour here by any methods than her own raising and spreading" (qtd. in Potts 111). In Bolton's view, Bowers' way of life was a deliberate provocation, a tactic intended to bring undeserved public attention. Bolton depicts Bowers as strong-willed and impulsive: she lives "free from Society as if she had lived in a cave under Ground or on the top of a high mountain"; she takes up vegetarianism on a whim; she exercises a "thirst for knowledge" that is "boundless," reading her Bible frequently "to no better purpose than to afford matter to dispute" doctrine with the preacher; and she is "a Quaker by profession but so Wild in her notions it was hard to find out of what religion she really was of" (qtd. in Potts 111–12). The evident scorn of these descriptions suggests that while Quaker theology might have authorized Bowers' lifestyle, it could not bring her widespread cultural acceptance. Yet, putting aside Bolton's disdain, the Bowers her account reveals is passionate, intelligent, and sharply independent in her thinking, a far cry from the quiet, humbly dependent creature her culture expects her to be.

Bowers' life is characterized by a set of opposing tensions—between solitary retreat from society's expectations and insertions into public conversation, and between the need to be faithful to her vision and cultural pressure to perform a specific kind of womanhood—and her spiritual autobiography mirrors these tensions. Bowers' introductory remarks suggest publication of *An Alarm Sounded* (1709) almost did not happen, mentioning "Repulses in my proceeding to print" that caused her to "weep before the Lord" and ask him to take her life (3); she nevertheless expresses belief in the rightness of her cause, identifying God as the "Author of this my Concern" (3). She also expresses a deep unwillingness to publish her work out of fear that she will "make a contemptible appearance in the world," becoming "the Object of Scorn and Ridicule" rather than the "subject of sober Consideration" she ought to be (4). She is torn between her "Obligation" to relate her spiritual experience and the pride that makes her fearful of a derisive reception (5), which she portrays as a battle between God's direct inspiration and her own sinful nature. In the body of the work, she similarly exults in the promise of God "that I had been faithful in a few things, and should be made Ruler over many things" (13), but also wrestles mightily with the call to preach, describing it as a "cross" that she must bear to rid herself of the evils of pride (11). She struggles with the need to claim her convictions publicly in speech or in text, knowing the likely result will be social condemnation. This oscillation between bold claims and fearful self-questioning plays out repeatedly in Bowers' text.

Bowers' narrative is emblematic of her continual resistance to cultural conformity. As Suzanne M. Zweizig notes, *An Alarm Sounded* departs from typical Quaker spiritual autobiographies in both content and structure. It begins as most spiritual autobiographies do, with Bowers' childhood understanding of faith and her fear of hell, then describes her prideful, error-strewn youth, a time when she was "extreamly addicted to decking up my self, going abroad and keeping of wild Company," even while gripped by a "secret terror" of the consequences of her behavior (Bowers 6). Bowers then describes a period of spiritual struggle and the search for inner light, the third stage in the Quaker autobiographical tradition, but unlike most authors she doesn't proceed to a dramatic conversion and then to resolution. Instead, Bowers spends the rest of her autobiography moving between "euphoria over her closeness to God and despair over his forsaking her" (Zweizig 70), and although she closes by reflecting that her "Fits are shorter and seldomer than they have formerly been," her final words emphasize the "long and tedious travail of my spiritual warfair" (Bowers 22–3). This refusal to bring closure to her narrative and "present a unified image of the self" (Zweizig 70) is another refusal of cultural expectations, perhaps intended to comfort others who were likewise committed to lives of faith but still felt unworthy. In addition, unlike most autobiographers, Bowers is largely absent from her text, focusing on her inward spiritual life to the exclusion of any specific details about her physical life. Zweizig suggests this erasure is Bowers' way of reconciling her desire to write publicly about her life with the "historical, cultural, and theological discourses about identity and self-hood" that forbade women to do so (71), an act of defiance that was also an act of self-preservation.

While undoubtedly more colonial women than Fiske and Bowers wrote religious texts in the seventeenth century, either they have not survived or have not yet been discovered. We do know that increasing numbers of women wrote and published accounts of their spiritual lives throughout the eighteenth century, but beginning in the late seventeenth century, the strength of religious convictions increasingly served as a justification not only for the publication of women's life stories and other religious texts—even if under various constraints and practices of masculine authorization—but also for women's participation in the political, cultural, and intellectual debates that would eventually turn a disparate group of colonies into a new nation.[15]

Native groups, New England captivity narratives, and Mary Rowlandson

As Europeans ventured farther from their home continent in the early colonial period, encountering new and different cultures, it became increasingly important to them to articulate European and specific imperial group identities, and the "daily presence of an 'other,'" particularly a strange and savage other, was one way to do so (K. Brown 45). By contrasting themselves with Native Americans, European colonists in North America could reassure themselves they were sufficiently English and that England stood for the spread of good and civilization throughout the world. In spite of their frequently brutal methods, Europeans considered their civilizing and saving work among the Indians to be a merciful and even benevolent duty stemming from their position at the height of human social, political, cultural, and moral development.

It is tempting to think of Native Americans as the helpless victims of greedy European settlers, but this view is a dramatic oversimplification of colonial history and does Native American tribes a disservice, falsely rendering them passive when they were themselves agents of history. They had complex interrelationships among themselves for thousands of years before Europeans came to North America and their own goals, plans, and ways of life that were not erased or overwritten by European arrival. Instead, they adapted in many ways to survive, incorporating Europeans into their trade networks and alliances and adopting European tools for use in existing practices and traditions without sacrificing their own sovereignty (Kidwell 94). Some Native Americans converted to Christianity and went to live in what are referred to as praying towns, English-style villages with schools and churches built to house and educate new converts (Lepore 32). Both colonists and Native Americans had deep investments in maintaining their ways of life in the face of great change, which frequently led to conflict, sometimes the "predictable disputes" of neighbors over land, debts, and livestock (K. Brown 164), and sometimes larger, protracted conflicts over issues of sovereignty; the most well-known of these is the conflict known as King Philip's or Metacom's War (1675–1676), during which several Algonquian tribes led by Wampanoag sachem King Philip fought the settlers of New England to protect their subsistence practices and prevent further erosion of their "cultural, political, and economic autonomy" (Lepore 8).[16] The resolutions of these conflicts led to further reconfigurations of both Native and European traditions and practices.[17] While the balance of power eventually did shift toward the colonists, it is important to remember that Europeans did not engage in one-way transmissions of civilization, and Native Americans were not simply humble, grateful recipients; they brought their own expectations of "reciprocity and exchange," and their own understandings of the "mutual obligations" involved in European–Native American transactions (K. Brown 72). To acknowledge these facts is not to ignore that the larger aims of imperial colonies directly violated the sovereignty of Native peoples, but to recognize that interactions between colonists and Native Americans were diverse and sometimes quotidian, and they did not fit neatly into the conquered–conqueror scripts so often found in early American colonial depictions.

Colonial writers documented the evolution of these relationships, exploring the cultural negotiations at their core and laying the groundwork for the stereotypical myths of Native American identity that still pervade American literature and cultural imagination. As Paula Gunn Allen (Laguna) notes in her landmark work of Native American feminist criticism, *The Sacred Hoop*, the two major stereotypes of Native Americans are the "noble savage" and the "howling savage." The noble savage is a romantic figure, the "appealing but doomed victim of the inevitable evolution of humanity" who serves as the "guardian of the wilds" and the "conscience of ecological responsibility," guided by a simple philosophy and a "transcendent comprehension of the laws of the universe" (4–5, 129). Howling savages, on the other hand, are the "denizens of a terrifying wilderness" who "capture white ladies and torture them, obstruct the westward movement of peaceable white settlers, and engage in bloodthirsty uprisings in which they glory in the massacre of innocent colonists and pioneers" (5). These descriptions might seem different, but Allen points out the fear of the howling savage is always lurking behind the veneration of the noble savage, and both conceptions lead to the conclusion that the elimination of Native Americans was inevitable and necessary (5).

These stereotypes have roots in European colonists' depictions of their encounters with indigenous people: the figures of Powhatan and Pocahontas in John Smith's *A General History of Virginia* (1605), Squanto in William Bradford's *Of Plymouth Plantation* (1656), and the numerous nameless, faceless heathens who appear in early American literature. The appearances of these figures represent colonists' attempts to grapple with the strangeness of cultural first contact and larger questions about the purposes and values that undergirded their presence in North America. It is no surprise, then, that during this time the Indian captivity narrative should become the first distinctly American literary genre, largely due to *The Sovereignty and Goodness of God* (1682), Massachusetts Bay colonist Mary Rowlandson's account of her captivity by Narragansett, Nipmuc, and Wampanoag Indians during King Philip's War. Rowlandson describes witnessing the killing of relatives and friends by Nipmuc and Narragansett Indians during an attack on her village, the journey she is forced to take away from her home and into the wilderness, the treatment she receives from her captors, and her eventual ransom and restoration to the colonial community. In her depictions of the Wampanoag and Narragansett Indians, Rowlandson frequently uses noble/hostile savage stereotypes but tries to reconcile these stereotypes with the reality of her lived experience, illustrating this process of colonial grappling with a cultural Other. As Joe Snader points out, Rowlandson did not invent the captivity narrative; however, *Sovereignty* was one of the earliest American captivity narratives to be published and is frequently described as the first American bestseller. It was so successful that it created a kind of template for the genre that would continue to be employed with only minor variations over the next two centuries, one emphasizing Native American violence and illustrating the role of providence in bringing about physical and spiritual redemption of the captives and their restoration to Christian community (J. Byrd 18). It was one of the earliest iterations of what we now recognize as a powerful American literary tradition, the figure of the American individual making her way through a dangerous wilderness.

While they frequently had white women and children as their protagonists, very few captivity narratives from the early American colonial period seem to have been written by the women themselves. Hannah Swarton's story of her three-year captivity among Indians and then French-Canadian Catholics and Hannah Dustan's dramatic account of being captured with her nurse and another young male, and of murdering and scalping ten of their captors with their own hatchets before they escaped, were retold by Cotton Mather in several sermons and in his epic colonial history, *Magnalia Christi Americana* (1702).[18] One of the most well-known stories is that of Eunice Williams: taken with her family by Kahnawake Mohawks as a child and adopted by a bereaved mother in the tribe, she opted as an adult to stay with the Kahnawakes when the other surviving captives were ransomed; her story is related through her father, renowned minister John Williams, in *The Redeemed Captive* (1707). As far as we know, Rowlandson stands alone as the author of her own text during the early colonial period, but even her narrative has been questioned; it features an anonymous preface believed to be written by Increase Mather, the influential minister and leader of the Massachusetts Bay Colony, which has led some scholars to question how much editorial oversight Mather exercised over Rowlandson's text.[19]

Why were Puritan ministers so closely involved in the retelling of women's captivity narratives? The answer lies in the genre's potential to disrupt the intertwined religious, political, and social structures of the colonies, which were predicated on prescribed cultural configurations of community and the wilderness (particularly a wilderness populated by heathen Indians), the individual's and the community's relationship to God, and the relationship of individuals to the community. The survival of the community depended on each member's perfect obedience to God's will and adherence to proper social order (Toulouse 939), and faithful individuals diligently searched out sin in theirs and their neighbors' lives so as not to invite God's punishment on the whole group. The unsettled wilderness was a place of temptation and certain destruction, and to enter it was to likewise endanger the community. These frameworks meant each individual bore responsibility for the entire community, and the entire community was likewise deeply invested in the obedience of each person.

These cultural configurations are dramatically encapsulated in the figure of a woman forcibly removed from the physical and spiritual protection of her community and taken into the wilderness among wild, unsaved people, where her survival depends as much on her resourcefulness and tenacity as on her obedience and submission to God's will. Stories of captivity and either redemption or misery and death were powerful object lessons that could reinforce the importance of collective repentance and obedience. However, they could also call into question the rightness and inevitability of colonial social, religious, and political structures, which made them dangerous (Fitzpatrick 16). In examining *Sovereignty*, the only surviving captivity narrative from this period written by a woman, we can see the specific ways these texts could serve as powerful metaphors to simultaneously call the community to repentance and revival and challenge community hierarchies; we can also see how the captivity narrative's emphasis on the sacredness of white, Christian community and the dangers posed by Native Americans contributed to an understanding of race that led to Native Americans' physical and cultural annihilation.

Mary Rowlandson was born Mary White in 1637 in the county of Somerset in England, the fifth child in a "middling" farming family (Salisbury 7). The White family sailed for the Massachusetts Bay Colony in 1639, some of the estimated 20,000 Puritans who left England between 1629 and 1642, and eventually settled in the frontier town of Lancaster, where Mary's father acquired considerable property. Few specifics are known about Mary's young life and education, but she was plainly taught to read and write, and her father's success suggests she and her family enjoyed a comparatively comfortable colonial life. In 1656, Mary married Joseph Rowlandson, the minister of Lancaster, a recent graduate of Harvard College, and an increasingly close associate of Increase Mather, and between 1658 and 1669, she gave birth to four children, the oldest of whom died in early childhood.

On February 20, 1676, Narragansett, Nipmuc, and Wampanoag Indians attacked Lancaster, killing thirteen colonists and capturing thirty-three, Mary Rowlandson and her three children among them. She had to carry her wounded youngest daughter, Sarah, who eventually died in her arms. Sold as a servant to a man named Quinnapin and one of his three wives, Weetamoo, Rowlandson was for the most part isolated from her fellow captives (Salisbury 25). Over a series of twenty "removes" (the term she uses to describe their frequent relocations), Rowlandson faced starvation, cruelty, grief, and despair; she sought comfort and discernment of the will of God in scriptures, fought for scraps of food and shelter, and eventually found a place in the Indian economy through her knitting ability. She remained in captivity for three months, ransomed for twenty pounds on May 2, and the last of her children was ransomed six weeks later.

It is believed Rowlandson wrote *Sovereignty* in May of 1677, after the family relocated to Connecticut (Salisbury 40). The narrative was initially intended for private circulation among friends, but the likely encouragement of Increase Mather led to its March 1682 publication in Boston under the full title *The Sovereignty and Goodness of God, Together with the Faithfulness of His Promises Displayed: Being a Narrative of the Captivity and Restoration of Mrs. Mary Rowlandson and Related Documents* (Derounian 246). The first edition sold so quickly that it was followed by second and third editions of about one thousand copies each and a London edition in that same year (Salisbury 49).

Sovereignty was carefully calibrated to be a cautionary tale, supporting a particular interpretation of Metacom's/King Philip's War as an "affliction" visited on the colony by God for its disobedience, but potentially offering redemption for those who would acknowledge God's sovereignty and their complete dependence on

Him. The title of the New England editions announces that the text is a narrative displaying God's power, goodness, and faithfulness, and minimizes Rowlandson's role as either actor or author (Salisbury 49), and the anonymous preface encourages readers to study Rowlandson's example so they can learn the same humility and dependence she did (Rowlandson 67–8). Rowlandson's narrative supports this position, repeatedly emphasizing that God has "strengthened [her captors] to be a scourge to His people" (105) and that her personal sufferings and the delay of her redemption are God's will, a position largely consistent with New England Puritan orthodoxy at the time. Rowlandson's text's exhortation for believers to commit to both "personal regeneration and rededication to the life of the whole" make it an excellent vessel for community revival (Vincent 31), and her ability to perform Puritan womanhood properly enables this message. In these ways, *Sovereignty* suited the didactic purposes of ministers whose theology was frequently tied to specific political and social goals.[20] This use of Rowlandson's narrative illustrates the ways in which women's captivity narratives became "sites for the articulation" of a masculine colonial authority that was constantly in flux (Wilcox 64).

But the text also shows Rowlandson's struggle between what she has been taught to believe about her experiences, her faith, and her role in her community, and her actual experiences as a captive, a grieving mother, and an increasingly independent woman. An obedient Puritan, Rowlandson spends time examining her thoughts and actions, repenting, encouraging her fellow captives, and seeking comfort in scripture. Yet, as Breitwieser points out, reflecting on the events of her captivity leads Rowlandson "primarily to mourning rather than to faith" as it should have done, so that the writing of the narrative itself "becomes a part of the work of mourning" (8). Even after her rescue, she reports being unable to sleep through the night, thinking of her dead daughter and remembering how "the other day I was in the midst of thousands of enemies, and nothing but death before me" (111). Rowlandson's gratitude for her rescue and awareness of God's sovereign hand in her life have not lessened her grief, and the act of remembering involves as much reawakening of grief as affirmation of God's goodness. In this way, Rowlandson's account offers a subtle but persistent critique of Puritan orthodoxy.

Rowlandson's adaptation to captivity also offers a critique of Puritan gender roles. In captivity, she finds that conformity to prescribed gender roles that dictated modesty, submission, and dependence on male authority will put her life in peril. While initially she struggles to eat what little food is offered her, describing it as "filthy trash" (79), she eventually forages for food in the woods, begs from other Indians, and literally takes food from the mouth of an English child who does not have the teeth to chew it, declaring it "savoury ... to my taste" (96). Determined to survive, she has become bolder, decisive, and even opportunistic. And the more independent Rowlandson grows, the farther her behavior drifts from orthodoxy. In spite of protestations of helplessness and submission to God's will, Rowlandson is far from passive by the later weeks of her captivity. She is "neither submissive nor despondent" with her master, mistresses, and the other Indians she encounters (Fitzpatrick 12). Instead she makes a place for herself in the Indian economy, bartering her sewing and knitting skills and the tobacco her husband sends for food, shelter, and other goods, even making clothes for King Philip's children and other members of his household. When she is threatened with violence because begging for food disgraces her master, Rowlandson argues that "they had as good knock me in the head as starve me to death" (96); yet, she reflects, "my Conscience did not accuse me of unrighteousness toward one or other" (91). That she sees nothing condemnable in behavior that before would have seemed immodest is a reflection of the degree to which she has, perhaps unconsciously, cast off the restraints of Puritan femininity. By the end of her captivity, Rowlandson is a different woman—enterprising, resourceful, and with an undeniable power—and the story of her experiences is one of "female strength, endurance, and even prosperity" featuring a previously unimagined, distinctly female subjectivity (Castiglia 4).

Perhaps the most visible of Rowlandson's struggles is her inability to reconcile her conceptions about Indians with her experiences with her captors. The English Christian sense of superiority over the Indians was, as Tiffany Potter notes, "deeply ingrained" (156), and Rowlandson often describes her captors as "ravenous Beasts" (70), "Barbarous Creatures" (70), and "mad men" (97). Some of these descriptions are borne out by Rowlandson's experiences—she has, after all, seen Indians kill her friends, relatives, and her daughter, and has experienced harsh treatment at their hands—but her cultural and gender biases are also a factor. Puritan culture valued femininity that was chaste, maternal, and performed gender-appropriate activities (Potter 156). In her relationships with Indian women, Rowlandson seems to respond best to those who take a maternal, reassuring role with her, offering food and shelter. What's more, her descriptions of her mistress Weetamoo, with whom she has a contentious relationship, never acknowledge Weetamoo's high political and military rank, the result of birthright in a matrilineal culture and marriage connections (Potter 154). Rowlandson could not have helped knowing of Weetamoo's importance, but she makes no mention of it, perhaps believing Weetamoo's position is inappropriately masculine (Potter 155–6).

Nonetheless, Rowlandson repeatedly comments on Indian behavior that contradicts her own depictions of Native depravity. She and Sarah are allowed to ride horseback when Rowlandson's strength gives out (73); an Indian gives her a Bible, which is a source of great comfort to her (76); and she is repeatedly offered food and shelter, even by an Indian she knows has "killed two Englishmen at Sudbury" (101). She also insists that in spite of the unusual group sleeping arrangements, "not one of them ever offered me the least abuse of unchastity to me" (107). Such acknowledgments may be "grudging," as Fitzpatrick suggests (12), and the avowal of her chastity may be intended to affirm Rowlandson's unsoiled Puritan femininity, but these details still speak to the kindness and civility of the Indians with whom Rowlandson has contact. Rowlandson may not have considered her opinions of Indians materially changed following her captivity, but her narrative is markedly ambivalent.

Many scholars have noted the existence of two voices in *Sovereignty*: one good Puritan woman and one colloquial voice that expresses "what Puritan ideology could not contain" (Faery 31). Rowlandson spends much of her text shuttling between these two voices, between her observations and experiences in captivity and the scriptural glosses she applies to them. For example, she comments on the failures of the English army during King Philip's War, noting how easy the Indians should have been to track and the army's general ineffectiveness (104–7). She repeatedly attributes these things to "the strange providence of God" (106)—the narrative that most heavily supports the Matherian interpretation of the war as God's punishment—and yet what shines through are a sharp critique of English military capability and "fairly seditious rebukes" of the patriarchal power structure using "providence" as a shield (Vincent 31). Such bold criticism under the guise of marveling at God's sovereignty suggests a writer not fully at ease with her professed ideology, and perhaps more savvy in her manipulation of religious and cultural tropes than she first appears.

Fitzpatrick observes that for all its apparent religious orthodoxy, *Sovereignty* demonstrates the possibility of an individual's salvation, not only outside the community, but in the wilderness, even among "demonic adversaries" (3); she argues the late seventeenth century saw a rhetorical shift from the idea of a covenanted community toward "personal agency" (3) in matters of salvation, a transition at least partly enabled by the ways *Sovereignty* and other captivity narratives portrayed individual suffering as evidence of God's grace as much as of his displeasure (3–9). However, while captivity narratives allowed certain kinds of resistance that might point to new freedoms for white women, they frequently reinforced stereotypical views of Native Americans as savage and dangerous; they also "engrained a certain expectation of subjectivity" in an American cultural imagination which dictated that only white women and children could be captives, effectively disregarding or invalidating the experiences of the many Native Americans also taken captive during King Philip's War and other armed conflicts (J. Byrd 18; Lepore 136–50). And, as Audra Simpson (Kahnawake Mohawk) argues, captives who chose to stay with their captors and "become" Indians, like Eunice Williams, may have caused settlers to question their "assumptions about the inherent desirability of *white* female identity" and civilization, as opposed to the undesirability of Native communities and female identity (254). However, in claiming Native identity for themselves, these captives also reenacted the cultural and physical appropriation that occurred through the colonial act of "*claiming* and *owning* land," thereby "contribut[ing] to the expropriation of land" and the destruction of Native ways of life (253, 255). Reasons such as these are why Native American women writers have considered captivity narratives one of the "literatures of empire" that must be responded to (J. Byrd 19).[21]

Over the course of the seventeenth century, the initially shaky foothold of European colonization in North America became a firmly established foundation upon which imperial powers would look to build: the English pushing westward from the Atlantic coast, the French moving across what is now Canada and the central continent, and the Spanish working their way through the South and West. Among the British colonies, cash crop farming was coming to dominate the middle Atlantic and southern regions, laying the groundwork for an agricultural economy built on racialized slave labor. Colonial settlements were expanding, and the Native Americans they displaced sought new means of resistance, prompting debates about sovereignty, land rights, and racial superiority while freighting the imagery of the frontier as a wilderness to be conquered in a nascent cultural imagination. And the Puritan preachments of a sacred calling in the New World were shaping a sense of colonial purpose in the Northeast, which would become the ideological cradle of the Revolution. While thoughts of an independent nation were still far off, by the end of the seventeenth century the elements that would shape its inception, its policies, and its defining conflicts and ideologies were moving into place.

Notes

1 See, for example, Thomas Harriot's account of Native Americans in his 1588 narrative *A Briefe and True Report of the New Found Land of Virginia*.

2 Columbus and other Spanish explorers believed they would find jewels and precious metals in the New World as well as a plentiful source of slave labor in the Native populations (see Chaplin 161–2). French and English imperial powers had similar goals. Richard Hakluyt wrote to Queen Elizabeth in 1584 that American colonies could solve a number of English economic problems, supplying raw materials for England, creating a new market for English manufactured goods, and conveniently solving England's overpopulation problem (Zahadieh 51).

3 As P. Jane Hafen notes, the inclusion of Native American texts in anthologies of American literature "claims Indian expression as a Europeanized literary 'art,'" but this inclusion does not take into account the layers of mediation involved in such an inclusion (234). There are questions of who is doing the translation and collection of these materials, and what interpretive and instructive frameworks these individuals and institutions bring to them, as well as the issue of attempting to recreate performance pieces in print.

4 See Mulford "Writing" 109–11 for discussion of the history of early American canon formation and revision; see also Wilcox for discussion of the ways the canon has expanded to include works in translation, as well as previously unpublished works such as letters and poetry manuscripts.

5 Leonor de Ovando, a nun living in Santo Domingo (now the capital of the Dominican Republic) in the late sixteenth century is believed to be the first woman poet in the Americas. See Chang-Rodriguez 117 for additional information.

6 In the last thirty years, anthologies of American literature have begun to include Native American origin stories and trickster tales in the early American section, but we have not done so here. While they are an important part of the cultural heritage of Native Americans and play significant roles in later works by Native American writers, it strikes us as appropriative to assume that seventeenth-century Native Americans would have considered their private and in some cases sacred traditional cultural transmissions to be part of a shared literary endeavor with the European settlers who occupied their land. What's more, while we know that women were involved in the creation and transmission of these stories over thousands of years, it would be impossible to tease out their individual or even collective contributions in any meaningful way. As Wilcox notes, the point is not to dismiss the contributions of women to these traditions, which were significant, but to acknowledge the "inadequacy of the methodological tools provided by the study of Eurocentric literary traditions" (56).

7 For additional discussion of Bradstreet's education, see White 42–70; for more on her reading, including potential sources for references in her poetry, see White 61–70 and Stanford's biography as well as Harvey 25ff. and Rosenmeier 59–60.

8 Bradstreet's poetry and prose make no mention of enslaved Africans. Simon Bradstreet's will dated December 23, 1689, specifies that upon his death his wife will inherit "my

negro woman Hannah and her daughter Bilhah" (qtd. in R. Anderson 211), but it is not clear whether Hannah and Bilhah were part of the Bradstreet household during Anne's lifetime.

9 While both groups of colonists are generally called Puritans and shared the same primary theology, the Scrooby Separatists on the Mayflower were more radical than the other Puritan groups who followed them to New England. The Scrooby Separatists wanted to break from the Church of England, while the Puritans were non-separating dissenters who disagreed with the Church of England's hierarchical structure but did not want to leave the church fold; for more on the distinctive religious culture in New England, see M. Peterson.

10 See, for example, Salska, Waller, and Martin *Triptych*.

11 See Rosenmeier 59–60, Merrim xxii, and Harvey 12–13.

12 All Bradstreet citations are from the *Complete Works* edited by Joseph R. McElrath, Jr. and Allan P. Robb. Parenthetical citations include both the page number of the poem and the line numbers of the respective quotations.

13 Sylvia Brown identifies Elizabeth Clinton (the Countess of Lincoln), Dorothy Leigh, and Elizabeth Joscelin as English women who wrote instructional texts for mothers (191–7). Marie de l'Incarnation, a French Ursuline nun who spent most of her life as a missionary in New France (now eastern Canada), did not write specifically for children but did write instructional texts for Native newcomers to the Catholic faith, including a history of the Catholic church in the Algonquin language and a catechism in the Iroquois language; she also founded the first school for girls' education in North America.

14 A "Notes and Queries" entry attributed to historian William John Potts in an 1879 issue of *The Pennsylvania Magazine of History and Biography* collects most of the known information about Bowers from Bolton's diary and an 1877 history of Cambridge by Lucius R. Paige. Bolton's diary, written in the form of letters to her physician, was published in 1923 but is now out of print.

15 One of these women was Sophia Wigington Hume, who became a prominent Quaker minister in South Carolina and England and advocated in her writing for greater austerity among Quakers who'd been led astray by cardplaying, fine dress, and the celebration of Christmas. Another was Sarah Osborn, who defied the religious leaders of her community when she led revival meetings in her Newport, Rhode Island, home and invited enslaved Africans to attend; Osborn left behind more than 2,000 pages of writing, including her published memoir and numerous letters and diaries that illuminate her active participation in the religious, political, and social conversations of her time.

16 There has been significant debate among scholars over what to call the Wampanoag sachem known as King Philip and the war that began in June of 1675. King Philip was the name English settlers gave to Metacom, the leader of the Wampanoags who succeeded Massasoit. Thus, some scholars believe "Metacom's War" is more accurate. However, as Lepore notes, while Metacom may have been the sachem's name in his youth, many Wampanoags changed their names multiple times, and there is evidence that Metacom adopted the name King Philip and was using it at the time of the war; given that Wampanoags rarely reverted to previous names, it may be most accurate to refer to it as King Philip's War—especially since we do not have any way of knowing what Algonquians called the war (Lepore xv–xxi).

17 As Holm notes, one of the key shifts related to these conflicts was in the styles and conceptualizations of warfare; as a result of wars between settlers and Native Americans, settlers eventually learned to adopt Native tactics, while many Native groups shifted toward the total–decisive war model practiced by most Europeans. See Holm 155–64 for more information.

18 Mather is also the source through which the captivity narratives of Mary Bradley, Hannah Bradley, and Mercy Short have been related (Wilcox 62).

19 See, for example, Fitzpatrick 2–4. Rowlandson's story had also been previously told by Increase Mather in his *A Brief History of the War with the Indians in New England*

(1676), as well as in other authors' texts about the war, and Mather is believed to have funded *Sovereignty*'s publication (see Derounian 241–2 for additional details). The next known captivity narrative claiming a woman author was Elizabeth Hanson's *God's Mercy Surmounting Man's Cruelty, Exemplified in the Captivity and Redemption of Elizabeth Hanson* (1728).

20 Mitchell Robert Breitwieser sees Rowlandson's text as part of Increase Mather's efforts to "*control the meaning of the war*" (6, italics in original); according to Fitzpatrick, the Mathers' purpose in collecting captivity narratives was to paint the war as punishment for the colony's departure from the ways of the first generation (14 and *passim*). And Teresa Toulouse argues that Increase Mather promoted *Sovereignty* as a means of advancing the cause of colonial sovereignty rather than imperial control (Toulouse 926).

21 Among those who have responded to the captivity narrative, Jodi Byrd (Chickasaw) includes Zitkala Ša's *American Indian Stories* (1921), which are about Indian children who were forced to go to boarding schools, and Louise Erdrich's poem "Captivity" (2003), which speaks directly to Mary Rowlandson (J. Byrd 19).

2

RHETORIC AND REVOLUTION

The women writers of the new republic

The eighteenth century was a period of energetic intellectual, political, and artistic activity in the North American colonies, and one in which colonial women played vital roles that blurred the lines between public and private. There were several decisive shifts in British North American culture over the course of the eighteenth century that helped create this more woman-friendly cultural environment. One key shift had to do with the role of religion in colonial life. While the Puritans had held New England in a powerful grip for many decades, the Enlightenment made its way across the Atlantic in the late seventeenth century, and the notions of a universe increasingly comprehensible through scientific development, of human sympathy and natural rights as the basis for moral relationships, and of the ability of rational men to govern themselves, were taking hold.[1] It was a turn toward a more benevolent and orderly universe, less frequently characterized by an unpredictable and chastising God, and toward explorations of human rather than divine nature.

The death of Cotton Mather, one of the last of the old-school Puritan leaders, in 1728, seemed to signal the end of the era of Puritan social and political control over much of New England. Religious faith was still very much a part of colonists' daily lives, but the Christian revivals that swept through the colonies from the 1720s to the 1750s, now known as the First Great Awakening, were based less on themes of judgment and election and more on individuals' emotional experiences of God. This emphasis on personal, emotional religious experience led to the formation of radical new Methodist and Baptist denominations that drew Christians away from more formal Congregational churches (Pearsall 129), but the traveling revival meetings of the Great Awakening also created ties of Christian sympathy among the colonies, "'awaken[ing]' all thirteen colonies to a common faith and … help[ing] to mobilize the forces of revolution" (Bercovitch *Puritan* xiv–xv; see also Gustafson 45–51). Colonial women continued to find inspiration and strength in their religious practices, and the role of sensibility—the ability to feel life's experiences deeply and express these feelings in ways that connected one person with another—in the evangelical fervor of the Great Awakening opened new spaces for women to act on their religious and political convictions.

One of the issues about which religious and political conviction empowered colonial women to speak was slavery. The North American colonial population grew sevenfold from 1700 to 1770, with the largest groups of European migrants coming from Scotland, Ireland, and German-speaking regions (Games 38; Jon Butler 29), but a nearly equal number of enslaved Africans were also brought to North America to supply the exponentially increasing demand for labor, particularly in the southern colonies.[2] Enslaved Africans had never passively accepted their captivity, but had pushed back against the "spiritual and cultural holocaust" of slavery by fighting to maintain their diverse religious and cultural traditions and engaging in forms of labor resistance such as "tool breakage, slack work, and running away" as well as violence against slave owners, organized rebellion, and even suicide (Jon Butler 44–6). But growth in the ranks of the enslaved was accompanied by growing restrictions on their activities, including the prohibition of reading, writing, and the use of drums as tools that fomented rebellion, and the unofficial discouragement of conversion to Christianity as a practice that might give the enslaved a "rationale for their emancipation" (Pestana 82). Literacy was thus not only a marker of gentility and culture, separating colonial elites from the laboring classes, but it was also recognized as a "critical tool of political power that must be restricted to whites" (Kerrison 12).

But some colonists began calling attention to the disparity between the justifications for slavery and Christian and Enlightenment ideals, and advocating for the emancipation and education of enslaved Africans. In spite of the legal restrictions in many colonies, Anglican missionaries taught some enslaved Africans to read and write (Kerrison 12), and after emancipation some wrote accounts of their lives and captivity, while others, including Lucy Terry and linguistic prodigy Phillis Wheatley, found expression through poetry. While Terry's songs and stories were not published in her lifetime, she was an important figure in her community. Wheatley's poetry eventually found a willing publisher in London, and its existence and obvious erudition called attention to both the artificiality of the supposed distinctions between Europeans and Africans and the hypocrisies of such justifications for slavery among colonists who increasingly proclaimed themselves lovers of humanity and freedom.

If the seventeenth century was a time of exploration and establishment, the eighteenth century was a time of expansion and development. The only new English colony founded in the eighteenth century was Georgia in 1730; the other twelve colonies, which stretched from present-day South Carolina to Maine, continued to extend their roots deeper into North American soil, not only by pushing farther into Native American lands and forcing thousands of Native Americans west, but also by developing intellectual and cultural communities. The colonies developed a thriving culture of letters in which political, philosophical, and artistic debates on natural rights, revolution, and the importance of sensibility in shaping civic and personal relationships were staged. Annis Boudinot Stockton, Elizabeth Graeme Fergusson, and many other urban women wrote letters, poetry, essays, plays, and fiction that were shared in privately hosted salons, circulated by manuscript among networks of interested people throughout the colonies, and printed in pamphlets, newspapers, and books, occupying spaces that were public, private, and somewhere in between. In the midst of this vigorous debate, colonial readers and writers acquired a stronger sense of themselves as distinctly North American subjects of the distant British Empire, and stronger—frequently conflicting—opinions about how such a relationship ought to look, particularly when it came to governance, representation, and taxation. England had initially intended its colonies to both provide raw materials for European manufacturing and serve as a built-in market for English goods, but they hardly counted on colonists developing their own industries and wanting a say in the economic and political decisions that affected them, or the military costs of maintaining the colonies.[3]

As the eighteenth century wore on, colonists agitated for levels of autonomy and participation that the English government was increasingly reluctant to grant, leading to the fierce and bloody Revolutionary War (1775–1783). During the buildup to the war and in the dawn of the republic that arose in its wake, women such as Abigail Adams, Judith Sargent Murray, and Mercy Otis Warren engaged in the questions of revolution and representation, wrote vividly about their experiences with the war and its effects on their lives, and argued for the extension of civil rights and responsibilities to those whom the rhetoric of revolution had bypassed altogether, including women and enslaved Africans.[4] Judith Sargent Murray proclaimed "a new era in female history" in 1798 (*The Gleaner* 3: 189), and she and other newly American women aimed to take their place in it. In the turbulent early decades of the republic, during which each line of the Constitution and each policy was hotly debated, women wrote plays, poems, essays, histories, textbooks, and novels that explored the "obligations of citizenship" (Baker 95) as well as the possibilities for women's civic and social engagement. Writers of sentimental novels, such as Susanna Rowson, Hannah Webster Foster, and many others, "drew on a language of liberation," slavery, and natural rights (Baker 105–8) that had been extremely powerful in the decades leading up to the Revolutionary War in order to critique the restrictions of their patriarchal society and to argue for greater freedoms, legal equality, and better education for women—but, as Gareth Evans points out, they also helped to reinforce middle-class values in a culture whose class system was far from established (*passim*).

The eighteenth century was a time during which women writers thrived. They increasingly employed the rhetoric of emerging images of womanhood to justify their writing activity, which often circulated far outside the bounds of the home and significantly blurred the lines between public and private realms. They wrote fiction, poetry, drama, religious tracts and spiritual autobiographies, advice and conduct books, textbooks, children's books, local-color stories, translations, biographies, histories, family memoirs, cookbooks and domestic manuals, editorials, essays, and manifestos and were "always conspicuously present in public life" (Baym *American Women Writers* 3). Sensibility was a key theme of many women's writings, providing justifications for their engagement in civic, religious, and artistic activities and suggesting non-martial ways women could serve the revolution and the republic. These women were still predominantly white and Anglo-American, but Wheatley, a notable exception, presented her readers with undeniable evidence that, as Henry Louis Gates puts it, "culture was, could be, the equal possession of all humanity" (*Trials* 89–90). While they frequently disagreed on what American womanhood and America itself should be, many eighteenth-century women writers felt they lived in a time that was alive with possibility, and they were eager to make the most of it. In addressing the complexities of their world through multiple genres, American women writers made valuable contributions to the conversations about governance, civil liberties, and human rights that shaped the new United States.

Cultural shifts in the literary Atlantic

The eighteenth century was a time of rapid growth in the transatlantic world of letters. In the early decades of the century, a literary culture that was sharply satiric emerged in England, fueled by the proliferation of newspapers and other periodicals. Inspired in part by Miguel de Cervantes' *Don Quixote*, the emerging novel form was revolutionizing English literary culture in the hands of Daniel Defoe, Tobias Smollett, Samuel Richardson, and Henry Fielding, as well as Fielding's sister Sarah, Eliza Haywood, and many other women writing "novels of sensibility" (Showalter *Jury* 15). Alexander Pope, Lady Mary Wortley Montagu, Richard Steele, Joseph Addison, Jonathan Swift, and Samuel Johnson were publishing highly stylized and formalized poems and moral essays that satirized contemporary political and cultural situations, and dramatists such as Fielding, Steele, Susannah Centlivre, and John Gay wrote plays that presented the lives of ordinary people and commented on current events for an avid theatergoing public. With increases in literacy and the availability of printed materials, more people were reading, and writing, than ever before.

Much of this literature found its way to the colonies, along with the philosophical writings of John Locke, Francis Hutcheson, and others, but it took some time for its influence to become visible in colonial print culture, which was quietly undergoing shifts of its own. In some ways, the literature of the early eighteenth century in the North American colonies looked much like the literature of the seventeenth century that had preceded it. Ministers frequently published their sermons, Cotton Mather put out his massive religious history of New England, *Magnalia Christi Americana*, in 1702, and many individuals published tracts on various moral and religious themes—including *The Selling of Joseph*, believed to be the first anti-slavery tract in the colonies, published by Massachusetts merchant, printer, and judge Samuel Sewall in 1700. Very few women colonists wrote for publication in the early decades of the eighteenth century, but those who did followed much the same patterns as those who had come before them. Jane Colman

Turell of Massachusetts wrote poems about childbirth and domestic life, her religious faith, and the deaths of loved ones, as well as some essays and hymns; these were published along with a funeral sermon by Turell's father after her death from a sudden illness in 1735, in the hopes that her testimony of faithfulness to God and her devotion to her family would be "of good Use to Parents and Children" (Colman i). While the Puritan hold on New England culture might have been loosening, in Massachusetts at least its influence was still strongly felt.

But at the same time, the colonial literary landscape was evolving. Although they differ on the degree and methodology, scholars generally agree that literacy rose across the eighteenth century for white colonial men and women, although men consistently read at a higher rate.[5] And the colonies were certainly developing an active periodical culture that would grow to be as politically pointed as its transatlantic counterpart and would help to decentralize cultural production, which had been hitherto dominated by Boston. The first colonial newspaper with continuous publication, the weekly *Boston News-Letter*, began printing in 1704 and was quickly followed by dozens more throughout the colonies, largely made up of reprinted materials from British publications, advertisements, poems, essays, and letters from local contributors—some of them women.[6] Many would take pseudonyms as a nod to the convention dictating that respectable women should not seek personal fame. One of the earliest known women to do so was Pennsylvanian Elizabeth Magawley, who engaged in protracted battles of the sexes through satiric poems and essays that were printed in the *American Weekly Mercury* from 1724 to 1731, signed "Generosa" (D. Shields 92–104). Other women wrote anonymously during that time—complaining about mistreatment from men, bad marriages, the lack of suitable men to marry, and the inequality of the sexes, and establishing newspaper letter and poetry columns as the "designated public sites for the discussion of gender issues" (Bennett *Poets* 6)—but Magawley is one of the few who wrote consistently and identifiably from this early period (Bennett *Poets* 6–10). She was an early voice heralding the numbers of women who would write political and cultural satire in the revolutionary era, but she was nevertheless a reflection of an at least sometime openness on the part of a colonial print culture that was still "profoundly masculinist and class-bound" (Bennett *Poets* 8) and a growing boldness on the part of some colonial women writers in challenging cultural hierarchies.

There may be no better figure than Sarah Kemble Knight to illuminate how much colonial culture was in flux in the early eighteenth century, and how women's shifting roles contributed to this dynamic environment. Born and raised in Charlestown, Massachusetts, Knight straddled the line between Puritan past and more secular, entrepreneurial future, embracing the conception of New England as culturally exceptional while matter-of-factly—and quite literally—moving through professional and legal circles from which women had traditionally been excluded. Born in 1666, Knight married the much older sea captain and businessman Richard Knight in 1688, and she took over as head of her family's household when her father died in 1689. Her husband was frequently in London on business, and in his absence she ran a boardinghouse and shop, wrote letters on behalf of petitioners, copied court records, taught school (Benjamin Franklin and the Mather children are rumored to have been among her pupils), and trained herself in the law, particularly in settling estates. An effort to settle her cousin's estate in New Haven, Connecticut, led to the text for which she is known, *The Journal of Madam Knight*, which documents her 1704–1705 solo travels from Boston to New Haven and then on to New York before her return home. The manuscript was compiled shortly after Knight's journey and may have been intended for publication at that time but wasn't actually printed until 1825, when it was published anonymously during a surge of interest in early American texts (Bush 215). Due to the loss of the manuscript shortly after publication, it wasn't identified as having been written by Knight until 1858; however, Knight's frankness, humor, and resilience as she documents the perils of the road, her meals and the bodily functions that ensue, and her scornful but humorous encounters with provincial people provide a revealing glimpse into the life and mind of a seventeenth-century woman during a period of significant colonial transition.

Knight's text offers intriguing glimpses into some of the ways cultural values began to shift in the colonial imagination as Puritan social and political influence waned in the early eighteenth century. Many of Knight's contemporaries wrote private accounts of their lives, but their examinations of conscience and emphases of God's faithfulness more closely resembled spiritual autobiographies than anything else; Samuel Sewall, whose diary records his daily activities and thoughts on various social and political events, is a notable exception. Knight, on the other hand, wrote vividly and humorously about her experiences traveling on horseback across the wintry northeastern countryside and her visits with family and new acquaintances in New Haven and New York. Her journey is frequently perilous, but she relates it with the clear intent to entertain. While being led across a river in a canoe, she describes herself as "greatly terrified," but if at one moment she can only "entertain my Imagination" with "blackest Ideas of my Approching fate" crossing a "dang'ros River," which she overcomes by "raly[ing] all the Courage I was mistriss of," at the next she finds herself in "Raptures" at the "friendly Appearance of the Kind Conductress of the night," the moon, which inspires "very diverting tho'ts" and a poem of celebration (9–11, 14–15). In spite of her professed fear, Knight clearly delights in the play of her imagination and her sense of humor in facing these challenges. Her focus is not on her fear or her dependence on God but on her determination, mental resourcefulness, and creativity as a means of survival. But if Knight has rejected this part of the Puritan mindset, she has retained its sense of exceptionalism and her own as "the emissary of New England in strange lands" (Balkun 12), a point she repeatedly emphasizes as she travels farther from Boston. She depicts Boston as a place of greatly superior culture and intellect and criticizes the citizens of rural New Haven for their moral looseness, their lack of education by which they "Render themselves almost Ridiculos," and their failure to keep Native Americans and slaves in their proper places (34–38, 44). As Scott Michaelsen notes, Knight might be a strong, independent woman, but the social superiority emphasized in her *Journal* reveals her independence is "linked …

to the domination of others" and to a "bourgeois passion for proper or right form" that frequently extends to sharp critique of other women (35). As humorously as it might be portrayed, her condescension reveals the racially tinged and class-related underpinnings of the sense of empowerment that allows Knight to move through these spaces. Knight's *Journal* has been heralded as an early example of the picaresque tradition and Knight as the "first significant female humorist in American literature" (Bush 215); in her depiction of herself we can see the roots of the rugged, resilient individual, an emerging literary conception of the American self that would be as relevant at the time of publication in 1825 as it was during Knight's itinerant journey through the northeastern colonies.

The rise of manuscript culture

If Sarah Kemble Knight's *Journal* shows the beginnings of the conceptual transition from British subject to American citizen in the colonial imagination, it is also suggestive of another pattern that grew more prevalent over the eighteenth century: the role of poetry in social and cultural life. After a fearful nighttime river crossing, Knight is comforted by the appearance of the moon and composes a poem as she rides, which she copies into her journal account of her travels later that night. This practice was not at all unusual. Among Europeans and North American colonists, poetry was one of the most commonly employed forms of verbal creative expression in the eighteenth century; unlike prose, poetry could be composed, remembered, and passed along to others even when writing materials and time were hard to come by (Steedman 17ff.). As such, it was well suited to the exigencies of colonial life, especially for women, most of whom would not have the leisure to sit and compose poetry but might share it orally or (as Emily Dickinson would do one hundred years later) slip a pencil and scrap of paper from their pockets and jot a few lines in between rounds of laundry, weaving, or cooking. The rise in colonial women's literacy in the eighteenth century meant that written poetry was accessible to more women, but neither reading nor writing skills were prerequisite for poetry's composition or transmission (nor did those who lacked these skills wait for permission to begin). There was, as Steedman notes, a "constant interaction of oral and literate knowledges" (3), which allowed women of all social standings to participate in more or less formal creative networks that existed in the spaces between public and private realms. Wilcox points out that poetry served important social roles in the eighteenth century (57), although such roles varied widely depending on the poet and her social status—as seen in the lives of Lucy Terry and Annis Boudinot Stockton.

The life of Lucy Terry suggests some of the social and political functions of poetry for women without the privileges afforded by wealth, formal education, or whiteness. Stolen from Africa as a child and brought via Barbados to Rhode Island in 1730, Terry composed the 1746 poem "Bars Fight," which is widely recognized as the "earliest known work of literature by an African American" (Gates and McKay 186). She was purchased by Ebenezer and Abigail Wells and worked with another enslaved African in the Wells home and tavern in Deerfield, Massachusetts, where she was something of a local legend for her "volubility," the "fluency of her speech," and her "tenacious memory" ("Mrs. Lucy Prince" 3). Deerfield was home to a fairly large African community, some free and some enslaved, who lived in "ones and twos with white families" in their homes, in a less formal setting more frequently found in "urban than rural slavery" (Gerzina 72). Literacy was not prohibited in Deerfield, and while Terry was apparently taught to read and write by the Wells family, Gretchen Holbrook Gerzina points out that the comparative benignity of such arrangements is deceptive; the law may have "recognized the rights of free blacks but [it] also upheld the institution of slavery" (75). Terry may have been lauded by her fellow residents for her ready wit and her "recitations, songs, and poetry" (Proper 6), but she was still not permitted to eat dinner at the same table as Ebenezer and Abigail Wells (Gerzina 75). It was in the context of this apparently comfortable but foundationally conflicted community that Terry composed the poem for which she is remembered.

While "Bars Fight" is Terry's only surviving poem, the other known details of her life provide an indication of the social and political power that her gifts with language gave her and the public spaces they created for her. "Bars Fight" was composed to commemorate a Native American attack on two white Deerfield families that occurred on August 25, 1746. It is a frankly violent poem in rhyming tetrameter couplets that is believed to have been sung as a ballad, preserved and passed on orally until it was published on the front page of the *Springfield Daily Republican* more than one hundred years later. There is some scholarly debate on the intent of the poem. It begins innocently enough by lamenting the death of Samuel Allen, whose "face no more shall we behold" (8), but by the end of the second stanza Terry is describing Simeon Amsden, whose body is found "Not many rods distant from his head" (16), and in the fourth we see Eunice Allen, whose heavy petticoats prevent her escape and lead to her being "tommy hawked" on the head (25), images which are somewhat less solemn than the occasion would seem to demand; the poem ends with "Young Samuel Allen, Oh, lack-a-day!" (27) being carried as a captive to Canada. While April Langley sees the absence of religious language or references to slavery in "Bars Fight" as leaving room for ambiguity about Terry's subversive intent (157), Sharon Harris reads the poem and its unresolved ending (for Samuel Allen, at least) as a satirical comment on popular captivity narratives, which emphasize the horrors of ransomed captivity for people who themselves perpetuated unending captivity for Terry and many thousands of others for whom "there could be no overt narrative" of lament (*Executing* 172).

Terry's intent for "Bars Fight" may have been unclear, but her position on racism and the systems that upheld it was not. In 1756, Terry married a free black man, Abijah Prince, and was emancipated; over the next several decades, Terry used her facility with words to advocate for greater social and political freedom for her family, successfully representing herself in two major court battles to protect encroachments on their property from racist neighbors and presenting a three-hour argument for the admission of her son, a Revolutionary War veteran, to Williams

College that was widely acknowledged for its legal, scriptural, and rhetorical skill (Harris *Executing* 155–6; Gerzina 154–62). As Langley notes, Terry did not "wait ... to be called into existence" by a culture that frequently denied her humanity (156); she was one of the earliest African American women to use her abilities and her personal experience with injustice to advocate passionately for social and political change.

At the same time that Terry was putting her gifts for poetry and oratory to political use in New England, Annis Boudinot Stockton was part of a developing culture of letters among colonial elites that spanned New Jersey, Pennsylvania, and other parts of the Northeast. As the daughter of a successful craftsman and wife of a prominent lawyer and eventual signer of the Declaration of Independence, Stockton traveled in the top circles of Middle Atlantic society. Her coterie of elite colonial women (and a small number of men) formed in the 1750s included Pennsylvania poets Elizabeth Graeme Fergusson, Fergusson's niece Anna Young Smith, Susanna Wright, Milcah Martha Moore (through whose commonplace book much of this group's circulated poetry survives), and Hannah Griffitts, as well as New Jersey writers Esther Burr and Sarah Prince. They shared the details of their lives in letters and journals, conducted extended debates on philosophical, religious, and political subjects, and circulated their poetry and other writings in manuscript form, memorializing their lives and experiences and creating what Susan Stabile describes as a material collective identity among themselves (153). It was an emphatically feminine community that stretched across hundreds of miles and was built on "intellectual and creative exchange" (Gustafson 76) between women who might otherwise be somewhat isolated. Letter writing had long been a common means of establishing a sense of community across distance, and while it was frequently personal it was rarely as private in the eighteenth century as it might seem. Letters were often written with the understanding that they would be copied and shared among friends and, as Showalter notes, among the elites they frequently employed the "elegant neoclassical imagery of Augustan poetry rather than the American vernacular," composed with the intent of "enter[ing] the public sphere" (*Jury* 18). In circulating their poetry and other writing along with their letters, Stockton and the members of her "sororal network" wrote with a certain expectation of privacy springing from their desire to be "independent of the implied social constraints of mixed-sex company" (Mulford *Only* 4), but they also wrote with a certain expectation of quasi-publicity among members of their recipients' social circles with a similar investment in women's intellectual and artistic exercise.[7]

As Felicity Nussbaum has demonstrated, there was a significant amount of anti-feminist discussion in the eighteenth-century Atlantic world suggesting that women were bound by their emotional passions and lacked the intellectual and moral capacity to own property or to reason properly, based on Protestant arguments that woman was to blame for the fall of man.[8] Stockton and her friends found a way to challenge such depictions of eighteenth-century intellectual life as a strictly male enterprise and achieve a measure of celebrity without appearing to step out of place.[9] Their ability to engage in this creative and political activity was predicated on their elite status, which provided them the necessary education and leisure for belletristic pursuits, and their poetry reflected this reality. While they came from a variety of religious and political backgrounds, their poetry was largely consistent in style and subject matter with the English neoclassical conventions of their day popularized by Pope, Dryden, and others. Neoclassicism was a highly elitist and even misogynistic movement. It emphasized "order, logic, and emotional restraint," characterized by a careful matching of subject matter and poetic form, and neoclassicists valued a poet's ability to work within the constraints of a particular poetic genre, such as an ode, an eclogue, or an elegy, while successfully evoking the proper response from the reader; Mulford notes it was a system designed to exclude women, who were naturally subject to "ruling passions" (*Only* 1, 15). But like her British peers, Stockton wrote in every major poetic form and addressed common subjects such as friendship, romantic love for her husband, death and mourning, the differences between country and city life, and the ongoing poetic battle of the sexes. And, as Gustafson observes, Stockton also frequently employed the language of sensibility when writing about both personal and larger civic subjects, emphasizing the importance of sympathy, benevolence, and deep feeling (78–9). The careful and skillful adherence to strict neoclassical guidelines served as an effective counter to claims that women were inherently incapable of reason, but the emphasis on the value of sensibility, linked to emotion, sensitivity, and perception, also reflected an increasingly "resilient theoretical position" among Stockton and her friends that women's more humane qualities could in fact give them a rational advantage over men (Mulford *Only* 6). For as much as the poetry of these women might have enforced particular cultural boundaries related to class and education, it also pointedly challenged cultural boundaries related to proper gender roles and the values assigned to women and men.

Sensibility would come to play a powerful role in eighteenth-century colonial culture, not just in conversations about women's and men's rational and moral capabilities, but also in conversations about human rights and governance as the influence of Enlightenment spread and republican voices began to grow louder—and as political rhetoric emphasized moral responsibility to others based on sympathy and common humanity, sensibility became an increasingly powerful justification for women's participation in public discourse. Stockton's undated "Sensibility[,] an ode" suggests the connection between powerful feeling and civic responsibility that would become an important part of revolutionary rhetoric. In it, Stockton asks sensibility to give her the "tender trembling tear" when she sees "human woe" (5–6), the strength to "stretch the hand to sorrows tutor'd child" (9) and greet with kindness those who repent of their errors, and the "sprightly wit and true benevolence" (25) to help her rejoice with her loved ones when good things come. These lines provide evidence of the strong link between the characteristics of sensibility—sympathy, empathy, kindness, forgiveness, and charity—and Stockton's sense of what she ought to give to those around her, especially those less fortunate than she. As the colonies inched closer to revolution and sensibility became intertwined with American patriotism in the eyes of many, Stockton and many other women would rely on this connection to publicly articulate their views on civic matters, particularly when it came to the threat of war, and to imagine new roles for themselves in the public arena.[10]

Writing the Revolution

In a letter to Hannah Winthrop in 1774, poet, playwright, essayist, and historian Mercy Otis Warren wrote:

> When I took up my pen I determined to leave the field of politicks to those whose proper business it is to speculate and to act at this important crisis; but the occurrences that have lately taken place are so alarming and the subject so interwoven with the enjoyments of social and domestic life as to command the attention of the mother and the wife who before the contest is decided may be called to weep over the names of her beloved sons, slain by the same sword that deprived of life their intrepid and heroic Father.
>
> (*Letters* 27)

Warren makes two important points in this passage: it is the "alarming" nature of recent events that "command" her attention and her pen, even in addressing a subject that is the "proper business" of others; and the important political questions she feels compelled to address are, in fact, "interwoven" with domestic life, an inescapable part of daily life even for the woman determined to confine herself to private concerns and leave public events to men. For many colonial women, the threat of war quite literally entered their households each day. The great men of the world, of whom Warren's husband was one, might wish women would leave "the field of politicks" to them, but when it came to the possibility of a revolutionary war fought across the farms and forests of North America by their husbands, brothers, and sons, the field of politics or even the field of battle might literally be one woman's field of grain or another's house. This dual argument about the deeply felt trauma of war as a justification for action and women's personal experience of war, even away from the heat of battle, would echo throughout the Revolutionary period as women found themselves faced with the growing certainty of a war in which they would be powerfully affected but were supposed to have very little say.

The first shots of the Revolutionary War were fired on April 19, 1775, in a series of small towns near Boston, but colonial residents in the middle and late eighteenth century were long accustomed to the idea of war; Joan R. Gundersen notes, between 1740 and 1790 "peace appeared more as short periods of regrouping than as an end in itself" (xii). France, Britain, Spain, and much of Europe had been involved for more than a decade in the group of wars that would become known as the War of Austrian Succession (1739–1748). Many of these parties would engage each other again when British colonial conflicts with the French and their Native American allies over control of western Pennsylvania erupted into the French and Indian or Seven Years War in 1754 (Dowd 59ff.); within two years it had become another international conflict involving Sweden, Austria, France, Prussia, and Britain and reaching from Nova Scotia to Virginia as well as across Europe, India, and the Caribbean. Although one of the major issues leading to the war was British colonial intrusion onto Native American lands, and Native Americans had fought alongside both French and British colonists, the Treaty of Paris that ended the war in 1763 demonstrated imperial Europe's disregard for Native sovereignty. Several groups of Native Americans, angered by the "sheer audacity" of the division of the North American continent between Britain, France, and Spain, banded together to reclaim their stolen lands, launching what is now known as Pontiac's War (Dowd 61). As Dowd and many other historians have noted, the repercussions of the Seven Years War, such as Britain's massive resulting debt and the perception that the British colonists were unable to defend themselves without imperial assistance, accelerated the "imperial crises" that led to the Revolution (62). Beginning in 1764, Britain levied a series of taxes on the colonies to help defray the costs of the war, and colonists from across the thirteen colonies began various kinds of organized revolt, including attempts at diplomatic outreach, intercolonial agreements to boycott British goods, and underground acts of rebellion like the Boston Tea Party in 1773. Some colonists wanted to make peace and maintain ties with the British Empire, including many elites who enjoyed positions of power, but the tide of public opinion seemed to be turning toward independence.

Women who felt the pull of revolution but were excluded from political and martial activities found other ways to express revolutionary or anti-revolutionary fervor. The organizing activities of Loyalist women are less well known, but the Daughters of Liberty, organized as a counterpart to the Sons of Liberty of Tea Party fame, called for women to boycott tea and make homespun fabric rather than buying British imports.[11] Unable to take up arms themselves, many colonial women raised funds for local militias and embraced the new political and revolutionary resonances of domestic tasks that had previously seemed innocuous, such as cloth-making and purchasing household stores (Baker 97, 102–3).[12] And while elite women such as Stockton, Fergusson, and Abigail Adams—whose husbands, fathers, and brothers were deeply involved in colonial political affairs and who had intimate knowledge of the revolutionary conversations taking place at the highest levels—found a wider audience for their writings both in letters and in public spaces like newspapers and other periodicals, women writers of lower status such as Phyllis Wheatley also found a space for their voices. In the formative years following the United States' Declaration of Independence, during which war and peace raged with equal volume as the shape of the new nation was fiercely contested, women writers such as Judith Sargent Murray and Mercy Otis Warren argued in their plays, essays, poems, and other works that women had a vital and necessary role to play. These women increasingly pushed themselves into the public arena, engaged in conversation with prominent leaders, and commented pointedly on both civic matters and the unfair treatment of women; in so doing, they proposed non-martial ways to practice civic responsibility and fought to shape the fledgling United States as a nation that placed equal value on women's contributions.

Without question, one of the most remarkable women to whom the Revolution gave a voice was Phillis Wheatley. Although an enslaved African woman, Wheatley's prodigy and her poetic gifts gave her access to people of great power, and her participation in the discourse of sensibility and freedom highlighted the injustice and deep inequities on which the revolution and the new republic were being built. Wheatley was taken as child from Senegal and purchased in 1761 by John and Susannah Wheatley, a wealthy Boston couple who quickly recognized Wheatley's astonishing facility with language and allowed her to be instructed not only in English and English poetry but in Latin and Greek, and Roman history. Her first published poem, an address to the students of Harvard University, was printed by the *Newport Mercury* in 1767, when she was only thirteen or fourteen; at around seventeen, her elegy for the popular Methodist preacher George Whitefield was published in broadside throughout the northern colonies and in London, earning her international attention (Gates *Trials* 20–22). In the decades of Wheatley's most active writing, enslaved and emancipated Africans throughout the Atlantic Rim region were beginning to publish accounts of their experiences.[13] Wheatley's poetic activity was part of a slowly growing movement to acknowledge the validity of enslaved Africans' cultural and intellectual contributions, which would fuel abolition movements on both sides of the Atlantic in the coming decades. But this movement seemed a long way off in 1772, when Phillis Wheatley was forced to endure an examination by eighteen of Boston's most prominent ministers, politicians, and poets to determine whether she had the ability and knowledge to produce her poems. Henry Louis Gates, Jr. describes that incident as "the primal scene of African-American letters," in which Wheatley was "auditioning for the humanity of the entire African people" (*Trials* 5, 27). She passed the examination, but she and her supporters were still unable to find enough colonial subscribers to publish her proposed volume of poetry. Only after a journey to London to round up support could Wheatley's *Poems on Various Subjects, Religious and Moral* be published in 1773, to mixed praise but near universal marvel at the speed of her learning and accomplishment (Showalter *Jury* 22; Shields 1ff.). She was manumitted shortly thereafter and married, continuing to write poetry while working as a seamstress to support her family. Wheatley corresponded with abolitionist Samuel Hopkins, English Methodist leader the Countess of Huntingdon, Mohegan Christian minister Samson Occam, and other notable eighteenth century Atlantic figures, and the poem she addressed to George Washington in 1775 earned her an invitation to visit him in Cambridge, Massachusetts. Yet, all Wheatley's abilities and energies could not keep her from sliding into poverty, and she died in poor health after the birth of her third child in 1784.

Like Stockton, Wheatley was heavily influenced by contemporary neoclassical and religious traditions, and many of her poems are odes, elegies, and commemorative occasional verses that rely on the "discourse of sensibility" (Gustafson 81) for their emotional, spiritual, and patriotic effect. While in a 1774 letter to Occam she makes mention of the "natural Rights" of Africans and the "strange Absurdity" of those who profess to love liberty and yet participate in the "Exercise of oppressive

Power over others" (152–3), Wheatley rarely speaks plainly about slavery or her own longing for freedom in her poetry. In "To the Right Honourable William, Earl of Dartmouth," Wheatley points to the "love of Freedom" (21) she shares with Dartmouth and her readers; she claims this love derives from her imaginative sympathy for her parents' suffering at losing their child to slavery—a claim consonant with the layers of mediation involved in claims of sensibility (Gustafson 82)—and asks rhetorically whether, given this sympathetic identification, she can be expected to do anything but "pray / Others may never feel tyrannic sway" (Wheatley 30–1). She may be playing on the language of tyranny and slavery, as Vince Carretta and others have suggested, and hinting at the ways in which the revolutionary rhetoric had co-opted and effectively "trivialized" the horrors of chattel slavery (Carretta xxviii), but she refrains from commentary on her own enslavement or on abolition, leaving readers to make the connection.

Wheatley has been harshly criticized by some scholars, particularly at the height of the Civil Rights and Black Arts movements in the 1960s, for not addressing slavery more directly.[14] She has been especially condemned for her short poem "On Being Brought from Africa to America," in which she declares that "'Twas mercy brought me from my pagan land, / Taught my benighted soul to understand / That there's a God" and concludes by reminding (white) Christians that although they may view Africans with a "scornful eye," even they can "be refined and join the angelic train" (Wheatley 1–3). While twenty-first century readers might rightly shy away from the assumption that chattel slavery was ultimately beneficial to Africans because it brought them in contact with Christianity, to focus disproportionately on these lines is to ignore the powerful ethical and religious argument Wheatley is making for the shared humanity of "Negroes, black as Cain" and the white men and women who have enslaved them (Wheatley 7). In addition, as others have pointed out, it would have been difficult for Wheatley to circulate a poem overtly depicting the traumas or injustices of slavery, dependent as she was on the goodwill of the Wheatley family, to whom she was still enslaved, and the white patrons who subscribed to her work (Glazener 143). Gustafson also argues that Wheatley intentionally avoids anything that would render her a figure of sympathy or "silent (and silencing) spectacle"; she prefers to observe and portray the suffering of others rather than making herself a "sentimental object [who] merely suffers" (83). Thus, in her poem to Dartmouth and elsewhere, Wheatley presents affecting images and then shifts her readers' sympathetic energies toward higher goals: appreciation of God's divine nature, the importance of political liberty, or the glories of military heroism (Gustafson 83). In thus retaining her subjecthood and humanity in her poetry while shifting the focus to higher objects, Wheatley suggests the ways in which human suffering and even enslavement can be usefully transformed and transformative for both sufferers and witnesses.

Wheatley lived in Boston through the Revolutionary War until she was forced to flee as a refugee in 1775, but Wheatley's personal experiences with the war scarcely make an appearance in her poetry—unlike many other women writers who, although far from the battlefront, found life to be profoundly changed. As

Mulford points out, the war was not just a revolution against a distant imperial government, but also for many colonists a civil war that divided towns and families (*Only* 19). Stockton and Fergusson, both married to influential men in the British colonial governments who were not fully committed to the revolutionary cause, undoubtedly felt the division deeply; Fergusson's poem "The Deserted Wife" explores the toll that the divided loyalties and the protracted separation took on her marriage and expresses her deep heartache.[15] Other women also wrote about their experiences of war's horrors. Hudson Valley poet and novelist Ann Eliza Bleecker was forced to flee British troops on foot with her two young daughters in tow, the younger of whom died of dysentery during their flight to Albany. Bleecker and her surviving daughter, Margaretta Bleecker Faugéres, both wrote texts about the war that were "haunt[ed]" by this experience and the murder of another local woman, Jane McCrea, by British-allied Iroquois, and these texts are justified by the writers' personal "Revolutionary sacrifices" (Baker 99). Women may not have been able to claim the glories of the battlefield, but such texts eloquently demonstrated the hidden costs of war exacted from women and other noncombatants; in turn, these women's personal experiences with the violent repercussions of revolution authorized their public writing.

If some women found their justification for taking up traditionally masculine topics such as war and politics in their profound suffering, others, particularly elites such as Abigail Adams, Mercy Otis Warren, and Judith Sargent Murray, sought to redefine the terms of civic participation in ways that included women. Intimately involved in revolutionary activity in the quasi-public world of letters, Adams saw the cause of freedom as intertwined with the acknowledgment of human rights for women. As the wife of a leading member of the Continental Congress, Adams was privy to a significant amount of information, but her importance is not only as John Adams' wife; the letters she exchanged with her husband during his extended absences demonstrate her role as an active co-participant with him in the cause of revolution and the debates over the new government. Adams' letters to her husband combine discussion of weighty political affairs ("If we separate from Britain, what code of laws will be established? How shall we be governed so as to retain our liberties?") and personal, familial concerns about the hardships of war ("The little flock remember Papa, and kindly wish to see him"), but they also hint at her restlessness and ardent desire for individual and broader corporate action: "We have too many high sounding words," she wrote on October 16, 1774, "and too few actions that correspond with them" (Adams and Adams 125, 25, 45).

Beyond debating questions of political philosophy, Adams also used her letters to attempt to exert her influence on public opinion on one hand and specific policies on the other. The letters provide evidence of what Parry-Giles and Blair describe as Adams' "social politicking" on behalf of John Adams and the Continental Congress, a practice she would continue as the first lady (572). The letters between Abigail and her husband were written with the intention of somewhat broader distribution, so that Abigail was able to use the information provided by her husband to both inform and influence her circle of acquaintance—though the occasional warning from her husband that "This letter must be secret my dear—at least communicated with great discretion" (83) gives evidence of the ways Adams was coordinating locally to assist the Congress' efforts. She reports to him on public attitudes on the war and support for congressional proceedings, relays information about local battles and the status of army camps, and describes her work to establish social and political connections with Generals Washington and Lee and many other leaders of the revolution (Adams and Adams 80–1, 99–104). But in the midst of discussing the work of the Continental Congress and army, Adams repeatedly pushes for the extension of the revolutionary rhetoric of liberty to women and to enslaved Africans. In one letter, she famously asks her husband and his fellow congressional delegates to "remember the ladies" as they write the laws of the new nation, warning that "If particular care and attention is not paid … we are determined to foment a rebellion, and will not hold ourselves bound by any laws in which we have no voice or representation"; while there is a slight archness to her tone, Adams subsequently presses her point with appeals to both reason and emotion (148–9). In another letter she highlights the inherent contradiction between revolutionary rhetoric and the colonial reality of slavery, declaring that "It always appeared a most iniquitous scheme to me—to fight ourselves for what we are daily robbing and plundering from those who have as good a right to freedom as we have" (Adams and Adams 39). In the letters of Abigail Adams, we can see the activism of an exceptional woman of her time whose clearsightedness about the racial and gender hierarchies built into colonial America did not preclude her endorsement of the new republic, but allowed her to look forward through the ugliness of war to what America might become.

Although Adams worked largely behind the scenes, Warren, Murray, and many other women took their battles to the pages of American periodicals. Two of the most active—and the boldest—intellectuals of the early national period, Warren and Murray wrote and published extensively on political and social issues, frequently using pseudonyms as a nod to the cultural convention that insisted women should not seek public recognition, in spite of the fact that their identities were often known. In the early years of the Revolution, Warren was more prolific than the much younger Murray and worked to build public support for a break with England. She and her husband hosted "revolutionary meetings and debate" in their home in Plymouth, Massachusetts (Showalter *Jury* 17); she also published poems, essays, and several satirical plays, including *The Adulateur* (1772), *The Defeat* (1773), and *The Group* (1775), in Boston newspapers under the name "A Lady of Massachusetts." As Sandra J. Sarkela and Jason Shaffer have noted, while the plays received mixed critical reception as pieces of theater, they were highly effective as pro-revolutionary propaganda, reinforcing the identification of the British colonial administration with "tyranny and its opponents with virtue" and rousing a "complacent public" (Sarkela 550, 562). *The Group* was particularly successful, winning praise from John and Abigail Adams for its service to the cause of revolution (Cima 489). By her continual activity on behalf of the revolutionary efforts, Warren demonstrated the ways women could and ought to be engaged in political and civic affairs.

In the years immediately following the war, fierce arguments raged over the shape of the United States government and Warren and Murray threw themselves into the debates, advocating for the improvement of women's legal and social status, challenging male-centered visions of civic responsibility, and countering with their own images of republican womanhood. Warren was an anti-Federalist who believed that the Federalist position presented in the proposed constitution was a threat to democratic principles and particularly to women.[16] Her three-volume *History of the Rise, Progress, and Termination of the American Revolution, Interspersed with Biographical, Political and Moral Observations* (1805), which she began in 1791, reflects her concerns about Federalist infringements on individual liberties, including her frustration with the hierarchies of sexual and racial patriarchy embedded in—and in fact necessary to—the newly approved U.S. Constitution (Schloesser 112), but it also suggests her view of appropriate republican womanhood. It was one of the earliest historical accounts of the revolution and was an incredibly bold undertaking, given that history and the public discussion of it were considered, as she acknowledges, "the more peculiar province of masculine strength" (Warren xli; see also Baym *American* 1). But in it Warren announces her belief that "every domestic enjoyment depends on the unimpaired possession of civil and religious liberty," which makes the cultivation of these liberties in others her duty as a republican woman and mother (xlii). Thus, she portrays her writing of history as an act of female civic virtue on par with military and political service, not contradictory to but part of her domestic responsibilities to home and family. Warren's history uses highly moral framing, emphasizing in black-and-white tones the villainy of the British and the virtue of the Americans, and expressing the secularized, eighteenth-century republican version of Puritan ideology which held that "God had played a special role in enabling Americans to secure their freedom and establish the United States as a beacon of liberty to other nations" (Zagarri 285). In Warren's view, even though the Federalist government that had resulted from the revolution would lead to the marginalization of women and their exclusion from politics, women had a duty not to "marginalize themselves" (Schloesser 113); this was an essential part of women's civic responsibility in the republic, rendered as an extension of the domestic realm, even—or especially—under a system with which they disagreed.

While Warren's writing often focused on specific political debates, much of Murray's political writing focused on the relationship between the rights of women and the rhetoric of freedom in the new republic. Beginning in the 1780s, Murray anonymously published more than one hundred poems and essays in various major periodicals, many of which were later compiled into a three-volume set that was subscribed to by nearly eight hundred readers, including George and Martha Washington and John and Abigail Adams.[17] Writing with a lively wit and sense of irony, Murray praises the potential of the new republic while arguing for the extension of the "political language of emancipation" to women and the full recognition of their rights and responsibilities as civic participants (Baker 95), emphasizing the need for women's legal equality, financial independence and, most importantly, education based on the language of natural rights. She values moderate ambition, which she believes should be encouraged in the "young minds" of both boys and girls through proper education; she argues that each girl should be taught "to reverence [her]self" by cultivating her "intellectual existence," without which she would be at best a "pleasing picture" to hang in a gallery and would be vulnerable to flatterers and deceivers (*Selected* 45–6). Her most famous essay, "On the Equality of the Sexes," had been written during the war but was not published until 1790—two years before Wollstonecraft's *Vindication of the Rights of Women*— in *Massachusetts Magazine* under the pseudonym "Constantia." In it, she imputes the apparent foolishness and lack of intellectual capacity commonly used as an excuse to deny women's rights to men, who "rob us of the power t'improve," and asserts that "nature with *equality* imparts" both intelligence and the "*noble passions*" that inspire patriotism, liberty, and love of learning (*Selected* 4, emphasis in original). Murray employs several ironic turns in making her case, suggesting that the qualities for which women are frequently criticized—an interest in changing fashions and tendencies to gossip and flirt—are in fact markers of women's imaginative and intellectual capacities, and that women need only proper education to help direct their imaginations toward reason and good judgment (Galewski 86). In fighting for women's equality and proper education, she believed she was fighting for a more virtuous republic, one in which women were allowed to meet their full potential as an act of patriotic duty.

Adams, Warren, Murray, and the other elite women writers of the revolutionary era took fairly radical positions on the rights and positions of women in early national American society, but it is important to remember their activism was a function of their privilege and was in many ways highly chauvinistic. Schloesser notes that Adams became more conservative and more invested in a "racial patriarchy" that elevated whiteness and protected her class status as her husband grew more prominent and faced greater public scrutiny (115, 147); as with many of her elite peers, Adams' feminism was ultimately undermined by its dependence on a cultural definition of worthy womanhood within a set of boundaries demarcated by race and class.[18] In appropriating and applying the language and imagery of slavery to white colonists and their British oppressors, Warren's *History* acknowledges the many wrongs of slavery and colonial treatment of Native Americans but ultimately uses this identification as a literary device that reinforces freedom as a concept indelibly associated with whiteness (Doyle 76ff.; Schloesser 103ff.). And Murray might argue for women's equality, but the effectiveness of her argument often relies on the ways improved legal rights and education make women better companions for men (Galewski 99). As Mulford observes, the emphasis on proper feeling, education, and participation in the republic by many early national intellectuals reflects a powerful desire to "contain" public tastes, attitudes, and behavior and direct them into the appropriate channels—those that affirm the values of the elites and preserve the status quo (*Only* 40). The revolutionary writing of these elite women helped expose the shortcomings of the new republic's gender ideology even as it embraced revolutionary rhetoric, but it often did so at the expense of those without their race and class privileges, reinforcing the patriarchal power structure they critiqued. They demonstrate "how easy and insidious it was to sign on to the terms of racial patriarchy" (Schloesser 152), even when they might ardently believe otherwise.

Taking up the flag: The cause of women in the new republic

The last decades of the eighteenth century and the first decade of the nineteenth century were tumultuous for the new republic as its citizens and leaders faced the practical difficulties of making a single, functioning, and peaceful self-governing nation from colonies that each had their own regional cultures, industries, political systems, and priorities. In the midst of what seemed like continual agitation over what the country had become and what it ought to be, many women took advantage of the ever-increasing popularity of print culture to make their own arguments about how the revolution had played out in the lives of women. The preamble to the U.S. Constitution declared part of its purpose was to "form a more perfect Union," a secular extension of the millennial rhetoric that had inspired Puritan separatists in the earliest days of English colonization, and many women took the Constitution at its word.[19] Fueled by the work of Murray, Warren, and others, the early national years were characterized by a growing conviction that "women were only limited by their lack of education, not their intellectual capacities" (Branson 44). In fact, the push to improve women's education became one of the chief reform movements during this period, tied largely to ideas of proper republican motherhood. If in the seventeenth century a woman's highest duty had been to train up good and faithful Christian children, by the late eighteenth century this duty had shifted in tandem with the colonial and now republican mandate: in the same way that the pursuit of God's glory had given way to the pursuit of happiness, the emphasis on raising good Christians had been replaced by a new emphasis on raising good citizens. The only way to fulfill this duty properly, women argued, was for them to receive better education.

While Warren and Murray were engaging in public political debates about the roles of women, Susanna Rowson and Hannah Webster Foster were writing immensely popular sentimental novels that examined how the conflicting demands of the new republican womanhood played out in women's lives and interpersonal relationships when it came to questions of marriage and independence. They were part of a group of emerging American fiction writers that included Charles Brockden Brown, Rebecca Rush, Tabitha Tenney, Leonorea Sansay, and S.B.K. Wood. In the quest for a distinctly American voice that has preoccupied scholars since the early nineteenth century, these authors have been frequently overlooked or dismissed as insufficiently serious, overly didactic, and derivative of Richardson and other British writers, but in the last thirty years feminist scholars have worked to establish the importance of especially Rowson's and Foster's novels in exploring the issues facing women and other marginalized groups in the early national period. The protagonists in Rowson's *Charlotte Temple* (1790) and Foster's *The Coquette*

(1797) find themselves caught between the rhetoric of classical republicanism, which invokes personal sacrifice for the good of the polity, and liberalism, which emphasizes liberty and the pursuit of happiness (Baker 91); in their bodies they bear both the tensions and the consequences of the inevitable clash of these philo- sophical positions. The novels also contradict the pull of the smoothing impulses of literary patriotism in the early republic, revealing in wrenching detail the illusory nature of the rhetoric of liberty for women while, in the case of Rowson's work, emphasizing the cultural continuity between the old colonial regimes and the new nation masked by the emphasis on a specifically American literature. While at face value they can be read as deeply conservative texts affirming middle-class republican values of restraint, rationality, and modesty, these novels are ultimately ambivalent about the possibilities for women, serving as illustrations of the very real shortfalls that occur when revolutionary political philosophy is put into practice.

While most of the scholarly attention Susanna Rowson receives is related to *Charlotte Temple*, Rowson had a long career as a novelist, playwright, actress, and educator in both London and North America, and her writing reflects the cultural fluidity of her experience. Scholars have historically tended to think of national literatures as discrete, but Rowson's work demonstrates what more recent critics have emphasized: the strongly transatlantic nature of eighteenth-century literature, the links between the "political, social, economic, and historical relationships" among the peoples of the Atlantic Rim, and the destructiveness of patriarchal colo- nialism that did not disappear when independence was declared (Doolen 134).[20] Rowson's seduction-and-abandonment novel *Charlotte Temple* tells the story of an innocent young girl lured from her English boarding school by a handsome and flattering soldier, Montraville, seduced, and taken against her will to colonial America, where she is assuaged by promises of eventual marriage while being kept a virtual captive. Repeatedly deceived by Montraville and his cohorts, Charlotte sinks into illness, gives birth to a daughter, and dies with words of repentance and sorrow on her lips. Charlotte is the model of the kind of daughter Murray warns about—one whose shoddy education renders her unfit to cope with the threats posed by self-interested flatterers. If, as Doolen suggests, the novel acts as an allegory in which the family is a metaphor for national progress (123), then naïve Charlotte, selfish and dishonest Montraville, and their orphaned child sug- gest the ways in which the patriarchal national family is highly compromised and vulnerable. Though Montraville takes Charlotte to colonial America during the Revolutionary War, when the rhetoric of liberty and freedom from oppression is at its height, she becomes not more free but less so, wholly isolated and dependent on the whims of a capricious and untrustworthy man. This depiction empha- sizes the precarious position women held in a corrupt world. And yet Rowson's repeated authorial intrusions entreating young girls to heed Charlotte's example and the conclusion of the novel, in which Charlotte laments her moral weakness, seem to endorse the "middle-class virtue" (Mays 337) that Charlotte's situation simultaneously mocks. It is a deeply contradictory text that emphasizes the chaos and instability of the eighteenth-century world even as it attempts to restore order.

Foster's *The Coquette* offers a similarly complex portrait of the conflicts between the pursuit of happiness and the domestic (and therefore private) performance of republican virtue for American women. Based on the true story of Elizabeth Whitman, *The Coquette* was published anonymously by Foster as "A Lady of Massachusetts" in 1797. In the epistolary novel, protagonist Eliza Wharton finds herself freed from an engagement contracted by familial obligation by the death of her suitor and is determined to enjoy her unexpected freedom while maintaining her virtue; unwilling to either refuse the attentions of charming scoundrel Sanford or accept the proposal of respectable but dull minister Mr. Boyer, Eliza eventually loses Boyer, succumbs to Sanford's seductions, and dies alone in an inn after giving birth to their child. Unlike Charlotte Temple, Eliza is no ingénue but a woman of lively spirit, humor, and character who is clearsighted enough to see that both of the options presented to her for the pursuit of happiness—the embrace of private, domestic virtue with Mr. Boyer or of pleasure and society with Sanford—are unsatisfactory; yet she is surrounded by people who see no such thing, and the consequences of Eliza's incompatibility with the requirements of polite society are deadly. Many critics, including Cathy Davidson and Elizabeth Dill, see Eliza's story as revealing the injustices and contradictions of patriarchal culture and the ways the notion of marriage and motherhood as a woman's civic responsibility "fail[ed] the republic" and threatened both personal and public virtue (Dill 258). But other scholars see Foster's novel as a cautionary tale about the dangers of female autonomy and a reinforcement of the middle-class virtues of conformity, modesty, and moderation, serving a deeply conservative agenda in depicting "existing institutional inequalities" as being in the best interests of women (Joudrey 67; see also Baym *Woman's Fiction* 51 and Korobkin). Both threads are present in Foster's text, which condemns Eliza to death while rendering her deeply sympathetic in her quest for a measure of personal freedom. Many contemporary readers found Eliza to be so: the book went through nineteen editions between 1797 and 1874, and Elizabeth Whitman became a kind of local heroine; however much a threat to republican virtue and civic morality an unconstrained woman might have seemed in 1788, Foster's novel helped to "[transform] public opinion," creating a public who saw Whitman as less a criminal than a victim herself (Jennifer Harris 378).

The post-revolutionary years were marked by sharp dissent and political chaos, amid which many women found opportunities to speak eloquently for expanded rights and recognition. However, these years were also marked by a conservative backlash in which traditional gender roles were sometimes emphasized (if couched in new language) even by the elite women who believed most fiercely in women's equality, as a means of protecting their own access to power (Pearsall 129–31). Women might have found greater access to print under their own names or under pseudonyms, and those with sufficient wealth might receive better education, but they were not allowed to vote or hold office except for during a short period in New Jersey, due to a legal loophole that was closed by 1807 (Mulford *Only* 35). In addition, as Pearsall observes, the ability of more women to write for publication was in part due to economic growth and rising consumption, which led to a larger middle class and more leisure—but such growth was built on the backs of the unenfranchised working class and the increasing numbers of enslaved African Americans (131), the disregard for whose humanity was enshrined in the U.S. Constitution itself. For these Americans, the Revolution was one in name only, and it had been accomplished by the displacement and death of the many thousands of Native Americans upon whose lands the halls of the U.S. government stood. As the United States sought to define itself politically and culturally in the nineteenth century, these issues would preoccupy the moral energies of Americans in their continuing fight to create a "more perfect Union."

Notes

1 Isaac Newton's *Philosophiae Naturalis Principia Mathematica* (1687) introduced the laws of motion and gravity, among other notable discoveries, revolutionizing physics and scientific knowledge. John Locke's *Two Treatises of Government* (1689) argued persuasively for representative government as the most effective means of protecting the natural human rights to life, liberty, and private property. Scottish Enlightenment philosophers Francis Hutcheson and Lord Kames (Henry Home) would also have a powerful influence on American thought in the eighteenth century, building on Locke's ideas in order to argue for a universal moral sense that bound people together and for unalienable rights that included the right to resist an immoral government. See Robert Ferguson's *The American Enlightenment, 1750–1820* for an overview of the development of Enlightenment ideas in North America.

2 European settlers in every North American colony held enslaved Africans, but by far the greatest proportions were in the southern states with cash crop economies; by way of comparison, New York had the highest percentage of enslaved residents in the northern states at 15 percent in 1750, while in South Carolina enslaved Africans outnumbered European settlers two to one by 1720. See Jon Butler 37–41 for additional details.

3 Throughout the eighteenth century, England struggled to maintain control over colonial economic practices. One example is the Hat Act of 1732, which attempted to prevent intercolonial trade in American-made hats, beefing up the market for English-made hats; but the law was unenforceable, and Americans increasingly relied on British manufacturers primarily for "conveniences" and "superfluities" rather than for essentials, which they made themselves (Zahedieh 64–5).

4 As Pauline Schloesser notes, the positions of these women on racial issues were complex and sometimes contradictory, but they tended to reinforce systems that benefited the elite class to which they belonged; most notably, Adams apparently shifted toward a pro-slavery position after her husband's election to the presidency, bringing her views in line with his. See Schloesser 145, 108–10, and *passim*, and 42–43 in this volume.

5 Literacy statistics in the eighteenth century are difficult to compile because recordkeeping varied so widely and so much went unrecorded. For example, measuring literacy by signatures on deeds, wills, and other public documents excludes those who did not own property, a figure estimated at 20 to 30 percent of the white population and likely the entire African population. See C. Davidson 55–79 for more details.

6 By 1775, there would be nearly fifty newspapers and forty magazines being printed throughout the colonies. For an overview of print culture in the eighteenth century, see Amory and Hall's *A History of the Book in North America, Volume 1*.

7 Elizabeth Graeme Fergusson often convened a group of local friends in Philadelphia for conversations on literature, art, politics, and philosophy in what became a distinctly American version of the British salon culture Fergusson admired; later, Stockton would begin a similar practice at her home Morven in Princeton, New Jersey. For more on Fergusson and her salon, see Ousterhout and Slotten.

8 See Felicity Nussbaum's *The Brink of All We Hate*.

9 It should be noted that Stockton and some members of her group did occasionally publish poems in newspapers and other periodicals in the 1750s and 1760s; in later

decades, Stockton would publish poems in almost every major publication in the United States, twenty-one poems altogether (see Mulford *Only* 60). However, in the early decades their writing was primarily circulated via manuscript.

10 See Eustace for a broader overview of the role of emotion in the American Revolution and the formation of American social and political structures.

11 Hannah Griffitt's "The Female Patriots," published in the *Pennsylvania Chronicle* in 1768, calls for women to "nobly arise" and boycott taxed British goods (6). In a parenthetical aside, she suggests, "(Then merchants import till yr. Stores are all full, / May the buyers be few & yr traffic be dull!)" (9–10).

12 In one example, farmer's daughter Betsy Foote of Connecticut wrote in her diary that making homespun cloth made her feel "Nationly" (qtd. in Norton 169).

13 In 1760, Briton Hammon, former servant to a Connecticut general, published a captivity narrative. At the same time, the unrelated Jupiter Hammon, born into slavery in New York, began publishing religious poetry in local periodicals. And in 1772, freed slave James Albert Ukawsaw Gronniosaw published what is considered to be the first slave narrative in the English language in Britain.

14 In recent years many scholars have worked to correct factual inaccuracies about Wheatley's biography and to rehabilitate her image in the wake of this criticism. Gates' *The Trials of Phillis Wheatley* was an important work in this project; another notable defense comes from poet June Jordan, whose magnificent "The Difficult Miracle of Black Poetry in America: Something Like a Sonnet for Phillis Wheatley" argues passionately and persuasively for the "miracle" of Wheatley's poetry amid oppressive and dehumanizing conditions, noting that Wheatley wrote in the traditions of the only kinds of poetry to which she had been exposed (177ff.).

15 See Mulford *Only* 19–22 for more information on Stockton and Ousterhout for a detailed discussion of this period in Fergusson's life. See Mader for a thoughtful examination of "The Deserted Wife."

16 After the generally acknowledged failure of the original Articles of Confederation and Perpetual Union, Federalists and anti-Federalists fought over the role and size of the central government. The Federalist Papers (1787–1788), a series of anonymous essays now known to be written by prominent Federalists Alexander Hamilton, John Jay, and James Madison, argued for the ratification of the proposed constitution, which featured a strong central government, in response to several essays that had appeared in various periodicals urging the constitution's rejection based on its failure to protect various civil liberties, among other issues. The Bill of Rights was amended to the U.S. Constitution as a means of appeasing anti-Federalist concerns.

17 This set, titled *The Gleaner* after the name of Murray's popular essay series that ran in *Massachusetts Magazine* from 1792 to 1794, was Murray's most financially successful writing endeavor. It included about a hundred essays, several poems, and two of Murray's plays, which had been produced in Boston. The *Gleaner* column was written under a pseudonym, Mr. Vigilius, but Warren unmasked herself in the afterword at the end of the *Gleaner* collection, confessing that she had used the pseudonym in order to gain a wider audience than she would have under a woman's name.

18 Adams wrote to her husband in 1774 that she abhorred slavery, but Schloesser describes the ways that Adams, Warren, Murray, and other elite women of the eighteenth century opted instead for the relative safety of protecting their own limited race and class privileges (see Schloesser *passim*).

19 Bercovitch argues that this construction, suggesting the existence of something that has been perfected in the past and can be perfected again, depends on a constant cycle of dissatisfaction, dissent, and the silencing of the dissenting position by its incorporation into the mainstream. It concentrates power in the hands of those who hold it already and relies for its force on idealized conceptions of "America" that have never been realized. See Bercovitch *Jeremiad* xvff.

20 See Rust's "Daughters of America," Sorensen, Kritzer, and Homestead and Hansen for discussions of Rowson's plays and other works that draw on the transatlantic nature of eighteenth-century culture.

3

SENTIMENTAL POETS AND SCRIBBLING WOMEN

The writers of the early nineteenth century

In the story "Cacoethes Scribendi" (1830), Catharine Maria Sedgwick introduces Mrs. Courland, a middle-class mother of six who secretly harbors aspirations to authorship and finally takes up her pen after seeing that the authors of many of the stories she reads are her childhood friends; she goes on to publish several stories and recruits several members of her community to write too. In the figure of Mrs. Courland, Sedgwick is gently teasing the women who eagerly transmuted the events of their personal lives into didactic tales for publication in the costly gift editions known as annuals that became popular in the early nineteenth century.[1] These publications, the seemingly constant throng of new periodicals out of New York, Philadelphia, Boston, and other cities, and growing public interest in literary endeavor led to many new opportunities for women writers to publish their work. And yet "Cacoethes Scribendi" is ambivalent about whether the increase in women's writing is positive. Mrs. Courland's elderly mother refuses to write, citing a lack of skill, and her daughter Alice prefers not to offer her private life for public consumption; at the end of the story, Mrs. Courland gives up her writing career because Alice reveals she is getting married, a seeming affirmation of the idea that writing was not so much a vocation as a distraction, largely incompatible with women's domestic and familial responsibilities (Scheiber 49). Yet it also depicts the relationship between women and writing as "natural and idyllic," and with its emphasis on the shifts in this relationship from grandmother (unlearned) to mother (fluent) to daughter (fluent but discerning about the use of her skills), it suggests future generations of women writers may be freer still (Sánchez 110).

Sedgwick's story encapsulates many of the tensions for middle-class white women writing in the early nineteenth century. What did it mean to be a woman writer, and what was the value of her contributions? Were some kinds of writing more suitable than others? Did greater opportunities herald positive change or negative? Women might have better success finding their way into print—the gender bias of newspaper and periodical editors and publishers did not run deep enough to refuse what was, after all, a highly profitable enterprise—but the act of writing still had clear "political stakes" (S. Williams 210) for white women. Just as important are the women Sedgwick's story leaves out entirely: the African American and Native American women over whose bodies and lands many thousands would take up arms in the coming decades. They too found greater opportunities to write, but they also frequently had to assert their own humanity, worth, and rights to autonomy in their texts, raising even more significant questions: What did it mean to be an American woman, and why was African or Native American womanhood less valuable than white womanhood? Could the deep cultural and political rifts between white Americans and the peoples they subjugated in their conquest of the North American mainland be bridged if such subjugation was ongoing? For these women, the personal and political stakes of writing were far higher.

The United States was still in its infancy and eager to assert itself as a nation in the early nineteenth century, although the kind of nation it ought to be was being hotly contested in newspapers and literature, in government halls, and in private homes. On one issue, at least, many agreed: the United States ought to be *bigger*. While the colonies had tripled in square mileage in the eighteenth century, in the first half of the nineteenth century the United States expanded exponentially, acquiring via purchase, agreement, or seizure lands from Florida to the Pacific Coast. Settlement of these new territories was fueled by the reports of explorers like Lewis and Clark and the discovery of vast natural resources such as Midwestern timber and California gold; the powerful national ideology of Manifest Destiny suggested that American imperial expansion across the continent was not only foreordained but was part of the United States' responsibility to the world as a beacon of freedom and democracy.[2] To many white Americans in the eastern United States the land seemed wide open, full of possibility and romance, and the Western frontier became a prominent theme in American literature as explorers, wagon trains, and eventually railroads snaked their way across the continent. Many writers, including Caroline Kirkland and Louise Clappe, wrote lively, humorous, and picturesque stories of their experiences, and the West became both a symbol of hope and a proving ground in which the young nation might come into its own by taming the wilderness.

But the spread of the American flag across the continent did not mean freedom or democracy to the Native Americans displaced by this growth. U.S. territorial expansion in the nineteenth century was matched by increasingly draconian anti-Indian policies aimed at opening up the most desirable lands to white settlers. But as Native Americans were pushed out of their lands, they began to figure more prominently as writers of their own stories. Some published autobiographical, religious, and political texts calling attention to injustices against Native nations, while others sought to document and preserve Native cultures. Among these writers was Jane Johnston Schoolcraft (Ojibwe), the earliest known Native American woman writer and poet. Native Americans also began to figure more prominently in American literature, most frequently as variations on the noble and hostile savage in historical fiction and poetry by writers such as Sedgwick, Lydia Maria Child, and Lydia Sigourney. Situating Native characters in the past was a memorializing move motivated in part by a powerful culture of white supremacy that saw Native cultures as the inevitable victims of (white) progress. But it was also in some cases tempered by a sense of the deep injustice of white treatment of Native Americans, and attempts to reconcile the past with the kind of country the United States was becoming. This simultaneous reach back to history and forward to the future in the image of the Western frontier was an important component of the quest for a national literature that occupied American writers and thinkers in the nineteenth century.

The antebellum years were also characterized by political and religious ferment in which many women writers worked to eradicate social injustice. The Second Great Awakening began in the 1790s and swept through the states and new territories, breathing life into reform movements related to temperance, poverty relief, women's rights and education, Native American rights, labor conditions, prisons, and mental health facilities. Many women, including Catharine Beecher, Margaret Fuller, and Fanny Fern, took to the printed page to advocate for various reforms. But at the same time that mainstream Americans were embracing Protestant faith, many New England intellectuals and writers, including Child and Sedgwick, were leaving Calvinist denominations for the more open Unitarian church, which did not espouse the divinity of Christ or require members to make personal declarations of faith. Emily Dickinson, Fuller, and others were also influenced by the Transcendentalist movement, which embraced the divine "universal soul" that indissolubly joined human beings with all of creation (Emerson 270)—a radical position mainstream Christians found heretical. The focus on spiritual and intellectual freedom and the inherent worth of all of creation placed these writers in opposition to the growth of industry, imperial expansion, war, and other policies that resulted in the oppression of various peoples or the destruction of the natural world.

Of all the reform movements of this period, none was as fervently debated as abolition, which ultimately led to the American Civil War (1861–1865). The cause roused many white women writers to action. Sisters Sarah and Angelina Grimké left their slaveholding family in South Carolina to write and give speeches, Child wrote tracts and edited abolitionist publications, and Harriet Beecher Stowe wrote *Uncle Tom's Cabin* (1852), one of the most influential texts in American literary history. But the abolition movement also gave formerly enslaved African American women a platform to speak for themselves. Among them were Sojourner Truth, an abolitionist speaker of great rhetorical force; Harriet Jacobs, whose autobiographical *Incidents in the Life of a Slave Girl* (1861) called attention to the psychological and sexual victimization of enslaved women; and Harriet Wilson, whose novel *Our Nig* (1859) exposed the deeply entrenched racism of which Northerners were also guilty. During the war, women in both North and South took charge of farms and businesses, served as nurses and spies, and offered their homes as hospitals;

women such as Louisa May Alcott in the North and Margaret Junkin Preston, Judith McGuire, and Mary Boykin Chestnut in the South published accounts of their wartime experiences, presenting the struggles of women as a "valid, indeed central, story of the war" (Fahs 1471) equal to the experiences and accounts of great men.

Writers were in the midst of the major cultural and political movements of the early and mid-nineteenth century, participating, recording, and helping to shape these movements and broader cultural perceptions of them as they occurred. Their texts were similarly in the midst of multiple genres and movements, blurring boundaries between fiction and nonfiction, prose and poetry, advocacy, education, and entertainment. Their influence was linked to a simultaneous cultural and economic shift in the world of letters that was bound up with issues of race, class, and gender. While many nineteenth-century writers came from the middle and upper classes and relied on their relative wealth and leisure, the rapid growth of the publishing industry meant that for the first time, individuals could support themselves and their families as writers, editors, and critics. Many white women took up writing as a profession, refusing to be limited by cultural expectations dictating that they must marry, raise families, and make their homes a haven from the immoral public world—a belief system that became known as the Cult of True Womanhood.[3] But along with professionalization and some democratization came a backlash in the form of the construction of hierarchies of writing, which predictably placed women's productions near the bottom and well-educated white men's productions at the top. Serious, artistically minded men wrote "literature" that offered transformative aesthetic experiences, while women were accused of pandering to their readers, settling for financial gain and popular acclaim rather than artistic truth or beauty, and feeding the materialistic culture all great literary artists ought to repudiate—a position which, like the Cult of True Womanhood, was only available to those with enough financial and social security.[4] Nathaniel Hawthorne famously complained that "America is now wholly given over to a damned mob of scribbling women" and described their work as "trash" written for a public he would be "ashamed" to please (*Letters* 75).[5] While women's writing continued to drive enormous sales, a vocal coterie denounced it as sentimental pablum and its readers as lulled masses. They were even more dismayed because their quest to define literature was coeval with the goal of establishing a specifically American literature that could compete in reputation with Shakespeare, Dante, and Goethe; what was the hope for literature and the country if America could not recognize the truly great work done in her midst? Women's writing was not serious enough, artistic enough, or American enough, and yet too popular by far for critics invested in a particular conception of American literary prestige.

These criticisms of nineteenth-century American women's writing have been remarkably persistent. Women's texts have historically been ignored, dismissed as sentimental, unrealistic, didactic, and shallow, trading in clichés rather than engaging with important issues.[6] All but a few women, such as Emily Dickinson and Stowe, were for many decades deemed unworthy to be compared to the great white men—Melville, Hawthorne, Poe, Whitman, Emerson, and Thoreau—whose work most often stands in for nineteenth-century American literature. But such characterizations fail to take into account the wonderful diversity of women's writing during this period, their deep explorations of important issues and, not least of all, the massive popularity and impact of their work at the time of publication, as many feminist scholars have more recently argued. Women worked as editors and journalists, wrote sketches, short stories, novels, autobiographies, poems, and political treatises, kept diaries and letters, and used their pens to call for and in many cases bring about widespread cultural change. Their texts are difficult to discuss because they often cannot be sorted into one clear genre, instead straddling the lines between fiction, autobiography, poetry, and reform literature in complex and compelling ways. Women faced cultural, economic, and legal barriers to public participation, but they increasingly refused to stay in the social, economic, and political spaces to which they had been relegated, and their perspectives shaped and even dominated public conversation in the antebellum nineteenth century.

The profession of writing

The early nineteenth century saw the creation not only of what we now think of as literature, but also of authorship and literary culture. The thriving print culture of the late eighteenth century had become a full-fledged industry. Newspapers and magazines sprang up in the Northeast and all over the country. The domestic book trade grew exponentially, and literary subjects became a prominent theme in periodicals in the form of published fiction and poetry, reviews, essays, advertisements, and articles featuring popular writers, about whom the public had a growing curiosity (S. Ryan 166). Some magazines still published today, such as the *Saturday Evening Post* and the *Atlantic Monthly*, were founded during this period; many more that are unknown to today's readers found hundreds of thousands of subscribers. *Godey's Lady's Book*, which published stories, poetry, dress patterns, sheet music, recipes, and fashion plates, had a subscription list of 150,000 at its peak (Mott 1: 581). Many smaller magazines lasted for only a few years or decades, but they contributed to an American middle-class culture that thought of itself as increasingly literary.

While the writing industry was dominated by men, many women fought for professional opportunities as writers, critics, columnists, journalists, editors, and founders of periodicals. Lydia Maria Child, inspired by the historical romances of Walter Scott and the call for a national literature, wrote a historical novel about Native Americans in New England; the publication of *Hobomok: A Tale of Early Times* (1824) launched a writing and editorial career that lasted several decades and included children's literature, domestic instruction manuals, and fiery anti-slavery texts. Sarah Willis Parton—more commonly known by her pseudonym, Fanny Fern—and Louisa May Alcott wrote to support their families after the men who were supposed to provide for them were unable to do so, and their writings are suffused with awareness of the deep poverty in which many nineteenth-century women and children around them lived and died.[7] Fern's work as a feature writer and columnist covering household topics and reform issues made her one of New York's first celebrity authors; she wrote primarily for the *New-York Ledger*, but she also collected her columns into several books and published three novels. Alcott is most famous for her many novels, but she also published stories and poems in a variety of genres under her own name and several pseudonyms.

Many women had long and distinguished publishing careers, working in so many genres, subject matters, and positions that the categories typically used to discuss literature and authors are difficult to apply. Such successes might make it seem as if the field was altogether clear for women writers, but this was far from the case. Writing was still considered somewhat morally suspect for women, as was the reading of fiction, so women's texts are often full of didactic disclaimers meant to exculpate both authors and readers (S. Ryan 168). And many women wrote anonymously or under pseudonyms, some even claiming to be men, as Child did in the preface to *Hobomok*. When it came to editorial positions, women were most welcome at publications that were closer to the margins: those affiliated with progressive or radical viewpoints or those intended for women and children. Child founded a children's magazine before editing an abolitionist paper, and Sarah Josepha Hale founded her own women's magazine before it was bought by Louis Godey and she joined him as an editor of *Godey's Lady's Book*. Women's rights activist Margaret Fuller was in many ways the most radical: she was one of the first women to support herself as a journalist, traveled alone to Europe to cover the Italian Revolution, and had a child out of wedlock with her much younger Italian lover; she was a popular literary critic and journalist for Horace Greeley's *New York Tribune*, but she found editorial work only with the Transcendentalist journal *The Dial*.[8] Women were among the most popular writers in newspapers and magazines for the general population, but it would be many decades before they reached similar positions of influence in the industry.

The women who became powerful in publishing were white and largely middle class; in spite of their interest in causes involving marginalized groups, they were no less invested in retaining their new authority than the men they worked with and for, which often led to a kind of professional gatekeeping. These women had relied on editorial goodwill from powerful men to reach the positions they held, and they often found themselves in the position to give or withhold similar goodwill from women of color. One notable example is the case of Harriet Jacobs, who sought help from female abolitionists in publishing her autobiographical novel. Jacobs initially approached Stowe through a mutual friend, but instead of helping her Stowe suggested Jacobs allow her to use the story in Stowe's upcoming *Key to Uncle Tom's Cabin* (1853), a text designed to respond to criticism of Stowe's novel. When Jacobs refused, insisting that publishing her story on its own "would do more good" for the abolitionist cause without the addition of any of Stowe's "romance," Stowe abruptly ended their communication (qtd. in Belasco 100). Jacobs felt this as a deep betrayal (Yellin xxi), but she eventually got help from Child, and *Incidents* was published in 1861. Both Stowe and Child had the power to bring Jacobs and her text to the reading public, and each attempted to mediate the text in her own way based on motivations with varying degrees of self-interest. They may have had benevolent intentions, but they also effectively delimited African American women's access to the literary marketplace.

Poetry and the politics of sentiment

As the publishing industry grew in the early nineteenth century, the U.S. market for poetry broadened. Newspapers and magazines spread poetry throughout the nation, and popular poems were often reprinted in multiple publications. Leather-bound and gilt gift editions of poetry flourished alongside their prose cousins, and many poets began producing collections out-of-pocket or through subscription in addition to those volumes released by publishing houses (Charvat 29–48, 100–5). The expansion in the publication of women's poetry was remarkable: according to one tally, only eighteen American women had published volumes of poetry prior to 1800, but more than 1,600 volumes by American women from a range of race and class backgrounds were published during the nineteenth century (Davis and Joyce ix–x). Poetry's rising popularity and the increase in publication venues meant women's writing was accessible to more readers than ever before.

Women's poetry from the antebellum period had a long history of critical neglect. As Elizabeth Renker notes, for much of the twentieth century, nineteenth-century poetry was seen as a vast wasteland, with the chief exceptions being Dickinson and Whitman, harbingers of the poetic glories the modernist movement would visit upon the civilized world (232). Virtually the entire century's poetry was rejected as too feminine, but women's poetry came under particular opprobrium, condemned as apolitical, domestic, and excessively emotional. It was an oversimplification that largely held for several decades. However, feminist scholars in the late twentieth century began to recover long-ignored poets and their texts and reevaluate not only the variety and achievement of women's poetry, but also its political and cultural implications. Foremost among recent scholars has been Paula Bernat Bennett, whose *Poets in the Public Sphere* (2003) argues that nineteenth-century women's poetry was part of public conversations about gender and social reform that led to the victories of first-wave feminism.[9] The work of Bennett and others has paved the way for new understandings of poetry in the antebellum world by women such as Frances Sargent Osgood, Lydia Sigourney, and numerous others as complex and multivalent, both reaffirming and manipulating ideological femininity to serve various social, political, and professional ends.

Women's poetry came in a variety of forms, including ballads, occasional poems, lyrics, and odes, and appeared in public and semi-public media, depending on the poet's fame, location, and opportunities for publication. Poetry might be published under a woman's actual name, a pseudonym, or anonymously; it might show up in a newspaper, magazine, a bound book, or perhaps all three; if in book form, it might be a poet's own collection, a gift volume, or an anthology authorized by an expert like literary critic Rufus Griswold or his rival, editor and poet Caroline Mays; or it might be read aloud by the poet herself at a private salon. These poetic practices and venues had shifted over time. In the early decades of the republic women participated robustly in public civic conversations, and the women's poetry that appeared in the columns of the nation's newspapers in the first two decades of the nineteenth century was an extension of these earlier traditions. Like Judith Sargent Murray and her peers, early nineteenth-century poets emphasized wit and participated in ongoing public debates, particularly the battle of the sexes. Many women writing in this tradition, such as Anna Maria Wells, wrote humorous, direct poetry that presented arguments based on reason rather than emotion (Bennett *Poets* 27–31). But by the mid-1820s, the genteel poetic tradition referred to as sentimental poetry had established itself and would dominate American poetry for the next several decades. While such poems have come to be associated with women, Mary Louise Kete argues that women did not have the monopoly on sentimental poetry (xii); men and women both wrote enough of the genteel poetry modern critics have loved to hate to fill several anthologies. This poetry is preoccupied with home and family as a sacred vocation, chaste romantic love, Christian piety, American nationalism, and reflections on the natural world, and it is often tinged with high flights of emotion, but it is far from the only type of poetry antebellum women wrote.

Writers of sentimental poetry were responding to traditions that originated in eighteenth-century discourses of sensibility and characterized the early Romantic literature written by men such as Goethe (Renker 240; Bennett *Poets* 23–7). For women, participation in such discourses involved self-effacement because they privileged a male subjectivity that anchored women to a domestic role—the bourgeois Angel in the House (Bennett *Poets* 27).[10] And yet, as Bennett notes, by publishing these ostensibly private poems in public spaces, women tested the bounds of this ideology even as they seemed to affirm it. The genteel literary traditions in which such poets as Sigourney, Osgood, Elizabeth Oakes Smith, Julia Ward Howe, and numerous others participated paid lip service to Victorian gender norms emphasizing womanly devotion to the home, but in practice their genteel poetry and their careers as poets often challenge the limits of such norms in semi-public and public spaces—including in the fact of publication itself.

Frances Sargent Osgood is a prime example of a poet who appeared to toe the line of domestic ideology but whose body of work reveals intriguing complexities. Much of Osgood's published poetry follows the genteel model closely, praising unspoilt maiden youth and beauty, the joys and sorrows of chaste romantic love, the innocence of children, the charms of home and family life, and the glories of nature. But the level of Osgood's craft is revealed most clearly in the unpublished/salon poetry discovered by Joanne Dobson.[11] For example, "The Wraith of the Rose" was likely read at a gathering of New York's literary elite in the 1840s (Dobson 632). In this poem, Osgood does away with propriety and reflects frankly on a long-ended love affair when her former swain comes to call, warning him he would "better far at home remain, / And save your time – and *knee!*" (7–8). She later confesses her regrets in a series of lines that begin with "I wish": that she had not burned his lock of hair, and that he had not *"drank champagne / So freely since we parted!"* (21–2); her anger grows, and she eventually cuts herself off mid-sentence, concluding with the wish that her lover will find "a peerless wife, / Whose wishes, Sense shall bridle!" (39–40). This closing acknowledges the unconventionality of all that has preceded it, hinting at the way a proper wife might—unlike the speaker—suppress such inappropriate wishes, and offering a glimpse of the unruly passion that might lurk behind even the prettiest feminine façades. Dobson argues this private poetry demonstrates an "urbane and sophisti-cated voice" that plays with the "dilemmas and absurdities" of sexual attraction within the limitations of Victorian society (632, 646); she and Eliza Richards use these salon poems as evidence to argue that the persona presented in Osgood's published poetry is the construction of a savvy businesswoman catering to popular taste in femininity (Richards 72ff.). Osgood styles herself as "the erotic dream of the nineteenth-century bourgeois everyman ... playful, fantastical, angelic, senti-mental, knowing, innocently perverse, always promising, never giving" (Bennett *Poets* 36), and yet she can drop any of these masks at will to reveal the real woman behind the poems. Her ability to manipulate these conventions calls attention to the space between performance and reality and pushes back against the idealization of domestic womanhood.

In addition to sentimental lyric poetry, many women in the nineteenth cen-tury wrote poetry of protest; African American poets Sarah Louise Forten and her niece Charlotte Forten Grimké, Quaker writer Eliza Earle, and career poet Lydia Sigourney wrote in the "high-sentimental" political mode (Bennett *Poets* 42), using their poetry to activate readers' sympathy and help rectify various social wrongs. Sigourney, the most prominent of these, has often been described as the "high priestess" of the sentimental poets (Bennett *Poets* 60) because her life and career fit a bootstrapping model that ultimately "affirm[ed the] traditional class structure" (Baym "Reinventing" 385). The construction of this reputation began during Sigourney's life, and she helped perpetuate it, churning out domestic poetry, funerary odes, and other typically sentimental poems in astonishing numbers in a career that spanned more than fifty years.[12] She is best remembered for poems such as "Death of an Infant" (1827), whose subject is a "cherub" with a beauty so divine it can charm even "ruthless" Death; while Death will close the blue eyes, he does not dare to erase the "smile, / So fix'd and holy" from the child's face because he "dared not steal / The signet-ring of Heaven" (1, 7, 13–15). Such poems firmly established Sigourney as a poet of feeling, piety, and homely devotion.

But Sigourney also developed an extensive body of historical poetry and prose that positioned her as an advocate of conservative republicanism and evangelical Christianity, writing narrative poetry that catalogued the mistreatment of Native Americans and explored the "insoluble *political* and *moral* problem" posed by the triumph of the American project at the cost of republican and Christian principles (Baym "Reinventing" 392, 394). In shorter poems such as "Indian Names" (1834) and much longer works such as her 4,000-line *Traits of the Aborigines of America: A Poem* (1822), Sigourney casts Euroamerican treatment of Native Americans in the uncomfortable light of Christian principles and asks readers to imagine having to defend themselves before God after having driven Native Americans "from their father's lands," violated treaties, and treated them like "the insects of the hour" ("Indian Names" 45, 46, 42). In the exhaustively footnoted *Traits of the Aborigines*, Sigourney documents Native history throughout the Americas and concludes with a call to action and a vision of an America in which white Americans and converted Native Americans live together in Christian harmony, a stance Baym describes as deliberately public and "thoroughly Utopian" ("Reinventing" 399). It is a perspective that Sigourney acknowledged in her memoir was "singularly unpopular" when the poem was published in 1822 (*Letters* 327), but it was one she held her entire life and never stopped expressing.

Sigourney's model of womanhood attempted to carve a public space for women's social and political engagement using the "range of allowed achievements" for women while exploiting their perceived "required inadequacies" (Baym "Reinventing" 385). It was no less opportunistic than Osgood's performative Victorian femininity; they may have worked to different ends, but both poets pushed for a greater range of political expression for women. For Osgood, Sigourney, and the thousands of other women who wrote in sentimental modes, poetic practice constantly blurred the lines between private and public space and utterance, and through it they sought to reshape the boundaries of acceptable womanhood beyond the confines of the home.

The poet of circumference

Unlike the poets who made a profession out of writing poetry obedient to nineteenth-century conventions, Emily Dickinson wrote in her own highly idiosyncratic style and refused to publish most of her poetry, instead circulating it among friends and family or hiding it away, stitched together in handmade books referred to as fascicles that were only discovered after her death.[13] And although early twentieth-century modernist critics dismissed most nineteenth-century women poets, they are largely responsible for launching Dickinson's reputation as one of the major poets in American history (Renker 232–5). They embraced her irregular syntax and punctuation, as well as her turn away from commercial endeavor and her lack of interest in pleasing the reading masses. Dickinson was aware of her difference from her peers, describing herself in a letter to mentor Thomas Wentworth Higginson as the "only Kangaroo among the beauty" (*Letters* 412), but her deliberate withdrawal from participation in the marketplace was not so much a matter of scorn for the work of other poets as a conviction about her own artistic values. Dickinson's writing practice involved no less a refusal of Victorian gender norms than many of her sentimental peers, but the result was an astonishing body of work produced by one of the most original voices in American literature.

Dickinson was born to a prominent family in Amherst, Massachusetts. As a child during the Congregationalist revivals of the Second Great Awakening that swept up most of her own family, Dickinson refused to publicly affirm her faith, confiding to a friend that she wanted to please her family but "it is hard for me to give up the world" (*Letters* 67). She was educated first at Amherst Academy and then at Mt. Holyoke Female Seminary, where she studied poetry, history, mathematics, Latin, and the natural sciences, developing an enduring love for the outdoor world that would reveal itself in her poetry. After reluctantly leaving school due to illness, Dickinson continued to read widely in the family library, devouring the newest releases in science, history, travel writing, poetry, and fiction in spite of her father's insistence that too much fiction-reading would "joggle the mind" (*Letters* 404).

Scholars speculate that Dickinson may have had several love affairs, possible with George Gould, Judge Otis Lord, Samuel Bowles, and her future sister-in-law, Susan Gilbert Dickinson, but she refused to marry and take up wifely and maternal roles. Instead, she devoted her adult years to cultivation of her poetic voice, writing on scraps of brown paper bags, in the margins of magazine clippings, and on the backs of recipes, envelopes, and old letters (Franklin "Fascicles" 16). Dickinson's career spanned nearly half of the nineteenth century and was stunning in scope. She wrote her earliest known poem as a teenager, and by her death in 1886 she had written nearly 1,800 more; though she initially sought publication and guidance from Higginson and others, after witnessing the liberties editors took to make her poems conform to contemporary conventions, she determined never to subject her work to editorial interference again (Dickinson *Letters* 450; see also Denman 23ff.). She continued to write in every spare moment, however, and was especially prolific between 1858 and 1865, when she wrote more than half her known poems. For reasons that are unclear, at some point in the 1860s she began wearing only white and eventually withdrew from social circulation, leaving the family grounds only rarely after 1869. Such resistance was not without cost; Dickinson was the subject of much mythologizing, even during her lifetime, marked as an odd spinster nursing a broken heart, a loner with a morbid streak, or a lunatic lost inside her own mind. And yet the Dickinson seen in her poems and letters is not a madwoman or an isolated, embittered recluse, but a woman deeply engaged in exploring the world around her through poetry.

Dickinson's refusal to publish and her social isolation are the parts of her biography that loom largest over her poetry. She has often been caricatured as a poet either deranged or romantic in her solitude, but such depictions are hardly accurate. Dickinson had warm and loving relationships with her family at The Homestead. She also maintained an active correspondence with dozens of friends and relations. Her letters were affectionate, deeply emotional, and in some cases even erotic— particularly many earlier letters written to Susan and three letters to an unknown lover known as the Master letters. And her correspondence often serves as an extension of her poetic practice. Many letters included partial or complete copies of her poems, and as Elizabeth Hewitt notes, later in her life Dickinson increasingly merged epistolary and poetic forms, infusing her letters with the dashes and fragmented phrases found in her poems and creating "peculiarly hybrid" texts (43). Her poem "This is my letter to the World" (1862) suggests the ways the two forms merged in Dickinson's conception; letter and poem are one, both consisting of the "simple News" she has heard from "Nature," a message Dickinson now entrusts to her reader with the plea to "Judge tenderly" of the messenger (*Poems* 442, ll. 3, 8).[14] As Hewitt notes, the analogy here suggests each poem is a "social document" as much as any letter, and each letter as fraught and prone to misunderstanding as any poem (54).

Dickinson was also an avid consumer of news and current events, which frequently appear in her letters and poems. Although physically isolated, she "allowed her intellect and imagination to trespass all boundaries" (Martin *Cambridge* 36). Dickinson was especially curious about the Civil War, which coincided with her period of greatest poetic productivity and which had a profound, lifelong effect on her. Images of and references to war make numerous if sometimes oblique appearances in her poems, as in "The Only News I know" (1864), "The name – of it – is 'Autumn' –" (1862), and "To know just how He suffered – would be dear –" (1862), which expresses Dickinson's grief at the death of friend Frazer Stearns. But though she came from a pro-Union family, her poetry does not repeat pro-Northern or anti-Confederate sentiments, nor does she "espouse the worthiness of dying" for a cause (Cappucci 262). Instead she probes the horrors of war and the uncertainties associated with death, wondering of Frazer Stearns "Was He afraid – or tranquil – / Might He know / How Conscious Consciousness – could grow –" (622, ll. 22–4). As Shira Wolosky argues, the Civil War was an "arena" in which Dickinson worked out difficult existential and spiritual questions (*Emily* 62), and a part of her deep and personal engagement with the wider world.

Though she repudiated the literary marketplace, Dickinson was nonetheless interested in the response to her poetry from other writers. She maintained a lengthy correspondence with Higginson, whom she often addressed as her "Preceptor," famously asking if he was "too occupied to say if my Verse is alive?" (*Letters* 403). She also wrote regularly to poet and school friend Helen Hunt Jackson, and they discussed whether some of her poetry might be included anonymously in an anthology (Martin *Cambridge* 115). Bennett suggests these engagements with the literary establishment "deeply compromised" the privacy of Dickinson's poetry (*Poets* 39), but this is so only if we accept that such exposure was cynically played, rather than the genuine desire to participate in a form of artistic community. Dickinson's refusal to publish after her initial forays and her close guarding of her manuscripts suggest the value she placed on privacy, and on the unique cadences and rhythms of her poetic style. "Publication – is the Auction / Of the Mind of Man," she declares in one poem, insisting that "Poverty" would be preferable to such transactions (709, ll. 1–3). But it should be clear that Dickinson's reticence and to some degree her idiosyncrasy as a poet were afforded by her middle-class status; she was subject to none of the financial difficulties that made Sigourney, Alcott, Fern, and many other women turn to writing for support, and was subject likewise to none of the artistic compromises.

There are many ways to characterize Dickinson's poetry, but one broad way is through the idea of "circumference," a term Dickinson used to denote her commitment to the exploration of the outermost limits of emotional experience, both pleasurable and painful. "I am in the business of Circumference," she announced in a letter to Higginson in 1862 (*Letters* 412), and her poetry reveals her willingness to examine physically, intellectually, and imaginatively, the farthest reaches of the universe, subjects as large as the solar system and as small as bumble-bees, as unknowable as death or as concrete as soil, as distant as South America or as near as her own garden. Many of her most powerful experiences occur in nature. There she finds the divine, marking the Sabbath not in church but in a wood with a "Bobolink for a Chorister," a place where "God preaches" and she can experience heaven on earth instead of waiting for an afterlife (324, ll. 3, 8). She is not starry-eyed about nature, which she recognizes "sometimes … sears a Sapling" (314, l. 1) and is as often as not "caught / Without her Diadem" (1075, ll. 7–8), but her willingness to represent even the destructive parts of nature points to her larger willingness to give herself—and her reader—entirely over to the truth of the experience. It is this openness and vulnerability that comes through in "I stepped from Plank to Plank" (1864), in which she crosses a fragile bridge with the glory of the night sky above her head and "About [her] feet the Sea"; though the next step may be her "final inch," she gains by it "that precarious Gait / Some call Experience" (875, ll. 4, 6–8). Dickinson is committed to her path of exploration and the wonder that comes with it, but she is aware that the potential for destruction is real. This risk-taking quality perhaps above all belies the caricatures of Dickinson as emotionally and socially crippled, highlighting her obedience to her own ethical vision and her right to live as she would or to lose all in the attempt. It is no wonder she declared herself "A half unconscious Queen — / … With Will to choose, or to reject" (508, ll. 16, 18) and "Royal — all but the Crown!" (1072, l. 5). Dickinson claimed a radical and radically un-Victorian measure of self-determination, and it is the power of such declarations that makes her poetry resonant for so many readers still.[15]

Indian removal, the West, and the vanishing race

Since the earliest days of colonization, European settlers had been confronted by the unpleasant reality that the lands on which their visions of prosperity depended already had inhabitants with their own claims. Conflicts between Native Americans and settlers only sharpened with the founding and subsequent growth of the new republic. Many Euroamericans saw the expansion of the United States as the divinely ordained future of the continent, and the presence of Native Americans as a hurdle to be overcome on the path of national progress. The result was a series of devastating anti-Indian policies that coerced Native Americans into exchanging their lands for territory west of the Mississippi River or much smaller tracts within their ancestral lands. The most notorious of these was the Indian Removal Act of 1830, which pushed the Creek, Cherokee, Choctaw, Seminole, and other Native nations out of the Southeast. In violation of treaties and multiple Supreme Court rulings affirming Native sovereignty—rulings then-President Andrew Jackson refused to obey—the U.S. military forced thousands of Native Americans to walk more than 1,000 miles to the newly designated "Indian Country" in present-day Oklahoma. Many died of hunger, exposure, and illness along the way.

These expansionist policies were enabled by the United States' role in global imperial struggles for territory. In North America, the United States largely had its way; various treaties and wars with European colonial empires resulted in the acquisition of vast new territories, and white Americans began to move west in droves. The Erie Canal, completed in 1825, connected the Great Lakes with the Atlantic Ocean, and the establishment of several wagon trails—including the Santa Fe Trail in 1821, the Oregon Trail in the early 1830s, and the California and Mormon Trails in the 1840s—made it possible for thousands of settlers to push into the interior plains, through the Rocky Mountains, across the deserts, and all the way to the Pacific, in the name of American progress and freedom.

Questions of progress and national destiny also emerged in literature about Native Americans and the Western frontier, much of it from women writers working at the nexus of literary and cultural movements. Some writers of historical fiction like Sigourney, Sedgwick, and Child criticized the treatment of Native Americans by their colonial forebears but tended to depict Native Americans as a "vanishing race," victims of the progress of Christian civilization who were incompatible with the American future (Deloria 63–5; Strong 5–6). Their accounts of the historical treatment of Native Americans could thus atone for past wrongs while offering something between justification and diminution of present ones. But writers of travel sketches and letters, such as Caroline Kirkland, found themselves in a position that more closely resembled that of the colonists. Like colonial writers describing the New World, they faced the question of whether the landscapes they encountered were empty or full, and their depictions frequently, paradoxically, indicated both: they were replete with natural bounty but largely without Native inhabitants, who were "here first but … simultaneously inevitably disappearing" (Bendixen and Hamera 4). Such portrayals exoticized the American West while also familiarizing and sanitizing it, making it seem habitable to lure settlers and their families to new territories while erasing Native histories and cultures. But concurrent with these portrayals, writers such as Ojibwe poet Jane Johnston Schoolcraft recorded, reshaped, and shared the traditions of Midwestern Native American cultures, illuminating the vitality and worth of Native American traditions and sounding a counternote to the cultural preoccupation with vanishing race mythology in the emerging United States.

In the early nineteenth century, historical fiction was enjoying a boom, and women writers were in the midst of it. The publication of Sir Walter Scott's *Waverley* (1814) had caused a sensation in Great Britain and the United States, where Scott's mixture of fictional and historical events and characters met with the American desire to establish its place in history and literature. The best known of the resulting throng of American historical novels are James Fenimore Cooper's Leatherstocking Tales, but Cooper was not first on the scene; responding to both Scott and the "call for a distinctively American literature" (Fetterley "My Sister" 491), Catharine Maria Sedgwick published *A New-England Tale* in 1822, a year before the first

Leatherstocking novel, and continued to write historical fiction for the next thirty-five years, along with didactic and instructional domestic texts. She was one of several women who saw in the early colonial period a wealth of material through which to examine what it meant to be an American, and an American woman.

Sedgwick was raised in a prominent upper-middle-class, conservative family in Massachusetts, but she was a figure of contradictions. She wrote many texts that can be read as conservative from a feminist standpoint, largely refused overt activism, and subscribed to the same republican motherhood view of women's letters that characterized many of her eighteenth-century predecessors, seeing her writing as "benevolent action" through which to inspire readers and effect cultural change (Homestead 188). But Sedgwick never married and rejected Calvinist theology for liberal Unitarianism; she also criticized Puritan authoritarianism and mistreatment of women and Native Americans while advocating for women's participation in public life in her fiction, offering an intriguing mixture of advocacy and ambivalence.

Sedgwick's fiction often calls attention to the wrongs of the past through its depiction of Native–Euroamerican relationships. In *Hope Leslie* (1827), a novel about mid-seventeenth-century conflicts with the Pequods in Connecticut, Sedgwick explores connections between Euroamerican and Native American women through the title character Hope, her sister Faith, who is captured and raised by the Pequods, and Magawisca, a family servant and the sister of Faith's eventual husband, Oneco. In Hope, who challenges the constraints on women's participation in public discourse, Sedgwick advocates for women's citizenship in the republic on an equal footing with men, and in Magawisca, the woman Hope repeatedly calls "sister" and who argues the Puritan justice system has no authority over her people, Sedgwick emphasizes the similarities between white and Native women while implicitly affirming the colonial violation of Native sovereignty.[16] Sedgwick's Native American characters are largely sympathetic, but Faith, who opts to remain with the Pequods rather than return to her family, reveals Sedgwick's ambivalence; in spite of Hope's declarations of sisterhood, she is disgusted by Faith's transformation and views her as in need of rescue. And like her peers, Sedgwick casts Native Americans as inhabitants of the past, not the present. Magawisca, who has loved Hope's childhood friend Everell since she saved him from execution (*à la* Pocahontas and John Smith), is ultimately unsuitable for him or for contemporary American life; at the novel's end, when Hope and Everell ask Magawisca to stay with them, Magawisca refuses, insisting that "the Indian and the white man can no more mingle, and become one, than day and night" (330).[17] And in *Redwood* (1824), Sedgwick describes Native Americans as "remnants," "monuments of past ages" rather than stakeholders in the present and future (2: 74). Sedgwick thus references Native American displacement as one of the injustices of colonization, revising national narratives that depicted Puritans as heroic tamers of the wilderness, while foreclosing Native American relevance to the national future—a future in which Sedgwick is implicated as a member of a politically elite family. Like many women writers eager to right the injustices they saw, Sedgwick was not immune to a self-protective chauvinism, even as she decried various cultural inequalities.

Sedgwick and other fiction writers turned to the historical record for stories of Euroamerican and Native relations—perhaps in part to make colonial injustices seem comfortably remote—but they did not have to. The conquest of the continent was ongoing, and as the growing ranks of known Native writers from this period attest, it was a time of significant cultural adaptation, transition, and mourning for the Native peoples whose lives were disrupted by American expansion.[18] One of the earliest of these writers was Bamewawagezhikaquay, the Ojibwe woman who is only slightly better known by her English name, Jane Johnston Schoolcraft.[19] She was born into a wealthy fur-trading family in Sault Ste. Marie (then a part of British Canada) during a time of mutual economic and cultural exchange characterized by relatively free intermarriage and cooperation between British and French-Canadian settlers and Ojibwe and other Native American peoples; Schoolcraft's Scotch-Irish father's fur-trading was largely successful because her mother, Ozhaguscodaywayquay, the daughter of a powerful Ojibwe chief, used her family network and social influence to help the business (R. Parker 4–12). After the War of 1812 (during which Schoolcraft's father and brother fought on the British side, and the Johnston family home and business were destroyed by American soldiers), Sault Ste. Marie and the surrounding areas became U.S. territory. Schoolcraft's eventual husband, anthropologist Henry Rowe Schoolcraft, came to the Michigan Territory as the first Indian agent of the new government in 1822 and was responsible for several land treaties with Native Americans, but he is better known for the collection and publication of Ojibwe and other Native American stories and traditions for American and European readers; Robert Dale Parker characterizes these as twin "acts of theft" that relied on the prevailing vanishing race mythology and the idea that land and stories both would go to waste without white intervention (26).

Like many women writers before her, Schoolcraft was educated at home by a father who encouraged her intellectual and literary pursuits, but she was also steeped in the stories, beliefs, and practices of her mother's Ojibwe culture, and she spoke, read, and wrote Ojibwe, French, and English (R. Parker 13). She wrote poetry that varied in language, form, and subject; she also worked alongside her husband to write, transcribe, and translate Ojibwe tales as part of his anthropological research. Schoolcraft refused wider publication of her poetry, but it was often circulated privately, and some poems and stories were included in a small manuscript magazine edited by her husband called *The Muzzeniegun, or Literary Voyageur*, the first known literary journal featuring Native American writing for Native American readers (R. Parker 33–6). In addition, her husband incorporated many of her stories (uncredited) into his 1839 collection of Ojibwe folklore, *Algic Researches*—a publication that earned him significant acclaim and established him as an influential figure in American ethnographic research.[20] After her death, Schoolcraft's husband published more of her work in his own memoirs and elsewhere, including his commentary and his translations of some of her Ojibwe poetry

(Schneider 112–13). Because Schoolcraft's most influential writing was either una-
vailable, published under her husband's name, or in other ways mediated, she has
been frequently overlooked in literary histories (Parker's introduction to the 2007
edition of Schoolcraft's writings is the most significant scholarship on Schoolcraft
to date). But she is nonetheless an important figure in nineteenth-century literature,
and her blending of Ojibwe and Euroamerican languages, forms, and literary
traditions attests to the mixed allegiances and complicated interrelationship of cultures
on the continually shifting terrain of the American frontier.

Schoolcraft shows remarkable adaptability in her writing, adjusting her style and
form to suit the topic and occasion in stories and poems. She read widely in English
poetic traditions, and she experimented with a range of poetic meters and stanzas,
sometimes within individual poems, as in the opening stanza of "Invocation, To
my Maternal Grand-father" (1823). But she also writes comfortably in more traditional meters, as in the rhymed couplets of "Pensive Hours" (undated). On deeply
emotional subjects, Schoolcraft sometimes turns to Ojibwe; she writes in Ojibwe
of being greeted by the pine trees of her beloved home after a childhood journey
in "To the Pine Tree" (undated), and of the pain of her husband's decision to
send her children to an Eastern boarding school in "On leaving my children John
and Jane at School, in the Atlantic states, and preparing to return to the interior"
(undated). Schoolcraft's husband printed what he described as a "free" translation
of this poem in his memoirs, a six-stanza poem that adhered to the sentimental conventions of the period, but the new translation included in Parker's 2007
volume reveals a poem that resists Euroamerican expectations of "conceptual or
rhythmic continuity" from line to line (R. Parker 49):

Nyau nin de nain dum	As I am thinking
May kow e yaun in	When I find you
Ain dah nuk ki yaun	My land
Waus sa wa kom eg	Far in the west
Ain dah nuk ki yaun	My land
Ne dau nis ainse e	My little daughter
Ne gwis is ainse e	My little son
Ishe nau gun ug wau	I leave them behind
Waus sa wa kom eg	Far away land
	(142–3, ll. 1–9)

As Parker observes, the poem refuses to clarify the subject of the poet's thoughts
or the "you" of line 2, leaving poet and reader suspended in "contemplation" (50).
The last two stanzas offer similar ambiguities around the word "land," which is
contrasted with "home": does "land" refer to Michigan, which had only recently
joined the United States? To the Eastern states where her children now resided?
To the United States itself, which had swallowed up Schoolcraft's home? It is a
poem that reflects the ways "both land and culture shift beneath Schoolcraft's feet,"

a poem in which "meanings do not replace one another ... but pile up, overlap, accrue" (Schneider 120) for Schoolcraft as she negotiates a changing world.

Schoolcraft is rarely overtly political in her poetry, but as she was married to a federal Indian agent during years of great social and cultural change, it is not surprising that political notes creep into her personal reflections. In one undated revision of "The Contrast," Schoolcraft criticizes the "busy strife" of life in the United States, characterized by "lawsuits, meetings, courts and toil" (118, ll. 43, 46), but she also remarks on her community's determination to "trim our sail anew" in the face of such changes and to "half in joy, half in fear, / Welcome the proud Republic here" (118, ll. 49, 53–4). Previous versions of this poem conclude instead with Schoolcraft's reflections on the transience of joy in her adult life. The shifts in tone and subject of the later version suggest that despite Schoolcraft's determination to adapt and proceed in good faith, the new republic into which they had been grafted was the source of much trepidation. These fears were perhaps already proving justified as the local representative of the United States, the man Schoolcraft had taken as a husband, was working to remove Native Americans from their lands. Schoolcraft lived in an era of transition, between a past in which her Ojibwe heritage was honored and an American present and future in which despite her education, skills, and social standing she was little more than "the northern Pocahontas" (H. Schoolcraft 208). But the complex subjectivities revealed in her work illuminate some of the ways she, like many Native Americans, resisted the homogenized white–red/self–racialized Other categories into which Euroamericans tried to sort them in the decades of westward expansion.

Popular travel writers like Caroline Kirkland, on the other hand, tended to reinforce vanishing race mythology. Travel vignettes had become popular after the success of Irving's *The Sketch Book* (1819–1820), and many women wrote travel narratives and letters for newspapers in the nineteenth century: Margaret Fuller, who is best known for her feminist texts, also wrote travel letters during her summer in the Great Lakes region that were published as *Summer on the Lakes, in 1843* (1844), as well as providing accounts of her travels in Europe; and Louise Clappe wrote letters about her years in the California gold mine camps in the early 1850s under the name Dame Shirley. But Kirkland was one of the few who made a sustained career out of it, following in the footsteps of writers of the American West such as Bayard Taylor and James Hall with her accounts of the years she and her husband spent settling a town near the then-rural outpost of Detroit. Under the pseudonym Mary Clavers, Kirkland wrote three books of frank, humorous vignettes about life in the undeveloped Midwest that are peppered with poetry, literary references, and reflections on human nature and the "compensating power of the wilderness" (*A New Home* 233). As Judith Fetterley notes, Kirkland's texts are attuned to the details of everyday life and especially how women are affected by their husbands' decisions to move west, providing a valuable woman-centered perspective on the frontier narratives so frequently dominated by tales of heroic men confronting the wilderness (*Provisions* 122–3).

Men writing "true accounts" of frontier life in the nineteenth century often categorized it as a place for American men to exercise their inborn independence and thirst for continual movement while women served primarily domesticating and civilizing roles, but Kirkland both broadens and narrows this scope.[21] The titles of her three collections, *A New Home—Who'll Follow?* (1839), *Forest Life* (1842), and *Western Clearings* (1845), underscore her literal homemaking role in this new life, but her texts shift between descriptions of the strange and beautiful wilderness she experiences and the effort involved in domesticating it. She emphasizes the appeal of the frontier for women as well as men, declaring the "natural and universal" nature of the "love of unbounded and *unceremonious* liberty" that draws people to unsettled country (*A New Home* 233). Kirkland's emphasis on the universal and personal appeal of nature and on the raptures of her own wanderings counteract the narratives of the West that name it a place for men only. But Kirkland's descriptions of the hard labor of frontier housekeeping also highlight women's difficulties in adapting their culturally defined roles as housekeepers and homemakers to the realities of rural life. Kirkland affirms the glories of the West and the freedoms it affords, but she is clear that these freedoms come at great cost for women.

Although Kirkland focuses on the experiences of settler women in a way that many of her fellow writers of the West do not, her account is far from unvarnished truth. Kirkland's texts notably overlook Native Americans almost entirely, in spite of the significant Native American population in her region and the fact that her Michigan years directly coincided with the negotiation and confinement of Ojibwe, Potawatomi, Ottawa, and other Great Lakes-area tribes to reservations; her cataloguing of the Western landscape and life and her erasure of Native Americans from that landscape reflects the inherently white supremacist method of "produc[ing] 'Americanness'" (Bendixen and Hamera 4) that so often appeared in the travel literatures of the West. Native Americans make scant appearances in Kirkland's books;[22] instead, Native American influence is found primarily in the form of linguistic remnants—potential names for the new village (*A New Home* 21), or "Massisaugas," the Native term for a rattlesnake (*A New Home* 27)—or as a vague menace, classed with snakes as a hazard that prevents her from taking walks outside her village (*A New Home* 236). And as becomes clear in a scene where Kirkland's narrator first mistakes a settler who has abandoned even an "outside show of humanity" (*Forest* 1: 151) for a Native American and then, with his wife, prods him to return to Euroamerican dress and habits, part of white women's frontier work involves policing racial boundaries and eradicating any potential Native influence on white "humanity" (Keetley 31ff.). The historical fiction of Sedgwick and others might suggest Native American groups were destined to vanish as distinct civilizations, but Kirkland's texts seem to enact such a disappearance with relish. Kirkland's was not the only perspective available in travel writing, but her view of Native Americans and of the Western frontier was the dominant cultural perspective, one which would play an even greater role in the settlement of the West in the decades to come.

The boundaries of domestic fiction

In 1857, a *New York Times* reviewer declared that "Courtship and marriage, servants and children" were "the great objects of a woman's thoughts" and the only appropriate subjects for women's writing ("Books of the Week" 2). He prompted a hot reply from columnist and author Sarah Willis Parton, better known to millions of *New-York Ledger* readers as Fanny Fern; she pointed out that male novelists such as Dickens and Thackeray undertook these same topics, and that women writing on a number of subjects had managed to find enthusiastic publishers and readers for decades ("Male" 285). But the *Times* reviewer was hardly alone in his condemnation of women writers who stepped outside the boundaries of the home. Many critics similarly dismissed women's novels as insufficiently compelling, plagued by unrealistic plots, melodramatic stock characters, unskillful execution, and overly pious themes, all contrived to evoke the maximum emotional response from readers.

Cathy Davidson, Jane Tompkins, and others began to argue in the 1980s for the reevaluation of the political work of women's fiction in the eighteenth and nineteenth centuries and the validity of the domestic as a subject, but a number of feminist scholars in the intervening decades have been more critical, suggesting that these texts tended to reinforce the heteronormative power structures of racial patriarchy.[23] Such criticisms are valid and call attention to issues with the unqualified celebration of women's writing as inherently feminist or woman-positive. And yet the work of many politically minded women in the early nineteenth century reveals that the domestic world could be as liberatory as any other setting, giving license to explorations of slavery, intermarriage and miscegenation, rape, women's economic dependence on men, and other important and controversial subjects. In their fiction, which encompassed genres from historical fiction to scarcely disguised autobiography and frequently overlapped with nonfiction modes such as reform literature, women challenged cultural definitions of appropriate womanhood and presented new models for engagement with important issues in texts that frequently questioned some of the logics of racial, economic, and gender power structures while reinforcing others.

Fanny Fern and E.D.E.N. Southworth both used their fiction to highlight the injustice of women's economic dependence on men. Fern's satiric *Ruth Hall: A Domestic Tale of the Present Time* (1854) was based on Fern's experiences as a widow trying to support herself and her two children. Ruth is an educated middle-class girl with a wealthy but parsimonious father and a prestigious literary brother; when her eldest daughter and husband unexpectedly die, Ruth is at the mercy of various relatives who all refuse to help her financially. After years of hardship while pursuing the genteel occupations allowed to women (sewing and teaching among them), Ruth turns to writing, eventually becoming one of the most popular newspaper columnists in New York. In Ruth's story, Fern recasts the virtuous, self-made American as an unmarried woman. She also exposes the real dangers of True Womanhood, which dictates women's financial dependence on men by keeping them in ignorance of business practices and economic realities and leaving them vulnerable to exploitation. With her biting satire, Fern argues that women can succeed in spite of the obstacles deliberately placed in their way.

Southworth's *The Hidden Hand or: Capitola the Madcap*, first serialized in 1859 in the *New-York Ledger*, tackles the question of women's dependence in a different way. The novel follows the exploits of mysterious orphan Capitola Black, adopted from the streets of New York by gruff but kindly old Major Warfield, who suspects Capitola is the long-lost heiress to a Virginia fortune held by her villainous uncle. Soon after meeting Warfield, Capitola is arrested for cross-dressing; during her hearing at the police station, she testifies that she cross-dresses to support herself because she is refused work when she wears girls' clothes. Although Capitola adopts feminine dress when she goes to live with Warfield in his Virginia mansion, she admits to being bored by the strictures of upper-class girlhood, where she keenly feels "the absence of the necessity of thinking and caring for herself" (Southworth 174); it is an indictment of the assumption that preventing women from bearing self-responsibility is a service performed on women's behalf rather than a stultifying restriction. And in one of the book's subplots, Warfield's estranged wife Marah Rocke and their son live in genteel poverty because her husband believes her guilty of adultery. Virtuous and penniless, Marah's fortunes depend on the generosity of the men in her world, who can grant her financial security or force her from her home at a word. If Fern's *Ruth Hall* reveals the oppression of poor women built into the American economic structure, Southworth's novel suggests that patriarchal benevolence is as destructive as patriarchal neglect and points to the illusory nature of women's financial security through marriage.

In spite of their progressive depictions of women's economic positions, the financial security women characters in these novels achieve is still largely dependent on the invisible labor of others. Southworth uncritically reproduces both slavery and racial stereotypes in her African American characters, who perform the household tasks that allow Capitola to be bored, and whom Marah supervises as the housekeeper of a family friend. And Gillian Brown finds in *Ruth Hall* an "unabashed" celebration of "market individualism" that culminates in Ruth's purchase of bank stock (G. Brown 140), a sign of Ruth's accession to the moneyed classes whose successes are built on exploitation as much as of Ruth's hard-won independence. Thus, sentimental fiction could be a powerful tool of social critique, "reorganiz[ing] culture from the woman's point of view" (Tompkins 124), while still relying on the subjugation of others for its force and meaning in claiming universality for a point of view that was largely white and middle class.

Women writers and the work of reform

One clear pattern that emerges from study of the fiction and poetry of the antebellum nineteenth century is the intertwining of women's writing with the impetus for protest and reform. Sigourney, Sedgwick, Southworth, Fern, and many others attempted to persuade readers to action by dramatizing injustice and immorality, blending fact and fiction in poem and story. But women also pursued more direct routes, arguing for their causes in pulpits, periodical essays, and full-length books. The overlap between these kinds of works makes them difficult to sort out: what makes a work a piece of sentimental literature, and what makes it reform literature? Is it a fiction–nonfiction divide? A generic or rhetorical divide? Sedgwick's *Hope Leslie* or Southworth's *The Hidden Hand* are closer to fiction and sentimental literature than to direct protest or reform, for example, considerably more about awareness and less oriented toward action than Sigourney's *The Traits of the Aborigines*. Catharine Beecher's *Suggestions Regarding Improvements in Education* (1829), Sojourner Truth's speeches, and Margaret Fuller's *Woman in the Nineteenth Century* (1845) are closer still to direct protest, nonfiction works rhetorically allied with argumentation, polemic, and history; Fuller's *Woman in the Nineteenth Century* was particularly effective in this regard, arguing that patriarchal social structures harm both men and women and transforming the central Transcendentalist tenet of the "continual spiritual growth of the soul" into a tool for practical social reform (D. Robinson 84). Many narratives by formerly enslaved African Americans, including Harriet Wilson's *Our Nig* (1859) and Harriet Jacobs' *Incidents in the Life of a Slave Girl* (1861), are either acknowledged or lightly fictionalized autobiography. And the most powerful work of literature from the nineteenth century, Stowe's *Uncle Tom's Cabin*, plays on the edges of all of these literary regions. These category-defying texts contain the germs of many of the major protest movements that would develop over the next hundred years.

Women reform writers were actuated by various causes. Some had experience with the wrongs they protested, and many others were inspired by the pervasive rhetoric of revolution, equality, and self-determination in American political thought. But many also partook in a developing middle-class reform ethos with roots in the Second Great Awakening.[24] As with the First Great Awakening and the Separatist movement, the Second Great Awakening emphasized a return to a purer form of religion. Converts believed they lived in a new millennial age in which they could prepare for Christ's return by ridding the world of social evils, a theology known as postmillennialism (Frederickson 115), and they directed their energies toward missionary activity and reform projects related to temperance, prison conditions, Native American rights, women's rights, and, most powerfully, the abolition of slavery. Many women took leading roles in these movements, spurred on by a moral imperative to right these wrongs in spite of condemnation from those who felt women's proper sphere of influence was private rather than public (Clapp and Jeffrey 13–14). As they had done for more than a century, American women questioned faith and shifted practice as they worked to improve their communities, motivated by Christian principles of justice, mercy, and charity.

Abolition, women's rights, and the Cult of True Womanhood

The two major reform movements of the antebellum period were women's rights and abolition, and for many of the women involved the two were deeply connected. Many white activists came to the cause of women's rights because of conflicts between their involvement with abolition and the ideals of Victorian womanhood. Sarah Grimké and Angelina Grimké Weld caused a scandal when they left their slaveholding family for a life of abolitionist activism; they began advocating for women's rights after facing vociferous criticism for daring to speak publicly and in front of men. Elizabeth Cady Stanton and Lucretia Mott were likewise moved to action by the shoddy treatment they received as female delegates to the World Anti-Slavery Convention in London in 1840.

African American women too felt the connection between women's rights and abolition, although their relationships with Victorian ideals of womanhood were decidedly more complicated. In Victorian culture, white womanhood was enshrined as the embodiment of domestic and moral goodness while black womanhood was denigrated as debased, sexually immoral, and inhuman, and black women's homes, families, and bodies were constantly vulnerable to the depredations of white men and women alike. For African American women, denied even the few rights granted to Euroamerican women, the fight for recognition of their rights as women was superseded by the fight for recognition of their personhood—and the fight for the rights of white women could only be seen as deeply compromised, even though its advocates were among slavery's fiercest opponents. The evils of slavery and cultural notions of womanhood were thus tightly bound together, and women's writing on these subjects often grapples with both.

The debate over slavery in North America was older than the United States itself. Several Northern states had moved to outlaw slavery in the late eighteenth century, and the nation quickly divided itself into slave and free states.[25] Slavery's defenders argued it was a benevolent institution without which millions of enslaved African Americans would be helpless and suggested that abolition would cripple the economy, but their opponents argued that any supposed African American helplessness was caused by slavery, a moral evil that could not be abided in a Christian nation. Westward expansion only caused further instability as Congress debated whether slavery should be allowed in new territories (and thus, which faction would wield more political power); even the resulting Missouri Compromise of 1820 did little to quell animosity in national and state legislatures and among the general population, where pro-abolition events were frequently met with violence, and their advocates with social reprobation. Lydia Maria Child is one example. Her 1833 *Appeal* was one of the earliest and boldest pro-abolition texts; it argues for abolition based on a historical, economic, and ideological analysis of slavery without sensationalizing slavery as a voyeuristic spectacle (Sorisio "Spectacle" 47–9). Child was publicly condemned, and her punishment was severe; she was essentially banished from polite society and the Boston Athenaeum library, and subscriptions to the children's journal she founded dropped so significantly that she was forced to surrender it to another editor (Mills 30–54).

While Child continued her advocacy, her story offers a potent reminder of the polarization surrounding the issue of slavery in the United States. This polarization only increased in succeeding decades as several major events in the 1850s fueled the sense of urgency on both sides. The Fugitive Slave Act of 1850 punished even free-state residents for failing to return runaway slaves to their masters, prompting many who had escaped slavery to tell their stories in slave narratives; it also became the basis for much of the action in *Uncle Tom's Cabin*, which was released serially in 1851 and as a book in 1852, provoking virulent reaction from slavery's defenders. The *Dred Scott v. Sandford* decision (1857), in which the Supreme Court ruled African Americans could not become citizens even if freed, was another catalyst for action, drawing the United States yet closer to war. And in 1859, radical abolitionist John Brown seized a federal armory in Harpers Ferry, Virginia, with the goal of freeing and arming the local enslaved population; when he and his men were executed for treason, they became martyrs for the abolitionist movement. Brown's raid and the immediate and deadly response from the citizens and government of Virginia revealed the violence, anger, and fear that rippled below the surface and would explode into war scarcely sixteen months later.

While it was less violent than the abolitionist movement, the women's rights movement likewise caused significant cultural conflict. The 1848 Seneca Falls Convention led by Mott and Stanton in Seneca Falls, New York, is often mentioned as the beginning of organized feminism in the United States, though Euroamerican women had been pushing for legal, political, and social recognition since the seventeenth century. Many Native American scholars trace the roots of American feminism farther back, arguing that equality-based western feminism owes much of its philosophy to the influence of Native American gynocratic cultures such as the Iroquois, and that the principles of "social justice" undergirding western equality movements were shaped by European interactions with Native Americans (Allen *Sacred Hoop* 212–13, 219ff.). The movement gained significant momentum in the mid-nineteenth century as women began speaking and writing publicly on the issue in greater numbers. Catharine Beecher, sister to the more famous Harriet Beecher Stowe, wrote numerous books and articles arguing for the expansion of girls' education, while Kirkland pushed for the reform of women's prisons in *The Helping Hand* (1853). Fuller took on broader questions of social and political equality; her *Woman in the Nineteenth Century* (1845) expanded an earlier *Dial* essay, "The Great Lawsuit," exploring the ways both women and men suffered under prescribed gender roles in patriarchal American culture. The 1848 Seneca Falls Convention was riding the crest of a wave of momentum: by 1850 women had made some inroads, with broader access to more comprehensive education, including women's higher education and medical schools, periodicals owned and edited by women, and the weakening of coverture laws through property rights legislation (Bennett *Poets* 41). These advances suggested that more significant change was possible.

For many white women, their desire for greater rights was related to a desire to work for other causes, particularly abolition, but this was also a kind of trap. Nineteenth-century women activists can be roughly divided into what Bennett calls "difference feminists" and "equality feminists." Difference feminists attempted to limn a "gender-specific form of female political power from within domestic ideology itself" (*Poets* 42), a task that proved rather slippery; they believed women and men had different strengths, and that women's public activism was justified because it stemmed from womanly compassion for the less fortunate. Difference feminists such as Sigourney and Stowe relied on the evocation of deep feeling for the victims of injustice as the catalyst for moral action. But equality feminists such as Fuller and the Grimkés relied on reason as the foundation of morality. They argued for abolition and women's rights on the basis of shared humanity and natural rights, frequently invoking slavery as a metaphor for women's lives under patriarchy.[26]

Many white antebellum feminists fell into one or the other of these camps and earnestly believed they were working for the good of both women and enslaved African Americans, but they were not immune to the white supremacy that permeated antebellum culture. Their texts have often been criticized as appropriative, and rightly so; in many cases they either adopt slavery as a metaphor for women's oppression, arrogating to white women the excruciations of the enslaved and obscuring the real suffering of African American women, or they rely on readers' identification with and assumption of the pain of others for emotional heft, in the worst cases making pity and sympathy the basis of political action rather than the acknowledgment of shared humanity and injustice (Sánchez-Eppler 14–49; Howard; Bennett *Poets* 53–6). It is, as Karen Sánchez-Eppler points out, a troubling image of female agency because the white woman's access to the "political discourse denied the slave" is authorized primarily by the "bound and silent figure of the slave" herself (19); it is a model of women's empowerment that needs slavery in order to survive.

In addition, while many African American women worked for the abolitionist cause, the mainstream women's rights movement largely excluded them. At the Seneca Falls Convention, for instance, 68 women and 32 men signed a Declaration of Sentiments proclaiming the same inalienable rights for all women and men, but there were no African American women present (Bennett *Poets* 50 n.2). African American women occupied a difficult position in the antebellum United States. They were black in a culture that viewed blackness with hostility and female in a culture that viewed women as naturally inferior, and they lived in a social system that viewed black women as wanton and unnatural, lacking the finer maternal and familial feelings inherent in white women. Even free women had to negotiate a world of constant racism in which their contributions were devalued and freedom could not guarantee safety for them or their families. In spite of these obstacles, many African American women led the charge for racial and gender equality. Maria Stewart, born free in Hartford, Connecticut, wrote for William Lloyd Garrison's *Liberator* and was one of the first women to publicly argue for abolition and women's rights before mixed-race and mixed-gender audiences. Harriet Tubman escaped from slavery in Maryland in 1849 but returned to the South numerous times, helping dozens of her family members and others escape; and as a Union scout during the Civil War, she led an armed assault that freed more than 750 enslaved people, the first woman to do so in the war. At least as early as the 1830s, African American women such as Sarah Mapps Douglass were working on a local scale as well, organizing literary groups, classes, and lecture series in free states, providing venues for public speaking—as Ernest describes it, oratory is "probably the most central and influential of all African American writings from the nineteenth century" (280–1)—and creating social, intellectual, and political communities.[27] In these communities, women could learn to read and write, practice public speaking, and create in a collaborative and supportive environment.

As the abolition movement gained momentum, African American women writers found increasing opportunities to write for abolitionist newspapers and magazines. Maria Chapman, Jarena Lee, and others published religious exhortations, lectures, and spiritual autobiographies in the 1830s, and writers such as Sarah Louisa Forten, her niece, Charlotte Forten Grimké, and Sarah Mapps Douglass published abolitionist and feminist poetry. The speeches of orators such as Sojourner Truth were printed and reprinted in newspapers throughout the country. And many women, including Harriet Jacobs and Harriet Wilson, made notable contributions to the slave narrative genre, presenting African American women's experiences of slavery as deserving of the same consideration as those of men like Frederick Douglass. These texts repeatedly challenge antebellum notions about black womanhood, cannily deploying the imagery of home, family, and Victorian womanhood in a complex interplay between repudiation and identification. They appeal to Victorian constructions of gender through the use of sympathy and ally themselves and their characters with their white female readership by dramatizing the repeated violations of home and family they experience—but they also hold white women accountable for their complicity in a system of subjugation and victimization. These texts are thus both a calculated embrace and a stinging indictment of nineteenth-century American womanhood.

The most famous of such texts is probably the Sojourner Truth speech most commonly known as the "Ain't I a Woman" speech, delivered at the Ohio Women's Rights Convention in 1851 and now a staple in nineteenth-century literary and historical curriculum. Truth was born into slavery in New York but escaped to freedom with one of her children in 1826. In 1843 she discarded her slave name and began speaking on anti-slavery and women's rights lecture circuits; she also owned property and successfully sued her former owner to get back her son, who had been illegally sold South. Truth's dictated memoirs (first published in 1850) recount her remarkable life up to that point, but she is best known for a single extemporaneous speech.[28]

Although it is rarely noted in the children's textbooks where most readers first encounter Truth, the text of Truth's famous speech has a contested history. There are dramatic differences between the earliest report of the speech, published by Marius Robinson in the New-Lisbon, Ohio, *Anti-Slavery Bugle* a few weeks after the convention—in standard English and without any appearance of the question "Ain't I a woman?"—and several later versions. The most well-known is Frances Dana Gage's 1863 version, which has Truth speaking in a southern African American dialect, adds the refrain "Ain't I a woman?", and makes both the speech and its reception more confrontational.[29] The corroboration of contemporaneous accounts and a rhetorical analysis leads Michael Phillips-Anderson to conclude that the Robinson version of the speech is the most authentic (30). He cites accounts of other speeches by Truth and dictated letters demonstrating that her spoken English and rhetorical style were closer to standard English and Truth's complaint to the *Kalamazoo Daily Telegraph* in 1879 about the tendency of writers to distort her words by giving her a "marked southern dialect" (28). Gage's version is certainly rhetorically effective, but it is highly unlikely the rhetoric was Truth's. In Robinson's version, the speaker is clear and unapologetic. "I am a woman's rights," she declares in a bold and unusual metaphor, equal to men in muscle, in work, in strength, and in appetite ("Women's Rights Convention" 1). She uses humor and scripture to refute common arguments against women's rights, and she makes herself an equal not to domestically focused white women, but to all men, offering a radical claim of equality that goes farther than many of her white peers. Gage's version construes Truth as powerless under slavery, and the contrasts she makes between Truth's reality and the claims of Victorian womanhood reveal how white feminists wished to see African American activists and Truth in particular: as highly romanticized and helpless victims rather than powerful and successful advocates for themselves and all African Americans.

Women's slave narratives written during the 1850s also offer revealing glimpses into African American women's lives and their vexed relationships with white womanhood. Hannah Crafts' unpublished manuscript *The Bondwoman's Narrative* tells the story of a woman's life under slavery and her eventual escape.[30] It examines among other subjects the issue of slave marriages, which were often illegal; Crafts presents these marriages as rebellions against both slavery and gender norms because they allowed enslaved couples to reimagine the husband–wife relationship unbound by legal considerations of contract or property (Chakkalakal 6–14). Crafts also contrasts the enslaved couple's choice to risk death in order to protect their marriage with the slaveowner's determination to "destroy" it (Chakkalakal 111), highlighting the arbitrary construction of whites as inherently virtuous and African Americans as inherently depraved. Harriet Wilson's autobiographical novel *Our Nig* (1859) debunks another cherished myth, that of Northern moral superiority. Wilson chronicles the experiences of Frado, a free orphan taken in as an indentured servant by the white Bellmont family in New England, and details the pervasive racism she encounters. Frado's new mistresses are the worst offenders, and the home becomes a literal battleground as these women bully, torture, and beat Frado while Frado resists as well as she is able. As R.J. Ellis notes, the primary contrast is between the respectable exterior of the Bellmont home and the cruelty and depravity Frado endures within its walls (15). The novel concludes not with Frado's dramatic escape but with her "anti-climactic recognition of uncrossable racist boundaries" (Ellis 74) and the lifelong legacy of fury and pain they engender.

Of the antebellum slave narratives, Harriet Jacobs' *Incidents in the Life of a Slave Girl, Written by Herself* (1861) features one of the clearest confrontations of Victorian womanhood in African American literature. Jacobs had difficulty finding a publisher for her book (published under the name Linda Brent), which recounts her subjection to continual sexual violence as an enslaved woman, her jealous mistress's cruelty, her desperate efforts to escape her master's advances, and her continued experiences with racism after her flight North. Jacobs eventually found a publisher in Lydia Maria Child; although the degree of Child's influence has been much debated, the narrative is clearly Jacobs', and the resulting text is carefully calibrated to create a strategic alliance between the African American female narrator and her white female readers through the use of sympathy while confronting them with the ugly truths of slavery and racial prejudice.[31]

Incidents is a book intended to delicately but clearly push its readers' buttons. Jacobs' title page features a quote from "A Woman of North Carolina" stating that Northerners "have no conception of the depth of *degradation* involved in that word, SLAVERY" because if they did they would work ceaselessly to abolish it; she follows with a biblical invocation to "Rise up, ye women that are at ease!" Jacobs wants to rouse her readers from indolence to action through the depiction of slavery's deepest evils, and she uses several techniques to do so. Johnnie M. Stover notes that Jacobs manipulates nineteenth-century generic conventions, most notably the sentimental novel, while also offering commentary that pointedly reveals her "dissatisfaction … with the social, political, cultural, and economic injustices" of the United States (134–5). Narrator Linda Brent describes the destruction of families under slavery, particularly the separation of mothers and children; she notes that her own mother was "weaned at three months" so her grandmother could serve as wet nurse to the mistress's child (7) and relates the story of another enslaved mother whose young daughter lies dying after giving birth to a "child nearly white" while her mistress gloats at her tragedy (13–14).[32] Linda also frankly recounts the sexual and physical violence she suffered under enslavement: a master who "began to whisper foul words in my ear" when she was fifteen and pursued her even to her mother's grave to remind her that "I belonged to him … [and] that he would compel me to submit" (28), and a mistress whose jealousy leads her to such great cruelty and violence that Linda takes a white lover as a means of protection. She acknowledges the wrongness of this action but insists that "so far as my ways have been crooked, I charge them all upon slavery" (165). Slavery, Jacobs' text is clear, renders both enslaved women and their mistresses unnatural and drives them to desperate, immoral acts.

Lest Northern readers grow too comfortable, Jacobs' text also details the racism Linda encounters in Massachusetts and New York after her escape, calling into question "Northerners' … conception of themselves as ideologically distinguished from their Southern neighbors" (Gunning 133). It is, as Gruesser notes, an act of shaming that Jacobs hopes will goad her readers into repentance and action (112). It is difficult to say whether Jacobs' book had the intended effect; anti-abolitionists immediately questioned its authenticity, but its reception was generally lukewarm, and it appeared too close to the start of the Civil War for its impact to be measured (Foster 64ff.). However, the body of scholarship on the book attests to its importance not only as a document of the realities of enslaved women's lives, but also as a critique of white American womanhood and American culture as a whole.

Uncle Tom's Cabin *and the transatlantic community of sympathy*

Any discussion of abolition literature would be incomplete without Harriet Beecher Stowe's *Uncle Tom's Cabin* (1852). One of thirteen children of famed New England preacher Lyman Beecher, Stowe became increasingly involved in abolition activities after witnessing pro-slavery riots in Cincinnati and controversies over abolition at the seminary where her father was president. She wrote several books and novels in her lifetime, but *Uncle Tom's Cabin* persists as her most significant legacy. The first American novel to sell more than a million copies, it was a literary and political sensation, so effective as anti-slavery propaganda that it has been credited with taking abolitionism from the fringes to the mainstream and accelerating the United States' descent into civil war (Painter 246, 252). In 1850s England, the book sold more copies than Dickens' works and inspired similar efforts from writers such as Dickens, Eliot, and Gaskell, an important part of what Susan David Bernstein describes as a nineteenth-century transatlantic "Anglo-American discourse of sympathy" (260). It was long treated as a historical phenomenon without significant literary merit, but the work of Tompkins and others in the last forty years has led to careful reexamination. Stowe's text has since come to be appreciated as the most effective deployment of sentimental tropes in international literary history, manipulating sentimental and religious themes to present the idea that personal transformation is the key to moral action and social and political reform.

Uncle Tom's Cabin follows two enslaved characters originally owned by the Shelby family of Kentucky: the faithful, virtuous Uncle Tom, who is sold South and endures the most inhuman treatment with patience and Christian forbearance, inspiring even his enemies' admiration, and the beautiful mulatta Eliza, who flees the Shelby home with her young son after discovering he is to be sold and escapes to Canada with the assistance of the Underground Railroad. As Bernstein notes, one of the engines of the novel's sympathy is the repeated theme of maternal loss and sacrifice (259). The threat of separation from her son drives Eliza to take significant risks with her own life to save his. In one striking scene, Eliza is chased by slavecatchers across ice floes on the racing Ohio River; it is one of the most frequently represented scenes from the novel, suggesting its emotional resonance for Stowe's readers, who are encouraged to identify with Eliza's sacrificial devotion to her son. Bernstein connects this emphasis with transnational literary precedents, including an 1847 Elizabeth Barrett Browning poem, "The Runaway Slave at Pilgrim's Point," in order to highlight Stowe's participation in a larger dialogue about maternal sympathy and children's suffering under various forms of oppression such as child labor (262).

Stowe evokes maternal anguish in her readers not only with sympathy, but also with a surprising amount of sarcasm, humor, and irony. She describes one character who violates the Fugitive Slave Law to help Eliza as someone with the "misfortune" of having a "particularly humane and accessible nature" that prevents him from refusing help to people in need (69). Later, she contrasts Tom's compassion for an enslaved woman whose child has been sold, the product of Tom's being a "poor, ignorant black soul" who had not yet "learned to generalize, and to take enlarged views" (113), with the trader's imperturbability, noting that his heart "was exactly where yours, sir, and mine could be brought, with proper effort and cultivation" (112). Stowe's narrator repeatedly and ironically refers to characters as "property" (as in the titles of chapters 10, "The Property Is Carried Off," and 11, "In Which Property Gets into an Improper State of Mind"), borrowing the language of pro-slavery advocates to create the emotional distance required to view slavery objectively (as slavery's defenders insisted they were doing), only to close the distance in dramatic fashion. The resulting disjunction between readers' expectations and reading experiences generates the same kind of productive discomfort as their sympathetic identification with maternal suffering.

The creation of productive discomfort is one of Stowe's strategies for political effectiveness both within and outside the text, as seen in the novel's conclusion and Stowe's postscript chapter. In Tompkins' reading of the conclusion, she points out that a major theme of the novel is Christian redemption, the promise Stowe offers that just as Tom's putatively evil final master Simon Legree has a change of heart and finds salvation after Tom forgives him on his deathbed, so can even the most hardhearted of slavery's defenders be transformed (133). The death of the innocent is already foreshadowed with Little Eva, the angelic daughter of another of Tom's masters, whose death likewise transforms the mischievous enslaved child Topsy into a humble, obedient Christian; this kind of repetition, according to Tompkins, is part of the Christian typology pervasive in American culture since its Puritan origins, the conviction that "human history is a continual reenactment of the sacred drama of redemption" through self-sacrifice found in the story of Christ (134). Slavery might transform human beings into monsters, but those monsters can be re-transformed by Christian love and kindness. In Tompkins' view, this is why *Uncle Tom's Cabin* was so effective: it dramatized "the culture's central religious myth" against the backdrop of its most significant political conflict and "most cherished social beliefs" about family and motherhood (134). In her concluding remarks Stowe insists the individual's highest responsibility is to "*feel right*" because the person who "*feels* strongly, healthily and justly, on the great interests of humanity, is a constant benefactor to the human race" (385, emphasis in original). The transformation experienced by Legree and Topsy leads to this right feeling, and to the moral action that brings about major change. In suggesting that reading *Uncle Tom's Cabin* can have the same effect on her readers, Stowe argues for the transformative power of her text and for the sentimental novel itself.

Although *Uncle Tom's Cabin* was a resounding success and made Stowe a celebrity reformer with an international reach, its legacy is complex and troublesome.[33] It may have contributed to the eventual freedom of millions of enslaved African Americans, but its reliance on racial stereotypes perpetuated persistent caricatures of African Americans, particularly through the influence of blackface minstrel shows.[34] As Sarah Meer notes, while Stowe hated minstrel shows, she populated her novel with stock characters like the mammy and pickaninny and mimicked minstrel show "patterns of dialogue" and plot structures, suggesting that such echoes of minstrelsy were among the drivers of *Uncle Tom's Cabin*'s international success (29–30). What's more, Stowe's novel was quickly co-opted and reabsorbed by minstrel culture, which turned its plots and characters into props to support the white supremacist ideologies circulated in shows, illustrations, and other visual materials (J. Morgan 20–63). Stowe herself was not immune to such ideologies, as her willingness to co-opt Harriet Jacobs' narrative indicates. Such issues suggest the vast and perpetually shifting ideological terrain in conversations about slavery and race in the antebellum decades.

The echoes of war: Women's Civil War narratives

The buildup to civil war in the United States was long and slow, and then very quick. Abraham Lincoln had promised to prohibit slavery in new western territories, and several slave states quickly seceded from the United States after his election in 1860, naming themselves the Confederate States of America; barely a month after Lincoln's inauguration, Confederate troops fired on Union-held Fort Sumter in South Carolina in April 1861. By the war's end in April 1865, more than 600,000 Union and Confederate soldiers were dead, along with untold numbers of civilians; only a few days after the April 1865 Confederate surrender at Appomattox, Virginia, Abraham Lincoln joined them, the first American president to be assassinated. These were years of chaos and staggering violence, of confrontation with the ugliest parts of human nature, and of the simultaneous destruction and reconstruction of various American mythologies.

As it had during the Revolution less than a century before, war again permeated every aspect of women's lives and found its way into their writing. The war is a significant focus in the poetry of Dickinson and of Margaret Junkin Preston, and women such as Emilie Frances Davis, Mary Chesnut, and Judith McGuire documented their wartime experiences in letters and personal diaries; some of them eventually adapted their diaries into texts that fell somewhere in between fiction, memoir, and history, narratives that helped them make sense of their experiences and interpret the war for their readers. Women were also among the earliest writers to attempt to translate the war into fiction, often using their work to probe the ways war reconfigured conventional gender roles and domestic life. Their texts helped them and their readers process the highs and lows of wartime—the exhilaration of service to a cherished cause, the devastation of loss, and the hopes, frustrations, and fears about the changing world. Such texts came in many varieties. Louisa May Alcott's *Hospital Sketches* (1863) is a fictionalized account of her experiences as an army nurse; Augusta Jane Evans' novel *Macaria; or, The Altars of Sacrifice* (1864) depicts the lives of two Southern women whose Confederate service functions as a path to self-realization and "single blessedness" (Faust xxi); and as Nina Silber, Alice Fahs, and Kathleen Diffley have noted, several women wrote "romances of reunion" that appeared serially in magazines beginning in the 1860s, stories that imagined the reconciliation of the broken national family through the marriage of Union soldiers and Southern belles.

While many women wrote Civil War narratives, Alcott stands out as an author whose work consistently and provocatively explores gender roles through the lens of the war, and for whom the war is a pervasive influence. Like her most famous character, Jo March of *Little Women* (1868), Alcott frequently bemoaned the limitations of her own femininity, declaring at fourteen that she was "born with a boy's spirit under my bib and tucker" (*Journals* 79). She had been raised in an unconventional family, the daughter of a "visionary but impractical" Transcendentalist father (Showalter *Alternative* xi) and a mother who strove to keep the family intact in spite of her husband's eccentric career endeavors while supervising her children's intellectual and moral development (Young 77). Alcott's resistance to culturally delineated gender roles ran headlong into her parents' insistence on self-denial as a moral good; and this interplay between societal and parental expectations and personal desires runs throughout her fiction and her personal writing. The Civil War offered Alcott a chance to combine her lifelong commitment to abolition and women's rights with her desire to flee the constrains of femininity, and to fruitfully explore her rebellions in texts such as *Hospital Sketches* (1863), *Little Women*, and *Work: A Story of Experience* (1873).

Hospital Sketches was the first work Alcott published under her own name, a fictional reworking of letters written to her family during her short-lived career as an army nurse in 1862. Alcott's war work had begun at home, where she made clothing for Union soldiers, but she longed for the field of battle. She found her opportunity at last in going to work as a nurse in Georgetown, the experience dramatized in *Hospital Sketches*; through the adventures of Tribulation (Trib) Periwinkle, Alcott presents war service as a duty both masculine and feminine and depicts wartime as an opportunity for women and men to be free from conventional gender roles, even if only temporarily (Cappello 63; Young 71). She draws specific parallels between nursing and soldiering; after securing a nursing post, Trib announces to her family that she's "enlisted" (4), begins saluting her family and referring to her meals as "rations" (5), and remarks on her mother's courage in sending her daughter "to the war" (7), just as later in *Work* the narrator Christie, also a Civil War nurse, determines she will wed her soldier-fiancé not in a fine dress but in her nursing garments, marrying "in my uniform, as David is" (272). Once at the hospital, appropriately named "Hurly-Burly House," Trib finds that the duties of war involve a gender reversal in which men and women adopt one another's traits as they confront the realities of male and female wartime bodies (Young 74). Men become meek "like bashful girls" when Trib bathes and dresses their wounds, and men blush at nudity and bodily contact while women push "manfully" through their discomfort in the name of duty (29–30). Later, when Trib falls ill and is confined to her quarters, she depicts her sickness as a "soldier's battle service" (Young 83) and casts the loss of her hair as a sacrifice for the cause of the war in the same vein as a soldier's amputation (*Hospital* 78). It is a sentiment echoed in *Little Women* when Jo March sells her hair to help send her mother to nurse her father on the battlefront: Jo confesses feeling "queer" seeing her cut-off hair and says of her shorn head, "It almost seemed as if I'd an arm or a leg off" (160).

In spite of her protests, Trib is eventually escorted home by her father to recover from her illness, a hint at the temporariness of the masculine freedoms and identity she can enjoy; however, the postwar world Alcott posits in her later fiction is one in which such imbalances can be corrected. As Young argues, in the second half of *Little Women* and its successors, *Little Men* (1871) and *Jo's Boys and How They Turned Out* (1886), Alcott reimagines a world in which legions of little boys are governed by Jo, who teaches them to internalize the self-regulation she and her sisters learned from their mother (101ff.). And in the concluding chapters of *Work*, Christie finds new meaning in widowhood when she starts a women's reform organization. In her Civil War writing Alcott thus not only insists that women can do work of equal value to men's work and at equal personal cost, thereby finding freedom from the restrictions of rigid gender roles; she also presents a vision of a postwar United States in which women exercise a restoring and regulatory power over a nation that, left to its own devices, had run amok.

The Civil War narratives of Southern women evince similar intentions to shape readers' interpretations of war, although in widely varying ways. While it is often convenient for the sake of discussion to refer to "Northern" and "Southern" sentiments, Americans in both regions were far from monolithic in their views of slavery, abolition, and the war, ranging from ardent support to deep ambivalence. The life writing and poetry of Mary Chesnut, Judith McGuire, and Margaret Junkin Preston offer illuminating insights into the multiplicity of Southern experience. Chesnut, who was the subject of a Pulitzer Prize-winning biography in 1981 and has received some scholarly attention, is the most well-known of the three, and she is a clear example of the deep ambivalence of some Southern women toward slavery—so much so that some readers hail her as a feminist and near-abolitionist hero where others find her a virulent racist who was deeply invested in Victorian Southern femininity.[35] Chesnut was the wife of a powerful Confederate politician who helped draft South Carolina's articles of secession; following the war she spent several years culling notes from nearly sixty journals and notebooks into a compelling narrative that criticizes the Confederate administration, the behavior of her slaves, and the leadership of the Union. She also criticizes slavery as a *"monstrous system of wrong and iniquity,"* primarily because of the sexual double standard that allowed white Southern men to have sexual relationships with enslaved women while strictly governing the sexual activity of white Southern women (29–31). Chesnut critiques a social practice that was undoubtedly a source of great pain for both white and black Southern women—and yet she reserves some of her sharpest criticism not for a social structure that devalues black female bodies and regulates white ones, or for unfaithful white men, but for the enslaved women, whom she sees as depraved sexual wantons (29). Chesnut's world is one full of injustice and evil, but one in which she sees herself as a primary victim.

The lesser known writings of McGuire and Preston sound counternotes to Chesnut's account. McGuire's family was forced to flee their Alexandria, Virginia, home when it was commandeered as a Union hospital, and her anonymously published *Diary of a Southern Refugee* (1867) recounts their difficulties as impoverished, economically and physically vulnerable refugees during the wartime years. Her diary provides insider accounts of daily life and her work in Confederate hospitals and administrative offices; it also documents the struggles of ordinary Southerners and the "internal tensions and conflicts that plagued the Confederacy," even among its most ardent supporters (Carmichael 68). And Preston offers yet another perspective: the sister-in-law of Confederate general Stonewall Jackson, she was as well connected in the South as Chesnut, but she was raised in the North and had deeply divided loyalties. She only shifted support to the Confederacy following Jackson's sudden death in 1863 and the ransacking and burning of her house by Union troops in 1864 (Klein 232–4). Preston had written poetry prior to her marriage, but her husband's disapproval and an extended illness curtailed her; however, her own ambivalence about the war pushed her to take it up again. Though it is rarely studied, her book-length poem *Beechenbrook* (1865) was an influential work of Confederate nationalist literature and became a bestseller when it was republished in 1866.

The field of women's Civil War literature has been particularly exciting in recent years. The texts discussed above are only the tip of what appears to be a sizable iceberg of women's writing on the effects and experiences of war, and more material is being recovered all the time. The pocket diaries of Emilie Frances Davis are one exciting recent discovery; they document Davis' daily life as a free African American woman living in Philadelphia during the post-emancipation Civil War. Thanks to the work of Karsonya Wise Whitehead, Davis' diaries are now published and available to students and scholars everywhere, offering a window into a previously unexplored world and a reminder that many more such texts from formerly un- or underrepresented writers may also be in existence and waiting to be found.

The end of the Civil War brought a host of changes to a nation that had spent decades nursing sectional hostility. Governments at every level had to determine how to accommodate and redress the wrongs of the four million newly freed African Americans, the Southern agricultural economic model had to be rebuilt, and mainstream American culture had to come to terms with the practical and psychological realities that followed the political acknowledgment of the humanity and rights of African Americans. These were projects and processes that would take more than a century, with varying and sometimes limited success. In the years following the war, women writers turned their attentions to other struggles and subjects in their attempts to move on from the years of intersectional strife. But just as the aftermath of the war created new political, social, economic, and psychological realities for the reunited nation, so too did it repeatedly manifest in the literature of the late nineteenth century as writers sought through their texts to make sense of the brutality and division of the previous years and imagine how the nation might recover as it moved into the modern era.

Notes

1 Sedgwick was a frequent contributor to these volumes, and the story was originally published in a gift annual, so some self-mockery was involved. Cacoethes scribendi is Latin for "writer's itch."
2 The term *manifest destiny* was coined in 1845 by journalist John O'Sullivan, but the sentiment was present in American cultural and political thought throughout the

nineteenth century. As many have pointed out, including Bercovitch in his introduction to the 2011 edition of *Puritan Origins*, this concept has been endlessly reworked throughout American history, beginning with Puritan settlers and continuing to this day in political speeches that proclaim a commitment to the spread of democracy throughout the world. The argument of manifest destiny was not as coherent as historical discussions make it seem, and its principles were fiercely contested between Whigs and Democrats (see D. Howe 705–6). However, it played an important rhetorical role in American expansion in the nineteenth century. See also Amy Greenberg's *Manifest Manhood*.

3 For more on the Cult of True Womanhood, see Welter, Kerber, and Elbert.

4 The sheltering from economic and political concerns involved in the embrace of both the Cult of True Womanhood and the hierarchies of literature was not an option for women of color and working-class women, who lacked the privileges of wealth and whiteness upon which such positions depended. Some wealthier women did repudiate commercial print culture, most notably Dickinson, whose early experiences with editorial demands made her unwilling to attempt publication of most of her work. See 59 in this volume.

5 Hawthorne did, in fact, succeed; as John T. Frederick points out, two of the eight novels from the previous five years that had sold more than 225,000 copies were Hawthorne's *The Scarlet Letter* and *The House of Seven Gables* (231). At the time Hawthorne wrote this letter, he was serving in the U.S. consulate office in London and had just met his savings goal of $20,000, which he hoped to live from so that he could devote himself to writing without having to work. Also, it should be noted that Hawthorne was rather mercurial in his positions on women's writing. In his next letter, he praised Fanny Fern's *Ruth Hall* (Hawthorne *Letters* 78), and in previous letters he admired the poetry of Julia Ward Howe (Hawthorne *Letters* 29–30).

6 See Tompkins 147ff. for an overview of and response to this vein of criticism.

7 See Showalter *Alternative* ix–xxvi for more on Alcott's support of her family and her famously unreliable father.

8 For an examination of the role of women, including Fuller, in the Transcendentalist movement, see Argersinger and Cole. Fuller was subjected to harsh criticism for her independent and sexually liberated lifestyle and was a controversial figure, in spite of her significant literary accomplishments; after her death in a shipwreck, a somewhat bowdlerized version of her *Memoirs* was published in 1852, and Hawthorne declared her to be "a great humbug," although one with "great talent," and a "ridiculous" figure (Hawthorne *French* 156). As a result of these enduring perspectives, Fuller was neglected for many years, but thanks to the work of dedicated scholars many of her books have returned to print in recent years. For more on Fuller's remarkable but brief life, see Charles Capper's two-volume *Margaret Fuller: An American Romantic Life* (1994–2002) and Megan Marshall's Pulitzer Prize-winning *Margaret Fuller: A New American Life* (2013).

9 Bennett followed the work of many earlier scholars, including Emily Stipes Watts' *The Poetry of American Women from 1632 to 1945* (1977), Erlene Stetson's anthology *Black Sister: Poetry by Black American Women, 1746–1980* (1981), Cheryl Walker's *The Nightingale's Burden: Women Poets and American Culture Before 1900* (1982), and Alicia Ostriker's *Stealing the Language: The Emergence of Women's Poetry in America* (1986).

10 See Brodhead in "Sparing the Rod," where he argues that the angel of the house discourse served a Foucauldian disciplinary function in nineteenth-century ideology because of the ways women internalized these norms. Bennett disagrees with the lack of agency Brodhead's larger argument implies (see Bennett *Poets* 49ff.), as do we.

11 See also Chaney and Petrino, who examine various ways in which Osgood's published poetry undermines its own apparent endorsements of Victorian values.

12 In Sigourney's posthumously published memoir, she identifies fifty-six published books in her name, including a significant amount of prose in various formats such as advice books, home instruction, history, biography, and fiction; she also suggests that her uncollected poetry published in various magazines and other venues would make up several more volumes. See Baym "Reinventing" 386 n.3 for more information.

13 The term fascicle derives from the Latin word for "bundle" and is also used in botany to refer to clumps of needles, flowers, or leaves; it has been applied to Dickinson's hand-sewn manuscript documents, the format and composition of which are viewed by many critics as intrinsic to an understanding of Dickinson's poetic process and philosophy. See Loeffelholz for more information.

14 All Dickinson poems are cited from the *Complete Poems* edited by Thomas H. Johnson. Because there are frequently multiple poems on a single page, parenthetical citations include the poem number rather than the page number, followed by the line numbers of the respective quotations.

15 For more, see Martin *Triptych* 79–83.

16 For more on Sedgwick's treatments of the women in her novel, see Fetterley's "My Sister! My Sister!"

17 Child's *Hobomok* (1824) offers a similar conclusion: the title character marries Mary Conant, a white woman whose fiancé is believed to be dead; though Mary comes to love him, when her fiancé returns several years later Hobomok nobly renounces Mary and their child and goes West alone to die.

18 As R. Parker notes, the work of several Native Americans writing in Euroamerican traditions has been uncovered in recent decades, and more writers are being discovered all the time. Parker lists, among others, David Cusick (Tuscarora), Elias Boudinot (Cherokee), and William Apess (Pequot), and notes other poets who closely followed Schoolcraft, including John Rollin Ridge (Cherokee) and Betsy Chamberlain (identified as "possibly Narragansett and/or Abenaki"); see R. Parker 74–5 n.1 for additional details.

19 We refer to this author by her English name throughout because it was the name she most commonly used to refer to herself, particularly in conjunction with her writing.

20 Henry Rowe Schoolcraft is considered one of the progenitors of American cultural anthropology because he was one of the earliest people to seek out and systematically document the beliefs and practices of several Native American nations. But Henry also tended to minimize the contributions of others, particularly Native Americans, in ways that privileged his own point of view as allowing for a more authentic representation of Native cultures than those of Native Americans themselves. R. Parker writes extensively about Henry's selective crediting of his wife and the other Ojibwe who collaborated with him in his research. Henry significantly rewrote stories for white audiences; in his memoirs, he noted that he removed "many vulgarisms" from the texts, worked to "restore the simplicity of the original style," and broke up or cut off stories in order to "avoid incongruity" (H. Schoolcraft 585), all while giving scanty credit to his sources (R. Parker 26–7). Some stories can be credited to particular writers, including Schoolcraft, based on the drafts found in Henry's papers. See R. Parker 61ff. for more information.

21 See for example Hall's *Letters from the West* (1828), Fowler's *Woman on the American Frontier* (1876), and Frost's *Thrilling Adventures Among the Indians* (1850). Women were occasionally portrayed as adventurers, as in Frost's *Heroic Women of the West*, but as Dawn E. Keetley notes, such women heroes were always pressed into action by the need to defend their homes and families, usually from Indian attacks (19).

22 Kirkland mentions that her husband encounters a party of drunken Native Americans while on an exploratory trip without her (see *A New Home* 47–9), but she only reports seeing one Native American in all of *A New Home* while out riding (135). In *Forest Life*, published in 1842 after Indian removal in Michigan was well underway, Kirkland makes joking allusion to it, noting in an aside, "I thought all our Indians had been persuaded off to Green Bay, at the point of the bayonet" (1: 151).

23 Hazel Carby's *Reconstructing Womanhood* is a key work in this vein, as are Hartman's *Scenes of Subjection* and Noble's *The Masochistic Pleasures of Sentimental Literature*. See S. Ryan 169–70 for an overview of this critical debate in the 1980s and 1990s.

24 As several scholars have noted, the Second Great Awakening was not a single coherent movement, and its origins are unknown, but there were some shared characteristics across the meetings (see Cott 15). Revival meetings led by itinerant preachers and denomi-national missionaries sent to the Western frontiers swelled the ranks of evangelical

Methodist, Baptist, and Presbyterian enrollees, and several new denominations were born, including the Church of Christ, the Seventh Day Adventists, the Shakers, and the Church of Jesus Christ of Latter-Day Saints.

25 Massachusetts was the first state to abolish slavery by a Supreme Court decision in 1783; in that same year, New Hampshire, Rhode Island, and Connecticut passed laws decreeing gradual emancipation, which meant that the children born to enslaved African American women in those states would be free. New York (1799) and New Jersey (1804) soon followed with gradual emancipation laws of their own. Ohio established itself as a free state in 1802, and Indiana emancipated most slaves in 1820. Texas and New Mexico were admitted to the Union as slave states, but California was admitted as a free state, even though some of its territory fell below the Missouri Compromise parallel. Pennsylvania was the last of the Northern states to abolish slavery in 1847 before the Emancipation Proclamation in 1863 and the Thirteenth Amendment to the Constitution in December 1865 abolished slavery throughout the United States. For more on the gradual abolition of slavery in the North, see Berlin 228–55.

26 See Bennett *Poets* 40–61 for a discussion of difference versus equality feminism and its application to the poetry of protest. See Grimké 112–13 for an example of the rhetorical linking between slavery and women's oppression.

27 See also Elizabeth McHenry's *Forgotten Readers.*

28 Truth's memoir went through several revisions in her lifetime, some of which are somewhat controversial. See Phillips-Anderson 36 n.8.

29 According to Albert Tricomi, it was uncommon in the nineteenth century for speech to be recorded in dialect, except for in the case of African Americans, a subtle but clearly "inequitable, problematic 'literary' decision" ("Dialect" 619); this makes both editorial choices—Robinson's to report the speech in standard American English, and Gage's to report it in dialect—suggestive of political motivation.

30 The manuscript was discovered in 2002 and has only recently been attributed to a self-educated enslaved woman named Hannah Bond. The attribution comes from professor Gregg Hecimovich at Winthrop University, who connects the text to Bond based on letters, diaries, and other texts (see Bosman).

31 See for example Mills 210 and Tricomi's "Harriet Jacobs' Autobiography and the Voice of Lydia Maria Child." For many years, *Incidents* was assumed by scholars to be a false slave narrative, written by Child and passed off as the work of an unnamed former slave. However, Jean Fagan Yellin has conclusively identified Jacobs as the author based on a series of letters and other corroborating historical documents. See Yellin xx–xxvii for more information.

32 While Jacobs' text is autobiographical, it is a mistake to confuse Jacobs' pseudonymous narrator with the author herself; following the lead of most scholars writing about Jacobs, we distinguish between Jacobs and her character by using the name Linda Brent where appropriate.

33 "Uncle Tom Mania" took hold in Britain as much as in the United States, and after its publication Stowe traveled to Europe several times, joining in a transatlantic literary community with her sympathetic peers (Kohn et al. xvi–xvii). The novel also prompted several pro-slavery response novels, including Carolyn Hentz's *The Planter's Northern Bride* (1854).

34 For a discussion of the evolution of the image of Uncle Tom, see Kathleen Hulser's "Reading Uncle Tom's Image: From Anti-Slavery Hero to Racial Insult."

35 See Catherine Clinton's introduction to *Mary Chesnut's Diary*, in which she outlines some of the critical debates.

4

FROM TRUE WOMAN TO NEW WOMAN

Redefining womanhood at the turn of the century

The signing of the treaty at Appomattox on April 9, 1865, heralded the end of Civil War combat, but the decades that immediately followed were hardly a time of peace. There were the immediate and direct repercussions of the war, beginning with a shocking act of violence: the assassination of Abraham Lincoln by a Confederate sympathizer on April 15, 1865, a reflection of the scarcely suppressed fury and bitterness of many in the defeated Confederacy that would linger for generations. Governmental and communal efforts to rebuild Southern infrastructure, bring recalcitrant states back into the fold of the federal government, and help emancipated African Americans adjust to their new freedoms were stymied by mismanagement, political wrangling, rampant corruption, the terror campaigns of the Ku Klux Klan, and the widespread establishment of segregation under Jim Crow law. But the Civil War also had unintended repercussions for the rest of the nation. It accelerated the processes of industrialization, particularly in the North, and led to the exponential growth of industries like mining and manufacturing, a development fed by an influx of European and Asian immigrants who were concentrated in urban areas.

This technological growth and the resulting cultural shifts fueled other conflicts that had receded in national importance during wartime. In the western United States railroads pounded their way across the prairies, bringing throngs of land-hungry settlers and making the hunting practices that had sustained many Native American tribes impossible; and skirmishes with Native Americans resisting the push onto shrinking reservations became full-fledged and bloody military operations. In eastern industrial centers, dangerous working conditions led to protests, labor unrest, and efforts to organize unions and care for the mushrooming numbers of urban poor, even while nativist resentment bubbled against the immigrants who filled the factories. The growth of immigration had its parallel in the United States' imperial action in Central America, the Caribbean, and the South Pacific, including embroilment in the 1898 Cuban Revolution (referred to in the United States as the Spanish–American War). And at the same time, reformers inspired by the success of the abolition movement continued to agitate for greater rights and recognition for marginalized groups. At scarcely a century old, the United States grappled with recovering from the deep national wound of civil war, adapting to the many social, economic, and political changes wrought by the war and the world's headlong rush toward modernity, and daily confronting the question of what it meant to be American in the midst of the cultural upheaval resulting from industrialization and ongoing imperial incursions around the world. There was no resuming business as usual after the war; for better or worse, life in the United States was irrevocably changing.

The literatures of the late nineteenth and early twentieth centuries reflect these issues, marked by preoccupations with cultural dislocation, reorientation, and deep ambivalence about change. African American writers and thinkers saw in this period opportunity to redefine African American identities and potential both within the African American community and in the eyes of dominant American culture. Many women took an active role in the public debates between those advocating a gradual approach to political, economic, and social equality, represented most famously by Booker T. Washington, and those demanding the immediate and full education and enfranchisement argued for by W.E.B. Du Bois and others. Anna Julia Cooper fought for educational equality and deliberately challenged members of the mainstream women's rights movement, especially the women of the South, arguing in her speeches and essays that white women should be working as hard for the equal rights of black women as for themselves. Frances E.W. Harper, Pauline Hopkins, and many others dramatized debates about race and women's roles in racial uplift in autobiography, fiction, poetry, and theater, presenting the relationships and fates of black and white Americans as inextricably enmeshed and working to rehabilitate dominant cultural conceptions of African American womanhood to include a broader range of black female subjectivities.

Many other writers were also working to bring previously unseen perspectives to the attention of the American public. Native American writers such as Sarah Winnemucca and Zitkala Ša wrote autobiographies, memoirs, novels, stories, and essays that documented threatened Native cultures and the constant shifts and renegotiations involved as they were forced into Euroamerican ways of life. Non-Native women also examined the Southwest and the ways it had changed under U.S. occupation. Helen Hunt Jackson used fiction and nonfiction to bring attention to the great injustices of the United States' treatment of Native Americans, early ecofeminist Mary Austin presented the redeeming power of southwestern landscapes and the spiritual influence of the natural world in her fiction and nature writing, and María Amparo Ruiz de Burton wrote political romances detailing the wrongs perpetrated against Mexican landowners who suddenly found themselves on U.S. property after the 1848 Treaty of Guadalupe Hidalgo.

Elsewhere in the country, the rapid growth of immigrant populations led to debates about what kinds of people ought to be allowed and whether they should or could be properly "Americanized" once they arrived. The deep poverty of many of these immigrants and their difficulty adapting to new cultural milieus fed prejudices against them that many writers sought to combat. Sui Sin Far's magazine fiction and essays explored the legal and social hardships faced by Chinese immigrants, Mary Antin's bestselling memoir documented her childhood as a persecuted Jew in Belarus and her process of eager Americanization, and Emma Lazarus wrote poetry and essays foregrounding the experiences of the growing Jewish population and other immigrant communities in New York. Writer and social worker Jane Addams dedicated her life to improving working and living conditions for urban immigrants; in addition to her writing and sociological research, Addams' Hull-House in Chicago provided classes, childcare, and other assistance for immigrants struggling to adjust to radically new ways of life. Each of these writers worked to draw readers' attention to perspectives far outside their own, to humanize their subjects and inspire respect, understanding, and cooperation between old and new Americans.

Still other writers worked to shift readers' attention to another group long neglected by the literary establishment: the inhabitants of the United States' small towns and villages. Author and editor of *The Atlantic Monthly* William Dean Howells was one champion of the literary movement known as regionalism. He sought to bring to light the farthest-flung corners of the United States by publishing stories that emphasized both the distinctive and the universal aspects of local ways of life in an effort to tease out the essence of an Americanness that seemed threatened by its traumatic past and uncertain future. While many authors wrote what could be considered regionalist literature, the genre was largely dominated by women. Regionalism involves specifically local landscapes, ways of speaking, and psychologically realized characters who often live in rural isolation, and it generally pulls in multiple directions: it is marked by a pervasive nostalgia and the sense that these ideal worlds are slipping away; and yet the stories and novels of women such as Mary Wilkins Freeman, Sarah Orne Jewett, and Kate Chopin also emphasize the desperation, stifling loneliness, and class and race struggles underlying the peaceful veneer of these rural communities, along with the strengths, hurts, and desires of the women who hold these communities together.

Regionalism is a branch of realism, which became the dominant mode of fiction writing in the late nineteenth century. In its simplest definition, realistic literature focused on truthful and unidealized depictions of ordinary life. It is an umbrella category that Elizabeth Ammons argues encompasses "the multiple realities figured in the work of the broadest possible range of authors writing in the late nineteenth and early twentieth centuries" ("Expanding" 100); it includes not only regionalism, but also psychological realism, which attempted to express psychological, moral, and emotional realities, and naturalism, which examined individuals' lives as products of the larger social, environmental, political, and economic systems within which they moved. Critics have been inclined to identify regionalism as a sentimental, nostalgic, and irrelevant women's genre and stylistically innovative, consciously political naturalism as a men's genre, but such classifications ignore the fluidity of these generic boundaries and the ways regionalism, psychological realism, and naturalism frequently bled into each other in turn-of-the-century texts. Among the most successful writers in these modes were Edith Wharton, Ellen Glasgow, and Kate Chopin, whose works explore the damaging effects of limitations placed on women in compelling and skillful mixtures of regionalist, realist, and naturalist tropes. Despite the efforts of some members of the literary establishment to marginalize them, these women shaped American literature in new and exciting ways and through their texts placed the lives and concerns of women at the forefront of literary innovation.

Cultural conceptions of womanhood were in flux and subject to transformation in the late decades of the nineteenth century. More women than ever before were challenging the notion of women's proper roles, asserting their rights to education, compensated work, suffrage, public life, and control over choices related to sex, marriage, and childbearing. These New Women, as they came to be known, pushed for greater personal autonomy and social freedoms, and many of them made activism and reform into careers. Such was the case with the sociological and political writing of Jane Addams, the pointedly reform-oriented fiction and journalism of Rebecca Harding Davis, the feminist fiction, poetry, essays, and speeches of Charlotte Perkins Gilman, the anti-lynching journalism campaigns for which Ida Wells-Barnett repeatedly risked her life, and the muckraking investigations of Ida Tarbell into corporate corruption and greed. Some of these women, primarily reformers and writers from the middle and upper classes, found a measure of independence in "Boston marriages," long-term, committed, socially sanctioned romantic and sometimes erotic relationships with other women.[1] These relationships, part of the long lineage of what Carroll Smith-Rosenberg terms the "female world of love and ritual" that resulted from the social separation of women and men (53), provided women with the support, companionship, and emotional and physical intimacy of marriage without the competing demands of pregnancy or childrearing. For these women, changing conceptions of womanhood allowed both personal and professional fulfillment.

But many other women greeted New Womanhood with ambivalence. The greater sexual freedom toward which it gestured was a double-edged sword for African American women looking to shed the Jezebel label, and some saw its emphasis on personal autonomy as incompatible with the political goals of a community focused on racial uplift. In addition, for most women of color and poorer white women, work outside the home continued to be an economic necessity as much or more than it was a meaningful personal pursuit. As Martha H. Patterson notes, New Women crop up in a range of turn-of-the-century literature, from the texts of Sui Sin Far and Pauline Hopkins to the novels of Wharton, Glasgow, and Chopin (4). All of these writers explore with varying degrees of enthusiasm and unease the ways in which the ability to exercise some measure of self-determination seemed a futile weapon against the power of the prevailing social order.

The texts from the decades bookended by the Civil War and World War I are marked by examinations of the ideas of cultural, political, social, and technological progress and change. As Anna Julia Cooper remarked in an 1892 essay, the late nineteenth century was "pre-eminently an age of organizations" (85) during which social and political reform groups flourished, including the settlement houses of Chicago and other cities, the National Child Labor Committee, local women's philanthropic and social clubs throughout the country, the Colored Women's YMCA, the Women's Christian Temperance Union, and the National Women's Suffrage Association. The work of women writers was central to these efforts. Stowe's *Uncle Tom's Cabin* had created a growing consciousness of the power of literature to effect social change, and many writers hoped to do the same for their own causes. But the spirit of protest and reform also suffused the works of writers who were not necessarily participants in specific movements but explored the dislocations and dissatisfactions of the age for women from a range of class, race, and ethnic backgrounds, pushing back against cultural perceptions of acceptable womanhood and the forces that attempted to dictate it. In their texts and speeches, women writers in the fin de siècle period emphasized the wide range of American female voices; they also worked to redefine American femininity to include those that had long been subdued or ignored, taking aim at definitions of Americanness that depended on race and gender and making the literature of this period above all else one of subjectivities.

The New Woman as race mother: Redefining black womanhood in the postbellum period

The decades immediately following the Civil War were a crucial transition period for African Americans. In the hubbub of newly realized freedoms and changing political, economic, and social configurations, there were numerous choices to be made that ranged from personal and practical (where to live and work) to broadly ideological (what it meant to be African American). Such decisions had to be made in the midst of a complex and evolving set of racially charged ideologies and practices. Beginning in the 1860s, the "Lost Cause" ideology valorized Confederate soldiers as the epitome of Southern masculinity defending not only white Southern women but a feminized South (Young 175–6), and the growing popularity of social Darwinism and pseudosciences such as scientific racism and eugenics, which claimed scientific evidence proving the superiority of the white race, were used to justify racist policies within the United States and imperialism without.[2] The 1870s and 1880s saw political gains such as ratification of the vote for black men and the first African Americans in Congress, but the 1890s saw "severe racial retrenchment" (Young 195), including the thriving practice of lynching and the enactment of Jim Crow laws across the South.

Against this shifting ideological terrain, two primary and opposing viewpoints emerged. Booker T. Washington and his followers advocated a gradual approach in which, by dint of hard work, an emphasis on technical education, and the absence of social and political agitation, African Americans could over the course of several generations earn the respect of white Americans and the right to full participation in American intellectual, economic, and political life. But W.E.B. Du Bois and his followers held that such accommodations only reinforced racial hierarchies and caused irreparable psychological damage in asking African Americans to internalize their inferiority; instead, Du Bois demanded immediate recognition, unrestricted voting rights, and equal access to higher education and the professions. Leading African American thinkers, writers, activists, and organizers explored the ramifications of pursuing these courses of action in speeches, poems, novels, and essays as they worked for the "uplift" of all African Americans. The richness of this intellectual output made what John Ernest describes as a "golden age" for African American historical writing, one in which the major terms of the debate about the future of the race were articulated in texts such as Washington's autobiographical *Up From Slavery* (1901) and Du Bois' *The Souls of Black Folk* (1903)—and one that also placed African American men squarely at the center as the "agents of African American collective self-determination" (283). But African American women were fiercely involved in the debate, and many saw in the centering of African American men the possibility of reinscribing the gendered power structures of white patriarchy. They viewed the struggle for women's rights as coequal with the struggle for African American recognition, but they faced the additional difficulty of white supremacy in the mainstream women's rights movement, which largely excluded them as a concession to Southern women who claimed African American women were sexually immoral (Carby *Reconstructing* 116). They were caught between the need to refute the common stereotypes of African American women as oversexed jezebels and tragic mulattas (linked with the politically radical claiming of marriage and domestic life that had been denied them under slavery) and the desire to assert the value of African American women's voices in shaping the future of the race, the nation, and the world. Their solutions were both political, in the formation of organizations such as the National Association of Colored Women in 1895, and textual, in the articulation of nuanced subjectivities that challenged dominant ways of reading African American femininity. In their life writing, essays, poetry, and fiction, African American women writers such as Mattie Jackson, Lucy A. Delaney, Frances E.W. Harper, Anna Julia Cooper, and Pauline E. Hopkins sought to redefine the meanings of African American womanhood and to rewrite cultural narratives of Americanness to reveal the ways African Americans were and had always been part of them.

Life writing was one significant way African American women worked to revise narratives of Americanness; in their texts, they posited the black woman's world and experiences during the Civil War and its aftermath as valuable, inverting the traditional "great men" mode of writing and reading history (Ernest 285).[3] Ernest identifies several key texts that work in this mode, including Mattie J. Jackson's *The Story of Mattie J. Jackson* (1866), which recounts Jackson's and her family's escapes to freedom, and Lucy A. Delaney's *From the Darkness Cometh the Light or Struggles for Freedom* (1891), which documents Delaney's and her mother's legal efforts to establish themselves as free women.[4] The Civil War looms large in these texts, and while the authors invariably praise Lincoln, Frederick Douglass, Ulysses S. Grant, and other heroes of the war effort, they insist on telling their own versions of history. They situate their own stories—their struggles to move from enslavement to freedom, to adapt to a post-enslavement world, and to gain legal recognition— and the larger account of Union victory and emancipation within the "providential realm" of history, and their own roles as actors, however small, in the divinely ordained progress toward justice (Ernest 286); they also point toward divine retri- bution, as in Jackson's text, in which she recounts her mistress vowing to see her children dead rather than "on an equal footing with a Nigger," only to encounter that mistress after the war, "trudging to market" along the same road as her former slaves and doing for herself and her children the jobs Jackson and her mother used to do (108, 126). The image suggests a divinely orchestrated comeuppance for the former mistress in which the author necessarily plays a part, including in her retelling of the story.

As Ernest notes, these women make "modest" claims (285) of their texts' unremarkableness but assert it is this unremarkable nature that makes them important. Delaney acknowledges her mother's life is not heroic by the standards of contem- porary history books, but suggests her story's ordinariness may help her reader resolve the question of whether "the negro race [can] succeed, proportionately, as well as the whites, if given the same chance and an equal start" (63–4). It is a claim that strikes at the very heart of national and international debates about racial equal- ity. In thus asserting African American women (and their texts) as actors in larger political and social movements, these narratives upend the model of understanding history, moving from a model that privileges great men, political action, and war to one that examines the "encompassing significance" (Ernest 289) of the lives of even the most obscure African American women.

Like Jackson and Delaney, Frances E.W. Harper worked to reshape concep- tions of the Civil War and African American women's history and potential, but Harper's most significant work was fiction rather than memoir. Harper was born free in Maryland and had a long career as an anti-slavery lecturer and writer prior to the Civil War; after the war she continued advocating for African Americans' rights and women's suffrage in speeches, essays, poems, and fiction, recognizing that, as Hazel Carby puts it, "organizing to fight meant also writing to organize" (*Reconstructing* 97). The most notable of Harper's texts from this perspective is her 1892 novel *Iola Leroy*. In the title character, Harper inverts the archetype of the tragic mulatta, showing how she discovers her mixed ancestry and is then taken into slavery, works as a Union nurse during the Civil War, refuses marriage to a white doctor, searches for her family after the war, and then returns to the South with her mixed-race husband to be of service to her people. Harper layers several critiques of dominant narratives of the Civil War and African American womanhood within this story and restores the culturally invisible wartime heroism of African American men and women in the figures of Robert Johnson, Iola, and others (Young 208). She also links women to the larger project of war, emphasizing the reunions of separated African American mothers and children and the restoration of families in order to present the war as a "maternal quest for women"; what's more, in aligning Iola's history of resistance to rape by white men with military combat, Harper reverses in one move the stereotypes of black women as seductresses and black men as rapists of white women (Young 211, 213). Finally, she creates a heroine who values independence enough to reject the patriarchal ownership model of marriage and only marry when she finds an "equal partner" (Young 216). At the close of the novel, Harper renders Iola as victor and a "symbol of honesty, purity, and achievement" (S. Smith 375)—anything but a tragic figure. Further, Harper makes Iola a potential author and posits the writing of a "good, strong book" as a work "of lasting service to the race" (Harper 262), arguing for the vital role of fiction in the pursuit of racial uplift. Gloria Naylor and others have criticized Harper's novel for going too far, "whiten[ing] and deaden[ing]" the sexuality of her black female characters during a time when white naturalist writers and others were pushing toward more open explorations of sex (22), but Claudia Tate argues that marriage and domestic life had long been denied to African American women and thus could in fact be aligned with liberation and political action for them (*Domestic* 7–15). In the figure of Iola, Harper asks readers to envision the contributions of African American women in new ways, rejecting passivity and dependence and embracing self-reliance, service to the race, and artistic endeavor as political acts.

Such an endorsement of domestic wife- and motherhood as civil service runs the risk of feeding into "anti-individualist doctrines of racial uplift" that ultimately silence African American women (Fleissner 247), a problem that Pauline E. Hopkins explores in her generically innovative fiction. Hopkins was born into the wealthy Black Brahmin community in New England.[5] A prolific writer, Hopkins had her first play, *The Slave's Escape; or, the Underground Railroad*, produced when she was twenty, and her long career included the genre-bending serial novel *Of One Blood* (1902–1903), an early piece of African American speculative fiction that combines gothic adventure with a reimagined, racialized novel of manners (Sherrard-Johnson 405–6). In her work as a founding editor of *Colored American Magazine*, her determination to "develop Afro-American popular fiction" (Carby "Introduction" xxix), and her aesthetic experimentation, Harper laid valuable groundwork for the Harlem Renaissance and prefigured some of the tropes of high modernism (Chapman 343), all while examining the roles African American women might play in the post-emancipation world.

One example is Hopkins' 1900 generational saga *Contending Forces: A Romance Illustrative of Negro Life North and South*, which fictionalizes the Washington–Du Bois debate in the lives of the racially mixed Montfort family and articulates the struggles for women within this framework in its two main female characters, Sappho Clark and Dora Smith. Over the course of the novel, Dora moves from a New Negro Woman figure who sees the subsuming of a woman's individuality into wife- and motherhood as "old-fashioned" to a "contented young matron," the wife of a Washington-like character who believes women should stay out of politics (Hopkins 176, 389).[6] Meanwhile, Sappho, who was a child prostitute under the slave regime, finds freedom from her "tainted history" in sharing her past with her future husband Will Smith, who represents the progressive

Du Bois perspective, but nevertheless ends up a "distinctly muted" maternal figure (Fleissner 244, 247). Critics have noted that these character arcs are somewhat discouraging in their suggestion of the silencing of African American women (cf. McCann 791), but Hopkins presents the issues dialogically, including a series of public oratorical debates and numerous private conversations between characters who question the proper role and attitude of the "race woman" (Fleissner 247). Chapman identifies this type of move as an alternate mode of persuasive writing that invites the reader's participation in the debate, as well as an antecedent to the "quoting" and "ventriloquizing" experiments in voice found in high modernism (337, 343). The shift of Sappho's political discourse from the auditorium to the parlor can thus be read as a troubling silencing on one level and a means of reaching outside the book to implicate readers in such debates on another. And in the undercurrents of sexual desire that link Sappho and Dora throughout the novel (Somerville 147ff.), we see flashes of all that "remains hard to say, yet is not merely unsaid" in the text (Fleissner 247). In this way Hopkins' *Contending Forces* offers the outline of a world in which a broader range of African American female sexual and political desires are visible but not expressible, in which what meets the eye is both more and less than what can be said.

If Harper and Hopkins explore African American women's roles in racial uplift, educator and essayist Anna Julia Cooper looks explicitly at the links between gender and racial dynamics within and outside the African American community. Born under slavery, Cooper witnessed the Civil War and the early years of the Civil Rights movement, and she was the fourth African American woman to earn a doctorate, at the age of 65. During her long career as a teacher, scholar, speaker, and community organizer, she worked ceaselessly for the intellectual and social advancement of African American women and the end of oppression around the world. Focusing on education and women's rights, Cooper's essays emphasize concentric circles of oppression within the African American community, the mainstream women's rights movement, and the imperial United States.

Cooper's most notable work is her lively, sharply ironic essay collection *A Voice from the South, by a Black Woman of the South* (1892), which evaluates among other things the roles white women play in perpetuating racial hierarchies and the damaging influences of patriarchal culture among African Americans. In "Woman Versus the Indian," Cooper addresses white women's reform organizations, noting the social influence of white women and their power to spur reforms on the one side and uphold racist values on the other; she also criticizes activists who would make the white woman "plaintiff in a suit versus the Indian, or the Negro or any other race or class who have been crushed under the iron heel of Anglo-Saxon power and selfishness" rather than see their oppression as connected to her own (123). In "The Higher Education of Woman," Cooper calls out African American schools and universities for encouraging male students toward intellectual and professional pursuits and supporting them institutionally while shunting female students into marriage, thus reinforcing the "ideology of true womanhood" (Carby *Reconstructing* 100). Cooper's larger argument in her collection is that the failure to see the elevation of any group at the expense of another as linked to every form of oppression around the world is a failure to recognize the "celestial kernel" at the core of all individuals, who hold the same "inalienable title to life, liberty, and pursuit of happiness" regardless of "accidents" of "race, color, sex, [and] condition" (125). By cloaking her moral argument in such powerfully American rhetoric, Cooper stakes a claim for the struggle for African American women's recognition as one intrinsic to American values.

Literatures of the West

Western expansion and the process of Indian removal had not ceased during the Civil War, but they became major focuses of the U.S. government and military in the decades that immediately followed the war as technologies like barbed wire and the completion of four transcontinental railroads dramatically changed the Western landscape. A series of events with significant bearing on the lives of Western residents marked the late nineteenth century: the 1851 Gwin Land Act essentially stripped Mexican landowners in new U.S. territories of their property; the 1871 Indian Appropriation Act made Native Americans wards of the state and subject to supervision by a network of government agencies; the 1887 Dawes Allotment Act broke up Native lands into family tracts; and there were a series of wars throughout the West, including the 1878 Bannock War in Washington, the Great Sioux War of 1876 in South Dakota, and the Wounded Knee Massacre in 1890, as Native groups resisted the U.S. government's repeated treaty violations, encroachments onto Native land, widespread corruption, and genocidal activity. The net effects of these transactions were the increase of power and land ownership by white Americans—to the tune of 90 million acres (Edmunds 401)—at the cost of thousands of Native American lives and a series of new and continually shifting allegiances as Native Americans struggled to survive and retain their ways of life. The literatures of the West from these decades produced by Native American writers such as Sarah Winnemucca (Paiute) and Zitkala Ša (Yankton Sioux), Euroamerican writers such as Helen Hunt Jackson and Mary Austin, and Mexican American writer María Amparo Ruiz de Burton reflect a sense of loss, instability, and constant renegotiation, even as they work to revise dominant cultural depictions of the West and its inhabitants and expose the corruption and hypocrisy of the U.S. government.

Many Native women wrote during this period, but as both writers and public speakers Sarah Winnemucca and Zitkala Ša offer compelling examinations of the series of renegotiations of identity and selfhood for Native individuals and groups during this period of rapid and dramatic change.[7] Winnemucca was born into a powerful family of Paiute leaders in Nevada, spoke five languages, and worked as a translator for the army and various Indian agencies in western states. She also traveled throughout the country delivering speeches about the mistreatment and starvation of her people at the hands of duplicitous U.S. agents and politicians and the repeated betrayals of her people by the U.S. government. Her autobiography,

Life Among the Piutes, Their Wrongs and Claims (1883), documents the process of acculturation for her people, including their forced transition to an agricultural way of life and repeated relocations, starvation, and mistreatment, her assistance to the U.S. army during the Bannock War, and her role as a translator and advocate for her people with the government, including the Secretary of the Interior and President Rutherford B. Hayes. Winnemucca is a figure of some controversy. Her position as translator for the army and the Bureau of Indian Affairs and her frequent billing as an "Indian princess" and public appearances in full Paiute dress seem to critics a betrayal of her people and an embrace of the project of Americanization, as well as acquiescence to the white American exoticization of Native cultures. But as many scholars have pointed out, Winnemucca's self-positioning and deliberate embodiment of popular conceptions of a Native American Other for white audiences allow her to articulate a sharp critique of the U.S. imperial and genocidal project even while working to find a common ground that would help save her people (Senier 87ff.; Sorisio "Sarah" *passim*). As Siobhan Senier notes, for Winnemucca, it was not a clear choice between capitulation and resistance to assimilation, between "merely speaking (open protest) or not speaking (silent self-preservation)," but a far more nuanced strategy of resistance that engaged with "the question of how to speak, whether to speak, and how one might—or might not—be understood" (28). What emerges from her autobiography is not only an unambiguous depiction of the pain, loss of agency, and vulnerability to predation of Paiute reservation life but also Winnemucca's concern for her people's survival and her recognition of this kind of barbed but adaptive cooperation with whites as the best hope of ensuring it.

The writings of Zitkala Ša present another view of Native American assimilation that depends for the force of its critique just as much on white conceptions of Indianness. Zitkala Ša was among the earliest generations of Native children to be lured to Indian boarding schools to be civilized and Christianized; her growing political activism cost her a teaching job at the Carlisle Indian Industrial School, but she went on to teach on various reservations and eventually became a leader in several Native American advocacy groups, including the Society of American Indians and the National Council of American Indians. While Zitkala Ša's texts cover a variety of subjects (and include the libretto for the first Native American opera, *The Sun Dance*), her autobiographical essays, published in *The Atlantic Monthly* between 1900 and 1904, explore the devastating psychological results of forced assimilation into a white supremacist culture. She describes her experiences in the "civilizing machine" of the Indian schools as a time suffused by grief during which her "spirit tore itself in struggling for its lost freedom" as she and her fellow Native students had their former ways of life literally stripped from them along with their blankets and their long hair (66, 52).

Zitkala Ša also presents the process of acculturation as one of distancing from nature, so that during times of deep feeling she comes to prefer her "small white-walled prison" of a room rather than finding "healing in trees and brooks" (96, 97); it is what Jennifer K. Ladino describes as an "inver[sion of] the idea of progress" that embraces the white conflation of Native Americans with the natural world in order to present the white world's version of civilization as "unnatural" (17, 35). But she consciously reverses this process in "Why I Am A Pagan" (1901) and describes her rejection of the converted "native preacher" with his "bigoted creed" (105) in favor of the "drifting clouds and tinkling waters" (101) where she can hear "the voice of the Great Spirit" (107), helping her to "see clearly again that all are akin" (104). Furthermore, in her presentations of the networks of social connections that constitute tribal life and her critiques of the forcing of Native Americans into individual property ownership and married single-family units in order to bring them into alignment with the civilized world, Zitkala Ša indicts white American hostility to "native traditions and extended kinship formations" and "contest[s] the political economy of imperial domesticity" visible in the work of other activist texts like *Uncle Tom's Cabin* (Rifkin 29–30). Thus, Zitkala Ša asserts an alternate feminist critique that reflects the way domestic ideologies are implicated in American imperialist activity, up to and including mainstream American reform movements.

Zitkala Ša was not alone in her critiques of the effects of patriarchal power structures on the American West. Euroamerican writers including Helen Hunt Jackson and Mary Austin also examined the exploitation inherent in the Euroamerican drive to colonize North America according to patriarchal notions of civilization and progress. Poet and novelist Jackson was spurred to activism late in her career when she heard a speech given by Ponca chief Standing Bear in 1879 (Phillips 141–2). Her initial political foray, *A Century of Dishonor* (1881), documented the histories of repeated treaty violation and abuse for seven tribes and advocated for Native property rights. After studying the conditions of the California Mission Indians for the Bureau of Indian Affairs, Jackson dramatized their plight in the hugely popular historical romance *Ramona* (1884), which she hoped would have "a thousandth" the effect of *Uncle Tom's Cabin* (H. Jackson 258). But the legacy of these works is ambivalent; in the mixed-race figure of Ramona and her repudiation of her adoptive white family Jackson offers a compelling rejection of whiteness and class hierarchies (Luis-Brown 66), but to Jackson's great disappointment, readers seemed to embrace the story's characters while disregarding its political content; they flocked to southern California to tour the novel's locations, which likely led to additional white settlement and loss of land (DeLyser x–xi). And many scholars credit Jackson with influencing the congressional reexamination of Native land rights that led to the Dawes Act and the break-up of Native landholdings through the application to Native cultures of the very patriarchal and capitalist values against which Zitkala Ša had protested.

The ecofeminist texts of Austin take what might be read as an oppositional approach to Jackson's. *The Land of Little Rain* (1903) and *The Basket Woman* (1904) feature nature writing about the American Southwest and its ecosystems that refuses patriarchal narratives of progress in which human civilization is the center of the created world. In Austin's Southwest, the desert is an impersonal force that shapes residents' lives rather than the mere backdrop for an anthropocentric melodrama like *Ramona*. Lawrence Buell reads Austin's refusal to name her locations and her repeated redefinition of their boundaries as a rejection of patriarchal and capitalistic views of the wilderness as a space to be conquered, mined, developed, or ticked off a tourist's checklist (80). Instead, the desert is a self-sustaining and perhaps even supernatural environment for those who are properly attuned to it (Hume 185). Under the inexorable and impenetrable movements of stars in the desert sky, both the "poor world-fret" of the human observer and the "howls and howls" of the "lean coyote" are of little account and no permanence, restored to their proper proportion at last (Austin 17).

The work of María Amparo Ruiz de Burton offers a strikingly different per-spective on the shifting allegiances and complex negotiations of subjectivity that characterized the late nineteenth-century West. As a wealthy resident of southern California during the transition from Mexican to U.S. rule, Ruiz de Burton had a complicated set of loyalties: she was "simultaneously Mexican, a U.S. (imperial) citizen, the wife of a U.S. army captain, and a non-Anglo landowner of a ranch formerly owned by a Californio" (Luis-Brown 49). She and her husband traveled in powerful American circles and had social relationships with the wives of both Union and Confederate presidents during the Civil War, and her plays and political novels reflect her insider's view of the machinations of American politics and her class-consciousness. The sharpest of these is *The Squatter and the Don* (1885), which chastises the U.S. government for repeated violations of the Treaty of Guadalupe Hidalgo while reinforcing the virtue, European sophistication, and above all the white-ness of the government's victims, wealthy Californio landowners. Ruiz de Burton draws parallels between the aristocratic Californios, surrounded by government-endorsed squatters, and the American South, both threatened by corruption and class instability; in this way, she works to expand definitions of whiteness to include the Mexican elite while attacking the foundation of social and political exploita-tion of marginalized groups through which that whiteness is constructed.[8] Ruiz de Burton's argument is not one of human rights but of property rights, positioning her, as Marcial González observes, "both against and in favor of the ideological interests of a rapidly changing capitalist society" (68), and struggling nonetheless, like so many writers of the West, for recognition and survival.

The Promised Land: Immigrant experiences and Americanization

The radical social transformations of the United States that began in the late nineteenth century were not limited to the South and West. Between 1860 and 1910, the U.S. population nearly tripled from 31.4 million to 92 million, and the number of foreign-born residents grew steadily along with it as millions of immi-grants passed through Ward and Ellis Islands on their way to New York, Boston, Chicago, San Francisco, Los Angeles, and many points in between. Most immi-grants came from Europe, but hundreds of thousands also came from Asia, other parts of North America, and Latin America, as well as from Africa and various island nations in smaller numbers (U.S. Bureau of Census 32–26). Their reasons for coming were many. Booms in the U.S. manufacturing, mining, agriculture, and transportation industries led companies to advertise for workers internationally and millions answered the call, hoping to earn enough money to support families at home, help others emigrate, or return home in triumph (Bodnar 52ff.; Takaki *passim*). U.S. imperial expansion in Hawaii, the Philippines, and Central America contributed workers to these industries, as did the border shift following the Treaty of Guadalupe Hidalgo, which disrupted preexisting seasonal migration patterns that brought thousands of Mexicans north to work in Southwestern mines and agriculture (Deutsch 13ff.). Still others left their homelands to escape economic hardship or political or religious persecution.

As a result of these mass migrations, major American cities underwent rapid population shifts within the span of a generation, which spawned resentment and distrust and the rise of a nativist ideology proclaiming that only Anglo-Saxons could be true Americans.[9] The rise of the industries that supported these workers also led to the concentration of fabulous wealth in the hands of a few hundred men and growing concern over the exploitation of their laborers—an exploitation that disproportionately affected immigrant women (S. Smith 377). Over the last half of the century, the working poor and the question of Americanization emerged as subjects of national concern and, concomitantly, as characters and themes in American literature. Many writers during this time, including Emma Lazarus, Mary Antin, and Sui Sin Far, worked to draw attention to immigrant experiences and the complex process of acculturation during a time when the definition of Americanness was subject to continual reinterpretation.

Violent and deadly anti-Jewish pogroms in the Russian Empire in the 1880s and again from 1903 to 1906 caused international outrage and resulted in more than two million Jews fleeing Eastern Europe, many landing in the United States. Responding to the resulting anti-immigrant and anti-Jewish public sentiment, Jewish American writers worked to represent the varieties of Jewish experience in their texts, making powerful cases for Jewish belonging in the United States and reaffirming the mythology of the United States as a place of refuge for the oppressed. Perhaps no one did so in a more visible or enduring way than poet and Zionist advocate Emma Lazarus. Lazarus had a sterling American lineage: she was the descendant of Jewish settlers of New Amsterdam who fled Spain during the Inquisition and a member of the American literary elite, was tutored by Ralph Waldo Emerson as a young poet, and corresponded with William James and many others (Lichtenstein 257). The Russian pogroms awakened Lazarus to Jewish activism, and she wrote numerous poems and articles on Jewish history and culture to educate readers, bolster Jewish pride, and "counteract" anti-Semitism (Eiselein n. pag.) while reinforcing the link between Jewish and American destinies embraced in Puritan mythologies. In "1492" (1883), Lazarus optimistically apostrophizes 1492 as a "two-faced year" in which Jews were "Hounded from sea to sea" after their eviction from Spain even as a "virgin world" was opened to them in which "race or creed or rank" were no longer the cause of hatred among people (1, 5, 10,

13; Schor 193); in her best known poem, "The New Colossus" (1883)—lines from which are mounted inside the pedestal of the Statue of Liberty—Lazarus replaces the "conquering" masculine form of the Greek Colossus with a "mighty woman with a torch," the "Mother of Exiles" who calls for the world's "tired, your poor, / Your huddled masses yearning to breathe free" (2, 4, 10–11). Scholars link this universal "Mother of Exiles" to Jewish heroines Rachel and Deborah, a move which positions the United States as a Jewish motherland not unlike the Puritan New Israel.[10] This overlaying of Jewish imagery with foundational American mythologies implicates Jewish immigrants in both the promise and the fulfillment of American freedoms.

Mary Antin makes this relationship explicit in her bestselling autobiography, *The Promised Land* (1912), in which she chronicles her young life in Polotzk, Belarus, part of the heavily restricted Pale Settlement on the edge of the Russian Empire, her family's immigration to the United States in 1894 after years of poverty and the continual threat of violence, and her enthusiastic Americanization. This transition is emphasized in her opening and closing words. She begins her text, "I was born, I have lived, and I have been made over," announcing her total separation from her previous life (xi). Throughout the text, she claims the United States as her own, presents herself as the ideal American, and declares the promise of the nation to be her inheritance: "I am the youngest of America's children," the last lines of the book read, "and into my hands is given all her priceless heritage ... Mine is the whole majestic past, and mine is the shining future" (364). This is the birthright of a woman who has worked to efface her difference through education and linguistic training and what Wirth-Nesher describes as her "unqualified embrace of the melting pot ideology" and its potential to give its adherents a new life (461). And yet, traces of Antin's past linger in her body: one day she eats a strawberry and is transported to her childhood to relive her whole life in an instant, so that she is "suddenly made aware of all that I had been, all that I had become ... a daughter of Israel and a child of the universe" (92–3). Later she describes herself as "pass[ing] as an American among Americans" (197), indicating her sense, however suppressed, of her own outsider status, of some invisible barrier that remains in spite of her attempts to master American English and ways of life. This doubleness mirrors Du Bois' double-consciousness and reflects Antin's awareness that no matter how much she works to become the ideal American immigrant, she will always bear internal and external marks of difference.[11] Her work to transcend such differences and universalize the American experience to include a Belarusian Jewish immigrant suggests the power of American mythologies to inspire, but her enduring sense of difference reinforces the deceptive nature of such promises.

The writings of Sui Sin Far also point to both the fluidity and the fixedness of national and racial identity for immigrants in the United States. Sui Sin Far was the pseudonym of Edith Maud Eaton, one of fourteen children born to an English father and a Chinese mother, and she was a truly transnational figure; her family moved from England to New York and then to Montreal, where Sui Sin Far grew up, but she spent most of her adult life in the United States, primarily in Seattle and Boston.[12] She helped support her family by publishing stories and essays in various magazines, and thirty-seven of her stories were later collected in her only book, *Mrs. Spring Fragrance* (1912). During a time of virulent anti-Chinese sentiment that led to the 1882 Chinese Exclusion Act forbidding male Chinese immigrants from being joined by their wives and families, and to cultural stereotypes of Chinese people as benighted, immoral, and hopelessly pagan, Far's texts provide a counter-perspective that marries the sympathy of the deep insider (Ling "Edith Eaton" 292) with the sharpness of a "clearly political" voice that examines misogyny, anti-Chinese bigotry, and the pull of both Western and Chinese cultures (Ammons *Conflicting* 109). In the stories of *Mrs. Spring Fragrance*, Sui Sin Far calls out the arrogance of white philanthropist women and Chinese men while picking apart the idea of distinct national traditions of literature ("Mrs. Spring Fragrance"), skewers Orientalist stereotypes by having Mrs. Spring Fragrance write a book about "these mysterious, inscrutable, incomprehensible Americans!" ("The Inferior Woman," 33), criticizes white middle-class feminists as actively harmful in their blithe ethnocentrism ("The Story of One White Woman Who Married a Chinese"), and demonstrates the devastating effects of institutional anti-Chinese racism ("In the Land of the Free") and the fear of silencing and erasure for Chinese women in the process of Americanization ("The Wisdom of the New" and "The Americanizing of Pau Tsu").[13] Far insists on the right to speak for herself and to articulate a subjectivity that is neither purely Chinese nor purely American or Canadian, but nevertheless gives her the authority to comment on life in the United States from a decidedly non-dominant perspective. For Sui Sin Far, as for many writers examining immigrant experiences in the fin de siècle period, Americanness is something that must be simultaneously asserted and redefined against a frequently hostile background.

Realism, regionalism, and local color

The growth in the immigrant population was one of several dramatic changes that many other Americans found bewildering in the late nineteenth century. Economic instability, the upheaval of industrialization, ethnic and racial strife, and the rapidity of technological change all contributed to what critics have described as a widespread sense of loss deriving from the shattered myth of a stable and unified country in the aftermath of the Civil War (cf. Brodhead *Cultures* 121, 115–76). For some Americans, particularly the comfortable and largely white middle and upper classes, the rate and scale of change during the late nineteenth century produced significant anxiety about the disappearance of what in retrospect seemed a much simpler, more homogeneous, and peaceful United States. And the popularity of regionalist fiction during this period suggests that for many readers it offered some reassurance in the face of these proliferating instabilities.

Regionalism's champions saw it as a "literary symphony of cultural difference" that would introduce the nation to itself and its heritage (Foote 298). While many men, including Mark Twain, Ambrose Bierce, Bret Harte, and Hamlin

Garland, published the realistic depictions of local particularities and personalities that would come to be associated with regionalism in American magazines, it was a field largely dominated by women. Elements of regionalism can be found in the work of Sui Sin Far, Zitkala Ša, Mary Austin, Harriet Beecher Stowe, Mary Noailles Murfree, Kate Chopin, Rose Terry Cooke, Sarah Orne Jewett, Mary E. Wilkins Freeman, and many others, covering nearly every corner of the country. New England regionalists such as Jewett and Freeman particularly took hold of the national imagination, working with powerful cultural mythologies about national origins; a characteristic review of Jewett's work from 1886 declares that it shows "the real motive and temper of life among the latest (and possibly last) distinct representatives of the English Puritan colonization of New England ... the true descendants in character as well as in blood of the original colonists" ("Recent Fiction" 440). But such readings of regionalist texts privilege a particular view, one whose focus on the preserved remnants of bygone eras ignores the very modern work of regionalist literature. Rather than simply offering nostalgic portraits of idyllic rural communities, regionalist fiction's focus on specifically local kinds of knowing upsets existing hierarchies of knowledge and cultural value, "developing the subjectivity of regional persons" (Pryse 86), particularly rural women, while often marking the stultifying effects such isolation can have on rural dwellers. And while regionalist literature often demonstrates cultural continuities tied to long-standing traditions, it also reproduces in rich detail the hierarchies of class, gender, race, and ethnicity that allow such ways of life to be maintained. Texts by authors such as Jewett, Freeman, and Chopin thus both reinforce some existing values and challenge others, building connections between rural and urban, local and national, past, present, and ambiguous future.

Sarah Orne Jewett and Mary E. Wilkins Freeman were two of the most prolific and popular contributors in a group of New England regionalists that included Stowe, Cooke, Celia Thaxter, and Alice Cary. In her fiction, Jewett repeatedly presents strong, self-sufficient women in communities whose idyllic appearances often mask the strict constructions of belonging and exclusion that inhere among their members. Jewett portrays a coastal Maine both remote and continually touched by urban life in stories that honor older traditions while critiquing the ways such traditions wear on and sometimes discipline their adherents. In spite of its bucolic appearance, Jewett's rural Maine is repeatedly intruded upon by industrial realities: its villages are marked by the absence of young men, who have been lost to war or the allure of life in the larger world, and urban outsiders are frequently found in their midst. Sometimes Jewett offers a sharp critique, as in "A White Heron" (1886), in which Sylvia, a child who was rescued from a "crowded manufacturing town" (3), must decide whether to protect the location of a white heron's nest— her own form of precious local knowledge—from the destructive, specifically masculine power of a visiting hunter whose idea of preservation is taxidermy. Jewett's best-known work, the 1896 "composite novel" *The Country of the Pointed Firs* (Dunn and Morris 36), and the follow-up story, "The Foreigner" (1900), present a more balanced picture. Dunnett's Landing is full of outsiders, starting with the visiting narrator, and independent, resourceful women, including the narrator's knowledgeable and voluble landlady, Almira Todd. Mrs. Todd is forever revealing the links of the community's vast kinship networks, and her family reunion is a paean to old New England stock where the narrator specifically invokes the Civil War and finds she "fancied that old feuds had been overlooked, and the old saying that blood was thicker than water had again proved itself true"—suggesting such small traditions offer at least a temporary sense of unity and belonging based on "common inheritance" (*Country* 179; see also 156, 163–4). Yet Mrs. Todd also works consciously and otherwise to police the boundaries of belonging, noting her own "particular animosities" even among her family (*Country* 171) and describing the community's shunning of a sailor's widow, a Frenchwoman by way of Jamaica whose crime was having "liked other ways better'n our'n" ("Foreigner" 243). Notably, Jewett does not endorse these exclusions, as Terry Heller reminds us (92); rather, she relates them, allowing her communities and characters to emerge as flawed for all their charm. Jewett's communities thus ultimately resist the idealization so many would read into them, insisting on their human frailty just as much as their exceptionalism.

Jewett's tales about rural Maine had a strong influence on Freeman, whose more than 250 stories often feature unusual heroines and plot and character twists that reveal the psychological effects of the strictly delimited gender roles found in New England towns as (to paraphrase Jewett's reviewer) the true legacy of their Puritan forebears. Freeman had a strict Congregationalist upbringing in Randolph, Massachusetts, a town with what biographer Perry Westbrook describes as a strict code of conformity and an "atmosphere of decay" that would make its way into Freeman's stories (17). While William Dean Howells published many of Freeman's stories in *The Atlantic*, he described them as triflingly sentimental and "peculiarly narrow" in spite of their being "true in the working out of character" (640)—but this depiction misses Freeman's point, which is to convey the validity, importance, and artistry found in even the smallest of lives. Her "The Revolt of 'Mother'" (1890) features Sarah Penn, a diligent and "masterly keeper of her box of a house" (555) who moves her entire household into the new barn when her husband breaks his decades-old promise to build a full-sized house; Betsey Dole in "A Poetess" (1890) writes soggy, cliché-ridden funerary poetry that nevertheless provides comfort to grief-stricken members of her community, and which comes to her as a spiritual experience during which "the room seemed all aslant with white wings" (200); she suffers great anguish when she hears that the minister, whose poems have been published in a magazine, derides her work as nothing "that could be called poetry" (202) but has her revenge in a deathbed request that the minister commemorate her life in a poem, forcing him into a new subject position in taking up Betsy's mantle as "sentimental village poet," a final act of resistance to the "translocal, patriarchal values" the minister embodies (Holly 96, 106). And in "A New England Nun" (1891), timid but resolute spinster Louisa raises her own independence and the delicate, feminine order of her home to the level of a sacred art, visible in her final refusal of an apparently advantageous and long-awaited marriage. Freeman's sympathetic presentation of these unorthodox heroines suggests that beneath a doily-covered, purple-prosed, or sparklingly clean surface there always lies the possibility of revolt.

Like Freeman, Kate Chopin frequently suggests hidden depths below misleading surfaces in her regionalist stories, which are set in New Orleans and rural Louisiana. Influenced by the work of Freeman as well as Guy de Maupassant, Flaubert, and Tolstoy, Chopin's stories deliberately exploit the market's appetite for regional writing in order to frankly explore female sexuality and refute racially and culturally monolithic ideals of American and Southern womanhood, even while sometimes reinforcing existing racial hierarchies. Kate McCullough identifies motherhood as one of Chopin's particular targets (209); in depicting the diversity of the Louisiana landscape in hundreds of stories, sketches, essays, and poems, as well as two novels, Chopin presents women of varying ages, races, backgrounds, and social classes wrestling with what it means to be a mother within specific sets of conditions. Grown and married foundling Desiree chooses (ambiguously) either flight or suicide when her child turns out to be of mixed-race descent, unaware that her wealthy planter husband carries the blood of a formerly enslaved mother, in "Desiree's Baby" (1893); in "La Belle Zoraïde" (1894), set during the antebellum period, enslaved, mixed-race Zoraïde finds refuge in insanity when her lover, Mézor, is sold South and their child is hidden from her by a well-meaning but cruelly self-absorbed mistress. Both Desiree and Zoraïde feel and express sexual and maternal desire, but Dagmar Pegues argues that by displacing such desires onto tragic mulatta figures who carry the dangerous potential to pass as white, Chopin reveals an "underlying racial anxiety" marked by "ambivalent feelings of fear and desire toward the racial Other" (1–2). Chopin continues this examination of motherhood in her controversial realist–naturalist novel *The Awakening* (1899), in which her main character struggles to reconcile the "mother-woman" Southern ideal with the physical reality and emotional demands of childbearing and childrearing, as well as the challenges of self-realization. During a time when white Southern women and families were portrayed as constantly threatened by black masculinity, the multiplicity of mothers in Chopin's fiction offer what McCullough describes as a "range of identities that make it impossible, ultimately, to essentialize maternity," which is revealed as a social construction based on race, region, and class (209)— and yet Chopin's reproduction of anxieties around miscegenation and passing suggest an apprehensiveness about what such a multiplicity of motherhoods might ultimately mean. Like many other women writing regionalist texts, Chopin uses the distinctive markers of regionalism to create equally distinctive and complex female characters who are both familiar and different enough to quietly challenge readers' underlying assumptions about American womanhood.

Naturalism and the question of New Womanhood

Although it bears many of the hallmarks of realism, regionalist literature was often implicitly contrasted with naturalist literature. Regionalist texts were frequently dismissed as "local color," especially when written by women, and were derided as amusing, insignificant, and, crucially, "apolitical" (T. Morgan 136), whereas American naturalist literature was a conscious literary movement read as masculine and political in its dealings with the relationships between individuals and the environmental forces in their lives in a supposedly objective way. For most of the twentieth century, scholars primarily considered naturalism in the work of its loudest advocates, including Emile Zola in the French tradition and Frank Norris, Theodore Dreiser, Stephen Crane, and Jack London in the American tradition, and within a fairly narrow set of texts. But as recent scholarship by Donna Campbell, Jennifer Fleissner, and others reveals, elements of naturalism are visible in texts across the turn-of-the-century literary landscape by both men and women, from the regionalist stories and novels of Freeman to the sociological essays of reformer Jane Addams and the novels of manners of Ellen Glasgow.[14] Far from being a male-dominated field, literary naturalism was a pervasive and vital element in the work of many of the most prominent American women in the fin de siècle decades.

Influenced by Darwin's theories of evolution and adaptation, Spencer's related social theories, the growing body of anthropological study by Franz Boas and his colleagues, and advances in medical and psychological knowledge, writers of naturalist texts portrayed individuals struggling—often futilely—to survive and find a measure of agency against the influences of biology and the environment amid the "vast and terrible drama" (Norris 3) of the powerful technological, social, political, and economic structures around them. In naturalism, human bodies are often read as animalistic or mechanical, but the consideration of women's naturalist texts alongside men's reveals that the pattern of naturalism is not one of marked determinism or inevitable tragedy but of the "ongoing, nonlinear, repetitive motion" and the "stuckness in place" of modern life (Fleissner 9), the unknowing or unintentional participation of individuals in the patterns created by industrial capitalism and the social structures it engenders. But naturalism's characters maintain their humanity and the possibility of moral complexity; Donald Pizer notes that what naturalism achieves is not complete dehumanization but instead the deflation of the concepts of love, morality, or heroism as ennobling or salvational (29).

For many women writers, the concepts of naturalism crystallized around the question of modern womanhood. One emerging model was the New Woman, empowered to autonomy through political action, education, work outside the home, and sexual independence. But while many women were discontented with their current roles and welcomed new freedoms such as better access to education and employment and looser divorce laws, they were also uneasy about how to transition to a new role, and whether such a transition was even possible. Many writers examined this subject in the fin de siècle years, including poet Sarah Morgan Bryan Piatt, whose "The Descent of the Angel" (1879) and other works reveal both the "folly" and "bliss" of domestic ideology in a world where "knowledge" offers as little redemption as "marriage and motherhood" (Bennett "Descent" 602). But this doubt about the possibilities of New Womanhood finds some of its clearest expressions in the hybrid realist–naturalist texts of the period. Such texts do not generally depict characters who explicitly identify as New Women, but they do dramatize the lives of women who pursue romantic, economic, or creative autonomy outside conventional social frameworks, and the consequences of their choices emphasize the "stuckness in place" and compulsion Fleissner identifies. The naturalism-inflected texts of Kate Chopin, Ellen Glasgow, Edith Wharton, and many others meld and reshape genre in order to make powerful cases for women's greater freedoms while looking frankly at the limitations of these freedoms to change women's lives in meaningful ways.

Chopin's *The Awakening* (1899) caused significant outcry at its publication from critics who thought its sensuality "trite and sordid" and its protagonist selfish and vulgar (Cather "Books" 153). The novel blends elements of regionalism, psychological realism, and naturalism in the story of Edna Pontellier. Edna is a wealthy New Orleans woman whose sense of her unfitness to meet the stifling expectations of wife- and motherhood leads her to shed conventions and obligations in pursuit of a vaguely realized idea of freedom that includes artistic endeavor, an adulterous affair, the embrace of sensual pleasures and, finally, an act that is frequently read as suicide. The structure of the novel mimics this shift in moving from "conventional techniques of realism" in the early chapters toward an "impressionistic rhythm of epiphany and mood" in the later sections (Showalter "Tradition" 43). While it is often seen as a literary oddity for its time and place because of its frank depiction of Edna's sexual desire, it is in some ways very much in step with its time, depicting Edna's quest for a New Woman-like autonomy within the confines of a social structure and biological reality that ultimately proves inescapable. There is a deep beauty in Edna's slow process of revolt and growing sense of her own power; she sets up a studio in her house and begins to paint, begins to read Emerson and other philosophers, and refuses to obey the social customs of her set. But there is also a dark, brooding edge to her new independence, a turning inward that many scholars read as narcissism, leading to Edna's rejection of her children and a series of self-deceptions that are the product of an "unrealistic and evasive inner life" (Glendening 70). She tries to produce meaning through her artwork and other creative acts, a means that is, as Maria Mikolchak points out, outside of the male-dependent paradigm of domestic life (44), but she also believes—wrongly, as she discovers—that her lover Robert will offer her something more fulfilling and less conventional than her loveless marriage. As John Glendening argues, in the figure of Edna, who is remarkably unsuited for the tasks her culture mandates for women based on a host of inherent and environmental factors, Chopin "refuses to avoid" the grimmer implications of Darwin's theories of evolution and adaptation, the question of what happens to those who find themselves ill-adapted to their world (70). Confronted by the "meaningless repetition of life" (Campbell "Women" 226) and the inescapable biological reality of perpetual childbirth for women, Edna apparently takes her own life; it is, in Deborah Gentry's formulation, the only act of "feminist self-definition" available to a woman trapped in a system over which she ultimately has little control, and the "visionary" quality of the final lines suggest Edna is "finally triumphant rather than defeated" (17, 44).

By contrast, the heroine of Ellen Glasgow's *The Descendant* (1897) is offered no such means of control. Glasgow most frequently receives scholarly attention for her depictions of Southern life and her later feminist novels, but *The Descendant* has a grimly naturalist bent, emphasizing the power of the physical forces of the universe over human lives and questioning whether individuals can assert any meaningful control.[15] Rachel Gavin is a promising young artist who chooses passion over marriage when she falls in love with Michael Akershem, the editor of a radical newspaper. She sacrifices her social standing by openly becoming Michael's lover, but she also sacrifices her career, wholly absorbed by a love that "supplants every concern," including her "masterwork" painting "Mary of Magdala" (Goodman 48). As William J. Scheick notes, Glasgow portrays Rachel's attraction to Michael as largely out of her control, the product of "aloof principles of physics" like magnetic "attraction and repulsion" (387). The end of the affair is equally a result of such internal and yet universal and impersonal conflicts: torn between his radical ideals and his middle-class yearnings, Michael leaves Rachel and ends up in jail for murder; at novel's end, torn between her artistic ambitions and her love for Michael, Rachel receives her ironic "reward" (Glasgow 276), the job of nursing Michael to a slow death from tuberculosis after his release. The narrator describes Rachel as the victim not of Michael but of nature, "a sacrifice to that force which draws the aberrant body to its orbit," while the man Michael kills is victim to "the velocity of the body in its recoil" (257); such fates are natural, the world restoring itself to equilibrium. For all of Rachel's liberation, she cannot escape or even understand the "warring elements in her own nature" (Goodman 49) that pull her back toward the culturally defined womanhood she tries to reject. Her efforts to be independent from the strictures of her culture are undone by her inexorable heart.

Without question, the most eminent woman writing in a naturalist vein was Edith Wharton, who stands alongside Henry James as one of the greatest American writers of the fin de siècle period and a master of psychological realism. Wharton herself was something of a New Woman, though it is doubtful she would have identified herself as such. She came from one of the most prominent families in New York society, but from childhood she held a literary and intellectual ambition that alienated many in her set and one would-be husband (McDowell 3); she did eventually marry, unhappily, but had a protracted affair before leaving her husband to settle permanently in Paris, finally (and scandalously) divorcing in 1913. Wharton's novels and stories frequently focus on women yearning for more than their social, cultural, and economic circumstances allow—most typically women who either travel in Wharton's own rarefied social circles or who aspire to do so—and they reveal her disaffection with upper-class life. Her critique of this social milieu is rooted in what she sees as its tragic frivolity, which has the power to destroy those who dare yearn for more, and its hypocrisy, revealed in the rigidity of the conventions and racially inflected class structures that are permeable not by art or ability but by money alone—a power that for women is obtainable only through men.[16] Thus, in Wharton's texts, the question of social mobility is always fundamentally one of gender.

Discussions of Wharton and naturalism most frequently address *The House of Mirth*, Wharton's wildly popular 1905 novel portraying the downward social mobility of beautiful but cash-poor socialite Lily Bart. Lily loves the sensual pleasures associated with wealth, but her dreams of a richer emotional life render her unable to make the loveless marriage that will allow her to obtain it. Desperate for money but determined not to sacrifice her principles, Lily discovers her upbringing has made her unsuited to even the most menial labor, and she eventually dies, financially, physically, and emotionally depleted, from an ambiguously unintentional overdose of sleeping medicine. Wharton's novel is a scathing indictment of what Thorstein Veblen identified in 1899 as the leisure class, whose hallmarks were the "non-productive consumption of time" (33) afforded by their extreme wealth and conspicuous consumption—both of which disproportionately affected the women whose largely decorative functions made them both prime consumers and objects to be consumed and displayed.[17] While such figures were objects of envy for most of the nation, as Ammons points out (*Edith* 25), in *The House of Mirth* Wharton draws back the elegant curtains on this world to reveal a structural moral bankruptcy that crushes those who are psychologically maladapted to meet its demands.

As Donna Campbell observes, most scholars tend to treat *The House of Mirth* as an aberration in Wharton's oeuvre ("Where" 152), but there are elements of naturalism in many of Wharton's texts, particularly when viewed through Fleissner's model of compulsion, repetition, and stuckness. The titular character of *Ethan Frome* (1911) is saddled with the care of not one but two querulous, demanding women after the wrecking of his plans to escape the misery of his small-town life and unhappy marriage through double-suicide with his sweetheart; and in *The Custom of the Country* (1913), the novel Wharton considered her masterpiece, relentless social climber and compulsive divorcer-remarrier Undine Spragg discovers to her dismay that "each of her marriages is no more than another mode of imprisonment" (Lewis 351). But perhaps the most naturalistic of Wharton's other published works is *Summer* (1917), a novella that takes on the supposedly romantic ideals of traditional small-town life found in some regionalist texts and emphasizes from the lower end of the economic spectrum the falsity of the American myth of social mobility. *Summer*'s protagonist Charity Royall was rescued as a child from the lawless, impoverished Mountain to be raised in tiny, genteel North Dormer by lawyer Royall, and as a teenager she dreams of escaping the crushing, perpetual sameness of small-town life for the wider world. She sees the fate of town pariah Julia Hawes, who has an illegal abortion in a nearby city and can never be spoken of again, as well as the numberless other "victim[s] of the perilous venture" that was "'going with a city fellow'" (40), but Charity still cannot help fantasizing a way out when she falls in love with visiting Boston architect Lucius Harney. But sexual awakening does not equate to liberation for Charity; it opens her eyes to love and passion only to finally confirm the narrow circumscription of her world when, abandoned by Harney and betrayed by her own body, pregnant Charity resigns herself to marriage to her guardian and to life in North Dormer forever.

Within the world of the novel Charity's fate appears inevitable, and even as she is caught up in her romance with Harney she receives constant reminders of its

imminence. The Mountain, linked with lawlessness, sex, and "monstrous" maternity (Campbell "Where" 166), looms always over the town, "cast[ing] its shadow"
and drawing storms to itself that "sweep back over the village in rain and darkness" (*Summer* 6); so too does the shadow of Julia loom over Charity's romance,
in conversation with Julia's sister Ally, in Charity's own recollections, and, most
dramatically, during her Fourth of July holiday with Harney, when Charity sees
the office of Julia's abortionist and then encounters mocking, vulgar Julia herself in
the company of a very drunk Royall. At this point Charity and Harney's relationship is still unconsummated, but these repeated presences affirm it will be, and to
Charity's harm. Her dreams of escape and love will be thwarted because her blood
will out, and the fact of her womanhood will keep her trapped in North Dormer
indefinitely. Harney can and does leave, free to marry the wealthy sweetheart
he has hidden from Charity, but Charity can only feel herself "slipping down a
smooth irresistible current" (179), a bird unable to lift even a "broken wing" to flee
(184). Social and spatial mobility and the larger myth of American success in which
they inhere are thus revealed as "distinctly male" properties (Pfeiffer 152) and the
promise of women's participation little more than a temporarily beguiling illusion.

Stephanie Smith describes these and other naturalist texts from the period as
extensions of the American captivity narrative tradition inaugurated by Mary
Rowlandson (371), an idea that dovetails neatly with Fleissner's "stuckness in
place." But while the existence of captivity narratives is predicated on the captive's
release and restoration to her community, the possibility of redemption for fin
de siècle women writers seemed far less certain. Their texts function, as Fleissner
notes, in a kind of "temporal *suspension*" that accepts the illegibility of the historical
moment and "defer[s]" its meanings to be "decided by an unknown future" (10).
This future was perhaps closer than it seemed, particularly for women with the
advantages of wealth and whiteness, as Wharton's *The Age of Innocence* (1921) hints.
In the novel, divorcée Ellen Olenska sees the futility of trying to live among New
York's wealthy without embracing their conventions and—like Wharton—leaves
New York for Paris; meanwhile, her former lover Newland Archer remains and
calcifies, so that when he has the chance to see Ellen many years later he is too "old-
fashioned" to take it (Wharton *Age* 297). In thus "stag[ing] its own obsolescence"
(Evron 49) and that of the Old New York culture and institutions it portrays, *The
Age of Innocence* suggests that for Wharton at least—and for women with sufficient
economic advantages to leave the United States behind—the shadow of stuckness
might be lifting. But the future would unfold unevenly for women of color and
the white women of the lower classes, as later naturalist texts such as Ann Petry's
The Street (1940) would articulate, a clear reminder that modern womanhood was
by no means a universal category.

Career women: Reform-minded writers at the turn of the century

The late nineteenth century saw the dramatic expansion of women's social reform
activity alongside the emergence of the New Woman and the women's rights

movement. While women had been involved in public reform work for some time, their activity increased after the Civil War as women from varying racial, ethnic, and class backgrounds organized to work toward temperance, literacy, urban poverty, labor reform, world peace, and, most prominently, women's rights causes in networks that extended from the highly local to the transnational.[18] Some of these groups, such as the Women's Christian Temperance Union headed by Frances Willard, clung to earlier justifications for their civic activity related to republican motherhood or women as the guardians of the family's (and thus the nation's) moral center, but as the years passed and arguments for women's equality began to take greater hold, fewer women felt the need to justify their work.[19] However, many white women, including renowned suffrage leaders Elizabeth Cady Stanton and Susan B. Anthony, found themselves in what they increasingly saw as a competition with African Americans and other groups who were also pushing for voting rights and political power;[20] for every Jane Addams, whose work with immigrant cultures focused on the recognition of their humanity, there was a Charlotte Perkins Gilman, whose equality-based socialist visions of the future had foundations in the eugenics and Nativist white supremacy movements then taking hold. It is no coincidence that the word *feminist* was coined in 1912 (Stansell 43). By that time, many women had come to see themselves as deserving of political, legal, economic, and social autonomy, and they were taking concrete steps to achieve it—but it is also no coincidence that such movements often privileged white women at the expense of non-white women.

Though not every reformer embraced women's rights, women's reform activity was fundamentally linked with questions of independence and gender equality, particularly for women who chose reform as a career. With better access to higher education, women were working in a wider variety of professions, including medicine, the sciences, law, journalism, higher education, and, of course, social reform; this economic autonomy was entirely linked to women's greater personal autonomy—the freedom to choose a career outside of marriage, and the freedom to choose not to marry at all. Where fifty years earlier Margaret Fuller's romantic and professional choices had been unthinkable for most women, by the turn of the century many more were openly rejecting marriage as their only available career option. While some reform-minded women did marry, including Rebecca Harding Davis, Ida Wells-Barnett, and Gilman, they often did so on their own terms and fought to continue their work after marrying. But many never married; for instance, Jane Addams lived in at least one long-term Boston marriage, and Ida Tarbell determined as a girl that she would never marry on principle. In choosing to prioritize careers dedicated to writing and speaking in the service of reform, these women fought for the rights of the silenced and marginalized in ways that sometimes contributed to the oppression of others but also affirmed the value of women's participation in civic and public life.

Rebecca Harding Davis was an early practitioner of realism with a naturalist bent whose most well-known writing depicts the psychological interiority and the stark realities of life for immigrant women, African Americans, and others living in the underbellies of American capitalism. Years before William Dean Howells and Emile Zola began publishing their realist fiction, she announced in an anonymous serial in the *Atlantic Monthly* that while her readers might want something uplifting, she desired them to "dig into this commonplace, this vulgar American life" to discover the "raw and awful significance that we do not see" (Davis *Margret* 6). Davis anonymously published *Life in the Iron-Mills* (1860) in the *Atlantic*, a grim exposé of the dehumanizing effects of industrial labor on Welsh mill workers in the figures of Hugh Wolfe, a furnace-tender whose backbreaking labor warps his artistic ambitions along with his body, and cotton mill worker Deborah, whose ill-conceived attempts to help Hugh realize his dreams end up costing Hugh his life. Davis' insistence on anonymous publication in the majority of her works reflects her desire to keep her characters in the foreground rather than their creator; as Arielle Zibrak argues, it is a refusal of a growing celebrity culture that tended to obscure the "beneficiaries of reform" in favor of more exploitative celebrity reformer-authors like Harriet Beecher Stowe, as well as an indictment of the economic, social and "representational systems" that conspired to "omit [industrial workers'] subjectivity" from public discourse (525, 547). Davis' epic novel *Waiting for the Verdict* (1868) depicts the complicated interdependence and twined fates of black and white Americans and portrays post-Civil War race relations as a crucial trial whose outcome is yet unknown; many of her other stories, essays, and novels focus on the lives of women and advocate for the broadening of cultural definitions of femininity (Harris "Redefining" 120–1). While Davis also wrote many less political stories and essays to support herself, her work always challenges readers to consider the lives of those outside their own circles and see the humanity of the people they might prefer to ignore.

Davis' career was primarily literary, but for Addams the literary component was joined with her settlement work and sociological research, in which she likewise labored for broader recognition of the shared humanity, beauty, and strength of immigrant communities as a means of reforming urban communities and thus the larger world. Addams' dreams of a medical career were thwarted first by her father, who wanted her to stay close to home for college, and then by her ill health, which required surgery, but she was still determined to use her life to alleviate suffering and do good. Influenced by visits to London's Toynbee House, in 1889 Addams and Ellen Gates Starr founded what became the most famous settlement house in the United States, Hull-House in Chicago, to provide education, childcare, arts training, and other social services to the immigrants in the surrounding neighborhood, as well as to build community relationships that would help ease the often shocking transition from rural to urban life.

Addams published numerous articles and books on her work and research at Hull-House, women's rights, social reforms, and pacifism. In her first memoir, *Twenty Years at Hull-House* (1910), Addams emphasizes her commitment to affirming the dignity of each person, no matter their age, gender, or place of birth; she describes hosting "Old Settlers' Parties," at which early Anglo-American settlers of Chicago could mingle with newer immigrants and bond through the relation of "early hardships" (87), as well as the celebration of various immigrant cultures in the Hull-House Labor Museum, which offered the increasingly Americanized children of immigrant parents the chance to see the value of Old World handcrafts and ways of life (137–40). In working to build relationships between immigrant groups, social classes, and generations, Addams helped provide a middle ground on which old and new Americans could meet to grapple with the everyday effects of a rapidly changing United States. But Addams was also a leader in domestic and international peace movements, and she would eventually become the first American woman to win the Nobel Prize. She opposed U.S. imperial action in the Philippines, World War I, and the use of poison gases in warfare; among her many texts on peace, her 1907 book *Newer Ideals of Peace* argued that peace was not just the absence of war but could only develop from social justice practices that joined concepts of broad democratic engagement among classes with an ethos of "social sympathy" (9). For Addams, local reforms and social cooperation were essential to effecting broader change.

The work of Ida Wells-Barnett was similarly local, national, and transnational in scope. Wells-Barnett was born under slavery in Holly Springs, Mississippi, and she had both white and Native American heritage on her mother's side. She attended a local Freedman's school and then Shaw University, but her education was cut short when her parents and brother died in 1878 during a yellow fever epidemic and Wells-Barnett took up work as a teacher to support her five surviving siblings. Though her work eventually took her around the country and to Europe, Wells' path to journalism and activism began on the smallest local scale, and local organizing was always an important part of her work. She started writing a pseudonymous newspaper column after taking part in a lyceum with other black teachers in Memphis, and by 1889 she had quit teaching to write and edit full-time for the *Memphis Free Speech and Headlight*, of which she was a part-owner. It was in this paper that her first radical editorials appeared in 1892, calling on African Americans to leave Memphis and boycott the streetcar system after the lynching of three Memphis men went unpunished. Enraged white residents responded by destroying the offices of the *Free Speech* and issuing death threats that caused Wells-Barnett to flee to Chicago.

Thus began a lifelong multinational campaign for racial justice, primarily focused on lynch law. Wells-Barnett's anti-lynching work included the publication of numerous articles and a series of pamphlets: *Southern Horrors: Lynch Law in All Its Phases* (1892), *The Red Record: Tabulated Statistics and Alleged Causes of Lynching in the United States* (1895), and *Mob Rule in New Orleans* (1900). Wells-Barnett relies on a compelling combination of evidence in her anti-lynching exposés, including the reports printed in white-run newspapers alongside those of black-run newspapers, condemning both the lynch mobs and the law enforcement and legal establishment who refused to arrest or prosecute the mobs for their crimes; in doing so, Wells-Barnett models the kind of critical, independent, and context-savvy engagement with published information she wants her readers to practice (S. Davis 77). Wells-Barnett also statistically refutes myths about black crime and the rape of white women that were commonly cited as justifications for lynching, presenting it as a form of social control designed to keep African Americans from economic and political participation. Under continual death threats for her work during what Patricia Schechter describes as "an intense period of personal dislocation and political movement" (4), Wells-Barnett traveled to England and Scotland in 1893 and 1894 to advocate for her cause and instigated the formation of European anti-lynching groups that pressured the United States to act to ensure African American safety—but she also continued her work on a local and national scale. After marrying a fellow activist (and hyphenating her last name, a radical act for that time), Wells-Barnett continued her work, often taking her children along as she founded a black kindergarten and orchestra and fought to prevent school segregation in Chicago, worked with W.E.B. Du Bois to found the National Association for the Advancement of Colored People (NAACP), and established the first African American women's suffrage club in Chicago and perhaps the country, the Alpha Suffrage Club, for African American women denied membership in the National American Women Suffrage Association. Her emphasis on community building is part of what Schechter identifies as a "distinctive tradition" of local organizing and protest among African American women (2), and it demonstrates the ways in which local activism was always much more than local.

Charlotte Perkins Gilman and Ida Tarbell offer glimpses into some of the deeper complexities in women's reform movements as staunch reformers whose philosophies are difficult to reconcile with present-day values. Gilman was a pointedly feminist social philosopher, speaker, and activist who wrote in almost every genre, including poetry, short and long fiction, drama, essay, and book-length nonfiction. Her 1898 book, *Women and Economics,* criticized the economic foundations of marriage and women's exchange of unpaid domestic labor and "sex-function" for financial support from men as a system that harmed both women and men (44), blending Marx and Engels' economic theories with the "American utopian socialist tradition" calling for "the elimination of the family as an economic unit" (Zauderer 152). In this text and *Human Work* (1904), Gilman envisions an economic solution in which childcare and housekeeping are professionalized for all households so women can expend in productive work the "social energy" wasted in inefficient domestic labor or idleness (192). In Gilman's view, this shift toward balance and the focus on cooperation to meet collective needs helps create an ideal environment for a "larger humanism" (Black 42) to flourish. And in her utopian novel *Herland* (1915), her religious treatise *His Religion and Hers* (1923), and elsewhere, Gilman presents motherhood as the purest expression of femininity and "true humanity" as she calls for the radical revision of social and economic structures on principles of harmony, growth, and shared humanity rather than patriarchal violence and combat (Carter-Sanborn 3–4; see also Gilbert and Gubar "Fecundate" 202ff.).

But the subject of maternity was vexed for Gilman, in both her life and work. Her often anthologized story "The Yellow Wall-Paper" (1892), which documents its unnamed narrator's descent into madness after postpartum depression and treatment by S. Weir Mitchell's famed and infantilizing rest cure, was based on Gilman's own postpartum struggles; Gilman eventually sent her daughter to be raised by her ex-husband and his new wife, believing they were better able to care for her (C. Rich 85). The depiction of motherhood here and in other of Gilman's short fiction works as having the potential to "breed ... animality, irrationality, and self-absorption" runs counter to the depictions of motherhood in *Herland* and other texts as leading to "spirituality, rationality, and benevolence" (Gilbert and Gubar 208). Further, Alys Eve Weinbaum and Kristin Carter-Sanborn argue the emphasis on maternal reproduction throughout Gilman's work is specifically racialized. The homogeneous, asexual maternal reproduction envisioned in *Herland*, for example, takes on a much more pernicious cast when put into the context of Gilman's nativist and eugenicist writings and speeches, which describe Asian and Southern/Eastern European immigrants as "low-grade humanity" and the ideal "American blend" as a mixture of Anglo-Saxon and Scandinavian races that specifically excludes African Americans (Gilman "America" 290). In *Herland's* utopian establishment of order through singularly white, female self-reproduction, Carter-Sanborn notes, Gilman both enacts a patriarchal and imperial form of violence through exclusion and "reinscribes a discursive link between violence and agency" (28). During a period of increasing anti-immigrant hostility in the United States, Gilman's models of white maternity as the guarantor of the future of the human race point clearly to the ways that ideas of social progress could serve very unequal ends.

Like Wells-Barnett, Ida Tarbell was a muckraking journalist, and like Wells-Barnett and Davis, her most famous reform work began in her own backyard, in response to the corrupt and monopolistic practices of John D. Rockefeller's Standard Oil Company, which had come to dominate the oil industry in which her father had worked for decades. Tarbell's mother was interested in women's rights, and prominent women were frequently in her home, including Frances Willard and Mary Livermore (Stinson 229). These women were undoubtedly a powerful influence on Tarbell, who vowed as a young girl not to marry so she could devote herself to improving work (Tarbell *Day's Work* 36). But Tarbell's feminism was an uneasy one, and her life and work were marked by its contradictions. Many women were finding work as journalists in the Progressive period, but Tarbell was one of very few who were able to break into the male-dominated field of front-page-worthy serious news (Stinson 236). Her first hugely successful stories for *McClure's* were historical and biographical in nature, and she always considered herself a historian (Tarbell *Day's Work* 242), but her major success came with the publication of a nineteen-part exposé of the Standard Oil Company (1902–1904), which transformed *McClure's* into the "leading voice of protest among the popular magazines" (R. Frederick 3948) and has since been recognized as one of the most important journalistic contributions of the twentieth century (Barringer C1).[21] Tarbell would later write a series on protective tariffs for *The American Magazine*, a publication she founded along with several other muckraking journalists; her clear presentation of complex subject matter and her sharp analysis of the ways high tariffs disproportionately affected the working class contributed to her reputation for working to protect the general public from corporate greed.

While Tarbell's career trajectory and life choices would seem to place her squarely in the suffragist camp, her position was far more ambiguous. As Stinson points out, some of Tarbell's early articles hint at an anti-suffrage position, suggesting that not having the vote posed no significant obstacles to women's professional success (232ff.), and beginning in 1909 Tarbell published a series of anti-suffrage articles arguing that the career of homemaker was a woman's highest calling and the home her most important sphere of influence. Tarbell also disputed that women as a group would prove any more peaceable or less conservative than men when they did get the vote (Stinson 220–6). As biographer Kathleen Brady notes, these puzzling articles "stopped just short of saying [Tarbell] had misspent her own life" (201). They prompted hot reactions from equally puzzled suffragists, including Gilman, with whom Tarbell debated via published essay (Cane 123), and Helen Keller, who suggested Tarbell was getting old (Stinson 219). This ambiguity in Tarbell's record may indicate her unfulfilled and previously unexpressed personal longings, as Stinson and Brady seem to suggest, or the remnants of the influence of Willard and other activists who hewed more closely to the ideas of True Womanhood; however, it clearly reveals the difficulty Tarbell and many other women faced in sorting out the competing cultural values related to womanhood in the Progressive Era. Tarbell, Gilman, and the many leading women's rights activists whose racial politics implicated them in the disenfranchisement of non-white Americans are difficult to embrace wholeheartedly. Their lives were complicated, in some ways ahead of their time but still very much part of it. Their internal contradictions and prejudices can make them figures of discomfort for twenty-first century readers, but in acknowledging their complexities and resisting oversimplification of their views, we can better understand the nature of Progressive reform and its influence on the generations of activists who have followed these women.

The postbellum decades were the launching ground for the United States' entry into technological, industrial, philosophical, and political modernity. While the literature of these years works to make sense of the American past and its historical moment, it also articulates many of the major social and political issues that would define the coming century: the deeply entrenched culture of white supremacy against which marginalized communities would continue struggling to assert themselves; the push for gender equality and the rejection of the cultural prescription that women's primary social responsibilities were marriage and reproduction; the relationships between rich and poor, labor and capital; the extension of U.S. policies, military force, and cultural products and values around the globe; and, above and through all, the effects on individual lives of the technologies—transportation, communication, manufacturing, life-saving, and life-taking—whose development seemed to accelerate at an exponential pace. These subjects would preoccupy American women writers in new and unexpected ways as the United States moved into the twentieth century.

Notes

1 The term "Boston marriage" is thought to derive from Henry James' 1897 novel *The Bostonians*, which depicts just such a relationship, and which was derived in part from the Boston marriage of James' sister Alice. See Faderman *Surpassing* 190–203 for more on Boston marriages.

2 Social Darwinism and pseudosciences such as eugenics enjoyed wide acceptance in the late nineteenth and early twentieth centuries, and only died out in the United States when the rise of Nazism in the 1930s made such positions socially and politically untenable. Leading thinkers, including Stanford University president David Starr Jordan, utopian novelist Edward Bellamy, and Charlotte Perkins Gilman (see 113–14 in this volume) argued for the supremacy of Anglo Saxons based on their historical accomplishments, most notably their record of military conquest. See Boeckmann 16–37 for more on scientific racism in the late nineteenth century. In addition, as Valerie Rohy notes, nineteenth-century evolutionary theory was used to link "sexual backwardness" with African American "racial backwardness" in order to justify racist, heterosexist policies and practices (1–2).

3 Much of our thinking on these texts is indebted to Ernest's compelling argument about the strategies of reading and writing presented in post-Civil War life writing, which he makes in "Nineteenth-Century African American Women Writers" 282–90.

4 Ernest also discusses Elizabeth Keckley's *Behind the Scenes* (1868) and Kate Drumgoold's *A Slave Girl's Story* (1898); other notable examples of life writing include Octavia Victoria Rogers Albert's biographical *The House of Bondage; or Charlotte Brooks and Other Slaves* (1890), Annie L. Burton's *Memories of Childhood's Slavery Days* (1909), and Susie King Taylor's *Reminiscences of My Life in Camp* (1902).

5 "Black Brahmin" was a term frequently used by Du Bois and others to refer to the community of wealthy, property-holding, established African American families in Boston; it was a riff on the "Boston Brahmin" nickname applied to Boston's white upper class.

6 What scholars have christened the New Negro Woman was a response to the postbellum embrace of Victorian womanhood that Claudia Tate has termed the "true black woman" (*Domestic* 97); while the true black woman saw domestic and maternal devotion as a form of political service, the New Negro Woman saw marriage and family as incompatible with work for racial lift and sought independence, "self-determination[,] and social advancement" (Wilks 570).

7 Other notable Native writers from this period include Muscogee novelist S. Alice Callahan, whose novel *Wynema: A Child of the Forest* (1891) responds to the Wounded Knee Massacre, and Mohawk poet E. Pauline Johnson, whose work reflects her complex relationships with both Mohawk and Euroamerican poetic and cultural traditions. Johnson lived and published in both Canada and the United States and is claimed by both literary traditions.

8 See Luis-Brown 50–3, Johannessen 66ff., Raab 78, and Ruiz 118ff.

9 For more on the long history of nativism in the United States, see Peter Schrag's *Not Fit for Our Society*.

10 See Wolosky "American-Jewish" 114, Marom 250, and Wirth-Nesher 460.

11 Du Bois' concept of double-consciousness comes from *The Souls of Black Folk*, where he describes it as the individual African American's awareness of the distance between their own sense of self and the way they are perceived by white Americans (11). As Wirth-Nesher notes, many Jewish American writers in the twentieth century saw connections between the plight of Jews and African Americans (465). See also Michael Rogin's *Blackface, White Noise*.

12 Sui Sin Far's sister, Winnifred Eaton, also wrote stories and novels from a purportedly Japanese American perspective under the pen name Onoto Watanna; see Birchall's *Onoto Watanna* for more information.

13 Ammons explores many of these stories in detail in *Conflicting Stories* 109–118. See also S-L. Wong "Chinese" 44ff. and Annette White-Parks' *Sui Sin Far/Edith Maude Eaton: A Literary Biography*.

14 See Campbell "Where" 153–6; see also Fleissner's *Women, Compulsion, Modernity* and Jennifer Travis' "Accidents, Agency, and American Literary Naturalism."

15 For an example of these analyses of Glasgow's later work and its relationship to the South, see Ellen Caldwell's "Ellen Glasgow and the Southern Agrarians."

16 It should be noted that Wharton generally reproduced the racial hierarchies of her time, particularly in her depictions of Jewish characters, who are often portrayed as grasping, tacky, and alarmingly effective social climbers. See Kassanoff for analysis of the ways Wharton's fiction is "profoundly invested in the imbricated logic of race, class, and national identity" (61). See also Higham's "Ideological Anti-Semitism in the Gilded Age."

17 Veblen is responsible for the introduction of the phrase "conspicuous consumption" into critical parlance; his *The Theory of the Leisure Class: An Economic Study of Institutions* was one of the first critical examinations of the gendered excesses and power structures of the United States' most wealthy citizens.

18 For example, as McHenry documents in *Forgotten Readers*, local women's groups were instrumental forms of community support, education, and political activity for African American women in the nineteenth century. Many women from this period attended and spoke at international women's peace congresses; in addition, as Bernstein notes, reform speakers and literature were part of transatlantic reform networks that helped to build broader international consensus for both national reform movements such as abolition and international movements such as labor reform.

19 This kind of conservatism was, at least in Willard's case, linked with white supremacy. Willard ended up in a public dispute with Ida Wells-Barnett while they were traveling separately in England when members of the British reform community took Willard to task for simultaneously preaching democracy and ignoring the implicitly government-sanctioned murder of African Americans via lynching; Wells-Barnett publicly called Willard out, including for the exclusion of African American women from southern chapters of the WCTU, and Willard attempted (unsuccessfully) to suppress Wells' comments. While British reformers largely sided with Wells-Barnett, she was subject to increased vilification in the American press. See Simone W. Davis for more information.

20 Stanton, Anthony, Lucy Stone, and many other white suffrage activists had come to suffrage campaigns through abolition activity (see 71 in this book), and their initial efforts were toward universal suffrage, working alongside Frederick Douglass and other African American leaders, but disagreements over whether the vote should be extended to African American men before women and Stanton and Anthony's association with opponents of African American suffrage eventually led to acrimony and division in 1869. The issues have been documented in numerous books, including chapters 6 and 7 of Paula Giddings' *When and Where I Enter: The Impact of Black Women on Race and Sex in America* and Faye Dudden's *Fighting Chance: The Struggle Over Woman Suffrage and Black Suffrage in Reconstruction America*.

21 Tarbell's series was published in *McClure's* from November 1902 to October 1904 and was later collected in the two-volume book *The History of the Standard Oil Company* (1904). For a thorough exploration of this subject, see Steve Weinberg's *Taking on the Trust: The Epic Battle of Ida Tarbell and John D. Rockefeller*.

5

CLASHES WITH MODERNITY

Women writers between the world wars

The two world wars are often used to demarcate discussions of American literature from the first half of the twentieth century, and for good reason: they bookend a series of dramatic, overlapping, and often cataclysmic worldwide cultural, political, and economic events. World War I began in Belgium and France in 1914 with the pounding of heavy artillery and the roar of machine guns—advances in weaponry with the ability to kill thousands of men at great speed which provided shocking evidence that the Victorian belief in the "benignity of technology" (Fussell 24) was terribly and ironically false. World War II ended in 1945 with the detonation over Hiroshima and Nagasaki, Japan, of two atomic bombs whose joint destructive power was equivalent to 165,000 tons of TNT, in addition to the devastations of radiation sickness and environmental contamination. In the roughly three decades between these two points—often referred to as the interwar period—there were massive movements of people worldwide, including the 6 million African Americans who moved out of the Jim Crow South in the waves of what is known as the Great Migration and the millions of Europeans who fled first the Armenian Genocide at the hands of the Ottoman Empire in 1915 and then the forced ghettoization and relocation of millions of Jews and other targeted populations to labor and death camps under Hitler's Third Reich. These decades also saw significant economic change, including the rise of communism in Russia following the overthrow of the czarist government in 1917 and the booming 1920s in the United States and Europe, which were followed hard by the stock market crash of 1929 and the Great Depression. In Europe, fascist leaders rose to power with promises to restore national pride and prosperity through authoritarian, militarized rule; in the United States, homelessness was rampant, unemployment reached 25 percent, and the nation hovered on the verge of revolution. It was not until the growth of wartime economies that meaningful recovery would take place. There were widespread cultural shifts, too, resulting from the mass production of the automobile and the birth of the airplane, the adoption of communication technologies like the telephone and radio, and the rise of two American art forms that would have profound cultural ramifications across twentieth-century American literature and around the world: the jazz music that came from the brothels, dance halls, and parade routes of New Orleans, and the motion pictures of Hollywood.

The enormous scale of change in these decades was a factor in both the modernist movement and the Harlem Renaissance, two major literary developments of the twentieth century in which American women writers played key roles. Narrowly speaking, modernism was an artistic movement among writers, artists, and musicians who found Victorian traditions insufficient to address the fragmented, incoherent realities of modern life, but who also viewed the rapidity of technological and social change and the rise of mass culture with no small horror. Consciously modernist women writers such as H.D. and Gertrude Stein created inaccessible, richly allusive, and formally experimental texts that drew upon an international range of mythologies and learned traditions and insisted on the unstable and highly subjective natures of truth, meaning, and experience. Some writers founded so-called "little magazines" like Harriet Monroe's influential *Poetry* specifically to publish these texts, rejecting the values of the larger publishing industry. The work of these artists, along with that of women such as Amy Lowell, Marianne Moore, and Djuna Barnes, is often referred to as *high modernism*, while the term *modernism* is also more broadly understood to refer to the work of writers like Willa Cather who wrote during the interwar period and whose texts responded formally and thematically to the shifting conditions of modern life. But this broader view of modernism also encompasses the experimental fiction, poetry, and drama of Greenwich Village writers like Susan Glaspell and Edna St. Vincent Millay; the acerbic, cosmopolitan literature of the Jazz Age and its discontents by writers such as Anita Loos and Dorothy Parker; the middlebrow "prestige" novels by Edna Ferber, Fannie Hurst, and others that thrilled members of the newly established Book-of-the-Month Club, filled the pages of popular magazines, and became Hollywood films; the politically tinged fiction, poetry, and drama of the 1930s and early 1940s by writers such as Katherine Anne Porter, Carson McCullers, Margaret Mitchell, Meridel Le Sueur, and Tillie Olsen; and the burgeoning literatures from Chinese American and Japanese American writers such as Jade Snow Wong, Helena Kuo, Chiye Mori, Toyo Suyemoto, and Mary Oyama. All of these texts incorporate elements of modernism without necessarily embracing high modernists' aims or attitudes.

While the Harlem Renaissance, the second influential movement of the interwar period, had few explicit ties to the modernist movement itself, it was no less influenced by the shifts of modern life. During the First Great Migration, which lasted from about 1910 to 1930, an estimated 1.5 million African Americans left the rural South for better working and living conditions in northern urban centers including New York, Chicago, and Boston.[1] In New York, Harlem became known as the primary center of activity for literature, photography, music, and art by black artists from the United States, Europe, and the Caribbean, affirming the value and importance of black experiences and cultures. Published in the growing numbers of African American-founded magazines, women writers including Jessie Redmon Fauset, Nella Larsen, and Zora Neale Hurston explored the richness and the challenges of black life in southern rural communities and northern and midwestern cosmopolitan cities, underscored by the cadences of African American vernacular speech and the rhythms of jazz and the blues.

The literary movements of the interwar period were part of larger debates that had political, economic, and artistic implications. One of the most prominent debates centered on the United States' relationship with the rest of the world. It was a difficult issue to resolve in 1914, as American politicians and intellectuals questioned whether the United States had any business interfering in the power struggles of European empires. American artists who had lived and worked in Europe—including Henry James, Edith Wharton, E.E. Cummings, Gertrude Stein, and Ernest Hemingway—pushed for American intervention in World War I and volunteered to serve Allied war efforts, but isolationism was such a powerful force among the American electorate that Woodrow Wilson defeated the pro-war Republican candidate easily in his 1916 reelection campaign under the slogan "He kept us out of war." The United States did declare war on Germany late in 1917, after German submarine attacks on U.S. ships became impossible to ignore, but the end of the war in 1918 brought retrenchment. An isolationist atmosphere tinged with xenophobia persisted for decades, marked by the violent, frequently immigrant-targeted Palmer Raids of the first Red Scare (1920–1921); the success of the Russian Revolution in 1917 and fears of the rise of communism; the politically charged arrest, trial, and execution of Italian American anarchists Nicola Sacco and Bartolomeo Vanzetti (1920–1927); and exclusionary immigration policies that placed quotas on or excluded non-white immigrants with the goal of "keeping American stock up to the highest standard" (*Congressional Record* 3 Apr. 1924 5467).

These abuses of civil and human rights and the rise of fascism across Europe in the 1930s led American leftists to advocate for the protections of civil rights and freedoms worldwide. Many were drawn to the egalitarian ideals of communism and volunteered to help the Spanish Republican Army fight fascist dictator Francisco Franco during the Spanish Civil War (1936–1939), but these women and men were in the minority among those across the political spectrum who saw the rise of Hitler after World War I as evidence that American military intervention could do little to make the world "safe for democracy" as Woodrow Wilson had promised (*Congressional Record* 2 Apr. 1917 104). Concern over how German and Japanese aggression in Europe and Asia might threaten its interests drew the United States closer to intervention in the early years of World War II (1939–1945), but it took a direct attack on Pearl Harbor in 1941 to reach consensus that American involvement was necessary. After more than four years of combat, during which the United States emerged as a technological, economic, and political leader even as it affirmed its equation of Americanness with whiteness in the internment of more than 120,000 Japanese American citizens in camps across the western United States, the question seemed all but settled.[2] After the bombing of Hiroshima and

Nagasaki and the signing of Marshall Plan legislation, it was clear that isolationism was no longer possible. The United States had become a global superpower, and there was no going back.

From an artistic perspective, the issue of the relationship between the United States and the rest of the world had a bearing on another central preoccupation of the period: what was the proper relationship between art and politics? American literature had always been part of transnational literary traditions and movements, but now the relationship between American and world (particularly European) literatures came more sharply into focus, and texts of the interwar period were marked by a tension between artistic and frequently transnational political objectives. Self-consciously American modernist writers living in Europe aimed to create works both American and international that were situated within the context of classical and European traditions, even as the movement rejected the certainty and coherence those traditions implied.[3] In spite of the political implications of this ironically anti-modern stance, high modernists explicitly rejected political concerns as valid subjects for art. But artists of the Harlem Renaissance saw their work very differently. They looked to reclaim their African heritage and connect it to African American folk heritage in a way that did not accede to the fetishization of primitivism by some modernists or the prevalent stereotype of African Americans as simple and unsophisticated. In these goals, they linked themselves to other international artistic movements aimed at restoring the voices of oppressed cultures, including the nascent Négritude and Negrismo movements spreading throughout the French and Spanish colonial worlds, the Irish Renaissance, and the Czech National Revival (J. Johnson xix–xli; Locke 7). One of the primary debates between generations of Harlem Renaissance artists involved the conflict between the desire to use African American art to serve the larger goal of racial uplift and the artists' freedom to depict African American characters and their ways of life as they saw fit. For African American writers, the relationship between politics and art was a process of constant negotiation.

In the 1930s, as Americans watched the rise of fascism in Europe and the devastation of the Great Depression across the United States, many writers on the left came to see the role of literature as more consciously ideological, a reflection of the growing belief that art could and should draw attention to the political and economic implications of human suffering and call to account those responsible. For these writers, political concerns trumped aesthetic concerns; for those involved with the Communist Party, this was nothing short of a Party imperative, a restriction which chafed many writers and led to some defections. And for Asian American writers, politics intruded into artistic pursuits during World War II as military enmity and alliance and Japanese American internment made questions of national identity central and unexpectedly thrust Chinese Americans into the role of "the 'good' Asians" (Wong "Chinese" 46). As these examples suggest, the relationship between art and politics was one of the defining issues of twentieth-century American literatures.

American literature of the interwar period pulls in several different directions, but on the most basic level it can be read as a constellation of responses to a world that seemed to be rapidly and simultaneously shrinking and expanding. Travel and communication across long distances was easier than ever before, and millions of people around the world could share cultural experiences in movie theaters or gathered around radios and phonographs. But technological progress could also seem like regression as weapons advances made warfare ever more deadly and impersonal. These world conflicts became local and issues that had seemed local or even personal were suddenly situated against the background of their larger contexts. Writers who tended toward high modernism viewed this progression with fear, distrust, sorrow, and anger; but their literature also reflects an absorption of the restless energy of the age, a feeling perhaps best expressed in Ezra Pound's now-famous resolution to perennially "make it new" and T.S. Eliot's long poem *The Waste Land* (1922), which became a metaphor for the barrenness of life in the modern era.[4] But Harlem Renaissance writers found something of promise in the speed and mobility of modern life and the broadening world, even if that promise was always undercut by racism. Members of the sophisticated literary milieu of 1920s and 1930s New York were more ambivalent, participating in the heady consumerism of the Jazz Age but sometimes unable to reconcile their roles in the production of mass culture with their disdain for it. And the political writers of the 1930s and the Chinese American and Japanese American writers of the early 1940s saw in the contractions and expansions of the modern world evidence demanding a verdict on the failures and successes of the American democratic experiment.

The high modernists have had a powerful influence over the formation of the American literary canon and our received understanding of what constitutes valuable literature, particularly for the interwar period. The enshrinement of high modernist criteria, including the distrust of anything mass-produced or popular and the emphasis on aesthetic experiences based on remoteness, irony, and effortful meaning-making, has led to the neglect of some of the most successful and critically acclaimed work from this period, including a significant amount of work by women writers.[5] But as scholars have begun to demonstrate in the last several decades, many women writers were invested in and affected by the shifts of modern life, and by the range of aesthetic concerns and movements these shifts engendered. They sometimes embraced the new freedoms heralded by the ratification of the Nineteenth Amendment in 1920, efforts to decriminalize birth control, and increasing economic and professional opportunities. But as their texts reveal, women writers across literary movements, class boundaries, and ethnic and racial groups were also sharply aware that the word freedom meant different things for men and women; their varied responses to modernity evince their deep engagement with the American cultural landscape and its national and international implications during the decades of the United States' major transformation on the world stage.

Women and the high modernist movement

The literary movement known as modernism began in the first decade of the twentieth century and was carried on in some form into the 1940s and perhaps later.[6] Hugh Kenner describes it as a "supranational movement" (367) influenced ideologically by F.T. Marinetti's 1909 manifesto of Italian futurism, which decried the "unending and futile veneration for the past" (15), and aesthetically by the radically non-representational Cubist and the chaotic collage-montage style of Dadaist art movements that sprouted in Paris and New York and attracted painters, writers, and photographers from across Europe and the United States. But modernism also had a strongly nationalist component in the United States grounded in explorations of American identity and artistic potential, frequently through regions and landscapes (Morrisson 15). The literature most often discussed under the modernist rubric tends to be poetry, from the short "one image" poems (Pound "Vorticism" 467) of early Imagism to the densely allusive long poems of late-phase modernism, most prominently featuring Pound, Eliot, H.D., Amy Lowell, Wallace Stevens, and Marianne Moore—but the movement also encompasses prose texts such as Gertrude Stein's experiments in subjectivity, Djuna Barnes' fantastic and lushly realized plots and characterizations, and Willa Cather's spare, simple fiction.

Many of the characteristics for which high modernism is known—fragmentation and irony, for example—developed after and in response to the devastation of World War I and its flat rebuttal of the Victorians' claim of human progress toward enlightenment. But such responses only highlighted or accelerated literary and cultural shifts that had long been in motion. The formal experimentation that was one of modernism's hallmarks can be found across a spectrum of literatures whose authors either preceded or did not necessarily imagine themselves as part of a specific movement. For example, scholars have found examples of Imagist-like poetry in the fin de siècle work of Lizette Woodworth Reese (Walker "Nineteenth" 241), and Chapman notes "aesthetic innovations" in Progressive-Era suffrage literature, including "quotation, ventriloquism, [and] collaborative authorship," which anticipated similar moves in high modernist works (343).[7] High modernism was thus part of these larger shifts even as it sought to differentiate itself aesthetically and philosophically from the literatures outside its boundaries.

Due in large part to the polemical rhetoric of its most famous contributors, the modernist movement can sometimes seem monolithic, but its practitioners were anything but uniform in belief or practice. Modernist poetry has often been read as a wholesale rejection of late Victorian literary traditions, a position predicated on a narrative of poetic decline from Victorian giants such as Tennyson into a feminized, decadent, and ultimately vacant sentimental morass, propagated by Pound and others (Lyon 230). In this view, masculine modernism rescues poetry from its terrible fate, a position tending to consider nineteenth-century poetry primarily in the light of its inevitable progression toward modernism (Ehlers 41–2). But for all its willingness to discard the old, modernists had a powerful investment in what Heather Love calls the "nonmodern," which can be seen in their interest in primitivism, in the "widely circulating rhetorics of decline and decadence," in its modernity-induced "melancholia," and in the very "concern with tradition" it evinces at every turn (6). And in spite of its wariness about mechanization and the rise of mass culture, modernism had roots in the technophilic futurist movement;

what's more, some artists were exhilarated by the way modernity's reconfigurations of the world seemed to explode the restrictions of earlier traditions, creating space for new imaginative freedoms. Then too, many modernists were more savvy in marketing themselves to a buying public—and more willing to do so—than their professed distrust of the masses would suggest (Bradshaw "Outselling" 142). And in spite of its masculinist position, many of the most influential modernist writers and thinkers were women. These women experimented with depictions of both male and female subjectivity and the fragmented self, explored the diversity of human sexuality amid the violence of rapid technological change, and reshaped literary forms to better express and resist the relentless motion of the modern age, illuminating the complexities and the diversity of the modernist movement.

Though she is not widely known today, Harriet Monroe was one of the most influential figures in American modernism, and her work embodies the tension between earlier poetic traditions and modernist innovations. She began her career as a poet in late nineteenth-century Chicago, persuading the Committee of Ceremonies for the Chicago World's Fair to give poetry its due among the other represented arts by commissioning her poem, "The Columbian Ode," for the 1892 Dedication Day ceremonies (Ehlers 44). Monroe went on to found and edit the little magazine *Poetry, A Magazine of Verse* in 1912 to publish the experimental modern poetry mainstream magazines would not touch, and she continued to write and publish poetry throughout her life, anchoring a Chicago literary renaissance that included modernist giants Carl Sandburg, Edgar Lee Masters, and Sherwood Anderson. In spite of the somewhat radical mission of her magazine, Monroe was known for her cantankerousness and for taking what many saw as a restrictive view of modern poetry: she published every major poet of the modernist era and several influential essays but famously hesitated to print T.S. Eliot's "The Love Song of J. Alfred Prufrock," declined some of Pound's poetry, chopped up Wallace Stevens' "Sunday Morning," battled with Amy Lowell over publication dates, and sharply criticized the work of William Carlos Williams and Marianne Moore (Schulze 50; A. Johnson 28–9).

The breadth of Monroe's career demonstrates the complexity of her commitment to modernist ideas. In her essays she draws on the modernist narrative of poetic decline, but with a twist that emphasizes her in-betweenness, calling for a rejection of the binding "tradition of external form" in favor of "direct and spontaneous" acts of artistic creation: "better the free foot in the wilderness," she proclaims in a 1913 essay, "better the upward flight of danger in a monoplane!" (67–8). But what Monroe seeks for poetry is not a break with the genteel past but a "generational shift" that allows for the "rebirth of the past in the new" (Ehlers 55, 57). Robin G. Schulze argues that Monroe saw the modern American poet's task as finding a way to "retain [the] defining relationship with American nature" that had distinguished earlier American literature while "reimagining nature as a viable subject of modernity" (51). Monroe attempts this in technological poems such as "The Turbine" (1910), exploring the relationship between a machine operator and his engine as a quasi-erotic one in which mechanical mythologies replace natural ones and machinery becomes yet another quixotic force—like women and their frequent analogue, the natural world—to be tamed and controlled. She also played a large role in the first surge of the short-lived but influential Imagist poetry movement, which Pound described in his famous 1913 essay in *Poetry* as characterized by "direct treatment" of the poetic subject, strict economy of language, and an obedience to the "musical phrase" rather than to a particular meter ("Retrospect" 3). As a poet, essayist, and editor, Monroe paved the way for two of the most significant poets to emerge from the Imagist movement, Amy Lowell and Hilda Doolittle, who published as "H.D."

Lowell was both an American modernist icon and iconoclast. Descended from the powerful Lawrence and Lowell families of Massachusetts, she came to poetry late in life but became one of modernism's most ardent and public advocates, producing nine books of poetry and four of prose, editing five poetry anthologies, and touring widely as a speaker and reader between 1912 and 1925. After reading H.D.'s poems she declared herself for Imagism and became heavily involved in its promotion, leading to a series of clashes with its loudest and most prominent champion, Pound.[8] Lowell's wealth and independence allowed her to travel and lecture, and she became known for her outsized personality—including her scandalous public cigar smoking—and her theatrical readings of her own and other modernist poets' work, which served to familiarize the public with the new forms of poetry and to make Lowell the kind of celebrity who was hounded at railroad stations and required police escorts (Bradshaw "Outselling" 144).[9] Such a careful construction of herself as a savvy businesswoman alienated Lowell from many of her fellow modernists, who preferred to see their art as serving cultural elites and themselves as above the commercial fray, but Lowell was convinced she could create appealing and accessible poetry without sacrificing her artistic ideals.

Lowell embraced Imagism as a form of poetry that was "hard and clear, never blurred nor indefinite" ("H.D." 240), but she also committed to continual experimentation in form and content; in later years, she developed what she called "polyphonic prose," a combination of free and formal narrative verse, and she was influenced by Chinese and Japanese poetry and visual art.[10] She also became known for her highly sensual imagery, particularly in her love lyrics, which shocked readers and have since been recognized by critics as explorations of lesbian eroticism and Lowell's most enduring poetic achievements. Dedicated to Ada Dwyer Russell, the retired actress with whom Lowell lived from 1914 until her death in 1925, innocuously titled poems such as "The Weather-Cock Points South" (1919), "The Taxi" (1914), and "Madonna of the Evening Flowers" (1919) and the forty-three poem "Two Speak Together" sequence in *Pictures of the Floating World* (1919) express Lowell's love, longing, and desire for Russell in what Lillian Faderman calls "some of the most remarkable, barely encoded, lesbian poems since Sappho" ("Which" 63). Lowell was committed to artistic and personal freedom and willing to compromise only so much as was necessary to "get over" in spite of the "prejudice and blindness" of many readers, which she saw as the best revenge (qtd. in Damon 483). It was an effective strategy, allowing some readers to read her love lyrics as "literary exercises" while making herself plain to "those who might welcome the revelation" (Faderman "Which" 65, 64). It was yet another way that Lowell challenged public expectations of how she ought to behave as an intellectual, a female poet, and an American heiress.

While Lowell cultivated her reputation as an Imagist, H.D. had become known as one of Imagism's primary practitioners almost against her will. She met Pound at 15 and developed a close friendship with him that outlasted their initial romantic relationship; it was Pound who edited the three poems signed "H.D., Imagiste" that appeared in Monroe's 1913 issue of *Poetry* and profoundly affected the direction of Lowell and other poets. As an adult, H.D. retained her American citizenship but divided her time between London, Switzerland, Greece, and Vienna. Her turbulent personal life was marked by the death of her brother in World War I combat, a painful divorce, and the dramatic end of friendships with Pound and D.H. Lawrence, but her lifelong and sometimes romantic relationship with Winifred Ellerman (who styled herself as Bryher) was a stabilizing force in later years, when H.D. produced her most significant work.

H.D. is most frequently remembered for the arresting images found in her early poems such as "Epigram" and "Hermes of the Way" (1913), but in her later career she turned toward long works that reflected her interest in mysticism, Hellenic studies, Egyptology, psychoanalysis, and astrology, most famously the three-part World War II series later published as *Trilogy* (1944–1946) and her heavily allusive and symbolic *Helen in Egypt* (1961). Unlike male modernists, H.D.'s project is one of consciously feminist deconstruction and revision of these mythologies. Instead of taking up the woman as "object of the artist's quest," as a long train of male poets have done, H.D. endows Helen with subjectivity and her own quest for "vision and selfhood," working to generate a "women's mythology" by setting Helen's quest against the "same cultural backdrop" and responding to the same "general crisis of the fragmented and drifting twentieth century" as male poets (Friedman 164–5). Her poetry deploys these allusions in order to present women not just as objects but as originators of mythologies and of their own selfhood against a male-dominated tradition that had very personal resonances in H.D.'s own life.

H.D. was instrumental in the careers of others poets, most notably Marianne Moore, whose first volume of poetry was published in 1921 by H.D. and Bryher without Moore's knowledge. Moore had met H.D. and Pound in her Bryn Mawr years, and when she and her mother moved to New York in 1916 she moved in rarefied poetic circles, eventually working as an editor and critic for the modernist magazine *The Dial* while working on her own poetry.[11] Moore had strong connections to the Imagist movement, but her poetry was difficult to categorize as anything but her own. Like the Imagists, Moore was able to distill meaning in a single image frequently drawn from the natural world so that readers might, in the words of William Carlos Williams, "[feel] the swirl of great events" while "looking at some apparently small object" (294). Like that of many other high modernists, Moore's poetry was erudite, full of quotations, footnotes, and references to history, science, and the arts, but with more "livel[iness]" and "winsome finesse" than the work of Pound or Eliot (Richart 338); but most of all Moore's poetry was characterized by precise, deceptively simple language layered over complexly textured rhyme and meter that revealed both the observed moment and something of the observer herself.

Like H.D., Moore's career lasted beyond modernism's peak period, but its arc reveals her commitment to the continual aesthetic and philosophical reinvention that characterized the best modernist literature—not least because she continually revisited and reworked her older poetry throughout her life. Her earliest poetry was characterized by the kind of personal "rectitude" of opinion (Harter 335) revealed in "Critics and Connoisseurs" (1916), in which she compares the beauty of "unconscious / fastidiousness" (1–2) to mindless poetic striving and pronounces her judgment: "I have seen this swan and / I have seen you; I have seen ambition without / understanding in a variety of forms" (21–3). But in the 1930s, as Odile Harter notes, confronted by the Great Depression and worsening political conditions in Europe, Moore was more aesthetically subdued, shifting away from certainty, "aesthetic rigor," and the didactic *I* and toward a "gentler" and "more communal" *we* in poems such as "Silence" and "The Frigate Pelican" (334–6, 338–9). In her later poems Moore moved farther still, toward greater accessibility and a "deeply ethical" humor based not on "ridicule" but on "fellow-feeling" and a shared "world of sympathy" that seemed increasingly important in light of World War II (Trousdale 121, 124). Moore's gentle responsiveness suggests the ways that in spite of its dictates modernist poetry was able to adapt in a constantly shifting world.

The formal and thematic experimentation of the Imagists and other modernist poets looks downright conventional next to the work of Gertrude Stein, who was at the nexus of several artistic movements. After stints at Radcliffe and Johns Hopkins University's medical school in Baltimore, Stein and her brother Leo moved to Paris in 1903, where they supported rising young artists such as Picasso, Matisse, and Braques by purchasing and privately exhibiting their paintings. They also hosted an artistic and literary salon in their Paris home, and Stein mentored many younger American writers in the expatriate set in the 1920s and 1930s, including Hemingway, Fitzgerald, and Sherwood Anderson. The visual art of the Cubists, which attempted to depict the planes and shapes the eye perceived rather than the translation of those shapes into a form dictated by cultural conventions, was highly influential in Stein's prose and poetry. Her work was also shaped by the theories of consciousness of American foundational psychologist William James, under whom Stein studied at Radcliffe, and her professional and romantic relationship with Alice B. Toklas, who was the subject of many of Stein's love poems, and with whom Stein would live and work for nearly forty years.

Much of Stein's writing was so controversially avant-garde that it was either delayed or unpublished during her lifetime, but based on what has been uncovered since her death, her work follows three roughly chronological phases. Stein's early prose reveals her interest in the highly subjective nature of consciousness. *Three Lives* (1909) explores the "baffled, unexamined states of desire" (S. Smith 378) in the interior lives of three working-class women in Baltimore, and *The Making of*

Americans (written from 1906 to 1911 but not published until 1925) traces the story of one family in a kind of perpetual present tense intended to represent the nature of consciousness: "There is repeating then always in every one," Stein declares, "that makes a history of each one always coming out of them. ... but such repeating always has in it a little changing" (191). Stein carried these experiments to their edge in her second phase, during which she worked to apply Cubist principles of perception to words, most notably in her 1914 collection *Tender Buttons*. In these prose-poems, Stein plays with words as sensual objects, focusing on the intersections of consciousness and "the process of experiencing each moment" (Dubnick 29); Sherwood Anderson described it as Stein "laying word against word, relating sound to sound, feeling for the taste, the smell, the rhythm" of each word ("Four American" 171) as she built sentences rather than obeying syntactical rules. But this playfulness obscures "highly condensed layers of public and private meaning" (Blackmer 684), part of Stein's lifelong practice of writing lesbian love poetry so deeply encoded as to be nearly indecipherable and hiding her culturally proscribed desires in plain sight. By the late 1920s Stein had become something of a literary celebrity, leading to the third phase of her career, during which she toured as a speaker, wrote an opera libretto, published several autobiographical texts, including her only commercially successful book, *The Autobiography of Alice B. Toklas* (1933)—Stein's memoir, written from Toklas' perspective—and embraced her role as an international public figure. While her work has always been controversial, Stein's playfulness and emphasis on even the most ordinary words as objects that could produce pleasure apart from historical or syntactical meaning profoundly influenced many writers who would follow her.[12]

Djuna Barnes is also preoccupied with questions of meaning, but where Stein plays with the representational and aesthetic qualities of words, Barnes pushes against the idea of literature as an inherently meaning-making art. Barnes was raised in a small village in New York by a highly unconventional father and grandmother who both advocated polygamy and free love, and sexual freedom was a persistent theme in her work.[13] She began her career as a reporter and illustrator, and her impressionistic interviews with figures like Coco Chanel and James Joyce and her experience-driven, actively feminist features such as "How It Feels to Be Forcibly Fed" (1914) made her a popular writer. But Barnes also wrote experimental poetry and plays for the Greenwich Village-based Provincetown Players, and she published her most acclaimed work as a member of the high modernist lesbian community in 1920s and 1930s Paris. She was thus able to move between the mainstream publishing world, Greenwich Village bohemians, and the high modernist avant-garde, one of its most remarkable figures.

Barnes' drama, poetry, and prose are radical in subject matter and construction. Her 1915 collection of "rhythms and drawings," *The Book of Repulsive Women*, contains an explicit depiction of lesbian sex (in defiance of obscenity laws), and her 1936 novel *Nightwood* is one of the earliest mainstream novels in English to explore queer sexuality. Her work deliberately resists order, sometimes presenting multiple viewpoints and styles within a single text, as in her satirical autobiographical novel

Ryder (1928); in the darkly gothic *Nightwood*, the best known of her works, a central character repeatedly offers monologues that mix "scatological and theological rhetoric, vernacular and dynastic culture, ornate metaphors and performative denunciations," refuting the concept of stable identity (M. Davidson "Pregnant" 215). As Katherine A. Fama argues, this strategy both reveals and frustrates the writer's and reader's "compulsions to pursue" the authority and meaning of the narrative (41). What reviewer Alexander Woollcott said of one of her plays might be said of Barnes' entire oeuvre: it demonstrates the capability of a work of literature to be "absorbing and essentially dramatic" without offering a clear meaning so that readers can "sit with bated breath listening to a playlet of which darkly suggested clues leave the mystery unsolved" (XX2). In creating works with the power to move readers without yielding neatly packaged meanings, Barnes dramatizes the sense of incoherence and ambiguity that pervaded the modern age.

Though she never identified herself as a modernist, Willa Cather can be understood as a sort of anti-modern modernist in her articulation of a distinct philosophy of art that resonated with modernist ideals.[14] She was born in Virginia but moved with her family to Nebraska at age ten, and though she lived in New York for much of her adult life, the landscapes of the West reverberate in her work. She published poetry and stories and worked as a journalist alongside Ida Tarbell at *McClure's* for more than a decade, but her period of most significant literary achievement began in her forties, when she published the first of the eleven novels for which she is best known. She is, as Stephanie Smith notes, an in-between figure (381), personally and culturally dislocated as a lesbian with deep ambivalence about the meanings and performance of womanhood and positioned generationally and ideologically between Victorianism and modernism. Many of Cather's novels share a strong sense of place as integral to the formation of their characters, which links her to the fin de siècle regionalists, and she lived and worked in the modern age, but much of her writing looks back to the late nineteenth century or earlier. She often focuses on pioneering figures, from the women and men who farmed the Great Plains in her Prairie trilogy, *O Pioneers!* (1913), *The Song of the Lark* (1915), and *My Antonia* (1918) to the railroad barons who opened the West to white settlement in *A Lost Lady* (1923) and the priests who brought Catholicism to New Mexico in *Death Comes for the Archbishop* (1927), but such figures are complex and not always heroic. More than a simple preoccupation with former ways of life or a rejection of modernity, this pattern reveals Cather's concern about the process and repercussions of change for a land and its inhabitants, a subject with insistently modern echoes.

Cather is a maze of contradictions, which makes it difficult to label her a modernist. She was largely uninterested in literary movements, but her 1922 essay "The Novel Démeublé" espouses modernist views in its preference for prose stripped of the excesses of realism so that the atmosphere of the story is "felt upon the page without being specifically named there" and each work is an "unfurnished" room made up only of "one passion and four walls" (6). Many of Cather's essays and novels express unease with the speed and ugliness of modern life, and her characters often indulge in a nostalgic mythmaking about simpler times that is only ambivalently undercut, if at all, by the distancing irony of the narrative voice. One clear case is Thea Kronberg, protagonist of *The Song of the Lark*, who retreats from "the competitive arena of modern life" to experience a more authentic Native American way of life in the Southwest (Clere 25), which inspires her greatest artistic achievements.[15] Many critics read this as an act of cultural appropriation mirroring the land appropriation of Thea's (and Cather's) "pioneering forebears" (S. Smith 381), and Sarah Clere observes it is anti-modern escapism in action, a flight from modernity into an oversimplified and idealized past (25). But tellingly, this flight and subsequent connection with ancient spirituality ultimately enable Thea to return to the modern world and fulfill her artistic ambitions, making the novel an interrogation, however flawed, of how a modern artist might retain earlier values and still be successful.[16] More than those of more overt modernists, Cather's depictions make transparent the tension between the revolutionary and deeply conservative impulses at modernism's core, one of the movement's larger contradictions.

Cather likewise has one foot in and one foot out of feminist territory. She was notoriously hard on her fellow women writers, proclaiming in 1895 she would have "no faith in women in fiction" until a woman had written "a story of adventure, a stout sea tale, [or] a manly battle yarn" (*Kingdom of Art* 409). Cather identified with traditionally masculine traits for most of her life: as a young adult she cut off her hair, wore boys' clothes, and insisted on being called William (Lindemann 20–31); though she eventually assumed more traditionally feminine habits, she continued to exhibit a deep ambivalence about womanhood and women's artistic production that verged on misogyny, and she saw herself as participating in a literary tradition that was masculine rather than feminine (Jeane Harris 81, 83). Her early novels feature independent, resourceful heroines doing work culturally assigned to men (and often more sensibly and efficiently), but a number of scholars have argued that Cather's most appealing characters are women with masculine traits, such as Ántonia Shimerda in *My Ántonia*, who sprouts a "little moustache" of sweat when she works, proudly shows off her muscles, and declares, "I like to be like a man" (Cather *Ántonia* 133).[17] But if Cather's work is not precisely feminist, it can certainly be read as queer. Marilee Lindemann explores the roles of queer bodies in Cather's texts—bodies with "perverse desires," with "markers of racial or ethnic difference" that make them superior or inferior, or those that are "physically 'extraordinary'"—as figures of fear, attraction and, ultimately "sameness," bodies that may be "embrac[ed]" insofar as they self-police or are "useful and entertaining" like barefooted mystic Ivar in *Pioneers*, but must be rejected if they violate the "bodily and social order" essential in the process of making the "meaning of 'America'" (33–4, 77). As Daniel Worden argues, particularly in the figure of Ántonia, Cather unmoors "masculinity" from an "essentially gendered body" (279), casting it as "pure becoming, a process that will not be stabilized" and can therefore have no "normal" state (273); she thus blurs the concepts of "time, gender, property, and family" (280) that undergird conceptions of what proves to be, in the words of *My Ántonia*'s narrator, a finally "uncommunicable past" (360). In reexamining the ways bodies can be read in narratives of the physical and conceptual making of America, Cather queers mythologies of American progress and asks whether representations of the past or of personal or national selfhood can ever be trustworthy. It is a position less mocking than other modernists but one no less inflected by modernism's pervasive sense of instability.

The Harlem Renaissance

For African Americans in the 1920s, Central Harlem was a place like no other. It was a largely black-populated city-within-a-city that stretched along the west bank of the Harlem River in upper Manhattan, with an area and population that nearly tripled between 1920 and 1930 ("Harlem in the 1920s"). By 1930, Central Harlem was home to more than 200,000 African American and West Indian migrants who came in search of work, followed family and friends out of the Jim Crow South or, like Claude McKay, Zora Neale Hurston, and Gwendolyn Bennett, wanted to join the growing communities of artists, writers, musicians, and activists leading the way in what seemed a new era of black pride and achievement. Harlem boasted a thriving black middle class, and its many artists, publications, and organizations helped launch an efflorescence of black American art, photography, and literature between 1920 and 1940 in many major cities in the United States. The energy of this activity drew to Harlem artists from around the world who were part of the larger African diaspora that had resulted from centuries of slavery, and its leaders saw it as linked in purpose and theme to various pride-based artistic responses to colonialism around the world. The American movement was made possible by the groundwork in arts, letters, and social reform laid by the women and men of the Progressive Era; the concentration of African Americans in urban centers across the North and Midwest; the economic boom years of the 1920s; and the growing interest in African American cultural productions, including the jazz and blues music of Louis Armstrong, Duke Ellington, Bessie Smith, Gladys Bentley, and Ethel Waters, the folklores, traditions, and dialects of African American communities, and the debut of African American actors and productions on Broadway.

Though it was a relatively brief period, one of the Harlem Renaissance's enduring legacies is the rich literary outpouring from artists such as Langston Hughes, Countee Cullen, Nella Larsen, Zora Neale Hurston, and numerous others, made possible by the increase in black publications during the 1920s. While some fortunate or connected writers were published in mainstream glossies such as *Vanity Fair* and the *Atlantic*, they were the exception. Instead, new publication venues for and run by African Americans were integral to the movement's growth, including the NAACP's *Crisis,* under the leadership of W.E.B. Du Bois and literary editor Jessie Redmon Fauset, the Urban League's *The Opportunity*, *The Messenger*, and Marcus Garvey's *Negro World*, and existing African American newspapers of major cities such as the *Chicago Defender*, the *Pittsburgh Courier*, and the *New York Amsterdam News*. Just as important were anthologies of African American literature and art like

Alice Dunbar-Nelson's *The Dunbar Speaker and Entertainer* (1920), James Weldon Johnson's *The Book of American Negro Poetry* (1922), Alain Locke's *The New Negro* (1925), and Countee Cullen's *Caroling Dusk* (1927), which did much among black artists and communities to invoke the sense of a movement, outline its philosophical parameters, and communicate the personal, political, and artistic value in celebrating black cultures and exploring both African and American heritages with racial awareness and literary and artistic excellence.

But for all its optimism, the movement was not without ideological conflict. Many were uncomfortable with the reliance on white dollars that helped make Harlem prosperous, from the patronage of wealthy and interested sponsors such as Carl Van Vechten and Charlotte Osgood Mason, whose insistence on oversight rankled Hughes and Hurston, to the primarily white-owned businesses that lined Harlem's streets and the money of wealthy white "tourists" (Hughes *Big Sea* 226) who came to Harlem nightclubs and speakeasies to drink, dance, experience exoticized black entertainment, and experiment sexually in an environment that seemed more permissive than their normal social milieu.[18] There were also debates between older members like Du Bois, who argued for artists' political duty to represent black life as positive and morally sound, and younger writers who insisted on artistic freedom unfettered by political concerns. And while the movement included celebrations of high and low, urban and rural black cultures, it was frequently criticized for its relative isolation from the lives of most black Americans, who did not travel in urbane, racially integrated circles or even necessarily know an artistic movement was taking place (Hughes *Big Sea* 228).

These conflicts are visible in the texts of black women writers who combated both raced and gendered oppression, longing for political and personal freedoms as much as any man but expected to perform a "New Negro womanhood" (Sherrard-Johnson 415) that combined the restrictive values of middle-class womanhood with the project of racial uplift. The tug of war between the respectability of the New Negro Woman and the personal ambitions and desires that simultaneously made women vulnerable and threatened to disrupt larger political goals can be seen in the prose and poetry of Dunbar-Nelson, Angelina Weld Grimké, Gwendolyn Bennett, and Marita Bonner, and in the passing novels of Fauset and Nella Larsen; and the tensions around the question of whether middle-class urban life or rural folkways constituted a more authentic black culture manifested in the fiction of Fauset and Hurston. The contributions of these women to the Harlem Renaissance demonstrate the complex and complexly motivated nature of African American literature during this period and call attention to the ways in which for women, the idea of freedom could be both a call to arms and a deadly siren song.

Many consider the inauguration of the Harlem Renaissance to be the publication of Claude McKay's defiant poem "If We Must Die" (1919) or the long-running production of the musical revue *Shuffle Along* (1921), the first Broadway show written and performed by black artists, but like all literary and artistic movements its influences can be traced to earlier writers. For the Harlem Renaissance, these influencers included Alice Moore Dunbar-Nelson, a teacher, editor, and writer of history, journalism, drama, poetry, and short fiction whose work has thematic and stylistic links to regionalism and modernism. Dunbar-Nelson, who published the first collection of short stories by an African American woman (A. Davidson 51), was born to multiracial middle-class parents in Creole New Orleans, was married for a time to poet Paul Laurence Dunbar, earned a master's degree from Cornell University, and became an ardent advocate for racial reform, education, and women's rights.

Dunbar-Nelson was criticized by her contemporaries and later scholars for her seemingly bifurcated life; she maintained a proper "post-Victorian" public image but engaged in secret "affairs and flirtations with both men and women" and illicit gambling and drinking with her "'roughnecky'" friends, a duality mirrored in her careful delineation between the political activism of her journalism and her more conventional imaginative literature (Hull "Two-Faced" 32–3). But recent scholars have contributed to a significant critical reevaluation of Dunbar-Nelson's work. Pamela Glenn Menke notes Dunbar-Nelson's subtle examinations of the color line in her regionalist stories about Creole New Orleans, and Gloria T. Hull calls attention to her use of "class signifier as a cloaked signifier for race," concluding that the apparent contradictions of her life reflect Dunbar-Nelson's struggle to be her "total self" in a culture that defined "blackness, womanness, and black/woman writer" in confusing and contradictory ways ("Shaping" 31, 33). And Adenike Marie Davidson argues that *Violets and Other Tales* (1895), Dunbar-Nelson's collection of stories, essays, reviews, poetry, and sketches, represents her attempt to "blend literary forms" into "prose poems" and anticipates the formal experiments of Jean Toomer's much-lauded 1923 text *Cane* (52). *Violets* and Dunbar-Nelson's other texts, taken together with her criticism and her production of *The Dunbar Speaker and Entertainer* (1920), reflect her efforts to expand the forms and conceptions of African American literature and establish an African American literary heritage. Poised between Victorian and modern generations, she balanced fierce advocacy for the race with a careful positioning as a woman and author, fighting to make sense of the conflicting demands of her era.

The work of Dunbar-Nelson and others of this in-between generation of poets and writers paved the way for the women that followed, many of whom actively supported each other as artists. While they are lesser known than their male counterparts or than female novelists, these women wrote poetry, essays, plays, and stories during the Harlem Renaissance, and most were, like Dunbar-Nelson, Ivy League-educated and deeply invested in the development of African American literatures. Georgia Douglas Johnson was the most prolific; she published three volumes of poetry between 1918 and 1928 in addition to numerous short stories, plays, and newspapers columns, and she hosted a salon in Washington, D.C., that drew the brightest of Washington's African American artistic and intellectual community. Many of the women in her circle had their own literary careers, some remaining in Washington and others moving on to Harlem or Chicago. One of Johnson's close friends was poet and playwright Angelina Weld Grimké, great-niece of the famed abolitionist Grimké sisters and an important part of

Washington's thriving African American theatrical community. Grimké's success-ful play *Rachel* was produced in 1916 in Washington and restaged in New York in the 1920s; initially titled *Blessed Are the Barren* (Perry 338), it examines the ethical implications of women bearing and raising black children in a culture determined to destroy them.[19] Others in Johnson's group, including Marita Bonner, also inves-tigated what was expected from African American women in the name of race service. Bonner won awards for her stories, plays, and music, but she is best known for her essay "On Being Young—a Woman—and Colored." Initially published in the *Crisis* in 1925, it pointedly pushes back against the sacrifices demanded of women to repay the "debt you owe 'Your People'" (63), the narrow view that assumes authentic black womanhood is "a gross collection of desires, all uncon-trolled," any deviation from which equating to a longing for whiteness, and the insistence that black women swallow the anger and pain of racism to maintain the "softness that makes you a woman" (64–5). The poetry of Gwendolyn Bennett, another member of Johnson's circle, celebrates the images of black femininity that figure so prominently in Harlem Renaissance poetry. In "Heritage" (1923), Bennett imagines "lithe Negro girls, / Etched dark against the sky" (4–5) and a "chanting / Around a heathen fire" in Egypt (10–11), which she links to her "sad people's soul / Hidden by a minstrel-smile" (16–18); in "To a Dark Girl" (1927) she declares, "I love you for your blackness," and beseeches the girl to remember her "queenliness," even though she has been "born for sorrow's mate" (1, 11, 10). Bennett's poetry reflects the hope and the sorrow that so frequently joined in Harlem Renaissance literature.

Jessie Redmon Fauset also played a key role in the Harlem Renaissance and, like Dunbar-Nelson and so many others, her career involved a careful—and not always successful—balancing act between the cultural demands of womanhood, her political aims, and her artistic sensibilities. Fauset was Ivy League-educated and worked as a teacher for a time while writing on the side. She began publishing stories and poems in *Crisis* and other black publications in 1912, and she worked as the magazine's literary editor beginning in 1919; she was also the most prolific of the Harlem Renaissance novelists, publishing four novels between 1924 and 1933. Fauset has a somewhat undeserved reputation for "Victorian primness" as a critic (Tomlinson 236) and has frequently been dismissed as a writer of bourgeois (and thus less authentically black) sensibilities (Jones 5), but such portrayals are oversim-plifications of her writing and her role in the development of literary talent.

Fauset's fiction deals primarily with the African American middle class, using the lens of consumption to probe the appeal and the trap of class aspirations for African American women. *Plum Bun: A Novel Without a Moral* (1929) tells the story of Angela Murray, a promising artist whose experiences with racial discrimination make her long for the unfettered opportunities whiteness seems to afford. Leaving her family in Philadelphia to pass for white in New York, Angela travels along the edges of several artistic communities, and along the way she becomes, like many of Fauset's characters, simultaneously consumer, producer, and consumed object (Tomlinson 228), the owner of a "voluptuously reported" catalog of goods and clothes (Christian 46), the creator of desires through the fashion sketches that pay her salary, the crafter of her own carefully calibrated image, and the object of wealthy white Roger's unremitting desire for conquest. This might seem like a situation ripe for a tragic mulatta plotline, but as the book's title suggests, this is no tale of petty bourgeois morality guided by propriety. Angela may come to New York an ingénue, but she guards—and ultimately relinquishes—her sexual innocence out of her own sense of rightness and taste rather than some externally imposed rule, and when Roger abandons her she is not crippled by regret, nor are her life or prospects for happiness ruined. In the end, if Angela has returned to her black roots it is not in defeat but in service to that same sense of personal rightness, now tempered by her experiences among both white and black people as she has struggled to balance her individual desires with the larger needs of her community. In refusing to judge her characters for their aspirations or choices, Fauset depicts African American women as neither morally lax, as the stereotype goes, nor rigidly sanctimonious, but as individuals making a difficult set of choices under the weight of raced, classed, and gendered cultural expectations.[20]

The novels of Nella Larsen also examine the pressures of sexuality, gender, class, and race in the lives of African American women, claiming for black women the quintessentially American literary theme of the relationship between the individual and society. Larsen's mother was Danish and her father a West Indian man who either died or disappeared when Larsen was a toddler. When her mother remarried a white man, Larsen became the only dark-skinned child in a white family, and the probing questions of identity, blackness, and cultural expectations about womanhood found in her fiction stemmed from her personal experience.[21] Her writing career was brief but brilliant: after attending Fisk University, training as a nurse, and working at the Tuskegee Institute and the New York Public Library, she took a leave of absence and wrote two acclaimed novels in quick succession, *Quicksand* (1928) and *Passing* (1929), but she never produced anything else. While like many women writers she was critically neglected for many years, Larsen is now recognized as one of the most important novelists of the Harlem Renaissance.

Quicksand and *Passing* offer extended analyses of the dangerous implications of repressed sexuality resulting from the internalization of white and black cultural expectations. *Quicksand*'s protagonist, Helga Crane, is a mixed-race woman who fits in with neither her fellow teachers at a Southern black college, the middle-class race women in Chicago and Harlem, nor her white family in Denmark, where she is courted as an "exotic Other" (Sherrard-Johnson 412), a role which she recognizes prevents real acceptance or understanding. Returning to Harlem only to become trapped by her inability to express long-suppressed sexual desires within the rigid morality of her middle-class social world, Helga flees into the arms of a storefront preacher who marries her and takes her South, where a string of physically and psychologically debilitating pregnancies draws her toward "certain death" (Carby *Reconstructing* 169). Larsen thus pushes on both the white view of "authentic" black womanhood as hypersexualized and "available for public consumption" (Silverman 601) and the black corrective that demands demure and obedient "domestic self-sacrifice" (Monda 23), decisively de-eroticizing both. *Passing* considers more deeply the demands of New Negro Womanhood, examining how the return of a childhood friend who now passes for white disrupts the life and marriage of Irene Redfield, who is the picture of the self-sacrificing New Negro Woman as the wife of a doctor who serves his people, the mother of two boys, and a tireless philanthropist. Clare Kendry is the opposite: a black woman who has abdicated her blackness and her wifely and maternal responsibilities to secure a life of luxury and leisure but who now wants to "reclaim her birthright as a black woman" apart from her racist white husband (Sherrard-Johnson 412). Clare's unrepressed sexuality and the frissons of desire that run between Clare and Irene threaten the stability of Irene's impeccably constructed and rigidly sexless world, and the novel ends with Clare's death when Irene cannot stop—or perhaps helps along—Clare's fall from a sixth-floor window. The police ruling of "death by misadventure" (Larsen 275) points to Clare's multiple violations of "both black and white social codes of conduct" (Sherrard-Johnson 415), and suggests that the costs of internalizing these demands are dangerously high.

The end of Larsen's *Quicksand* depicts Helga Crane's rural world as one of kindly but superstitious ignorance, bound by a set of expectations for women that are different from but no less stifling than those of Harlem's middle class; it is a stinging critique of the view of African American folk cultures as somehow more authentic and thus more valid subjects of African American art. But if this stance diminished the work of writers like Fauset and Larsen, it elevated the work of Zora Neale Hurston, whose vivid depictions of rural culture and reputation as a born story-teller contributed to her image as the intellectual representative of "the people" (Carby *Reconstructing* 161). Hurston was born and raised in the all-black town of Eatonville, Florida, a community that plays an almost mythical role in her folklore collection *Mules and Men* (1935) and her acclaimed novel *Their Eyes Were Watching God* (1937). After traveling as a lady's maid to a white actress, Hurston landed at Howard University, where she met Alain Locke and Georgia Douglas Johnson; under their guidance, she began publishing her stories of rural life and eventually moved to New York in 1925, during the peak of the Harlem Renaissance. While there, she continued to write, completed her degree at Barnard College, and studied anthropology under Franz Boas, which provided an intellectual framework for the folk cultures she depicted and helped her keep working as a writer through the Great Depression.

Between 1924 and 1951, Hurston published dozens of stories, essays, and articles, collections of folklore and travel essays, anthropological studies, plays, a memoir, and several novels. Her work celebrates African American folk traditions centered on the uses of language, including preaching and oratory, storytelling, vernacular language, and the acrobatic verbal sparring matches known as playing the dozens.[22] Hurston's texts combine colloquial, informal, and formal modes of speech, and her narrative voice "luxuriat[es] in ... the nuances of speech, ... recording and promoting ... the beauty of the black voice, and particularly that of the female voice" (D. Davis 269–70). Gary Ciuba links Hurston's emphasis on language to the project of identity formation, arguing that her texts issued a "hermeneutical challenge to know the self by way of the spoken and written word" (119); this process of self-knowing is a major thematic element in *Their Eyes Were Watching God*, in which protagonist Janie is silenced during her marriage to a domineering, abusive man, but eventually comes to a powerful sense of self by reclaiming her voice. Hurston faced significant criticism from contemporaries like Richard Wright for the apparently apolitical nature of her work in the 1930s and 1940s, but more recently scholars have investigated the subtle forms of activism in Hurston's texts. David G. Nicholls examines Hurston's depictions of "'everyday acts of resistance' carried out by working people" in *Mules and Men* (467), and Tanya K. Kam argues Hurston's memoir *Dust Tracks on a Road* employs "double-voiced discourse" that "subverts social structures and norms even as it seems to project a frictionless portrait of black-white relations" (74). And several scholars have noted Hurston's depictions of power dynamics between African American men and women, arguing that she presents language and folklore as a means for women to achieve measures of autonomy, creative expression, and power.[23] In these ways, Hurston's work examines the beauties and strengths of African American folk cultures while remaining critical of the oppressive structures they sometimes endorse.

The bursting of the Harlem Renaissance bubble, coincident with the onset of the Great Depression, signaled the end of relative financial security and literary production for some women writers. While many tried to keep their careers alive, they faced a disinterested literary market fighting its own economic battles. With help from the Works Progress Administration, Hurston continued to write through the 1930s and into the 1940s before being derailed by personal crises; despite her prior successes, she fell into poverty and obscurity and worked a string of low-paying jobs before her death and burial in an unmarked grave.[24] Hurston's story has echoes in the lives of too many others; while the Harlem Renaissance offered unprecedented opportunities for women, this pattern renders painfully visible the persistently vulnerable and precarious nature of creative pursuits for African American women in the early twentieth century.

Coast to coast: Defining cultures of the 1920s

When we think of American women in the 1920s, we often picture the gangster's moll or the flapper, newly liberated from the constraints of traditional womanhood and dancing at the licentious parties described in Fitzgerald's *Gatsby* or talking tough on the bullet-riddled streets of Al Capone's Chicago. These images have a historical basis. Women gained a host of new freedoms during these years, including the right to vote in 1920, increased opportunities to work outside the home, the dress reform that freed them from the constraints of corsets, ankle-length hemlines, and long hair, and, crucially, the greater availability of birth control. And the economic boom of the 1920s seemed to betoken a limitless prosperity which, joined with the restless energy of a younger generation that had survived the horrors of modern war, signaled an embrace of consumption and pleasure-seeking, often fueled by the bootlegging operations of organized crime. These shifts gave rise to images of the modern 1920s woman as sexually liberated, largely apolitical, and above all "interested in herself, her freedom and her pleasures" (S. Smith 380), a woman found in the bohemian artists' studios of Greenwich Village, the silent films of the period, and the stories of Fitzgerald's Jazz Age. But these images tell only part of the story of 1920s womanhood. As Joan Shelley Rubin points out, the prosperity of the period hardly touched "farmers, immigrants, and racial minorities," and even white, middle-class women found that sexual liberation had its limits, so that the "New Woman" was more often someone in the middle, "confront[ing] both professional opportunities and domestic constraints" (xv) as she picked her way between traditional and modern worlds.

This contested middle position between radical and conservative, new and old, was manifested in the struggle to delineate worthwhile artistic and intellectual pursuits during an era of heady consumerism fueled by the rise of advertising, the mass production of entertainment, and a growing celebrity culture. New York had forged a reputation as the modern cultural center of the United States, the home of most of its major publishing houses and magazines, its most important theater district, and new artistic movements, including the Harlem Renaissance and the avant-garde radicalism of Greenwich Village. It was also home to a set of elite literary and cultural tastemakers who held court from the Rose Room of Manhattan's Algonquin Hotel and the pages of New York's magazines and newspapers. Taking their cues from the high modernists, writers and critics such as Alexander Woollcott and H.L. Mencken denounced what had become known as "middlebrow" literature and culture, produced primarily by and for women, neither "vulgar" enough to be low culture nor "sophisticated or experimental" enough to be high culture, but safe and undemanding to appeal to the masses of undiscriminating (female) consumers (Botshon and Goldsmith 3–4).[25] Not surprisingly, one of their primary targets was Hollywood, seen as the crassest of the purveyors of the feminized middlebrow.

But for all the posturing and distinctions of these cultural critics, the elites of New York, the upstarts of Hollywood, and the writers who moved in between had much in common. Greenwich Village was home to radical experiments in theater and poetry by playwrights like Susan Glaspell and poets like Edna St. Vincent Millay, but many of them also enjoyed wider success and cultivated public images in mainstream magazines and newspapers. And while the narrative experiments in middlebrow novels might be less "confrontational" than in avant-garde and other modern literatures (Lutes 439), bestselling writers like Edna Ferber and Fannie Hurst, cultural elites like Dorothy Parker, and screenwriters like Anita Loos all grappled with the implications of modernity in their heroines' lives along with the implications of their own literary celebrity. What's more, for all the proclamations of a cultural hierarchy, many writers circulated in and between New York and Hollywood both socially and professionally, arguing, collaborating, and contributing to a vital and relatively elastic literary community. The false distinction between highbrow and middlebrow tends to diminish women's contributions to the literature of the 1920s: the literature of modernity written by women encompassed the liberatory political works of Greenwich Village, the urbane verse, criticism, and drama of the Manhattanites, the bestselling novels of the Book of the Month Club, and the films they engendered. These works differed in tone and style but were linked by a deeply modern sensibility and a concern with the freedoms and constraints of women's lives in the modern world.

Greenwich Village had its own Little Renaissance in the first two decades of the twentieth century, driven by an admixture of modernist, feminist, progressive, and avant-garde artistic ideals (Murphy 356). Artists, writers, and intellectuals interested in avant-garde experimentation flocked to the village to be part of an open, collaborative artistic and social community known for its radical politics and its "penurious and promiscuous bohemian lifestyles" (Keyser "Edna" 66). It was especially an "incubat[or]" for a kind of "young American feminism" that encouraged "solidarity" as a means of achieving political results and individual "female self-discovery" (Fletcher 244). The experimental ethos of Greenwich Village also spawned the Little Theater movement, which was committed to social and philosophical critique through experimental, small, specifically American theater (Shafer 76). The movement was welcoming to women: of the 145 plays produced between 1915 and 1922 by the most well-known of these groups, the Provincetown Players, 60 were written by women, including Millay, Glaspell, Ferber, Alice Brown, Djuna Barnes, and Neith Boyce (Murphy 357).

Susan Glaspell was instrumental in the Little Theater movement; she and her husband helped found first the Washington Square Players in 1914 and then the Provincetown Players in 1916, through which Glaspell had eleven plays produced. Her plays are noted for their blend of realism, symbolism, and expressionism (Gainor 153), which Katherine Biers links to the influence of Emerson and Maeterlinck and Nietzsche's call for playwrights to "reunit[e] philosophy and theatre" in modern drama (457). Her most well-known works, *Trifles* (1916), *Inheritors* (1921), and *The Verge* (1922), are social protest plays that explore what it means to be a non-conforming citizen in a democracy, and specifically the power available to women occupying devalued and marginal spaces in American society.[26] *Trifles* analyzes the tensions between the requirements of the law and justice in the case of an abused woman who kills her husband, and *Inheritors* and *The Verge* demonstrate the after-effects of restrictive and xenophobic wartime policies and the "chaos and destruction" of war in "postwar life" (Gainor 147). But Glaspell's Provincetown years were only part of her career; she also enjoyed mainstream success as a writer of novels and short fiction for popular magazines such as *Harper's* and the *Ladies' Home Journal*. Her fiction has historically been read as conventional (cf. Waterman 175), but more recently Colette Lindroth has found in Glaspell's stories subtle challenges to early twentieth-century American "sacred cows" of "rugged individualism" and "faith in progress" (265), and Martha Carpentier reads Glaspell's treatment of the same narrative in multiple genres—as with *Trifles* and its fiction analogue "A Jury of Her Peers" (1917)—as a continuation of Glaspell's experiments in narrative and genre that reveals the "vital continuum" between forms in her work (50).

Like Glaspell, poet Edna St. Vincent Millay was a member of the Provincetown Players and is often considered the chief of Greenwich Village's young feminists, the "standard bearer for the breakdown of futile conventions and of taboos" (Colum 17). But her iconoclastic, sexually liberated celebrity persona was a savvy construction she diligently cultivated through her poetry and public performances. Millay's poetry combines traditional sonnet and lyric forms with emotionally expressive, frankly erotic content. While it was praised for its emotional qualities, it was also dismissed by contemporary critics as too feminine and insufficiently intellectual (Ciardi 8);[27] but several critics have argued that Millay deliberately cultivated an excessively feminine image precisely to mine the contradictions between surface and substance, particularly in her challenges to sexual double standards. As Andrea Powell Wolfe argues, Millay adopts an aggressive and independent "sexual subjectivity that was traditionally only available to men" (155) in her poems, which she insisted on performing in "long dresses, trailing ones … very graceful and floaty" (Millay 76), creating productive disjunctions between appearance, expectation, and reality. But Millay also acted as an ironic "mouthpiece for the cosmetics-wearing and cocktail toting sophisticates of midtown" in essays published pseudonymously in *Vanity Fair*, which allowed her to skewer the sophisticated set's emphasis on "cleverness" and "consumption" in modern women rather than real intelligence (Keyser "Edna" 66, 90), an extension of her broader challenges to the links between surface and substance. With one foot in the Village and the other in midtown Manhattan, Millay bridges both literary worlds while pushing against cultural constraints on appropriate femininity.

Dorothy Parker extended Millay's critiques of the smart magazine set's conceptions of womanhood from a position that was squarely within New York's literary elite, even as her career revealed the deep and enduring links between these elites and the middlebrow mass culture industry. Parker had her first poem published in *Vanity Fair* when she was 20; she replaced P.G. Wodehouse as the magazine's drama critic three years later and published poetry, reviews, and stories in the *New Yorker*, *Vanity Fair*, and other prominent magazines throughout her career. Parker was the undisputed queen of the circle of acerbic cultural tastemakers known as the Algonquin Round Table, whose core group included critic Woollcott, playwrights Robert Sherwood and George Kaufman, and writer Robert Benchley. Known for her darkly humorous poetry, ironic short stories, and biting theatrical and literary criticism, she reserved much of her disdain for writers whom she saw as overestimating their own talents. She also criticized women writers whom she believed produced "fantasies" rather than the truths of the world, however unpleasant—including playwright-of-manners-turned politician Clare Boothe Luce and sometime Round-Tabler Ferber, writers she and her fellow suffragettes "did not foresee" when they "chained ourselves to lamp posts to try to get our equality" (80). Like several of the Algonquin writers and many more of the supposedly non-commercial modernists, Parker worked in the 1930s as a screenwriter in Hollywood but abhorred its crassness and described it as full of writers whose best work was "garbage" and offering continual "indignity" for anyone with real ability (86). She was frank about the economic realities of writing; when an interviewer asked about the inspiration for her work, Parker replied, "Need of money, dear" (79) and acknowledged making money often involved a tradeoff between artistic inclinations and market demands. This self-deprecating and distancing stance allowed Parker to maintain her position as a critic of discerning taste and a member of the cultural elite, working to shore up the boundaries of cultural hierarchies even while she repeatedly crossed them.

Parker's reputation for caustic wit and critical acuity made her a literary celebrity and a rather unwilling symbol of the kind of clever, cosmopolitan modern womanhood she deplored, and she returned to these subjects repeatedly in her writing, even as she was pushed into performance of the cosmopolitan role by economic demands. She frequently dismissed her own poetry as mere "verses. I cannot say poems" (78), but she also critiqued those who inflated her reputation for cynical, sophisticated humor into a particularly gendered caricature. As Keyser notes, Parker often adopted the pose of femininity to critique the "over-sexed images" of women in mass culture (*Playing* 53), but she also found herself (sometimes literally) reduced to a flapper cartoon, stuck with a "publicity double" in a literary culture that valued women's "attractiveness and whimsy over cultivation and wit" and transformed their pain and disillusion into "adorable" marketing tactics (67–8). Parker acknowledges this fragmentation of the female celebrity self in autobiographical monologue stories such as "The Garter" (1928), whose premise—author Dorothy Parker's garter breaks at a party—hints at the allure of the celebrity female body while exploring the threat of exposure and lack of control such celebrity involves (Helal 96–7). She also emphasizes the strain of the expectation that modern women continually perform this "attractiveness and whimsy," most famously in her award-winning story "Big Blonde" (1929), but also in her "Constant Reader" book reviews for the *New Yorker*, in which she declares herself a "representative for the limited body and exhausted resources" of the modern woman (Keyser *Playing* 53).[28] It was a position uncomfortably reinforced by Parker's ambivalence about her own place in such a scheme and her lifelong struggle with depression. In exposing the performative and constricting nature of female celebrity, Parker critiques a view of supposedly modern womanhood that celebrates surface forms of liberation while obscuring the emotional and physical price the performance of such a womanhood can demand.

Many scholars have been more comfortable with Parker's tortured celebrity and the literary hierarchies it implies than with the comparatively untroubled popularity of writers like Edna Ferber. Of all the perennially bestselling female fiction writers generally classed as middlebrow, including Fannie Hurst, Zona Gale, and Dorothy Canfield Fisher, Ferber is a particularly large target. She wrote magazine fiction and numerous bestselling novels—one of which, *So Big* (1923), won a Pulitzer—collaborated with George Kaufman and others on several successful Broadway plays, including *Dinner at Eight* and *Stage Door*, and negotiated contracts for award-winning Broadway and Hollywood adaptations of many of her works, including *Cimarron* (1929), *Show Boat* (1926), *Saratoga Trunk* (1941), and *Giant*

(1952), all while traveling in the rarefied social air of the Algonquin Round Table and Manhattan's theatrical elite.[29] Ferber was prolific and unabashedly canny about the business end of her work: she built up her readership by first serializing her novels in major national magazines such as *Woman's Home Companion* and *Ladies' Home Journal* and negotiated film contracts prior to publication, ensuring a longer period of public conversation and the kind of book sales that led to repeat appearances on *Publisher's Weekly*'s bestseller lists (Smyth 17, 13). And Ferber's Hollywood contracts were unprecedented (Smyth 13), guaranteeing her not only top prices and percentages but also above-the-title billing, so that every audience member knew they were watching "Edna Ferber's *Show Boat*." Unlike Parker, Ferber worked to manufacture and maintain a celebrity status and have it proclaimed from advertisements and movie screens just as much as from the title pages of her books.

For all the popularity of Ferber's works, they were hardly the "fantasies" Parker labeled them; they were often multigenerational, regionally focused historical epics that challenged American mythologies of origin, success, and national belonging, what Ferber described as works of "loving protest" against American "naïveté" that combined political argument with a strong story and "vitality" in its "theme background plot characterization dialogue" (*Magic* 261, 262). During a period when consumerism was flourishing, the Nineteenth Amendment was fighting for ratification, Congress was debating anti-miscegenation and anti-immigration laws, and the discovery of oil in Texas was set to permanently reshape the landscape, Ferber's novels took on materialism, sentimentality, environmental destruction, nativism, racism, and the treatment of Native Americans in the West, Southwest, and Alaska, repeatedly revising American histories and mythologies. In narratives of westward expansion, she shifts the focus from individualist he-men who tame the wilderness toward complex women who are strong, independent, and not always likable; they are sometimes progressive, like Leslie Lynnton Benedict in *Giant*, and sometimes "narrow-minded, racist, and utterly conventional" (Campbell "Written" 30), like Sabra Cravat of *Cimarron*. Ferber's communities include Native American, black, brown, and mixed-raced characters, and she presents race-mixing as a beneficial, empowering, and historically pervasive form of cultural exchange rather than a kind of contamination (Campbell "Written" 27), challenging the prevalent "myth of white America" (Smyth 12). And in her passing narratives, including *Show Boat* and *Saratoga Trunk*, Ferber dramatizes the anxieties about cultural acceptance that led many Jewish Americans to identify with "African Americans who crossed the color line" (Wirth-Nesher 465; see also Gubar 234). Ferber believed in telling compelling and dramatic stories, but she had no interest in lulling her readers into comfort, or in others' delineations of cultural hierarchies.

On the other hand, cultural distinctions between middlebrow and highbrow play a significant role in Anita Loos' satirical novel *Gentlemen Prefer Blondes* (1925), an indictment of the vacuity of modern womanhood that ends up skewering pretty much everything else along with it. Loos, a longtime Hollywood screenwriter with deep New York ties, claimed to have written the sketch that grew into *Blondes* after watching famously snobbish cultural critic and longtime friend Mencken pursue one too many women whose most outstanding characteristic was their blonde hair (Loos *Gentlemen* xxxvii–xxxviii). The diary of acquisitive social-climbing flapper Lorelei Lee, *Gentlemen Prefer Blondes* was initially serialized in *Harper's Bazar* and then published in novel form by Boni and Liveright, an immediate bestseller that spawned a sequel and multiple stage and film adaptations.[30] According to Loos, Mencken refused to publish the text in his elite magazine *American Mercury* out of concern it would offend his readers: one Loos memoir records him as saying, "Do you realize, young woman, that you're the first American writer ever to poke fun at sex?" (*Kiss* 191). But while many of Loos' critics focus on the expert manipulation of the sexual economy by Lorelei and her best friend Dorothy as they journey from Manhattan to Europe and back, sex is only one of the novel's many targets; Loos also takes aim at New York high society, moral reformers, the movie industry, the judicial system, consumerism, flappers, intellectuals, Christian Scientists, the English aristocracy, American tourists, and advertising. Loos' ultimate critique is of "social pretension" of all kinds (Churchwell 145), and her text works to collapse middlebrow and highbrow distinctions, both within Lorelei's world and in the production and reception of the text itself. For all Lorelei's efforts to acquire "refinement," she and Dorothy are "socially disruptive," continually infiltrating the highest social echelons while remaining "unassimilable" (Barreca xiii–xiv), and they facilitate the collapse of social barriers; at Lorelei's belated coming-out party, judges and intellectuals are indistinguishable from the elite members of the Manhattan's Racquet Club and the Italian bootleggers from Brooklyn (*Gentlemen* 105). The text itself similarly cuts across class lines, operating both within and on the periphery of the worlds it critiques. *Harper's Bazar* was, as Churchwell notes, "an instruction manual in middlebrow social pretension" for "arrivistes" looking to buy their way into the cultural aristocracy (142), and "highbrow institution" Boni and Liveright's publication of the novel capped off a year in which they had also published Hemingway, Sherwood Anderson, Eliot, Dreiser, and Pound (McGurl 109). What's more, the novel was admired by millions of readers as well as by Joyce, Faulkner, Wharton, Santayana, and a slew of other cultural elites (Barreca x–xi; Churchwell 153). Loos is perfectly aware of the socially anarchic potential of her text; when Dorothy announces in Munich that Lorelei can "be a high brow" at German museums but she is "satisfide to be a Half brow and get full of beer" at the world's largest beer hall, the "Half Brow house" (*Gentlemen* 86), Lorelei declares Dorothy will always be unrefined—but the reader knows the refinement Lorelei seeks has only ever been a show, a kind of advertisement that promises what it can never deliver.

Forgotten women: Writers and politics in the Great Depression

The Crash of 1929 and the following massive economic depression rapidly made the flush years of the 1920s seem a distant memory. In the United States, unemployment soared and millions became homeless as businesses failed, industrial production went into steep decline, and the devastating conditions of the Dust Bowl destroyed thousands of Midwestern farms. While images of "forgotten men" have long dominated historical depictions of the Great Depression, the situation was particularly fraught for women, many of whom lost their means of economic support, or faced accusations of "stealing jobs from men" or dereliction of their domestic duties if they did manage to find paying work (Hapke xv). The increasingly hostile responses of local and national governments did much to destroy public trust and confidence, most visibly when the "Bonus Army" of thousands of World War I veterans demanding payment of long-owed service bonuses was driven out of Washington, D.C., with teargas and tanks under the orders of President Herbert Hoover in 1932. Even with the election of Franklin D. Roosevelt and the enactment of his New Deal policies, which included the establishment of Social Security, unemployment insurance, and the jobs-creating Works Progress Administration, it was hard for some to shake the conviction that capitalism had failed. Membership in the Communist and Socialist parties and the radical left rose, international labor unions grew in strength and power, and the United States seemed to hover on the brink of economic and political collapse.

The literature of the 1930s reflects these cultural anxieties over who had the right to work, the proper relationships between laborers and the products of their work, and the obligations individuals, communities, and governments had to one another from a range of political positions. John Marsh observes that the political literature of this period, which mostly tends toward the "proletarian and radical," has been frequently dismissed as too agenda-driven to be literary, and until the last twenty or thirty years, discussions of this literature had been largely limited to mainstream male figures like Steinbeck, Richard Wright, and Woody Guthrie (477). And while more recently scholars have examined the work of women writers like Tillie Olsen, Meridel Le Sueur, Muriel Rukeyser, Genevieve Taggard, and others who published poetry, journalism, and fiction in leftist publications, they have largely been inattentive to the less radical but no less political writing of the period that Laura Hapke terms "nonprotest fare" (xiv). Political and economic concerns infused a broad spectrum of literature, from the politically pointed journalism and fiction of Le Sueur and the poetry of Olsen to the more mainstream fiction of Katherine Anne Porter and the bestselling novels of Carson McCullers, Fannie Hurst, and Margaret Mitchell—works linked in their considerations of the realities of political revolution, labor conditions, and of women's place in the working world.

Her fiction was generally published in prestigious literary magazines, but Katherine Anne Porter was no stranger to leftist political activism. While supporting herself as a freelance journalist, she moved from Dallas to Denver and then Greenwich Village before settling in Mexico for several years, where she became involved in the Mexican Revolution; it was a place to which she would repeatedly return both in life and in the deeply symbolic, politically charged fiction that would become her literary hallmark. Porter's fiction examines the tensions between her female characters' desire for independence and artistic expression and the external expectations they face (DeMouy 6, 16). In her most well-known story, "Flowering Judas" (1929), Porter explores the politics of lust, betrayal, and disillusionment in the figure of Laura, an American girl confronted by the "disunion between her way of living and her feeling of what life should be" as a female worker for the Mexican Revolution (Porter *Flowering* 142). Laura is paralyzed by her realization of the distance between the clarity of her political ideals and the confusion of her reality, what Jane Krause DeMouy sees as a confrontation with her own limitations and the cultural boundaries she faces as a woman in the supposedly liberatory situation she has sought (79). Laura's disillusionment mirrors Porter's, who had come to Mexico in a primitivist search for truth, simplicity, and beauty in Mexican folk culture and the people's revolution only to find in the chaos of the movement's infighting and struggle a "battleground of death and destruction" (Brinkmeyer 200). Porter's increasing disillusionment about political ideals in her fiction points to the difficulties she and other women faced in trying to navigate radical politics in a world that still saw revolution as the province of men.

While Porter explored the possibilities for women in political revolution, Tillie Olsen and Carson McCullers gave attention to the economic and political forms of oppression that prompted such revolutions. Olsen was raised in a socialist family and spent most of her life as a political activist. Most of her work in the 1930s was published in leftist publications such as *The Daily Worker* and *New Masses* and included accounts of the labor strikes in San Francisco, in which she participated, as well as poems and stories examining the exploitative working conditions of the people who produced consumer goods. In "I Want You Women Up North to Know" (1934), for example, Olsen exposes the dehumanizing machinery of consumer capitalism, juxtaposing the language of saleswomen in "macy's, wannamakers, gimbels, marshall fields" (3) and the "exquisite pleats" (8) of the children's clothing they sell with the faces and consumptive bodies of laborers like "catalina" (11), whose "bright red blood embroiders the floor of her room" (20); published in *The Partisan*, Olsen's poem had a specific political message for a receptive political audience. On the other hand, McCullers' first novel, *The Heart Is a Lonely Hunter* (1940), reached a very different audience as a bestseller from major publishing house Houghton Mifflin. It has often been considered an apolitical novel by critics such as Malcolm Cowley because it "steadfastly refuses to make broad sociohistorical generalizations" (Kaiser 290) in examining the alienation of the residents of a small Georgia town, but it has many political resonances. It connects agricultural and industrial working conditions with larger political and economic forces in the figure of itinerant socialist Jake Blount, who fights to convince his mill coworkers to organize, arguing that the mistreatment of Southern sharecroppers due to the greed of "Northern corporations" was worse than the treatment of the "lowest peasant in any European fascist state" (226). McCullers also suggests a link between economic exploitation and racial oppression in the figure of African American doctor Benedict Mady Copeland, who reminds Jake that "So far as I and my people are concerned the South is Fascist now and always has been" (228). In spite of the common ground they find, Jake and Dr. Copeland are ultimately unable to agree on methods, and their idealism keeps them from entering into real community or effecting any lasting change; nevertheless, together they suggest the "widely divergent personal experiences" (Kaiser 294) through which Americans understood the economic and political forces at work in their lives.

Women writers from an equally broad range of careers and readerships considered the implications of the idea of appropriate and inappropriate work for women during the Depression. Meridel Le Sueur was the most politically active of these writers; she came from a long line of women activists and supported herself by writing for a variety of publications, but she was best known for her radical fiction and journalism. Her 1932 article "Women on the Breadlines" compares the "public spectacle of men in breadlines" with women's more private suffering (Marsh 479), noting that most jobs open to women would take only "attractive" or "adroit" candidates, leaving millions of women to live on "a cracker a day," go mad, or "go on the street" (Le Sueur 138–41). Fannie Hurst was known for her bestselling "woman's weeper" melodramas (Hapke 118), but she had worked in factories and shops and frequently featured working women in her texts (Burke 442). In *Back Street* (1931), the story of a successful working woman who leaves a good job at her married lover's insistence only to descend into "nightmarish" and "dehumanized" poverty after his death (Hapke 123), Hurst demonstrates the economic and psychological toll of obeying a culture that dictates women's economic dependence on men and values the self-esteem of working men over the actual lives of women facing dire economic straits. But Margaret Mitchell's Southern antebellum escapist fantasy, the Pulitzer Prize-winning *Gone With the Wind* (1936), pulls in the opposite direction, praising heroine Scarlett O'Hara for the resourcefulness that helps her feed her family while the men are off at war before condemning her for the business acumen that makes her rich in the postwar years; as Hapke argues, it is an "allegory of 1930s professionalism" that grudgingly accepted the necessity of working wives while deploring the "unnatural role reversals" that followed the end of slavery (214–16). As these works demonstrate, while popular texts like Mitchell's, Hurst's, and McCullers' might express varying political views and aims from the overtly political writing of the period, they shared with leftist texts a preoccupation with the economic and political concerns of the Great Depression and its implications in the lives of women.

The contests of war

Many women were moved to write by the troubling spread of fascism and anti-Semitism in the lead-up to World War II. Edna Ferber's first memoir, *A Peculiar Treasure* (1939), was written as a rebuttal to European anti-Semitism and ends with her declaration of gratitude for her Jewishness and the challenge, "So come Revolution! Come Hitler! Come Death! Even though you win—you lose" (398). Along with Hurst, Ferber went on to witness the horrors of the Holocaust firsthand as a war correspondent. Many other women channeled their World War II experiences into poetry and prose, including H.D. in *Trilogy*, Marianne Moore in "In

Distrust of Merits" (1944), and Gertrude Stein in *Wars I Have Seen* (1945). These texts document the fear, excitement, anger, and deep grief of war in complex and moving ways. But some of the most important—and perhaps most neglected— literature that emerged during World War II is the literature by Japanese American and Chinese American women.

There are few texts by Asian American women from this period, in large part because Asian women faced significant legal and cultural obstacles in the United States. Anti-Asian immigration policies effectively prevented most Chinese and Filipino women from coming to the United States beginning in 1882, and while Japan permitted men and their families to immigrate to the United States after 1885, land-ownership and naturalization policies generally barred them from owning land or obtaining U.S. citizenship, creating a cultural distance the younger genera- tion sought to bridge in part through literary and artistic endeavors (Yogi 128). But shifts in international political allegiances in the 1930s and 1940s that made Japan an aggressor and China a U.S. ally, the internment of more than 120,000 Japanese Americans during the war, and the repeal of the Chinese Exclusion Act in 1943 also caused a shift in the focus of the texts of the period. Many Asian American women writers found themselves unwitting actors in international political agen- das, seeking to articulate their experiences during a period when the question of whether one could be both Asian and American was fiercely contested.

Internment had profound psychological, political, and economic ramifications for Japanese Americans, and their wartime texts explore their conflicting senses of betrayal, pride, optimism, and disillusionment. Second-generation Japanese Americans, referred to among Japanese Americans as nisei, occupied a middle ground between Japanese and American cultures; in the 1920s and 1930s, young writers like Mary Oyama had published English-language poetry and fiction in Japanese American newspapers and magazines and worked to cultivate a literary community among nisei writers through salons and small literary magazines. Some, like the editors of *Gyo-Sho: A Magazine of Nisei Literature*, saw themselves as "an interstitial cultural group" linking Japan and the United States (qtd. in Yogi 130), but others were more ambivalent about this connection, like Chiye Mori, whose poem "Japanese American" (1932) depicts Japanese Americans as painfully vulner- able (Matsumoto 92), "Helpless targets" in a double-sided "shooting gallery of political discord" (Mori 4). But it became difficult for Japanese American writers to maintain any optimism during internment, when questions of loyalty pushed some into defiant American patriotism and others into "bitter disillusionment" (Yogi 132). Poet Toyo Suyemoto's "Gain" (1942), published in camp magazine *Trek*, masks a sharp critique in an apparently "apolitical" nature poem (Schweik 186) in which the speaker recalls her quest to "seed the barren earth / And make wild beauty take / firm root," not knowing how much "The waiting long would shake / Me inwardly" (1–5). As Suyemoto's poem suggests, the fruit of internment is a bitterness and pain the cessation of military hostilities will do little to repair.

For Chinese American writers, the shifts tended to be more beneficial but were no less politically fraught. Helena Kuo was a Chinese-born journalist and writer who advocated for modern education and women's rights in China before moving to the United States in 1939 at the invitation of Eleanor Roosevelt. As Amy Ling notes, Kuo was one of a group of well-educated Chinese American writers during World War II who were "prepared to be unofficial diplomats and bridges between the East and West" (*Between* 173) but were caught up willingly or otherwise in an American campaign to define Chinese Americans as desirable in comparison to the hated Japanese (Wong "Chinese" 46). Kuo's autobiography *I've Come a Long Way* (1942) and her novel *Westward to Chungking* (1944) explore this contested position between images of East and West in the contexts of the Sino-Japanese War (1937–1945) and World War II. American-born Jade Snow Wong's *Fifth Chinese Daughter* (1945) performs a similar diplomatic function, offering what Sau-Ling Cynthia Wong calls "autobiography as guided Chinatown tour" ("Chinese" 46); and in the State Department-sponsored speaking tour that followed, Wong worked to smooth relations between the United States and Asian nations in the postwar period. While Chinese American writers such as Kuo and Wong were the recipients of official American goodwill rather than enmity, the sudden political shifts pointed toward the precariousness of their position in a political world whose allegiances were unstable at best.

As these literatures suggest, the defining preoccupations of the interwar period were with how the world was changing, what it meant to be American, and who was allowed to make such a determination. The economic and political turmoil of these years led many to question the efficacy and the rightness of existing structures of power, which concentrated political, economic, and cultural decision-making in the hands of the few. These questions would take on even greater urgency in the second half of the twentieth century as various social movements grew in force and power, demanding the recognition of a more diverse group of American stakeholders and continuing to change the face of American literature.

Notes

1 The Second Great Migration lasted from about 1940 to 1970 and involved the movement of an estimated 5 to 6 million people. See Chatelain's *South Side Girls* for the most thorough examination of women's participation in the Great Migrations, focusing specifically on Chicago.

2 For more on the Japanese American internment, see Brian Masaru Hayashi's *Democratizing the Enemy* and Alice Yang Murray's *Historical Memories of the Japanese American Internment and the Struggle for Redress*.

3 See Eric Bulson's "Little Magazine, World Form" for an analysis of the ways little magazines functioned powerfully in both local and global contexts.

4 As Michael North notes in *Novelty: A History of the New*, Pound's slogan was itself an amalgamation of various historical sources, which makes the slogan as contradictory and multivalent as modernism itself; North also observes that the slogan first appeared in Pound's writing in 1928, after many of high modernism's most famous works had been written, and did not achieve much cultural currency for several decades (162–70). However, the late arrival of the slogan does not preclude its ability to express the pre-existing modernist emphasis on newness, even if its over-adoption by critics in the years since has been generally misleading.

5 See Renker 232–3, Lauter's "Melville Climbs the Canon," Lutes 422–3, and Showalter *Jury* 294ff. for discussions of modernism's masculinist influences on canon formation in the early twentieth century.

6 There is some critical debate about the dates of the modernist movement because of its looseness (it might more accurately be described as a collection of interrelated stylistic, formal, and thematic literary developments). Some scholars place its beginning as early as the 1890s, while its end is generally considered to be marked by World War II; however, several modernist writers, including H.D., continued to write in what could be considered modernist modes throughout their careers.

7 Reese did not identify her poetry as Imagist, a designation which had not yet been created when she was writing in the 1880s, but Walker notes that the poetry in Reese's four volumes "meets most of Ezra Pounds rules for the new poetry of imagism" ("Nineteenth" 241). Amy Lowell claimed Dickinson and others as modernism's nineteenth-century predecessors; see Lowell's essay "Emily Dickinson," as well as Munich 20–1 and Donaldson 31–4.

8 After the publication of one of Pound's Imagist anthologies, Lowell insisted that the selections in subsequent anthologies be more democratically selected and the revenues shared. Pound, outraged at what he saw as Lowell's appropriation of the poetic form he had helped to pioneer, eventually renounced what he derogated as "Amygism," which he insisted had become full of "emotional slither," "mushy technique," and "general floppiness" under Lowell's guidance, in favor of the new Vorticist movement (qtd. in Healey and Cushman 8). As Bradshaw notes, Pound's public feminization of Imagism under Lowell also linked it to his similarly feminized denunciations of mass culture ("Outselling" 159). Lowell would go on to edit three anthologies of Imagist poetry, *Some Imagist Poets 1915, 1916*, and *1917*, which featured John Gould Fletcher, H.D., Richard Aldington, D.H. Lawrence, and F.S. Flint, along with her own poetry.

9 See also Bradshaw's "Remembering Amy Lowell," which examines critics' emphasis on Lowell's weight and physical appearance, which Bradshaw argues becomes "a text onto which cultural anxieties are projected" in relation to discourses on the proper way of "inhabiting a woman's body" ("Remembering" 170).

10 Along with other Imagists, Lowell saw a relationship between Chinese and Japanese poetic forms, particularly the haiku, and the sharp impressions of single images they believed poems should express. In the preface to her fifth volume of poetry, *Pictures of the Floating World* (1919), Lowell says that several of the included poems "owe their inception to the vivid, realistic colour-prints of the Japanese masters" (*Pictures* viii).

11 The modernist edition of *The Dial*, which was the first American publication venue for Eliot's *The Waste Land* and many other works of modern literature and art, was the third reincarnation of the Transcendentalist magazine Margaret Fuller had worked for eighty years earlier (see 54 in this volume).

12 Stein faced significant hostility from contemporary reviewers who saw her work as devoid of both meaning and discipline. For example, critic James Thurber described her as "one of the most eminent of the idiots" whose work was passing for great art among the modernist literary set (32). She was often criticized for the way her wordplay served to democratize literature so that, in the words of one writer, "no knowledge of the English language whatsoever" was needed to appreciate it (Lambert 93). While some of her fellow writers praised her, others were ambivalent about her radical democratization of language. Anderson remarked on Stein's decision to give up poetic acclaim to "live among the little housekeeping words, the swaggering, bullying, street-corner words, the honest working, money saving words," a project he believed was more important for other writers than for the public ("Work" 8). Katherine Anne Porter was more clearly bemused: "Wise or silly or nothing at all, down everything goes on the page with an air of everything being equal," she wrote in1947 ("Gertrude Stein" 521–2).

13 Barnes' family life was somewhat unstable and may have involved sexual abuse. There are hints in Barnes' work, particularly in her final published work, the play *Antiphon* (1958),

that she may have been raped as a teenager with her father's knowledge, and some letters indicate that her relationship with her grandmother may have been incestuous. At the age of 18 she was pushed into a private marriage of sorts with the much older brother of her father's lover, but the marriage was never legally binding and Barnes soon left him. Shortly thereafter, Barnes' mother left her father and she moved with Barnes and some of their other children to New York City, where Barnes began her career as a journalist. See Herring's biography *Djuna: The Life and Work of Djuna Barnes* 1–58 for more on Barnes' family life.

14 See Lutes 424–5 for a review of the ways in which scholars have increasingly read Cather as a modernist in the last three decades.

15 See also Debra Cumberland, who argues that Thea's experiences in Panther Canyon help her to reject the gendered Victorian "anti-physiological school of singing" instruction that prevented female singers from understanding their own bodies (61); in rejecting these singing techniques, Thea is able to connect with her body and sexuality as a "whole person," making her a better artist (63).

16 Smith contrasts the eventual artistic success of opera singer Thea, inspired by her time in Panther Canyon, with the protagonist in Okanagan writer Mourning Dove's *Cogewea* (1927), in which Mourning Dove "records the destructiveness of modernity" for women of color who do not have the privileges of Cather's white protagonists (S. Smith 382).

17 See Bailey 396, Jeane Harris 87, and Worden *passim*.

18 As Lillian Faderman notes, African Americans were not necessarily more accepting of homosexuality in general than white Americans, but bisexuality seems to have had some measure of acceptance, particularly among women. See Faderman *Odd Girls* 67–79. Langston Hughes offers one of the most stinging indictments of this kind of tourism in the frequently anthologized "When the Negro Was in Vogue" (*Big Sea* 223–33).

19 As Robin Bernstein notes, *Rachel* was written in response to the NAACP's call for plays that would counter the depictions of African Americans in D.W. Griffith's popular and acclaimed silent film *Birth of a Nation* (1915), whose climactic scene features the riding of the Ku Klux Klan to save a white woman from being raped by a black man and whose happy resolution involves the suppression of African American votes by armed force on election day; see R. Bernstein 61ff.

20 See Carby *Reconstructing* 166–8 and 198 n.14, in which she argues that while *Plum Bun* is ultimately conservative, Fauset does not endorse white middle-class morality; instead, she portrays a black middle class that was "more moral and more civilized than ... white racist society" (198 n.14).

21 Comparatively little is known about Larsen's early life; much of what is currently known is due to the diligent recovery work of Thadious M. Davis, whose *Nella Larsen, Novelist of the Harlem Renaissance: A Woman's Life Unveiled* (1996) was one of the earliest and most significant treatments of Larsen's life and work.

22 Many scholars have examined Hurston's use of language. For example, Deborah Plant traces Hurston's emphasis on the language and cadences of the folk sermon to Hurston's preacher father, especially as revealed in her autobiography *Dust Tracks on a Road* (1942); Ann L. Rayson also considers *Dust Tracks* in order to argue that Hurston experiments with both the style and form of African American autobiography, using multiple registers of language as she "indulg[es] in exuberant self-examination" rather than chronological depictions of events and "famous acquaintances" (44). Henry Louis Gates (*Signifying Monkey* 184–232) and Alice Walker (*In Search* 83–92) are two among the many who have considered Hurston's depictions of playing the dozens in *Their Eyes Were Watching God, Mules and Men, Dust Tracks*, and other works.

23 See, for example, Lupton, Wall, and Doris Davis.

24 Hurston's burial site was unmarked until 1973, when Alice Walker erected a headstone in the location where it is believed to be. For more, see Walker's "Looking for Zora" in *In Search of Our Mothers' Gardens*.

25 Mencken lived in Baltimore for most of his life, but he edited two prominent and scathingly critical New York-based magazines, *Smart Set* and *American Mercury*, which he

co-founded; while he is not technically from New York, his prominent association with New York magazine cultures and his unabating vitriol toward the middlebrow make him an essential part of this conversation.

26 See for example Winetsky, who reads Glaspell's "performative liberalism" in *Inheritors* (1921) as a form of non-violent political protest (5); Holstein, who sees the conclusion of *Trifles* (1916) as revealing how the "discounted" female characters' "low status allows them to keep quiet," withholding valuable knowledge overlooked by the men in authority and thus rendering their silence as an act of power (284, 290); and Dymkowski, who sees Glaspell's plays as informed by a "consciousness that identifies women as outside the mainstream of life and thus capable of shaping it anew" (91–2).

27 See also Parks and Colum.

28 See Scott Ortolano's "Liberation, Degeneration, and Transcendence" for a deeper analysis of how Parker's "Big Blonde" critiques the liberatory potential of 1920s womanhood, which he examines in conjunction with Ferber's 1911 novel *Dawn O'Hara: The Girl Who Laughed*.

29 Among her lifelong friends, Ferber counted Broadway royalty Alfred Lunt and Lynn Fontanne, Noel Coward, and acclaimed playwright and director Moss Hart; among her enemies was Alexander Woollcott, unofficial head of the Round Table, where Ferber was a frequent attendee in the 1920s. See Gilbert 336–40 and 272–3 for more on the Round Table and Woollcott, and Ferber's *Treasure* 394ff. for more on her New York social circle.

30 The magazine title was initially spelled *Harper's Bazar* until 1929, when it adopted its current spelling, *Harper's Bazaar* (Churchwell 160 n.1).

6

LITERATURES OF WITNESS

Women writers after 1945

The United States emerged from World War II in a position of great strength. It had lost nearly half a million men and women, but geographically isolated from combat zones and the ensuing devastation, its infrastructure and industries were largely intact and flourishing. Its military strength and relative economic and political stability compared to the other Allied nations meant the United States was poised to take the lead in a new world order, one that quickly resolved itself into sharp ideological opposition between capitalism and democracy on one side and socialism and communism on the other. Any goodwill between the Allied powers after their victory soon disintegrated in the debates over how best to govern defeated Germany and facilitate European recovery, and the United States and much of Western Europe were soon embroiled in a cold war with the Soviet Union that took on the rhetorical overtones of good and evil as both sides sought global dominance. Determined to save the world from what Winston Churchill described in his famous "Iron Curtain" speech as a "growing challenge and peril to Christian civilization" (7291), the United States employed a dual strategy of deterrence, which involved stockpiles of increasingly powerful nuclear weaponry and the promise of nuclear retaliation to Soviet aggression, and containment, in which the newly launched Central Intelligence Agency and the U.S. military intervened in world conflicts to limit the spread of Soviet influence. This commitment to anti-Communist action led to the nation's involvement in seemingly unending proxy wars in Korea (1950–1953) and Vietnam (1955–1975) and shaped American policies, world politics, and increasingly connected global cultures for the rest of the twentieth century.[1]

The early Cold War years in the United States were characterized by contradictions between apparent stability, economic prosperity, and assertions of international authority and the shadow of constant danger and imminent annihilation. The 1950s and 1960s were prosperous as manufacturing continued to grow significantly after the war, powerful labor unions meant healthy incomes for many American families, and American corporations expanded their overseas operations. With the help of the GI Bill (1944), millions of returning soldiers attended college, bought houses in the suburbs, and started businesses, swelling the ranks of the white middle class. Such policies encouraged a return to normalcy—including to the "traditional gender roles" that undergirded American democracy (May 87–8)—after the turmoil of war. But at the same time, politicians such as Wisconsin Senator Joseph McCarthy stoked public fears with increasingly hysterical claims that communist operatives were infiltrating the U.S. government and Hollywood movie studios and plotting the destruction of everything Americans held dear. The imposition of loyalty oaths on government employees, the House Un-American Activities Committee and Army–McCarthy hearings about Communist activity (the live broadcast of which was one of the first major events on television), and the casting of political dissenters and other nonconformists—including people suspected of homosexuality—as dangerous subversives helped create an atmosphere of fear, suspicion, and secrecy that lurked beneath the period's outward placidity and was reflected in the literature and film of the time.

Although the United States projected itself as the moral and political leader of the free world, such assertions were jeopardized by the domestic unrest that grew over the 1950s, 1960s, and 1970s. During these years, a series of overlapping radical social movements arose that questioned the idea of American progress and the social and political institutions that upheld it, including the government, free market capitalism, racial segregation, Christianity, marriage, and the nuclear family. The African American Civil Rights and women's liberation movements were the most prominent and widespread. African American veterans who had fought in segregated armies overseas hoped with their service to secure a "double victory" over tyranny abroad and racial discrimination in the United States ("Courier's Double 'V'"), but they returned home to find that the provisions of the GI Bill did not apply equally to non-white soldiers, and that many white Americans were as resistant to racial equality as they had been before the war (Katznelson 113–41). The ensuing non-violent Civil Rights movement made significant legal gains, such as the striking down of the "separate but equal" justification for segregation in *Brown v. Board of Education of Topeka* (1954), the enactment of federal affirmative action policies, and the passage of the 1964 Civil Rights Act, but the hostility and state-sponsored violence with which these gains were met, particularly in the South, led to a splintering of the movement and to growing anger and militancy. The women's rights movement also gained momentum as many women who had patriotically joined the workforce during the war were no longer willing to accept that their proper place was in the home. Sparked in part by Civil Rights activism and a growing awareness of the ways women were denied full economic and political participation, the second-wave feminist movement that began in the 1960s pushed for equal rights and women's control over their own bodies, most famously with the decriminalization of abortion in the 1973 *Roe v. Wade* decision, and the reconfiguration of the male- and heterosexual-dominated social and political structures that had led not only to gender and racial oppression in the United States but also to ecological destruction, a nuclear arms race, and the globally dominant military industrial complex.

These movements stemmed from more than a sense of injustice; radical social activists were also motivated by awareness of the United States' place in the world, its relationships and responsibilities to other nations, and the broader international shifts taking place due to U.S. global military activity and decolonization. Across Africa, Southeast Asia, and Central and South America, long-colonized peoples were moving toward self-governance through treaty, political negotiation, and violent revolution. The advent of television, which was in 90 percent of U.S. households by 1960 (Spigel 1), meant these national and international events were broadcast into millions of homes every night, rendering them more vividly and personally than ever before. African American activists saw their struggle for equality as connected to the global push for freedom against oppressive political and cultural regimes, and women's rights activists viewed their fight against gendered inequality within the United States as having international implications for peace and nuclear disarmament movements, as well as for the rights of women and children around the world.

The Civil Rights and women's rights movements also helped catalyze the growth of several other domestic movements within the United States. Inspired by the insistence on visibility and the racial pride of the African American Civil Rights and Black Power movements, Asian Americans, Chicana/o and Latina/o Americans, and Native American groups united among themselves to fight for political change, express racial and ethnic pride, embrace their cultural heritages, and promote political, social, and artistic solidarity. Queer women and women of color also began to push back against what they saw as the reproduction of racist, masculinist, and heteronormative values within radical movements, articulating the multiple forms of discrimination to which they were subjected and giving rise to what is now known as intersectional feminism.[2] College campuses across the nation also became centers of protest as leftist students pushed for peace and political change, disaffected with the difference between American rhetoric and reality, continuing racial injustice, and the violence and imperialism of American military interventions worldwide, especially in Vietnam. And after decades of quiet resistance to legal and medical persecution, gays and lesbians began their own campaigns for liberation and equal rights, a movement unofficially inaugurated by the Stonewall Riots in Greenwich Village in June of 1969. All of these movements shaped public discourse in what has become known as the Civil Rights Era in U.S. history.

While protest movements tend to dominate our view of the 1960s and 1970s, conservative political and social currents were just as powerful. Many strongly believed in small government, the power of the unregulated free market, and the moral value of the American system of government. The 1970s in particular were full of economic and political turmoil. President Richard Nixon resigned after a series of embarrassments culminating in the Watergate scandal, the United

States was plagued by stagnation and rampant inflation as domestic manufacturing declined in the face of greater global competition, and U.S. foreign policy led to conflicts with Middle Eastern oil suppliers and significant domestic oil shortages. These years were also marked by violence. Abroad, more than 200,000 U.S. soldiers were killed, wounded, or missing in action in the unpopular and ultimately unwinnable Vietnam War. Within the United States, these years saw riots and race-related violence, National Guard, state, and local police shootings of anti-war and anti-segregation protesters in Orangeburg, South Carolina, at Kent State University in Ohio, and at Jackson State College in Jackson, Mississippi, and multiple assassinations, including African American leaders Martin Luther King, Jr., Malcolm X, and Medgar Evers, President John F. Kennedy and his brother, presidential candidate Robert F. Kennedy, and openly gay San Francisco politician Harvey Milk. These issues increased distrust in established authority and made cultural and political change seem all the more urgent for countercultural activists. But to those who feared the United States was entering a period of moral and political decline, the violence and instability only seemed to confirm that such changes posed a significant threat to the future of the country.

The Cold War ended in 1991 after several years of decreasing tensions and the economic collapse of the U.S.S.R., but the 1980s and 1990s were still marked by significant cultural and political upheaval in the United States. President Ronald Reagan presided over what was ultimately a decrease in the nuclear stockpile, but the United States continued its military action around the world, most notably in the Middle East, and was rocked by a series of terrorist attacks on U.S. soil, the largest of which was the 1995 Oklahoma City bombing, carried out by U.S. citizens retaliating against what they saw as government overregulation of independent militias. From an economic standpoint, conservatives' hopes had seemed to be realized with the election of Reagan, who delivered on his promises to cut taxes, deregulate swaths of industry, and strengthen the military——but the combination of reduced taxes and higher military spending led to the exponential growth of the national debt. The 1990s saw a series of economic swings, from the recession that ended George H.W. Bush's presidency to the bubbles that accompanied the rise of computer technology and heralded the arrival of the Internet and global e-commerce. But this prosperity primarily benefited the wealthiest Americans, and gaps between rich and poor only widened.

For civil rights and human rights activists, this period was marked by both progress and regression. A swell in immigration from Latin America, Mexico, and Asia after the loosening of immigration restrictions in 1990 led to even greater visibility for long-marginalized racial and ethnic minority groups, and affirmative action policies continued to improve access to services and opportunities for many, especially in education. But this period was also marked by sharp anti-immigration public sentiment, directed most prominently at Mexican immigrants, a swell in prison populations (one result of the so-called war on drugs that disproportionately punished African Americans), and high-visibility eruptions of simmering racial tensions across the country after juries failed to convict the police who beat Rodney

King in 1992. While gay, lesbian, bisexual, transgender, and queer Americans gained some political and cultural acceptance as their visibility too increased, they also faced moral vituperation during the HIV/AIDS crisis and the staunch opposition of religious conservatives to the recognition of sexual orientation as a legally protected class deserving of equal rights. Such issues suggested that the gains of civil rights, equality, and diversity initiatives had been less effective than they seemed.

As this brief overview suggests, the period from 1945 to 2000 was tempestuous, characterized by conflict, dislocation, disillusion, and strife; by the expansion of U.S. military, political, and economic influence around the world; by outcries against oppression through revolution and slow gains in freedom and equality against entrenched and often violent resistance; by economic boom and bust and the expansion of class wealth and poverty; and by increasing comforts enabled by new technologies, often accompanied by increasing economic instability. Many scholars have acknowledged how difficult it is to categorize the literature from this period (cf. Ashton "Periodizing"); while there are some distinct movements and schools, the poetry, fiction, and drama of these years is diffuse and sometimes seemingly inchoate, and most writers and their texts exceed the boundaries of any one movement or style. This is particularly true for women writers, many of whom grew less interested in subterfuges, justifications, or excuses and wrote in whatever style, genre, or form they deemed appropriate. Nonetheless, it is possible to trace some broad themes and commonalities among women's writing in this period.

One important set of concerns was linked to the intellectual and theoretical shifts that occurred during these years. The development of postmodern literary and cultural theories had lasting implications for how literature was written and read. Rife with political and social tumult and haunted always by the specter of nuclear destruction, life in the Cold War twentieth century could be profoundly destabilizing and disorienting. This led many writers and intellectuals to question what had long been accepted as true, good, or apparently self-evident, including the relationship between language and truth and the ability of words or symbols to accurately express the chaos of thought, reality, or the individual self. Deconstructionist and poststructuralist theorists like Jacques Derrida and Michel Foucault began in the 1960s to examine the ways language was used to construct meaning and govern society through the production and reproduction of inherently conservative power structures. Feminist theorists such as Adrienne Rich, Judith Butler, and Eve Kosofsky Sedgwick pushed these ideas further, examining how gender and sexual identities are constructed and enforced through language and working to undo the false dichotomies that organized the world into male/female-coded binaries.[3] As literary scholars and writers questioned the underlying assumptions governing language use, literature and criticism grew to be characterized by a deep skepticism of purported coherence. Many writers rejected the unities of realist fiction and lyric poetry as inherently false and sought new ways to express the discontinuities of the age. The diverse literature that came out of this skepticism is often referred to as postmodern, characterized by emphasis on the fragmented and dislocated self, the deconstruction of language and meaning, pastiche, collage, and self-referentiality, parody, irony, absurdity, and the blurring of distinctions between literary genres and forms, high and low culture, and fiction and nonfiction.

At the same time, the study of literature and the structure of universities were undergoing significant and related change. Many writers and poets developed close relationships with universities that established creative writing programs, giving rise to the Master of Fine Arts (MFA) programs and workshops through which poets supported themselves while developing their craft and mentoring young artists. And in the 1950s, various groups began pushing for visibility, recognition, and inclusion in higher education and the study of American literature and history, part of the larger postmodern questioning of the veracity and dependability of a received history dominated by white men. Feminist scholars from diverse racial and ethnic backgrounds were an important part of this movement, and the shape of the American literary canon began to change as they fought to recover long-lost or ignored women writers from across American history and recuperate the literary reputations of women who had been dismissed as derivative, imitative, or historically irrelevant. This push evolved into a redefinition of American literature under the rubrics of multiculturalism and then pluralism, related movements that recognized the heterogeneity of American experience across racial, national, ethnic, class, gender, and sexual identities. By the close of the century, new collections like the *Heath Anthology of American Literature*, which first appeared in 1989, were introducing readers to a host of Native American, African American, Asian American, Chicana, and Latina women writers, as well as to previously excluded Euroamerican women writers, helping to establish women's place in American letters.

Such study was fueled in part by the feminist, gay rights, and cultural nationalist movements of the 1960s and 1970s. An important element of late twentieth-century cultural nationalisms was the recovery of previously disregarded or ignored literary and artistic traditions and the development of new forms of expression that reflected each group's political and cultural goals. The most cohesive of these movements was the Black Arts movement, which developed in the 1960s out of the protest literature of earlier decades and the militant separatism of the Black Power movement. Its goal was to create a new kind of literature that did not imitate Western models but accounted for African and African American heritages and was targeted to black audiences. Asian American, Native American, and Chicano literary movements took inspiration from the Black Arts movement, making concerted attempts to assert literatures that were culturally distinct but still merited a place in the larger field of American literature, and throughout these movements, women writers sought new ways to represent their own roles and experiences as equally valid. These movements were supported by new organizations like the Asian American Writers' Workshop in New York, which united writers from various national backgrounds in a network of mutual support, encouragement, and activism, and small, radical presses like the African American-owned Broadside Press in Detroit and the Feminist Press in New York, which published works by contemporary writers who had difficulty with mainstream publishers and reissued texts by earlier writers such as Zora Neale Hurston and Charlotte Perkins Gilman.

Such efforts contributed to the growing understanding that American literature incorporates a multitude of perspectives, what Jennifer Ashton describes as a move from universalism toward an ever more finely differentiated "particularism" ("Lyric" 524), and the recognition that each of these perspectives allows for a fuller understanding of what it means and has meant to be a resident of the United States.

While women's literature in the second half of the twentieth century sometimes seems to move in several directions simultaneously, it is above all responsive to its cultural moment, a quality that is reflected both formally and thematically. In the early decades of the Cold War, when the government touted the home and family as a form of national defense against Communism, writers such as Sylvia Plath, Anne Sexton, and Mary McCarthy challenged the cultural impetus to secrecy and conformity with texts that laid bare subjects previously considered taboo, including depression, suicide, substance abuse, premarital sex, and infidelity, while writers of so-called women's fiction, including Grace Metalious, Shirley Jackson, and Flannery O'Connor, exposed the fear, oppression, selfishness, and misery that lurked beneath the surfaces of women's domestic and small-town lives. Throughout the realism and naturalism-centered literature of black protest and the radical Black Arts movement, the works of Ann Petry, Gwendolyn Brooks, Lorraine Hansberry, Lucille Clifton, Audre Lorde, June Jordan, and others insisted on the importance of African American women's experiences and challenged the patriarchal and heteronormative power structures of the Civil Rights and Black Power movements. And during a period of global conflict, revolution, and refugee flight, many women writers called attention to American involvement in this upheaval and the connections between international unrest and domestic inequalities, especially as they figured in the experiences of marginalized communities in the United States.

Feminist writers across various literary movements also reflected the critical and intellectual destabilization of the postmodern period as they searched for new ways to express women's experiences outside of the patriarchally and racially inscribed forms of traditional literature. Poets such as Denise Levertov and Adrienne Rich interrogated womanhood, motherhood, and the histories of oppression while embracing to varying degrees the postmodern deconstruction of language, metaphor, and the declarative subject; others played with the limits of literary forms, like Joan Didion's melding of journalism and imaginative writing into New Journalism, or Ursula Le Guin's and Octavia Butler's examinations of gendered and raced power structures and history through science fiction and fantasy. Gloria Anzaldúa and other Chicana writers adopted the metaphor of the U.S.–Mexican borderlands with their mixtures of languages and cultures to express the in-betweenness of being multiethnic, multilingual, and queer. Many women of color, including Maxine Hong Kingston, wrote texts that blended memoir, mythology, fiction, and fantasy in their depictions of marginalized communities, while writers such as Julia Alvarez, Jessica Tarahata Hagedorn, Louise Erdrich, and Toni Morrison contributed generically fluid texts that contextualized the experiences of women of color within American, regional, and global history. While writers like Susan Howe fully embraced avant-garde postmodernism, many others chose instead to incorporate elements of postmodernism into works that drew on the realism and relatively coherent subjectivity of lyric poetry which still dominated mainstream literary productions, engaging with postmodern theoretical concerns in practical ways.

Above all, American women's writing in the second half of the twentieth century was about bearing witness: to traumas ranging in scale from personal to global, to the social, political, and psychological dislocations of the age, and to the human implications of American policies and ideologies. Their writing was an act of testimony, bringing forth unheard voices, unearthing and reclaiming lost or suppressed histories, and affirming the value and power of women's experiences. In texts that were often politically charged and international in aspect and focus, women writers worked to expose and deconstruct unjust power structures, but they also participated in imaginative acts of reconstruction, repeatedly reconfiguring the ways literature is used and understood, recognizing the creative power of language and putting it to work to reshape the world around them.

On the home front: Women writers and Cold War ideology

Secrecy, privacy, and the sanctity of the home were central and linked cultural preoccupations in the first two decades of the Cold War. As women who had gone to work during World War II were encouraged to return to the home, the domestic world was imbued with political significance as the haven of democracy and American values and the properly functioning home and family as the best defense against Communist infiltration. The home was thus a beacon of safety, American freedom, and prosperity that was perpetually vulnerable and in need of protection—a paradox neatly captured in the image of the backyard bomb shelter (May 1–2). At the same time, the primary threat to the safe space of the home—encroaching Communism—was the mechanism through which people's private, political, and sexual histories were made the subject of public inquiry in sensationalized congressional anti-Communist hearings that riveted the nation. Writers and filmmakers were among the high-profile targets of the House Un-American Activities Committee, which subpoenaed individuals suspected of having subversive ties and pressured them to prove their loyalty to the United States by outing Communist friends; those who refused to comply faced social and professional blacklisting and even imprisonment.[4] The privacy that was sacrosanct in the home was thus transmuted in the congressional hearing room into a dirty secret and national security threat deserving of exposure on televisions and newspaper front pages across the country. Debates over whose secrets were whose business continued even after HUAC's power declined in the late 1950s, marked by a series of Supreme Court cases over the use of birth control culminating in the 1965 *Griswold v. Connecticut* decision, which established a legal right to privacy in the home and within the "sacred precincts of marital bedrooms" (Cushman 192); yet the links between secrets, the home, and the moral and political fate of the nation persisted in the American cultural imagination.

Viewed in this context, the frequent characterization of women's fiction and poetry from this period as domestic and apolitical takes on new resonances. As Deborah Nelson notes, the confessional poetry that "reported the conflicts internal to the family and to the self" was sometimes criticized for its supposed triviality and self-absorption in the face of larger national and international conflicts (35), and even the most successful women fiction authors have often been classified as "niche" writers—Flannery O'Connor as a Southern gothicist, Mary McCarthy as a satirist of the New York intellectual scene, and Eudora Welty as a regionalist, for example (Hutner "Modern" 501)—especially when they have dealt with domestic life in a primarily realistic mode. But with the home as the locus of cultural and political anxiety, these domestic texts become sharply political. Writers such as Anne Sexton, Sylvia Plath, and McCarthy contrast popular culture representations of American femininity and domestic life with the far messier realities, revealed in confessional texts that straddle both imaginative literature and autobiography; and realist fiction writers like Grace Metalious, Shirley Jackson, O'Connor, and Joyce Carol Oates explore the vulnerabilities underlying idealized images of American domesticity, locating the home as a "crisis zone" (Vincent 47) characterized by a violence, grotesquery, and depravity that belies its placid exterior. During a time when the concepts of privacy and domestic life were politically and ideologically fraught, women writers resisted secrecy in their texts, examining what Nelson calls the "doubleness of the home" (37) and interrogating Cold War mythologies of gender, family, and the American way of life.

The confessional poetry of the mid-twentieth century is one strand of the lyric mode that has dominated popular American poetry since the mid-twentieth century. It draws from the lyric tradition its emphasis on subjective experience, which critics often read as a reaction against the impersonality of the modernist poetry, but it adds an element of "rawness," exposing taboo subjects such as marital infidelity, divorce, mental illness, prescription drugs and alcohol, suicide, abortion, and the limitations of the messy and inconvenient human body in a direct and apparently artless way (Nelson 34).[5] Ashton observes that confessional poetry's emphasis on subjective expression, its directness, and its controversial examination of subject matter often drawn from the poets' own lives have sometimes led to the "conflation" of the poems' speakers with the voices of the poets themselves ("Lyric" 518), but critics such as Christina Britzolakis have more recently begun to examine the careful construction of such apparent sincerity (6–8). As she and Nelson have argued, confessional poetry asks readers to confront the realities of middle-class domestic life that polite society does not acknowledge while simultaneously "theatricaliz[ing]" the intimacy such confessions create (Nelson 35), making it a medium for questioning both public and private performances of the self.

Though neither embraced the designation, Plath and Sexton are two of confessional poetry's most well-known practitioners; their depictions of domestic life, and particularly kitchen scenes, suggest how the acts of confession staged within their poetry mirror the theatricality of the domestic spaces they are expected to inhabit and the precariousness of the illusions they are expected to maintain. Plath's "Lesbos"

(1962) suggests the artificiality of domestic life with its empty, gossipy performance: "It is all Hollywood, windowless" (3) the poem's speaker says of her kitchen, "Coy paper strips for doors— / Stage curtains, a widow's frizz" (5–6). She gossips with an unknown woman, but "Meanwhile, there's a stink of fat and baby crap. / I'm doped and thick from my last sleeping pill" (33–4), and she eventually grows "silent, hate / Up to my neck, / Thick, thick" (64–6). In the lengthy conversation between the two women, the speaker reveals and acknowledges nothing, papering over her rage with silence and "lies" (91); her performance points to the "enforced silence among and between women" (Nelson 40) and presents an image of the kitchen as a place of stifling misery and blunt "hate" rather than wifely and motherly bliss.

Sexton likewise draws on kitchen imagery in her examinations of domestic performance. In "Self in 1958" (1966), the speaker describes the alienation from self that results from working to meet cultural expectations of domestic womanhood in four carefully rhymed ten-line stanzas. Unmoored from reality, she is a "plaster doll" (2), an "I. Magnin transplant" with "nylon legs, luminous arms / and some advertised clothes" (6, 9–10), placed by an unknown "Someone" in an "all-electric kitchen" (22) and expected to "smile," "shift gears," and "spring the doors open" to reveal only "wholesome disorder," with "no evidence of ruin or fears" (33–5). The poem suggests the strain of maintaining this performance, which involves designer costumes, takes place in a set designed to specification—"all-electric"— and even prescribes the acceptable forms of deviation from the model; it is a home life that is anything but safe, characterized by a lack of agency and the constant fear of exposure. Elsewhere, in the poem Nelson describes as Sexton's poetic manifesto (36), Sexton offers confession as a healthier alternative to this polished facade, defending her choice to publish poems about her time in a mental institution as a means of counteracting the alienation revealed in "Self in 1958." "Not that it was beautiful," she acknowledges of the mental hospital,

> but that I found some order there.
> There ought to be something special
> for someone
> in this kind of hope.
> This is something I would never find
> in a lovelier place, my dear.
> ("For John" 33–9)

For Sexton, there is value in acknowledging and sharing the ugliness; it is the lack of pretension to loveliness that tears down the "invisible veil" of fear that separates people even "sometimes in private, / my kitchen, your kitchen, / my face, your face" (41–4). In this second kitchen image, Sexton suggests that the value of staging confession is its ability to connect people, a performance that joins instead of isolating. The domestic realm does not have to be a trap, but it requires a vulnerability and openness to the unbeautiful that not everyone (including the "John" to whom the poem is addressed) may be able to accept.[6]

The growth of confessional poetry was part of a larger artistic shift toward experiments in personal revelation in the twentieth century that was magnified by the advent of psychotherapy (Nelson 33), and the autobiographical novel was one such development of this confessional move in literature. Plath's *The Bell Jar* (1963) and McCarthy's *The Group* (1963) are two such novels that draw heavily on the authors' own experiences in fictionalized examinations of the traps of social conformity for women viewed, as Catherine Keyser notes, through the lens of conformity to women's magazine culture. In Plath's novel, protagonist Esther Greenwood wins a coveted summer job at a fashion magazine only to find herself, like the speaker in "Self in 1958," deeply alienated by her failure to conform to the magazine's ideal of femininity, as exemplified in photo shoots, luncheons, and her unsatisfying closet full of "uncomfortable, expensive clothes" (2). Comparing a photograph of herself in the magazine supposedly "having a real whirl" at a party with her own much less glamorous memory of the event (2), Esther is confronted by the hollowness of the ideals she helps peddle and the depths of despair such images can mask (Keyser *Playing* 176); it is part of a depression over the limitations of culturally prescribed gender roles that results in Esther's attempted suicide and a stay in a mental hospital that may or may not be ending as the novel closes.

McCarthy's *The Group* also links attempts to conform to social standards with institutionalization in one of its main figures, Kay Strong. McCarthy was known for her sharp satires of New York's intellectual left, part of her larger campaign to puncture the pretensions of various social conformers, as the novel's title suggests. Following the lives of a set of friends after graduation from Vassar, McCarthy links progressive Kay's desire for domestic sophistication acquired through women's magazines, a charming and elegantly designed apartment, and a witty and accomplished husband, with a "self-destructive passivity" (Keyser 175). Kay's passivity is so ingrained that when her pretentious, self-absorbed husband commits her to a mental hospital so he can do as he wishes without her interference, Kay eventually determines to stay there, where she finds other women who "looked completely normal" but were unable to function in the outside world (330); after her release, Kay either falls or jumps to her death from her window at the Vassar Club while, as Keyser points out, one of her classmates reads a magazine (Keyser *Playing* 175). For Kay, as for Esther Greenwood and the women in Sexton and Plath's kitchen poems, the pressures of conformity to a particular standard of glossy domestic femininity exact a terrible toll.

Much of the fiction of the early Cold War decades also troubles the images of safe and cozy family life that found cultural and political purchase during those years. While many post-World War II "readjustment" novels served as a kind of "tranquilize[r]" for the middle class, helping them cope with veterans' trauma and reaffirming their roles in a "coherent, comprehensible society" (Hutner *What* 243), there were also novels like Maritta Wolff's *About Lyddy Thomas* (1947), whose depiction of a woman's abuse, rape, and attempted murder by her veteran husband points to the dehumanizing effects of military training and war and contradicts the "daily tributes to domestic bliss" found in newspapers, television shows, and other mass media outlets (Vincent 46–7). Other women's fiction dealt less explicitly with the repercussions of war but nevertheless undermined the domestic and nationalistic ideology of the age, sometimes by focusing on a particular region. Grace Metalious declared that her scandalous bestseller *Peyton Place* (1956)—a story of incest, rape, illegal abortion, domestic violence, murder, and racism in a seemingly orderly and appealing New Hampshire community—was intended to expose the "peaceful as a postcard picture" of small New England towns, like "turning over a rock with your foot—all kinds of strange things crawl out" (Boyle 1). Many of Shirley Jackson's stories and novels are also set in New England, and they are sometimes suffocatingly domestic; her female characters are often bound to houses and families that are isolated and mysterious, as in *We Have Always Lived in the Castle* (1962), and sometimes malevolent, as in *The Haunting of Hill House* (1959), and the result is psychological disunity and "disintegrat[ion]" (Hattenhauer 3) rather than growth or success. And in what is probably her best-known work, "The Lottery" (1948), in which a small New England town's annual ritual centers on the communal stoning of a townsperson to ensure a good harvest, Jackson points toward the ideological violence that serves as the guarantor of American freedoms and prosperity. While Jackson refused to provide explanations of her work, after her death Jackson's husband described the claustrophobia, anxiety, and violence found in her fiction as part of her intention to provide "a sensitive and faithful anatomy of our times, fitting symbols for our distressing world of the concentration camp and the Bomb" (Hyman viii); like Cold War messaging, Jackson's texts freight domestic and small-town life with global significance, but rather than suggesting them as family refuges or fortresses of American values, she links them with psychological fragmentation and destruction, the sources and amplifiers of the wider world's distress.[7]

Flannery O'Connor similarly examines the violence, danger, and cruelty hiding in plain sight in her short fiction, which is often set in the salt-of-the-earth rural communities of the South. In her darkly comic stories, O'Connor repeatedly presents fractured families; her characters are men and women with thwarted and generally uncommunicable ambitions whose misplaced confidence in their own ideas and abilities leads them to points of crisis. In "Good Country People" (1955), stifled philosopher Joy Hopewell clumps around on an artificial leg and renames herself Hulga, "purely on the basis of its ugly sound" (174), in order to spite her pious, platitudinous mother, who herself despairs of Hulga ever finding a husband. When her mother declares that painfully earnest traveling Bible salesman Manley Pointer is "good country people" (184), Hulga determines to seduce him as a kind of revenge, but her plan backfires when Manley reveals himself to be a con man and steals Hulga's wooden leg, leaving her helpless in a hayloft. And in "The Life You Save May Be Your Own" (1955), widow Lucynell Crater believes she has finally found a husband for her deaf and mentally challenged daughter in one-armed handyman Tom T. Shiftlet, who declares he'd "give a fortune" to have a porch to sit on and watch the sunset every night (54), but on their wedding day Tom drives off with Lucynell's money and car, abandoning his new wife at a roadside diner on the way to Mobile. In both stories, O'Connor presents women who are taken in by hollow platitudes while convinced of their own cunning and are eventually rendered immobile by their own foolishness, which revolves around rituals of courtship, marriage, and family. In depicting what Jon Lance Bacon calls the "invaded pastoral" (8) and more specifically the invasion of disordered homes whose inhabitants are incapable of defense, O'Connor satirizes both the "combination of fright and self-righteousness of many Americans" that sociologist David Riesman found pervasive in Cold War culture (76) and the idea of home, family, and marriage as a kind of personal or national salvation.

Perhaps one of the most compelling images of domestic vulnerability is found in Joyce Carol Oates' frequently anthologized "Where Are You Going, Where Have You Been?" (1966). In this story, originally published in literary magazine *Epoch*, teenager Connie is drawn out of her home against her will by the menacing, seemingly omniscient stranger Arnold Friend, who announces his intentions to "hold you so tight you won't think you have to try to get away or pretend anything because you'll know you can't" (24), while her parents are away at a family barbecue. In the images of her clueless parents, the backyard barbecue, and the suburban home, which Arnold Friend dismisses as a "cardboard box I can knock down any time" (29), Oates portrays the much-mythologized American middle-class home as incapable of offering protection, always permeable by an ineluctable violence. These inversions of the domestic as a space of danger, misery, and emotional and physical violence show Oates' and other women writers' increasing resistance to the gendered ideology of the home. Such domestic images would continue to play a significant role in women's writing as the second-wave feminist and other protest movements gained momentum in the late 1960s.

The emergence of feminist literatures

If collective cultural memories of the 1950s in the United States are dominated by the images of happy suburban conformity exemplified in sitcoms like *Leave It to Beaver*, memories of the 1960s and 1970s are dominated by images of radical departure from and protest against this conformity, more likely to come from news media than scripted television shows. While these images are oversimplifications of their respective times, the shift from one to the other gives a sense of the cultural transitions that were taking place, from glossy to gritty and sometimes chaotic, from a period of relative placidity to one of cultural upheaval. Change was undoubtedly in the air as marginalized groups took inspiration from one another's successes and determined to fight, sometimes literally, for their own freedoms and for human rights worldwide. The movements that arose during these years were often linked to literary experimentation; radical activist writers built on postmodern and deconstructionist ideas about the social and political uses of language to assert linked political and literary identities and experimented with form and genre in the search for new ways to express marginalized identities and viewpoints. Women played important roles in these political and literary movements, most prominently the feminist movement, which went mainstream with the publication of Betty Friedan's *The Feminine Mystique* in 1963 and gained force with the establishment of the National Organization for Women in 1966 and the passage of Title IX legislation in 1972 prohibiting discrimination in education on the basis of sex.[8] There was increasing visibility in these movements for women of color and for queer women, who more openly began to reject what Adrienne Rich would famously term "compulsory heterosexuality" in a 1980 essay ("Compulsory" 23), and for the first time, literatures arose that strove to be distinctly feminist in form and theme as women began to connect their experiences to larger political and social structures under the rallying cry "the personal is political."[9]

However, the mainstream feminist movement was not without conflict. It was largely led by white women such as Friedan and Gloria Steinem, and in spite of the significant contributions of queer women and women of color, for many there was the increasing realization that mainstream feminist initiatives "tended to be driven by and benefit" heterosexual, privileged white women (Ashton "Lyric" 526) and often sacrificed the needs of non-white, non-privileged, and non-heterosexual women to achieve those goals. These concerns were echoed by participants in the other contemporary movements who saw women's concerns repeatedly subordinated to men's.[10] One result was the rise of a range of feminist literatures by women who felt the need to articulate more specific feminist identities at the intersections of race, ethnicity, gender, and sexuality. Working within and in contradistinction to various political and literary movements, women in the 1960s and 1970s began to explore the implications of writing and the use of language as political actions, using their texts not only to "war against the tyrannies of silence," as poet Audre Lorde put it ("Transformation" 41), bringing to light histories and perspectives that had been suppressed or ignored, but also to assert the particularities of women's experiences in increasingly radical ways.

Radicalism and form in feminist poetry

For many women poets in the 1960s and 1970s, formal experimentation was linked to political radicalization stemming from a growing sense of urgency about the need for change. For several years Denise Levertov had experimented with a formally organic lyric style in which the rhythm and melody of each line and stanza grew out of her relationship as poet to the poem's subject; this experimentation took on a new shape in the 1960s and 1970s as Levertov's opposition to involvement in Vietnam and examinations of racial violence pushed her poetry closer to versified prose, influenced by what she jokingly described in one interview as her "ranting and roaring and speech-making" (Moffet 3).[11] Muriel Rukeyser was another feminist poet with a long career who "abandon[ed] formal and rhetorical restraint" during the radicalizing 1960s, "engaging in a looser line of language that is distinctly unpoetic, though full of urgency" as she addresses subjects like women's sexuality and the female body (Sewell 111).

But if any single poet can be said to embody the combination of evolving feminist radicalism and aesthetic experimentation of these decades, it is Adrienne Rich. Rich began her career as a poet in the 1950s but she struggled to continue writing after she married and had children. Her "resentment and dismay" (Martin *Triptych* 179) at the expectation that her career would end when wife- and motherhood began were an important part of Rich's dawning radicalism, which led to political protest, her eventual divorce, and her embrace of lesbianism as an expression of both personal desire and a form of activism. The radicalization of Rich's life, which she described as "the process of going from the conflicts and strife of the unconscious into the sayable, into the actable" (Martin *Triptych* 169), is mirrored in her poetry, which progresses from a formal, controlled style that W.H. Auden described as "neatly and modestly dressed" (11) to an urgent, formally flexible style in lyric poems that frankly interrogate the patriarchal mythologies structuring contemporary life. Rich's collection *Snapshots of a Daughter-in-Law* (1963) marks the moment when she took off the "asbestos gloves" of formalism and propriety (Rich "When We Dead" 40), moving from conservatism to radicalism in style and content as she addresses the personal and career sacrifices expected of women. Her subsequent collections are marked by the growing sense that individual lives are indivisible from their historical contexts and the exploration of the links between the personal and political. *Necessities of Life: Poems, 1962–65* (1966) examines global unrest, including the human costs of the Arab–Israeli and Vietnam wars of the 1960s, and Rich's sequence *Twenty-One Love Poems* (1976) offers an exploration of lesbian sexual desire as a revelation of the "immediacy of political questions in the lives of ordinary women" undertaking the "private negotiations of same-sex love" (Collins 142). And in *The Dream of a Common Language* (1978), Rich moves toward conceptions of a community premised not on masculinist hierarchy or mastery but on "a multilayered conversation or chorus" (Garber 134). Throughout her lengthy career, in both poetry and polemical prose, Rich increasingly "challenge[d] the most fundamental precepts of patriarchy" (Barry 301), including motherhood, domestic ideology, heterosexuality, the military–industrial complex, technological consumerism, and global imperialism. As her life and writing attest, for Rich the feminist poet has a role that is simultaneously personal and public, carrying with it an imaginative and psychological responsibility that is both individual and communal in scope.

While Rich wrote numerous works that have shaped feminist poetry and consciousness, the title poem from *Diving into the Wreck* is emblematic of the overarching themes of her career, reflected in prose such as "When We Dead Awaken: Writing as Re-Vision" (1972), *Of Woman Born: Motherhood as Experience and Institution* (1976), "Compulsory Heterosexuality and Lesbian Experience" (1981), and in so much of her poetry: the stripping away of patriarchal mythologies that have confined women and the process of helping women "re-vision" themselves and a world outside these strictures. "Diving into the Wreck" uses the metaphor of a deep-sea dive to describe the process of excavation necessary to uncover the possibilities buried under the "wreck" patriarchy has made of human civilization. The work is often solitary, the direction is uncharted, and the process is uncomfortable: Jacques

Cousteau's "assiduous team" is nowhere to be found (10), "there is no one / to tell me when the ocean / will begin" (31–3) and the poet's speaker must "learn alone / to turn my body without force," to move in a new way in an unfamiliar substance (41–2). "I came to explore the wreck," she announces as she descends, "the damage that was done / and the treasures that prevail. / ... something more permanent than fish or weed" (52, 55–6, 59–60), but she will not accept prevailing interpretations of what she finds; she wants to know "the wreck and not the story of the wreck / the thing itself and not the myth" (62–3). Once there, the speaker finds what Ashton calls an "abiding androgyny" ("Lyric" 527) in the figures of a mermaid and merman, and it enables further discovery. "I am she: I am he" (77), the speaker reveals,

> We are, I am, you are
> by cowardice or courage
> the one who find our way
> Back to this scene
> Carrying a knife, a camera
> A book of myths
> In which
> Our names do not appear.
> (87–94)

As Sewell suggests, Rich's metaphor of a dive functions as an exploration of the unconscious that ultimately unearths a shared history and way of being that have long been suppressed (112), and the process has brought the speaker to greater awareness, giving her what she needs to "find our way / back" and continue the work. This process is the mapping of what Rich would later call "a whole new psychic geography" ("When We Dead" 35) that can be used to develop a language, imagery, and poetry by and for women and expressive of their experiences and desires.

Rich develops this theme of the process of discovery and coming to consciousness throughout *Diving into the Wreck*, especially in the ten-part poem "The Phenomenology of Anger" (1972). She also points toward this kind of world outside of patriarchal interference when she references the eternal "homesickness for a woman" and a sense of her origins that is the woman's birthright in "Transcendental Etude" (122) and touches on the "pure invention" ("Twenty-One" 13.6) that is possible in a woman-centered, woman-identified civilization (Oktenberg 85). What Rich consistently proposes throughout her six-decade career is a world constantly subject to "re-vision," so that both individuals and communities can move from inchoate unawareness toward a consciousness that enables action, drawing on the power of language to bring about social change.

Poetry is not a luxury: Women in the Black Arts movement

Literature by African American women underwent a process of radicalization in the post-World War II decades that mirrored developments in both second-wave

feminist and Civil Rights movements and found its clearest expression in the Black
Arts movement of the 1960s and 1970s. The realist and protest literature of writers
like Richard Wright, Ralph Ellison, and Ann Petry in the 1940s and 1950s and the
social realist drama of Lorraine Hansberry and others was powered by an under-
current of anger that was yet mingled with hope; by the 1960s it had grown into
the relatively brief but powerful Black Arts movement, described by Larry Neal
as the "aesthetic and spiritual sister of the Black Power concept" (29). Inspired by
the fearless honesty of separatist leaders such as Malcolm X and Stokely Carmichael
and driven by a sense of revolutionary urgency, writers worked to create direct,
politically engaged, emotionally spontaneous, and distinctly African American art
for African American audiences primarily in the form of poetry and drama, whose
forms suited the immediacy and urgency of the movement.[12]

For many, this movement toward a black national literature involved an embrace
of their African roots. Africa had long been dominated by European colonial powers,
but the late 1950s and 1960s saw a wave of revolutions, with seventeen African
nations gaining independence in 1960 alone. Many African Americans saw this
revolutionary fervor as twinned with their own, just as Western colonialism in
Africa and slavery in the Americas were linked; and African American artists saw
in the embrace of African themes, history, and traditions in literature and in daily
life an opportunity to combat the cultural erasure brought about by colonialism
and enslavement. Unlike the Harlem Renaissance and protest writers who had
preceded them, the writers of the Black Arts movement were not interested in
working in Western literary modes or gaining the acclaim of the artistic mainstream. Recognizing that Western artistic achievements were indissoluble from
(and impossible without) Western oppression and exploitation, these writers
looked to revolutionize literary forms and find new modes of expression that took
into account their African cultural heritage. These elements remained important
in African American literature long after the Black Arts movement tapered off in
the mid-1970s.

But women writers who embraced the aims of the Black Arts movement were
also aware that its male leaders primarily envisioned the struggle for equal rights
and black artistic expression as a reclamation of black manhood, which relegated
women to marginal supporting roles or excluded them altogether. The misogynistic and homophobic rhetoric of leaders like Eldridge Cleaver led many women to
create literature that pushed back, building on the work of earlier writers such as
Petry and Hansberry, calling out misogyny within radical African American communities, and articulating woman-centered and non-heteronormative visions of
African American history and culture. Poetry took on a prominent role for women
in this countermovement; as Audre Lorde insisted, "poetry [was] not a luxury" for
women but the means by which "we help give name to the nameless," clearing
the way for substantive action and change ("Poetry" 37).[13] Lorde and many other
women, including Gwendolyn Brooks, Lucille Clifton, June Jordan, and Nikki
Giovanni, drew on their African heritage, their own experiences, and the language
and rhythms of African American life in creating new, experimental literatures

that bore witness to the particular joys, sorrows, and challenges of life for African American women.

While Petry and Hansberry cannot be said to be part of the Black Arts movement, they were two of its forerunners; they wrote key texts in the years leading up to the movement that anticipated many of its concerns, including the search for African heritage, the psychological damage caused by racial oppression, and the experiences of African American women within a social structure that prioritizes the concerns and successes of men. While scholarly considerations of African American fiction from the postwar decades have tended to focus on male writers like Wright, Ellison, and James Baldwin, Petry was one of several women fiction writers from this period, along with Paule Marshall, Gwendolyn Brooks, and others. Petry wrote several stories, three novels, and a series of children's books, and her work functions as an early link between the leftist protest literature of earlier decades and the more radical nationalist literature that would come (Lubin 11). She is best known for her social realist novel *The Street* (1946), which is frequently compared with Wright's *Native Son* (1940) due to its naturalist elements, urban setting, and depiction of psychological and physical violence as an inevitable outcome of racism. With its examination of the damaging effects of the continual objectification and attempted sexual exploitation of its main character, Lutie Johnson, *The Street* is often read as a corrective to the violent misogyny of Wright's novel. But Petry's incorporation of a wide range of literary tropes also places her fiction in conversation with popular culture, noir literature and film, and the horror-tinged examinations of Cold War domestic and small-town life of writers like Jackson, O'Connor, and Metalious.[14] As Bill Mullen and Rachel Peterson note, Petry focuses on the labor of black women's bodies in *The Street* and her subsequent novels, *Country Place* (1947) and *The Narrows* (1953), emphasizing the alienation of African American domestic laborers while also making them visible and bringing their "experiences and knowledge … to the foreground" (R. Peterson 76).[15] Petry's fiction thus testifies to the realities of African American women's lives and counteracts literary silences in ways that link her with the more radical feminist writers who followed her.

Hansberry's *A Raisin in the Sun* (1959) likewise gives significant attention to the realities of African American women's lives. It was the first play by an African American woman produced on Broadway, and it was popular with both critics and the theatergoing public. Hansberry took the play's title from Langston's Hughes' poem "Harlem" (1951); in the play she answers the question posed in the poem's opening line, "What happens to a dream deferred?" ("Harlem" 1) in the story of the Younger family. Walter Younger is an African American man whose dreams of success, wealth, and respect are systematically denied; the play charts his mounting desperation after years of being ignored and unheard, forced to swallow slights and endure poverty. But Hansberry also shows how the same pressures are brought to bear on the women in Walter's life—women whose lives, dreams, and bodies are expected to be sacrificed to assuage Walter's wounded pride and meet broader cultural expectations. Walter's mother, Lena, has spent her life in backbreaking labor as a cleaning woman; she longs to buy a house for the family and send her daughter to medical school with her husband's life insurance money, but Walter demands that she give him the money for a business venture whose dubiousness everyone but Walter can recognize. His sister, Beneatha, is likewise expected to postpone her dream of being a doctor to fund this venture, and to give up her political activism and her interest in her African heritage to marry a rich man; and Walter's wife, Ruth, is repeatedly accused of holding Walter back when she questions the wisdom of his investment, and she faces significant pressure from her husband and mother-in-law when she wants to terminate an unintended pregnancy she knows will lead to deeper poverty. Although the play ends with Walter's regained self-respect and the family's impending move to a suburban house, the fate of the women is ambiguous: Walter's failed investment means Lena must continue working into her old age to help pay the mortgage on the new house, Beneatha's schooling will be postponed, and Ruth is resigned to keeping a baby they can afford now less than ever. While Hansberry was criticized by Amiri Baraka and others for being insufficiently political (Baraka 19–20), *A Raisin in the Sun* offers a vivid depiction of the costs that a cultural focus on the restoration of black manhood as a marker of racial progress can have for women.

If Petry and Hansberry are literary antecedents to the women of the Black Arts movement, Gwendolyn Brooks is a writer whose career bridges the radical formal and ideological transitions of African American literature in the 1960s. Brooks was educated broadly in Western poetic traditions and began writing for publication while still in high school. She found major success early in her career, winning acclaim for her first poetry collection, *A Street in Bronzeville* (1945), and the Pulitzer Prize for her second collection, *Annie Allen* (1949). These collections and her lyrical novel *Maud Martha* (1953) reflect her lifelong commitment to documenting plainly and with a sharp sense of irony the intimate lives and everyday experiences of African American women; they cover such subjects as abortion, sexual desire, religious faith, and the struggle to retain a sense of dignity through the degradations of poverty.

Brooks had long resisted mainstream publishers' attempts to classify her work as "Negro" poems, seeing her subject matter as an "organic" outgrowth of her life and preferring to present African Americans "not as curios but as people" (Brooks 146), but she awakened to black nationalism in the late 1960s after attending a series of conferences with writers including Baraka and Neal. One major shift was Brooks' move away from the major commercial presses she increasingly saw as exploitative; after 1969, she published small, inexpensive volumes of poetry exclusively with smaller black-owned presses such as Broadside Press and Third World Press, a reflection of her commitment to addressing her work to African American audiences and ensuring it was accessible to as many people as possible, regardless of status or education. Brooks' later poetry, including *In the Mecca* (1968), *Riot* (1969), and *The Near-Johannesburg Boy and Other Poems* (1986), reveal the development of her black nationalism and her connections to the African continent. As Annette Debo argues, Brooks' growing identification with Africa, figured in the use of the Kiswahili spelling "Afrika" beginning with *Riot*, reflects her desire to connect her work and her readers with their African heritage and to embrace Afrika as an "appellation for all Blacks fighting racism and imperialism" around the world (169).

The Black Arts movement brought with it a host of women poets and writers who extended black nationalism's trenchant critiques of racial oppression and celebrations of black cultures to include considerations of gender. Margaret Walker drew on the history of militant black resistance to racial oppression, debunking nostalgic depictions of slavery in her 1966 novel *Jubilee* and connecting Nat Turner's rebellion in 1831 with the civil rights and black nationalist movements in her 1970 poetry collection *Prophets for a New Day*, in which she praises Malcolm X for the beauty of his "sand-papering words against our skins" ("For Malcolm X" 10). Poet and essayist June Jordan sought to connect the African American struggle for civil rights with human rights movements around the world, including in Guatemala, Palestine, and across Africa, but she also worked to make such connections closer to home, especially for the women whose lives and ambitions were sharply affected by the violence of racism and misogyny but whom historical narratives tended to ignore: "momma," she writes in "Getting Down to Get Over" (1972), help me / turn the face of history / *to your face*" (91–4). Lucille Clifton speaks plainly about poverty, sexual abuse, and racism in poems that remain defiant celebrations of blackness and femininity, including the appreciation of the black female body and rejection of white standards of beauty in "homage to my hips" and "homage to my hair" (1980); as Cherise A. Pollard notes, Clifton's work is characterized by joy in survival, though it is a joy tempered later in her career by grief and the "need to speak the truth of her entire experience" (22). And poet Nikki Giovanni became an overnight celebrity with her advocacy of violence as the appropriate response to global racial oppression in collections such as *Black Feeling* (1967), *Black Judgment* (1968), and *Re:Creation* (1970). Giovanni's simple, clear language and truncated lines reflect her sense of the urgent need for revolution, as when she replies to a neighbor who asks her to write a rhyming "tree poem" instead of her revolutionary verse,

> maybe i shouldn't write
> at all
> but clean my gun
> and check my kerosene supply
>
> perhaps these are not poetic
> times
> at all
>   ("For Saundra" 24–30)

As even this quick and by no means comprehensive survey reveals, women shared and fought for the goals of the black nationalist movement, but they also insistently pushed back against a masculinist culture that privileged a male-centered view of the beauty and power of blackness.

The writer who most vividly combined the aims of the Black Arts movement with feminist concerns was Audre Lorde, whose embrace of multiple political identities—her "consciousness as a woman, a black lesbian feminist mother lover poet all I am" (*Cancer* 25)—afforded her what she called the "sister outsider" position, allowing her to participate in and critique multiple movements from a space that was both within each movement and on its periphery (R. Byrd 5). These multiple, simultaneously held and shifting positions were the framework for Lorde's arguments for the right of self-determination and her radical critiques of racist, homophobic, misogynistic, and imperialist practices. Lorde believed one key to this self-determination was in learning to separate herself from the ingrained but deceptive Western value systems and to unearth "our own ancient, noneuropean consciousness" ("Poetry" 37), especially the power of feeling and intuition as sources of strength and resistance for women. This position is most clearly articulated in her essay "Poetry Is not a Luxury" (1977), in which Lorde describes the ways Western cultures subordinate feminized feeling to masculinized thought, arguing that "honest explorations" of feelings are essential to meaningful change because only the scarcely imaginable hopes and fears on the "farthest horizons" carry within them the seeds of revolution (37). By disciplining themselves to listen to the "it feels right to me" instinct (37), to trust feelings that cannot yet be fully articulated, and then to give license to the poetic impulse that can translate those feelings into a language that "does not yet exist," women can bring what has before only been possible into the realm of the real (38). Lorde thus theorizes poetry as something that enables women to turn what had long been considered a feminine weakness into a powerful asset for change.

For Lorde, self-expression through poetry offers women an essential means of claiming identity, building community, and resisting oppression. In her collection *The Black Unicorn* (1978), Lorde situates herself and other African American poets as the inheritors of an essential and sustaining African matriarchal tradition in poems such as "A Woman Speaks"; and in "A Litany for Survival," Lorde reminds readers who have been "imprinted with fear" by which "the heavy-footed hoped to silence us" and who are afraid "our words will not be heard / nor welcomed" that remaining silent does nothing to ease the fear, while speaking up is itself an act of defiant power (16, 21, 38–9). "So it is better to speak," she concludes, "remembering / we were never meant to survive" (42–4). Bearing witness, especially through poetry, can help make the invisible visible; it can build connections between the "dark mangled children / [who come] streaming out of the atlas" so that

> Hanoi Angola Guinea-Bissau Mozambique Pnam-Phen
> merged into Bedford-Stuyvesant and Hazelhurst Mississippi
> haunting my New York tenement that terribly bright summer
> while Detroit and Watts and San Francisco were burning
> ("Equinox" 30–5)

Bearing witness can reveal the linked acts of racialized, imperial violence embedded both in foreign war zones and in American neighborhoods. Speaking from a marginalized position and emphasizing difference can also provide the energy needed for change, creating a "fund of necessary polarities between which our creativity can spark" across sexualities, races, genders, and nationalities ("Master's" 111). The recognition of difference can catalyze discussion, understanding, and revolution rather than automatically leading to division, and the embrace of feeling, the inheritance from "the Black mother within each of us" ("Poetry" 38), can set women free. These ideas continued to influence Lorde's poetry and the texts of numerous other women long after the fire of the Black Arts movement subsided.

Cultural nationalism and feminism

Like the linked Black Power and Black Arts movements, the many political campaigns of the Civil Rights era also inspired connected artistic movements, most of which began in the 1960s and persisted over the following decades: among them, the pan-Indian Red Power movement among Native American writers and artists, which celebrated Native traditions and cultures, the Asian American movement, which united writers and artists from several countries under one encompassing label to promote "political solidarity and cultural nationalism" among Americans with Asian heritage (Cheung "Re-Viewing" 2), and the Chicano movement, which sought to combat negative stereotypes and build ethnic pride among Mexican Americans through literary and visual art. In tandem with political efforts and helped by the introduction of new publication venues and community organizations, artists and writers demanded recognition as Americans while also working to assert distinct cultural and artistic identities and traditions—and within each movement, women fought against masculinist assumptions and offered their views on the questions of national and cultural representation and self-expression these literatures examined.

The rise of Native American literary nationalism

The pan-Indian Red Power or American Indian Movement that began in the late 1960s worked to ensure the legal and physical safety of Native Americans, reaffirm Native sovereignty, reclaim Native lands, and provide counter-narratives about the history of Native–U.S. relations through protest, political activism, education initiatives, and the peaceful occupation of sites such as Alcatraz Island and Plymouth Rock. The literature that developed alongside the Red Power movement has sometimes been called the Native American Renaissance, but this is a contested term that ignores more than two hundred years of Native American texts in English, as Craig S. Womack (Creek-Cherokee) points out (16). Nevertheless, there was a marked increase in Native American fiction and poetry during these years, and this literature includes many of the most commonly taught Native American novels today, including N. Scott Momaday's Pulitzer-winning *The House Made of Dawn* (1969), James Welch's *Winter in the Blood* (1974), Gerald Vizenor's *Darkness in Saint Louis Bearheart* (1978), and Leslie Marmon Silko's *Ceremony* (1977).[16] These and the many other texts produced during this period reflect the growing nationalist currents in Native American literature.

Silko (Laguna Pueblo) is the most prominent woman to emerge from this period. While she does not generally identify as a feminist writer and has spoken plainly about her disaffection with mainstream white feminism, the Laguna Pueblo traditions in which she was raised are structured by matriarchy, and many of the most powerful figures in her work and the mythologies that inform it are female;[17] her texts reflect the "wholeness" and lack of gender segregation or rigid divisions of labor in her community (*Conversations* 55), and they emphasize the sustaining continuity of Native traditions, often passed on by women, in the midst of the repeated cultural upheavals of Euroamerican colonialism.[18] Her most well-known novel, *Ceremony*, tells the story of mestizo Laguna Pueblo Tayo, a World War II veteran who returns home after several months in a rehabilitation hospital to find himself "still not at home, ... far away from himself" (Ortiz 258). He and many of his fellow Laguna are distracted by what Silko calls the "witchery" of colonial influences and value systems, and his alienation from himself is only restored through his return to Laguna spiritual practices. Silko's mixture of Laguna chants and songs with prose and the use of white space to indicate pauses and breaks reflect the musicality and rhythms of Laguna oral traditions, emphasizing the role of storytelling and generational cultural transmission in Tayo's process of recovery.

Simon Ortiz describes the continuity of storytelling in Native American cultures as one of the primary acts of "resistance against loss" and identifies *Ceremony* as a "complete example" of the "affirmation of knowledge of source and place and spiritual return" that characterizes Native American nationalist literature (258–9). But the novel has also been criticized by Paula Gunn Allen and others for revealing sacred tribal knowledge (Allen "Special Problems"). *Ceremony* thus raises important questions about ethical conflicts within Native American literary nationalism, but it also demonstrates Native American concerns with the ongoing damage of settler colonialism and the importance of maintaining sustentative Native traditions and rituals in the face of cultural erasure.

Theorizing Asian American literatures and identities

The term Asian American was coined in the late 1960s as a means of generating political and cultural unity among Americans of Asian descent during a period of increased political activism that grew out of civil rights and anti-war protests. The 1965 lifting of Asian immigration restrictions only highlighted Asian Americans' status as the most discriminated-against immigrant group, having historically faced small national quotas, restrictions on the immigration of women and children, and in many cases the denial of citizenship and property ownership after immigration. The internment of Japanese Americans, the history of American colonial activity in Hawaii and the Philippines, and military interventions in Korea, Vietnam, and throughout Asia only reinforced the sense among young Asian American radicals that it was time to push back against popular perceptions of Asian Americans as perpetually foreign, fetishized either as exotic or as the dangerous political enemy (Cheung "Re-Viewing" 5). As Juliana Chang observes, several notable collections of Asian American poetry and literature were published in the following years, produced within the "context [of] the incipient formation of a politicized Asian American collective consciousness" (xx; see also Chiang). These collections, like *Roots: An Asian American Reader* (1971) and *Aiiieeeee! An Anthology of Asian-American Writings* (1974), were part of larger attempts to establish a fully American literary history and tradition which were nevertheless marked by a "sensibility" that was "neither Asian nor white American" but somewhere in between (Chin et al. xxi; see also Kim 88). The editors of *Aiiieeeee!* and other leaders of this cultural movement emphasized it as a fight primarily against the cultural "emasculation" of Asian American men (Cheung "Re-Viewing" 10), prompting many women writers to challenge this narrative in texts that prioritized the experiences of Asian American women, illuminating the questions of loyalty and responsibility that have accompanied women's participation in cultural nationalist literary movements.[19]

Poetry was a vital part of Asian American women's negotiations of cultural nationalism and feminism, grounded in both local and international political contexts. Japanese American poet and community activist Janice Mirikitani's poetry reflects her determination to break generational and cultural silences about subjects such as internment, U.S. involvement in Vietnam, sexual abuse and incest, misogyny, and anti-Asian racism and stereotypes, informed by her childhood experience with internment, her sexual abuse at the hands of her stepfather, her involvement with the radical Third World liberation movement at San Francisco State, and her anti-war and feminist activism. For example, in "Attack the Water" (1978), the speaker describes seeing a newspaper photograph of a "Vietnamese woman / her face etched old / by newsprint/war" and thinking it could have been her grandmother's face, "back then/just after / the camps" (16–18, 5–6), linking the two women, both non-combatants, as equal sufferers under U.S. policies. Mirikitani also helped to establish Asian American literary traditions, working with Third World Communications as the editor of *Aion*, the first Asian American literary magazine, and several anthologies of poetry and other writing, including the Japanese American collection *Ayumi* (1980). Other poets, including Mitsuye Yamada and Jessica Tarahata Hagedorn, likewise published poetry in these years that confronted the lasting legacies of internment, American colonial and military involvement in the Philippines and Vietnam, and the pervasive influence of American consumer culture on Asian American women, especially its images of acceptable female beauty. Like Mirikitani, Yamada's and Hagedorn's poetry reflects their desire to be heard and seen.[20] "They have looked away / From us before," Hagedorn declares in "Fillmore Street Poems: August 1967," "But not again" (41–3).

Of the many texts from women writing in or against culturally nationalist traditions, Maxine Hong Kingston's *The Woman Warrior: Memoirs of a Girlhood Among Ghosts* (1976) did the most to shift Asian American literature toward the mainstream in the 1970s.[21] As Shirley Geok-lin Lim famously described it, *Woman Warrior* is "part biography, part autobiography, part history, part fantasy, part fiction, part myth, and wholly multilayered, multivocal, and organic" (x). Kingston blends reexaminations of Chinese folklore with her experiences as a second-generation American child dealing with generational conflicts, expectations of cultural assimilation, anti-Chinese racism, and misogyny, especially within traditional Chinese culture, in a text that engages in postmodern explorations of narrative authority and subjectivity. Cheung argues that Kingston uses silence in *Woman Warrior* to challenge both masculinist Asian American critics such as Chin who seek to "refute stereotypes by renouncing silence" and mainstream feminists who value "voice and speech indiscriminately" (*Articulate* 1), but the text also "circumvent[s] authoritarian narration," positing silence as a "spur" to "creativity" rather than a sign of stereotypically Asian passivity (*Articulate* 24). In addition, Kingston's melding of fantasy, mythology, and memoir calls attention to the ways the supposed unity of subject implied by a speaking "I" in a text is always part-fantasy (Bow 559–60).

Woman Warrior was the first in a line of Kingston's texts to use generic and formal experimentation to examine political issues, including *China Men* (1980), *Tripmaster Monkey* (1989), and *The Fifth Book of Peace* (2003).[22] With its interrogations of women's oppression within Chinese and Chinese American cultures, *Woman Warrior* countered the emasculation narrative that dominated Asian American literary nationalism in the 1970s, prompting fierce criticism and raising the "gendered loyalty/betrayal complication" that women writers from marginalized groups frequently face (H-H. Chang 15). But its popularity as a memoir, especially compared to Kingston's subsequent novels, also points to broader issues that have troubled Asian American literature, namely the difficulty of finding mainstream success for texts that do not hew to an autobiographical line or tell an ethnographic rags-to-riches assimilation story that reinforces model minority discourse (Cheung "Re-Viewing" 18). Such tensions between reception, public appetites, and literary freedom only underscored the difficulties Asian American writers had in being read as both Asian and American and the importance of their struggle for recognition.

The figure of the mestiza in Chicana literature

Many Chicana women writers in the United States were, like their peers, first moved to radical protest by the Civil Rights, anti-war, and feminist movements in the 1950s and 1960s, as well as by El Movimiento, the Chicano civil rights movement that had developed in the Southwest. But also like their peers, Chicana women had to fight both the Chicano movement that envisioned itself as the patriarchal and fiercely heteronormative la familia and the "white bias" of mainstream feminism (O'Neill 591).[23] This struggle led to the development of a body of literature in the 1970s and 1980s that resists both in its efforts to retain Chicanismo values such as workers' rights, justice for the oppressed of the Third World, the reexamination of history, and the celebration of mixed-race Chicana identities and cultures while also working to locate a distinctly Chicana and queer subjectivity. Writers and theorists such as Cherríe Moraga, Gloria Anzaldúa, and Sheila Ortiz Taylor reconfigured Mexican cultural symbols, mythologies, and spaces in their efforts to articulate a radical feminist vision flexible enough to include people who identify with and can move between a variety of cultural identities and value systems.

For Moraga, Anzaldúa, and many others, the United States–Mexico border-lands became a powerful metaphor for their position as queer Chicana feminists with mixed racial and ethnic backgrounds, articulating the sense of alienation that comes from being both Anglo and Chicana, of "speak[ing] two tongues, one of privilege, one of oppression," along with the warring *"deseo para las mujeres, anhelo para la familia"*[24] (Moraga xiii, x)—the anguish of being between multiple groups and fully accepted by none. Yet the metaphor also offers a compelling image of hybridity as the place where, as Anzaldúa describes it, "the Third World grates against the first and bleeds …, the lifeblood of the two worlds merging to form a third country" (25), with the opportunity to break down the insider/outsider and us/them dualities that the borders of nations, cultures, social movements, and gender identities tend to produce. Anzaldúa calls this Anglo-Chicana-indigenous position "*mestiza* consciousness," which alone has the potential to "break down the subject–object duality that keeps her a prisoner and to show in the flesh and through the images in her work how duality is transcended," leading, it is to be hoped, to "the end of rape, of violence, of war" (102). The borderlands thus becomes a place of linguistic, cultural, and geographical conflict and coexistence, and the mestiza consciousness becomes the process of learning to "'see' the arbitrary nature of all social categories but still take a stand … to exclude while including, to reject while accepting, and to struggle while negotiating," holding these contra-dictions in tension while committing to fight oppression in its "concrete material forms" (Cantú and Hurtado 7).

This theory of literature and Chicana consciousness is manifested in texts that move fluidly and without translation or explanation between languages, genres, and forms, such as *This Bridge Called My Back: Writings by Radical Women of Color* (1981), an "ethnically, racially, and generically mixed" (Sewell 115) anthology of poetry, life writing, and essays highlighting the relationship between its authors' "feminist poli-tic" and their "cultural oppression and heritage" (Moraga and Anzaldúa xxiv); Ortiz Taylor's often neglected lesbian Chicana novel *Faultline* (1982), which presents a queer-inclusive revision of the patriarchal conception of la familia in a patchwork narrative of court testimony and submitted evidence (Rojas); Moraga's revolution-ary collection of essays, memoir, and poetry on Chicana lesbianism, *Loving in the War Years: Lo Que Nunca Pasó por Sus Labios* (1983); and Anzaldúa's *Borderlands / La Frontera: The New Mestiza* (1987), which offers the clearest articulation of the borderlands/mestizaje framework in a combination of poetry, polemic essay, myth, and memoir. These texts helped many women to conceptualize productive and vital spaces for themselves in and across multiple social movements.

Postmodern interventions in genre and form

As writers in the 1960s and 1970s grew progressively radical, they also came to reject earlier formal and generic practices as incapable of adequately expressing contemporary viewpoints. This was particularly true for many feminist writers, who seized on Audre Lorde's proclamation that "the master's tools will never dismantle the master's house" ("Master's" 110) and searched for wholly new forms of expression not bound by male-dominated literary traditions and conventions. Poetry was an apt vehicle for postmodern feminist experimentation, especially the work associated with the movement known as the Language school. Language poetry rejects the "false hierarchy" of poet over reader implied by a single, unified speaking voice (Ashton "Lyric" 521), particularly the overpolished lyric "workshop" poems produced by poets in MFA programs (Perloff 526), opting instead for deconstructed poems that allow reader and poet to cooperate in making meaning. As leading Language poet Lyn Hejinian describes it, this participatory model "rejects the authority of the writer over the reader and, thus, by analogy, the authority implicit in other (social, economic, cultural) hierarchies" (43). Susan Howe is one of many poets who began working in this vein in the 1970s. She is a visual artist who creates layered and disjointed poems from "collage fragments" (Perloff 533), using historical and literary texts to confront what Ming-Qian Ma describes as the two disparate versions of history: the powerful, male-dominated "record of winners" (S. Howe 15) and the "actuality" outside that historic discourse, the version "with which women identify themselves" (Ma 718–19). In breaking down, reformulating, and realigning sentences, words, and even syllables in her visually striking poems, Howe refuses the "dominant systems of meaning, value, and power" (DuPlessis 14), offering her readers the opportunity to reread and reinterpret history in new and provocative ways.

Experimental theater also became an important vehicle for feminist commentary in the 1960s and 1970s. "Collaborative and anti-hierarchical" feminist theater groups such as the Omaha Magic Theater, Split Britches, and At the Foot of the Mountain sprang up across the country, drawing on postmodern and avant-garde rejections of realism, linear plot structure, and "integrated characterization" to create plays that challenged patriarchal and heteronormative power structures (Murphy 361–2). Cuban American playwright María Irene Fornés began writing and directing avant-garde plays primarily with the New York Theater Strategy and other off-off-Broadway groups in the 1960s; her works include the absurdist *Tango Palace* (1964) and her most famous play, the all-female *Fefu and Her Friends* (1977), which examines the isolation, entrapment, and conflicts in the lives of women who struggle with cultural expectations and their lack of self-determination as women (Sofer 444–6). *Fefu* plays with the conventions of realistic theater: it is set in a country house that resembles the settings of many 1930s Broadway plays, but it shifts from a traditional staging to one in which the audience moves as multiple scenes are played simultaneously; it returns to traditional staging at the end only to break sharply from realism with a symbolic act of murder, "offer[ing] an oblique critique of reality" (Cohn 69) with its defiance of the conventions of representation. And Ntozake Shange and Jessica Hagedorn were among a group of poets, playwrights, actors, and dancers with roots in the San Francisco Renaissance who produced individual and collaborative projects. Among these projects are

Hagedorn's mixed-media solo project *Mango Tango* (1978) and Shange's unplotted, minimalist "choreopoem" *For Colored Girls Who Have Considered Suicide / When the Rainbow Is Enuf* (1974), in which seven unnamed African American women explore love, sexual violence, racism, misogyny, and self-expression in twenty interconnected and choreographed poems before coming together to declare in the end, "i found god in myself / & i loved her / i loved her fiercely" (63).[25] Such plays found ways to present women's experiences and stories and affirm their value in distinctly feminist modes outside of the "phallocentric" realistic traditions that dominated mainstream drama (Murphy 362).

Women writers were also working to reveal the constructedness of authority and truth in generically experimental forms of prose that disrupt the immersive reading experience and blur the lines between fiction and nonfiction. Grace Paley's short stories are often disarmingly realistic but nevertheless remind her readers that she is always present as a shaping force. This is perhaps most visible in "A Conversation with my Father" (1974), in which the narrator's dying father asks her to write him a simple story, "just recognizable people and then write down what happened to them next" (161). Her father argues with the narrator's successive versions of the story, but when he is finally, grimly satisfied with its end, the narrator is not. "I'm sorry for her," she confesses of her tragic main character, "I'm not going to leave her in that house crying," and she continues the story (167). In taking apart the pieces of her narrator's story and refusing its ending, Paley highlights the arbitrariness of narrative conventions and the interrelatedness of the fictive world within a story and the circumstances through which that story is produced.

Joan Didion similarly plays with the boundaries of fiction in texts like *Play It as It Lays* (1970), an elliptical novel whose fragmented narrative and suggestive use of space on the page call attention to all that the narrative erases, elides, or otherwise leaves out. Didion was also a prominent figure in the development of New Journalism, a blend of journalistic and imaginative literary techniques in which the writer's voice and experiences become part of the narrative and the journalism "read[s] like a novel," as Tom Wolfe put it in his manifesto (Wolfe 9). In the essays collected in *Slouching Towards Bethlehem* (1968) and *The White Album* (1979), Didion displays her subjectivity in interviews with movie stars, politicians, and homeless teenagers, examinations of true crime, and conflicts over the water supply, relying on her presence within each story as a source of credibility and questioning the claim to objectivity made by traditional journalistic institutions.

Fragmented texts and the rejection of linearity are also characteristics of the feminist science fiction and fantasy that emerged from writers such as Ursula K. Le Guin and Octavia Butler. Le Guin was an epochal figure in this movement, making radical interventions in what had been a male-dominated genre with her breakthrough novels *The Left Hand of Darkness* (1969) and *The Dispossessed* (1974); in the words of Harold Bloom, she elevated science fiction and fantasy "into high literature, for our time" (10). In these novels, both from her Hainish Cycle, Le Guin explores issues of utopia, violence, industrialization, revolution, war, and hierarchies of gender through outsider figures who must learn to exist in radically different societies. Genly Ai in *Left Hand* is a diplomatic visitor to Gethen, an androgynous world in which sexual attributes are changeable and only expressed during periods of high fertility. The novel is structured as a series of dispatches Ai sends to his superiors that intersperse ethnological reports and local myths with Ai's first-person narrative, a dramatic departure from the linear plots of Le Guin's science fiction-writing contemporaries. As Martin Bickman argues, the novel's complex structure accomplishes a merging of form and content as Ai's "story" is told not only through his own narratives but also through "the selection and ordering of everything that appears" (42). *The Dispossessed* employs a more traditional narrative form but moves between past and present on two worlds: the planet Urras, dominated by a patriarchal capitalist system, and its moon, Anarres, populated by exiles determined to establish a utopian, cooperative, and anti-authoritarian society. In the outsider figure of Anarresti physicist Shevek, who must navigate life on Urras as he works to complete his research, Le Guin examines the relationship between capitalism and academia, the limitations of political ideology, the sexual objectification of women, and the possibility of utopia itself, which in Le Guin's figuration is "ambiguous" and ultimately undetermined (Hanson 256). Le Guin's science fiction thus demonstrates both a commitment to and a perpetual skepticism about "ongoing utopian progress" (Hanson 247) and the possibilities for widespread cultural change.

If Le Guin uses imagined future worlds to explore power relationships and political ideologies, Butler intertwines science fiction and fantasy with African and American histories and futures in her examinations of human tendencies toward the domination of the weak by the strong, self-destruction, and survival in the *Patternist* series (1971–1984) and *Kindred* (1979). The *Patternist* series, published non-sequentially and moving in time and space from ancient Egypt to a distant, interplanetary future, presents the secret history of a telepathic species that comes to dominate the rest of the human race after millennia of selective breeding and social and biological engineering. In these and many of her later novels, Butler counteracts the drive toward dominance throughout human history with the literal reconfiguration of human bodies via gene manipulation, mutation, and inter-race and interspecies breeding (Ferreira *passim*), a move mirrored in her creation of hybrid communities that are multigenerational, multiethnic, and multispecies.[26] And in *Kindred*, Butler engages with American history in the story of Dana, a twentieth-century African American woman with a temporal link to her white slave-owning great-grandfather in nineteenth-century Maryland. The increasing fluidity of time and the compromises Dana must make in the past to ensure her survival in the present point to the embedded nature of past and present and the contingency of concepts like history and memory, suggesting that humans move in a "much greater temporal web of action" than we prefer to admit (LaCroix 109). Butler's fiction thus engages with the materials and themes of science fiction and fantasy while participating in what would become a major element of African American literature in coming years: the need for confrontation with the repercussions of history.

Literatures of witness: Moves toward pluralism

By the early 1980s, the work of feminist and cultural nationalist advocates had begun to have a visible effect on the American literary canon, marked by growing recognition from the academy and the reading public of what literary scholar Werner Sollors called "the whole maze of American ethnicity and culture" (6) and the diverse racial and ethnic influences that produced it. Scholars within the academy advocated for greater inclusivity in literature courses, anthologies, and the range of scholarly publications, particularly for the representation of women—including queer women and women of color—and other "silenced voices and abjected bodies in need of valuing and recognition" (Ashton "Lyric" 524; see also Bona and Maini 4–14). There was significant pushback to this pressure. National debates spread across campuses, the halls of government, and even the pages of *Newsweek* and *Time* (Gilbert and Gubar *Masterpiece* xii) over the sanctity or falsity (depending on one's perspective) of the traditional American literary canon. Nevertheless, the mainstream popular and critical recognition of writers such as Maya Angelou, Alice Walker, Toni Morrison, Rita Dove, Louise Erdrich, Amy Tan, Sandra Cisneros, and so many others in the 1980s and 1990s seemed to signal a growing consensus about the diverse character of the past, present, and future of American literature.

Even as cultural nationalist movements were shifting toward an emphasis on the representation of the plurality of American voices as a form of cultural justice, writers were aware of the dangers this emphasis posed, including the rendering of race, ethnicity, and sexuality as exotic cultural commodities and the resulting literature as a form of anthropology (Katrak 195), the unfair pressure of being asked or expected to represent an entire group based on the myth of internal consistency within that group (Mathur 2–5) and, at the root of it all, the assumption of an "irreducible" link between the physical body of a writer, marked by a given gender, sexuality, race, or ethnicity, and their literary expression (Ashton "Lyric" 515). Perhaps as a result, there was a turn in the literature itself toward the exploration of a range of exilic and diasporic identities, particularly in relationship to U.S. colonial and military activities in Asia and throughout the Americas (Cheung "Re-Viewing" 8; O'Neill 594). In the 1980s and 1990s, women writers often explored U.S. and global history, revising existing narratives, extending critiques of U.S. colonialism, imperialism, and global capitalism, and bearing witness to their ongoing effects in the lives of women, men, and children around the world.

Community and history in African American women's writing

The 1970s, 1980s, and 1990s saw the growth of what Hortense Spillers called "the community of black women writing" as a "vivid new fact of national life" (249). In these years, African American women's literature and art gained acceptance as part of the American cultural and academic landscape through the publication of anthologies like Toni Cade Bambara's *The Black Woman* (1970) and Mary Helen

Washington's *Black-Eyed Susans* (1975), the recovery of texts from earlier writers like Nella Larsen and Zora Neale Hurston, the theorization of African American creative practice and influence in texts like Alice Walker's "In Search of Our Mother's Gardens" (1972) and Toni Morrison's *Playing in the Dark: Whiteness and the Literary Imagination* (1992), and the emergence of significant new literary talents including Walker, Morrison, Maya Angelou, Gloria Naylor, Rita Dove, and Anna Deveare Smith. The international recognition for their work, including Dove's two terms as the United States' Poet Laureate (1993–1995) and Morrison's Nobel Prize in literature (1993), reflects the widespread acknowledgment of their importance to American literature. Much of the poetry and prose from these women is concerned with the recuperation of African American histories, addressing what Morrison has called the "national amnesia" around slavery (Angelo 257). In examining the beauty and strength in the everyday life of African American communities alongside the ugly cultural and psychological ramifications of slavery and racism, these writers create alternate histories that testify to the complex and enduring legacies of the American past.

Maya Angelou's long and remarkable career included touring Europe as a dancer, working with Malcolm X and Martin Luther King, writing several volumes of poetry and autobiography, writing, directing, and performing for theater, television, and film, and reading her commemorative poem at the inauguration of President Bill Clinton in 1993. Her early poetry shows her clear inheritance from the Black Arts and feminist movements, seen in the visceral anger of poems like "No No No No" (1971) and in the celebration of the determination, power, and beauty of black women's ability to survive and rise from "the huts of history's shame, ... / Leaving behind nights of terror and fear" to emerge as "the dream and the hope of the slave" in "Still I Rise" (29, 35, 40). In the acclaimed first book of her autobiography, *I Know Why the Caged Bird Sings* (1970), Angelou employs her characteristic frankness, humor, and vernacular rhythms in relating her childhood in a small Arkansas town, St. Louis, and San Francisco in the 1930s and 1940s. Her young life holds many harrowing experiences, most significantly her rape at eight years old, the resulting trial, and the murder of her rapist by her uncles, but through it all Angelou emphasizes the community of African American women who support her and teach her how to go on, particularly her grandmother Annie Henderson and their aristocratic neighbor, Mrs. Flowers. What comes through in all of Angelou's texts is the enormity and power of her will, her sense that, as she put it in one interview, "You may encounter many defeats but you must not be defeated" (Tate "Maya" 154).

Alice Walker's texts also attest to both the trauma and violence in African American women's lives and the legacies of dignity, resilience, and joy they pass on to one another. Walker practices what she has called womanism, an alternative to feminism that draws on African American vernacular language and the traditional strength, creativity, and spirituality of African American women, and her stories, poetry, essays, and novels often examine the lives of those most frequently overlooked: the rural, poor, and sometimes barely literate women who hold their families and communities together.[27] Her landmark essay "In Search of Our Mothers' Gardens" explores the artistic legacies found in the gardens, quilts, and cooking of the generations of African American women denied more traditional forms of creative expression, a theme given more humorous treatment in her frequently anthologized story "Everyday Use" (1973). And in her controversial and celebrated Pulitzer-winning novel *The Color Purple* (1982), Walker examines the incest, domestic violence, and psychological abuse inflicted on protagonist Celie by the men in her life and the healing and wholeness found in Celie's enduring friendship and love affair with blues singer Shug Avery. In more recent years, Walker has focused on environmental and international human rights activism in poetry collections like *Horses Make a Landscape Look More Beautiful* (1986), her novel about female genital mutilation, *Possessing the Secret of Joy* (1992), and her many essays and interviews.[28] Her clear, straightforward prose and willingness to confront difficult subjects with grace, humor, and passion have made her one of the leading voices in contemporary American literature.

Past and present in the work of Toni Morrison

Toni Morrison's insistence on confronting the uglinesses of the past and the power of her rich, original voice have made her one of the most significant American writers living today. She was born in Lorain, Ohio, a center of abolitionist activity in the nineteenth century, and attended integrated schools throughout her young life. After earning degrees in English and classics and teaching literature at Texas Southern and Howard universities, Morrison worked as an editor at Random House and published texts by prominent African American writers, including Toni Cade Bambara, Lucille Clifton, and June Jordan, as well as *The Black Book* (1970), a scrapbook of African American folk history. She published her first novel, *The Bluest Eye*, in 1970, and has since written ten more novels in addition to significant works of literary criticism and theory, short stories, essays, a play, and several children's books. Her first major acclaim came with *Song of Solomon* in 1978, and the publication of *Beloved* in 1984 moved her to "the forefront of American letters" and established her as a leading voice in the debates about "what could or should be included in historical accounts of slavery and emancipation" (N. Peterson 463). Her winning of the Nobel Prize in 1993, her teaching career at universities throughout the Northeast, and her subsequent novels, lectures, and essays have cemented her reputation as a respected public intellectual and a writer of lasting importance.

Morrison's novels are most often set in the past and frankly confront the histories of slavery and racism in the United States, but they also work to construct African American histories and cultural identities, depicting the richness of daily life in African American communities and her characters' efforts to construct "a clean-lined definite self" (Morrison *Song* 184) in the multigenerational wake of the "core cultural trauma of slavery" (Schreiber 1). They often involve elements of magical realism and are layered with allusions to Greek mythology, the Bible, Western literature, African lore, and African American creative traditions, echoing the kind of "classical, mythological archetypal stories" that used to be transmitted orally from generation to generation (Morrison "Rootedness" 340) and helping to create a specifically African American cultural mythology. In their explorations of African American communities across U.S. history, Morrison's novels emphasize the eternal and inescapable presentness of the past, and they model through the narrative construction of cultural histories and identities a means of transcending the legacies of trauma.

Morrison's novels blend Western literature, classics, and African lore in their constructions of African American cultural mythologies. Perhaps most notably, *Song of Solomon* mimics Homer's *The Odyssey* in the quest of its main character, Milkman Dead, to trace the history of his great-grandfather Solomon, who according to family legend escaped slavery by flying back to Africa, leaving his wife and family behind. Milkman follows a series of clues found in the fragmented oral traditions that have constituted so much of African American history, including songs, nursery rhymes, stories, memories, and jokes. As Milkman traces these clues through his family and community, including his aunt Pilate, a mystical wood-dweller who guides him when he seems to have lost his way and who ultimately gives her life to save him, he moves from a self-centered, materialistic, linear orientation to a community-centered orientation that acknowledges the continual return of the past in the form of familial and cultural inheritance; as Valerie Smith suggests, this shift allows him to "burst the bonds of the Western, individualistic conception of self [and accept] in its place the richness and complexity of a collective sense of identity" (283). And in constructing a familial history that relies on a syncretistic "mixture of cosmologies" (Wilentz 156) and exists entirely outside of traditional means, Milkman offers a compelling alternative to dominant Western modes of knowledge- and meaning-making that affirms the validity of African American experiences.

Like Walker and others of her contemporaries, Morrison focuses not on the interracial clashes that preoccupied earlier writers but on the violence, misogyny, rape, and internalized racism within African American communities, the hidden echoes and most damaging effects of centuries of slavery and institutionalized racism. *The Bluest Eye* (1970) pursues this subject through its protagonist, Pecola Breedlove, a young African American girl who prays for blonde hair and blue eyes. In her foreword to a recent edition Morrison describes the novel as an exploration of "how something as grotesque as the demonization of an entire race could take root inside the most delicate member of society: a child; the most vulnerable member: a female" (*Bluest* xi). And in *Sula* (1973) and *Jazz* (1991) Morrison presents characters who must deal with a "weakened family structure, modeled on separation, loss, abandonment, and faulty attachment" (Schreiber 92), the psychic inheritance of the children and families subject to the constant threat of orphanhood and separation under slavery. In both novels, the formation of "sisterhoods" allows the main characters to talk about their trauma and "thus begin the process of healing" (N. Peterson 472). Within these mutually supportive African American communities, Morrison's characters find the most painful and persistent consequences of slavery and the means to overcome them.

Morrison's most striking exploration of the legacies of slavery is found in *Beloved*. It is set in rural Ohio during the Reconstruction period and tells the story of Sethe, who escaped slavery in Kentucky with all of her children but one—a two-year-old daughter known only as Beloved. Over the course of the novel, which moves freely between past and present, the reader learns that Sethe slit Beloved's throat to protect her from being returned to slavery, but Beloved comes back to Sethe first as a vengeful supernatural presence and then as a silent, demanding woman whose presence threatens to destroy Sethe and her relationships with her surviving daughter, Denver, and her lover, Paul D. In addition to its biblical and mythical resonances, *Beloved* draws on the traditions of nineteenth-century slave narratives and the challenges to conceptions of justice, morality, and motherhood found in the texts of Harriet Jacobs, Harriet Wilson, and many others. The novel juxtaposes the rape, violence, and torture Sethe and other characters experienced under slavery with Sethe's decision to kill Beloved so she can "put my babies where they'd be safe" (*Beloved* 193); in this way, Morrison exposes as fictional the concept of impartial justice in a legal system that sanctions one kind of violence and forbids the other (MacPherson 546) and demonstrates with devastating effect the ways slavery and racism twisted the concepts of justice and moral responsibility. More than this, *Beloved*'s world is haunted by those who have been betrayed and destroyed and by the traumas of the United States' past, from the "Redmen's Presence" in a deserted building left over from "back when they thought the land was theirs" (*Beloved* 29) to the child murdered by her own mother. Morrison suggests that these traumas may be ultimately inescapable, but they must be confronted before they lead to even greater destruction.

Morrison has always been unapologetic about her desire to write chiefly for African American audiences; in a series of interviews promoting the release of her most recent novel, *God Help the Child* (2015), she reaffirmed this desire to present "African-American culture and people—good, bad, indifferent, whatever," but always for black audiences, "without the white gaze" (Ghansah n. pag.) or "the white critic [to] sit on your shoulder and approve it" (Hoby n. pag.). It is not an antagonistic stance, but one which demonstrates Morrison's lifelong investments in building cultural and literary traditions anyone can appreciate but that are first and foremost *for* African Americans; in countering the centuries-old American precedent of freely appropriating African American artistic, aesthetic, and linguistic innovations while attempting to erase African Americans themselves; and finally, in acknowledging the persistent legacies of slavery and white supremacy in the United States while refusing to accept that such realities are all we have.

Latina literatures in the multicultural age

U.S. Latina literature went mainstream in the 1980s, led by Chicana writer Sandra Cisneros. Her first novel, *The House on Mango Street* (1984), and her 1991 collection, *Woman Hollering Creek and Other Stories*, were the first texts by a Mexican American woman published by mainstream presses, and their popularity helped create space for many other women writers with Cuban, Puerto Rican, Dominican, Mexican, and other Latin American heritages. These literatures often examine culturally specific histories and traditions that share a broader concern with the representation of disparaged, ignored, and oppressed communities, especially women, within the context of "US military and economic control of the hemisphere" (O'Neill 596). Many Latina writers have embraced the concept of mestizaje advanced by earlier Chicana writers as a way to "reconcile the multiple, often conflicting allegiances" of diasporic peoples (O'Neill 593), recognizing mestizaje's blend of African, European, and indigenous cultures, languages, and identities, deeply inflected by U.S. economic, military, and political activity in the Americas throughout the nineteenth and twentieth centuries, as a uniquely Latin American quality. Throughout the 1980s and 1990s, Latina women wrote mestiza texts that often reimagined personal, national, and transnational Latin American histories, bringing the stories of the disempowered to light and examining the ongoing effects of U.S. influence and interference in Latin America.

Sandra Cisneros' texts are layered, multilingual mixtures of poetry and prose that explore how women's identities are constructed amid fluid and overlapping cultures, languages, chronologies, and geographical spaces. She accomplishes this in part through reconfiguring U.S. and Mexican cultural icons, including American Barbie dolls in "Barbie Q" and Mexican icons the Virgin of Guadalupe in "Little Miracles, Kept Promises" and La Gritona in "Woman Hollering Creek" (1991).[29] Cisneros also employs fragmented narratives in her short stories and as the structuring principle of *Mango Street*, a novel told in a series of vignettes about growing up in a poor Mexican American Chicago neighborhood in the 1960s; As Lois Parkinson Zamora argues, this fragmentation "undercut[s] rationalist notions of progressive history" but still allows Cisneros' female narrators to "oversee the fragments of their own histories and the histories of their cultures" (157). And in her epic historical novel *Caramelo* (2002), Cisneros rewrites popular U.S. narratives of the Mexican Revolution through the figure of Celaya, a Mexican American woman who processes her adult identity through exploration of her family history and her own homesickness as an exile from a country "that doesn't exist any more" (434).

Latina writers from other cultural traditions have also explored themes of exilic and diasporic identity in their chronologically fluid texts. Cuban American writers Cristina García and Achy Obejas explore the strangeness of being exiles with "symbolic value" (O'Neill 598) as refugees from Castro's Cuba during the Cold War and the combination of alienation and nostalgia that results from Cuba's political isolation from the United States.[30] The mother–daughter writing team of Rosario and Aurora Levins Morales portray their lives as women in New York's Puerto Rican communities in their prose–poetry volume *Getting Home Alive* (1986), in which they locate themselves as mestiza women at a cultural "crossroads," the daughters of the many indigenous, African, and European women who "*have kept it all going* / All the civilizations erected on their backs" ("Ending Poem" 42, 4, 36–7)—yet this multiplied heritage does not leave them broken but "*whole,*" "*made*" by history and complete as they are (44, 46). And Dominican American writer Julia Alvarez examines the "trauma of exile" (O'Neill 595) in New York for the four daughters of a father whose role in a failed CIA-backed coup of the Trujillo regime forces them to leave their homeland in *How the García Girls Lost Their Accents* (1991) and its sequel, *Yo!* (1997). The work of these women emphasizes the commitment of Latina writers to reexamining the linked and perpetually relevant histories of individuals and cultures across the Americas.

Asian American women writers and the literary marketplace

Kingston's *Woman Warrior* opened new avenues for Asian American women writers in mainstream literature, but its frequent classification as an autobiography despite its formal and structural experimentation highlighted a salient difficulty for Asian American writers: the literary marketplace's longstanding interest in their texts primarily as representational, ethnographic texts rather than as works of literature.[31] The publication of Amy Tan's blockbuster novels *The Joy Luck Club* (1989) and *The Kitchen God's Wife* (1991) and the dozens of similar mother–daughter narratives that followed fed into this cultural preoccupation.[32] Asian American writers have examined the tension between maintaining cultural values and assimilating into the dominant culture through the lens of intergenerational conflict in enough numbers to make the second-generation bildungsroman a "master narrative" in Asian American literature (Lowe *Immigrant* 63). The rise of "mother–daughter romances" in the 1980s and 1990s offered a corrective to the "abjected Asian mother" figure found in earlier masculinist texts (Chu "Bildung" 410), establishing daughters as symbols of the United States' potential and mothers as, among other things, "witnesses and victims of a backward, oppressive, ahistorical culture; as feminist tricksters and critics of American Orientalism; and as the empowering sources for Asian American feminist consciousness" (Chu *Assimilating* 22). But while these texts may have drawn readers' focus toward Asian American women's struggles with acculturation and diasporic identity, they also contributed to the cultural preoccupation with Asian American literature as sociology. Sau-ling Wong reads *The Joy Luck Club* as a participant in "quasi-ethnographic Orientalist discourse on China and the Chinese" ("Sugar" 184), and Christopher Douglas sees texts like Tan's as works that reinforce Asian American marginalization because the "cultural confusion" of Tan's protagonists helps white readers confirm the relative clarity of their own positions in American society (Douglas 119; see also Gunew 53). Further, they run the risk of fetishizing Asian American women's suffering under "semi-feudal gender codes" and fostering an uncritical acceptance of the United States as the site of "women's progressive advancement" (Bow 564).[33]

At the same time that mother–daughter narratives surged in popularity, other Asian American writers were moving away from the emphasis on national identity and toward what Aiwah Ong has termed "flexible citizenship," a rubric that allows for examinations of multinational capitalism, migration, and the persistent effects of military, cultural, and economic imperialism across time and space for diasporic communities. Genny Lim's plays *Paper Angels* (1978) and *Bitter Cane* (1989) portray the experiences of poor Chinese immigrants held in San Francisco's notorious Angel Island facility in the early twentieth century and the exploitation of Chinese laborers by American sugar plantation owners in late nineteenth-century Hawai'i; Lim uses these settings to explore how the "history of oppression of Chinese in the United States" affects present and future generations of Chinese Americans, to bear witness to "where we've been as a people" in order to effect social change (Houston 158). More experimental writers such as Theresa Hak Kyung Cha and Jessica Hagedorn also revisit U.S. "colonial and neocolonial influences in Asian countries" (Chu "Bildung" 408), offering alternate versions of Euroamerican coming-of-age stories that challenge the coherence and linearity of U.S. narratives of history and immigrant assimilation. Cha's *Dictée* (1982) is a fragmented text made up of images, maps, letters, diagrams, language exercises, poems, and prose narratives in English, French, Greek, Korean, Latin, and Chinese that examines the narrator's childhood in Korea under Japanese colonial rule, her French Catholic education, and her adulthood as a Korean American immigrant. Lisa Lowe argues that *Dictée*'s refusal to adhere to conventions of fiction or even any particular interpretive critical theory reflects its rejection of clear-cut national identity, the fixity of time or location, and U.S. narratives of immigrant assimilation as progress toward wholeness ("Unfaithful" 36–8). And Hagedorn's temporally fluid *Dogeaters* (1989) examines the devastating legacies of Spanish and U.S. colonial activity in the Philippines through several figures, including beauty queen Daisy Avila and queer mestizo DJ Joey Sands, engaging both U.S. colonialism's "instilling [of] a U.S. cultural orientation" (Tolentino 270) through movies, music, and consumer products, and the possibilities for anti-colonial resistance. In texts like these, Asian American women writers have imagined formal and aesthetic modes of resistance to dominant historical and cultural narratives about race, gender, and global power.

The expansion of Native American literatures

The publication of Ojibwe writer Louise Erdrich's first novel, *Love Medicine* (1984), and its subsequent national acclaim marked a significant point in the production and popular reception of literatures by Native American women, which continued to grow in the 1980s and 1990s. The roles of women in Native American communities were fruitfully explored by Native scholars such as Paula Gunn Allen (Laguna Pueblo). Writers such as Joy Harjo (Muscogee Creek), Janet Campbell Hale (Coeur d'Alene), Anna Lee Walters (Pawnee/Otoe-Missouria), Linda Hogan (Chickasaw), Susan Power (Standing Rock Sioux), and Carole La Favor (Ojibwe) joined Erdrich in publishing fiction and poetry that examines broader themes of land, kinship and community, sovereignty, exile, survival, and the relationships between Native American women and the U.S. government institutions that regulate Native land, women's bodies, and historical narratives about colonialism and its results (J. Byrd 24–5). Native American women's writing at the close of the twentieth century is part of the much longer Native tradition of a "literature of resistance to colonialism" (Warrior 30), challenging Euroamerican conceptions of history and literature and revising accepted American narratives of colonialism, linearity, and progress through explorations of tribal cultures and histories and the "reimagining of decolonial futures" (J. Byrd 13).

While Erdrich has written poetry, nonfiction, and children's literature, her most significant body of work is the set of interrelated but non-chronological novels and stories following the lives of three families on the Turtle Mountain Indian Reservation in North Dakota: *Love Medicine, The Beet Queen* (1986), *Tracks* (1988), and *The Bingo Palace* (1994).[34] These narratives explore the change, loss, and cultural conflicts across the history of Ojibwe interaction with Euroamericans, and they are marked by fluidities: the mingling of ancestors, mythical figures, humans, and all the "other-than-human" members of the community (Gross 49); shifts between various points of view; and the movements between past and present within and across the novels, which combine to "make divergent versions of a single event possible" (Silberman 106). The alinear chronological and narrative structures of Erdrich's texts are tied to what Craig Howe (Lakota) describes as a specifically indigenous form of history relying not on sequential time but on relationships between "landscapes, waterscapes, and skyscapes," the events that occurred there, and the "particular person or being" who was there (162). This approach allows Erdrich to develop a complex depiction of the adaptive, protective, and sometimes destructive ways individuals and communities respond to and survive what Lawrence W. Gross has called the "Anishinaabe apocalypse" (49). The weblike, alinear connections between her texts also resist conclusiveness, suggesting the perpetual possibility of regeneration for characters and communities in the tribal histories she constructs.

Joy Harjo's poetry similarly reexamines tribal histories and asserts the role of art in the construction of individual and communal identity amid the violence of colonialism. Since 1975 she has published several collections that often combine photographs and visual imagery with prose and poetry that incorporate myths, chants, storytelling, and autobiography. The first part of her 1991 collection *In Mad Love and War* testifies to the violence, dislocation, and fragmentation of life under U.S. colonialism, while the second part examines the possibilities for transcendence through acceptance of the "ultimate laws of paradox and continual change" (Ullman 182). In her poem "A Postcolonial Tale" (1996), Harjo demonstrates the political and artistic ethos that informs her work; she first draws on Iroquois traditions in describing colonization as being "stolen" by a "whiteman / who pretends to own the earth and the sky" and then falling from his back through the sky, but then she reminds readers that stories and songs "are like humans who when they laugh are indestructible" (5–6, 18), that the act of creation is a potent form of resistance and a means of "disrupt[ing] the violences of colonization" (J. Byrd 26) which will exist as long as Native Americans are under colonial rule.

While few today would argue with the need to broaden the understanding of American literature beyond the select group of white men and women considered worthy at the mid-century, many readers, writers, and scholars are nonetheless troubled by multiculturalism's focus on the representation of identity-based groups, which tends to "circumscribe" expectations about the value, content, and purpose of these literatures as well as the "range and force of [their] cultural and aesthetic innovations" (Bow 558). While visibility for underrepresented and marginalized groups has significant cultural and political value, the difference that marks Native American or African American or queer literatures for categorization can also function in markets, in universities, and in readers' minds as a form of discipline, a boundary not to be exceeded. What's more, the continual drive toward particularities based on race, gender, sexuality, religion, region, and economic class requires either ever "finer instruments of differentiation" (Ashton "Lyric" 524) or categories so broad as to be practically "incoherent" (Bow 563). But for all the problems posed by the pluralistic emphasis on representation, the diversity and complexity of late twentieth-century literature underscores the multiplication of women writers that occurred in the five decades between the end of World War II and the close of the millennium. The field of American women's writing was transformed during these years even as the study of American literature itself was being radically reconfigured, and as American literature itself was being redefined.

Notes

1 There is significant debate about the dates of the Vietnam War, also known as the Second Indochina War. U.S. troops were stationed in Vietnam and Southeast Asia throughout the 1950s, and a recent three-volume history puts the start of the war in 1945, when Truman accepted the French reoccupation of Vietnam, which triggered the First Indochina War (Gibbons I: vii). The U.S. government officially identifies the start of the war as November 1, 1955, the date when the Vietnam-specific U.S. Military Assistance Advisory Group was established. The first battle between the Viet Cong and the South Vietnamese army took place on September 26, 1959, and the first major increase in U.S. military forces in Vietnam occurred in 1961.
2 The term intersectional feminism was coined by Kimberle Crenshaw in her landmark article "Demarginalizing the Intersections of Race and Sex" (1989), but its philosophical origins can be traced much farther back, into the nineteenth century. In its broadest definition, intersectional theory holds that individuals are subject to multiple interacting and interdependent forms of oppression based on their points of identification with various regimes of social, cultural, and biological categorization, including gender, race, ethnicity, religion, ability, socioeconomic status, and sexual orientation.
3 See Butler's *Gender Trouble* (1990) and *Bodies That Matter* (1993) and Sedgwick's *The Epistemology of the Closet* (1990).
4 For a detailed account of congressional anti-Communist activity, see Ellen Schrecker's *Many Are the Crimes: McCarthyism in America*.
5 M.L. Rosenthal first used the term "confessional" to describe the poetry of Robert Lowell, Plath, Sexton, and John Berryman in a 1959 review of Lowell's work ("Poetry as Confession"). Confessional poetry wasn't an organized movement or school, but Plath, Sexton, and other poets commonly considered as confessional writers took classes with Lowell at Boston University and Harvard, and many of them knew each other and corresponded. See Nelson 31–2 for more.
6 The poem was addressed to Sexton's poetry teacher, John Holmes, who thought Sexton's poetry was too revealing. See Fields 258.
7 As Darryl Hattenhauer notes, the relationship between Jackson and her husband was a complicated, tempestuous, and dangerously codependent one (15–27). Hyman had

significant control over Jackson's marketing and public image, and his commentary on Jackson's work should be read as his heavily invested view rather than Jackson's own. However, it still offers insight into the way the person closest to Jackson, and perhaps Jackson herself, thought of her work.

 8 While gender is now the preferred term in discussions of identity rather than sex, which limits identification to a biological male/female binary, sex was the term used in Title IX and other legislation until only recently.

 9 This slogan was in wide use across several movements in the 1960s, but its prominent association with the feminist movement seems to have begun with Carol Hanisch's 1969 essay with the same title, which was published in the collection *Notes from the Second Year: Women's Liberation: Major Writings of the Radical Feminists* (edited by Shulamith Firestone and Anne Koedt). For more, see D. Smith 153 n.41.

10 Transgender activist Sylvia Rivera is one notable example: she was a regular patron of the Stonewall Inn and an important part of the Stonewall Uprising and the gay rights movement that grew out of it, but she split from the movements in the 1970s when they decided to drop protections for trans individuals from their initiatives. See Michael Bronski's obituary of Rivera for more. Another is Betty Friedan's decision to exclude the lesbian organization Daughters of Bilitis as a sponsor from the First Congress to Unite Women in 1969 out of concern that the causes of the feminist movement would be endangered by too close a link with lesbianism. See Jay 137–46 for one account of lesbian conflicts with the National Organization for Women and mainstream feminists.

11 Levertov's later work, such as *To Stay Alive* (1971), juxtaposed lyric poetry with letters and snippets of other prose documents. For detailed analysis of Levertov's radical and stylistic shift, see Mersmann's *Out of the Vietnam Vortex: A Study of Poets and Poetry Against the War* 77–112.

12 The Black Arts movement was clearly defined with a specific set of goals; Neal articulated these goals in an article for *The Drama Review* in 1968 calling for "nationalistic" literature with a "separate symbolism, mythology, critique, and iconology" that would help lead to a "radical reordering of the western cultural aesthetic" (29).

13 This position has much in common with Rich's depiction of poetry as a process of exploring the unconscious; Rich and Lorde were close friends, colleagues, and collaborators, and their work is often in conversation in this way. See their joint "Interview: Audre Lorde and Adrienne Rich," included in Lorde's *Sister Outsider*, and Lisa L. Moore's "Sister Arts."

14 See Keith Clark's *The Radical Fiction of Ann Petry* for readings of the elements of horror, terror, and monstrousness in various of Petry's novels and stories; see also the collection edited by Lubin, which examines the variety of Petry's work and her relationship to the political left in the early Cold War decades.

15 Mullen gives a Marxist reading of *The Street*, examining the social relations that structure the fetishization of black women's labor, while Peterson looks at the roles domestic servants play in Petry's novels as invisible and yet intimately involved members of elite white households.

16 As Womack notes, between 1970 and 1990 Native Americans published more than 2,000 books, but these four novels, along with Louise Erdrich's *Love Medicine* (1984), still receive the most scholarly attention and classroom time; Womack suggests that a shift away from these novels would involve a pedagogical recalibration, one that would broaden Native American literary study beyond "recovery, ethnography, homecoming, retribalization, and oral tradition modes" (17).

17 Silko comments on her complicated relationship with mainstream white feminism in *Conversations* 26, 28, and 142, and on the ways her matriarchally inflected upbringing affects her perspective on gender in 2–3, 75–6, and 140–2.

18 See for example the end of "Lullaby" (1981), in which elderly woman Ayah, out at night in a snowstorm with nowhere to go, sings her husband to sleep with "the only song she knew to sing for babies," one that had been sung by her grandmother and her mother before her, ending with the words,

> *We are together always*
> *We are together always*
> *There never was a time*
> *when this*
> *was not so.*
> (Silko "Lullaby" 51)

19 For more on challenges to women's loyalty in articulating criticisms of cultural nationalist movements, see Velia Garcia 200.
20 See for example Hagedorn's selections in Rexroth, and Yamada's *Camp Notes and Other Poems* (1976).
21 As Sau-ling Cynthia Wong notes, *Woman Warrior* was preceded by Chuang Hua's *Crossings* (1968), a high-modernist text that explores the "deracination" of its Chinese American protagonist Fourth Jane, and Hualing Nieh's *Mulberry and Peach* (1976), the story of a refugee woman who wanders across the United States; it was originally published in Chinese and only republished in English in 1981 ("Chinese" 49–50).
22 Kingston has repeatedly noted that *Woman Warrior* and *China Men* are meant to be read together, providing a balance between depictions of men and women in Chinese American culture; see Sabine for a reading of the two texts together. In addition, *Tripmaster Monkey* has been described as a "sharp-edged, Marvel-style comic book about an imagined sixties-style carnival of American literary production" (Mackin 513), and Hsiao-hung Chang's "Gender Crossing" looks at the ways *Tripmaster Monkey* works to destabilize a series of binaries that include "male/female, ethnicity/gender, and racism/sexism" and presents gender as "both a *product* and a *process*" (15). And see E. San Juan, Jr. for an examination of the ways *The Fifth Book of Peace* is a "hybrid testimony conflating fiction and history" (182).
23 The Chicano movement of the 1970s and 1980s was largely hostile to gay and lesbian perspectives, and many queer writers found that the nascent Chicano literary canon did not have room for the articulation of queer sexual identities (Rojas). Moraga suggested that it was this hostility that kept her from political activism in the 1960s and early 1970s, insisting that "I would have been murdered in El Movimiento—light-skinned, unable to speak Spanish well enough to hang; miserably attracted to women and fighting it; and constantly questioning all authority, including men's" (104). For more on the concept of la familia, see Blackwell.
24 Desire for women, yearning for family (our translation).
25 The San Francisco Renaissance was a leftist literary movement in the 1950s and 1960s most commonly linked to the romantic and radical traditions of the Beats. See Davidson "San Francisco" for a review of the movement and 74–5 for a discussion of Hagedorn's and Shange's connections to it.
26 See also Johns' "Becoming Medusa: Octavia Butler's *Lilith's Brood* and Sociobiology."
27 See Walker's definition of womanism in *In Search of Our Mothers' Gardens* xi–xii.
28 As Thadious M. Davis argues, Walker is "the exemplar par excellence of the southern writer evolving over the course of an active career into a writer of the Global South" (*Southscapes* 337); see Davis' chapter on Walker in *Southscapes* 335–74.
29 As O'Neill and others have noted, many Chicana writers, including Anzaldúa, Alma Villanueva, and Lorna Dee Cervantes, reexamine and seek to reclaim female icons in Mexican culture, which include the Virgin of Guadalupe, La Malinche, and La Llorona (also called La Gritona). See O'Neill 591–3 and 605 n.4.
30 See García's *Dreaming in Cuban* (1992) and Obejas' *We Came All the Way from Cuba So You Could Dress Like This?* (1994), *Memory Mambo* (1996), and *Days of Awe* (2001).
31 See for example Cheung "Re-Viewing" 17ff. and Bow 559.
32 Other examples include Denise Chong's *The Concubine's Daughter* (1994), Kyoko Mori's *The Dream of Water* (1995), Helie Lee's *Still Life with Rice: A Young American Woman*

Discovers the Life and Legacy of Her Korean Grandmother (1996), and Adeline Yen Mah's *Falling Leaves: The Memoir of an Unwanted Chinese Daughter* (1997).

33 Bharati Mukherjee's novels, while not strictly concerned with mother–daughter relationships, have faced the same criticism; see for example Cheung "Re-Viewing" 12.

34 Erdrich's novels are often compared to William Faulkner's Yoknapatawpha novels, which similarly explore a "fictional terrain, a coherently populated geography" (Owens 54), and Erdrich cites Faulkner as a key influence on her work (Weaver 55–6).

CODA

The literatures of the twenty-first century

It is difficult to discuss women's writing from the first fifteen years of the twenty-first century with any real clarity. It isn't just that women are writing more kinds of texts in an uncountable variety of genres and formats and in greater numbers than they ever have before (although they are). But more than this, we are sharply aware of the benefits of hindsight in discussing literature and history. With the distance afforded by time, the patterns of earlier periods seem to emerge clearly—accompanied always by the great temptation to project the present backward, seeing past events and trends as the inevitable precursors to the present. But looking at literature and world events in real time, it is easier to be aware of the ways that they pull away from coherence. It is only in our active constructions of the stories of past and present that they begin to hold together in any meaningful way, but we must still keep in mind that even such meanings are constantly subject to revision. It is not just the historical and cultural moment of the production of a given text that guides interpretation, but also the moment of its reception, and overlap between the two can sometimes muddy the waters. Given this slipperiness, rather than attempting to impose coherence on recent literatures we would like to offer some reflections on the events of the last several years and their effects on writing, literature, and publishing for women in the United States.

The first fifteen years of the twenty-first century have been momentous ones for the United States. The Al-Qaeda-sponsored terrorist attacks of September 11, 2001, in which nearly 3,000 people died, sent the nation into mourning and have dramatically affected political and cultural discourse in the years since, so that a freedom/enemies-of-freedom binary is once again one of the primary frameworks through which life in the United States and the nation's relationship to the world are construed. In the midst of this global political instability, the United States was at the center of a massive economic recession from 2007 to 2009, spurred by its financial and subprime lending crises, and from which it still struggles to recover. There have also been significant cultural shifts in the United States as LGBTQ groups have won major legal battles, including the repeal of the Don't Ask, Don't Tell military policy, the inclusion of sexual orientation as a protected class in various federal, state, and local laws, and, most recently, the Supreme Court's *Obergefell v. Hodges* decision, which found anti-gay marriage laws to be unconstitutional; these victories have been met with legal and social pushback from religious conservatives who fear encroachment on their freedoms of religion, but these dissenters are a shrinking (if vocal) minority in a population whose views on gay rights have shifted dramatically in the last few decades. And the United States elected its first African American president in 2008, leading some to proclaim that the United States had entered a post-racial era—but the disproportionate incarceration of African Americans, a seemingly unending spate of high-profile murders of unarmed African American men, women, and children by police officers and civilians, and the reluctance of local and state governments to prosecute their killers in the last several years have proven otherwise.[1] These events have crystallized for many Americans the significant and persistent cultural tensions in the United States and have made civil rights one of the defining issues of the period. And throughout and across all of these events, the expansion of the Internet and information technologies has revolutionized the ways people communicate, do business, socialize, and conduct their everyday lives in ways that seemed unimaginable only a few years ago, making the world feel like a much smaller, busier, and sometimes noisier place. All of these changes have affected the production and consumption of literature in subtle and not-so-subtle ways.

By far, the development of the Internet and various digital technologies is the change with the most profound impact on women writers. While the Internet had been in existence for decades and in relatively wide use since the late 1990s, in the last ten to fifteen years it has become ubiquitous, an essential part of the daily lives of the billions of people who rely on various digital technologies for communication, news, information, and research, photograph and document storage, personal banking, entertainment, directions, and a host of other applications, for many people supplanting earlier methods and technologies almost entirely (encyclopedias, Thomas Guide neighborhood maps, and answering machines immediately come to mind). Increasingly portable devices, from desktop computers to laptops to tablets, smartphones, and now wearable technology such as smartwatches, have made it possible to share information immediately with people from all over the world, revolutionizing the ways we conceive of the exchange of ideas. These cultural shifts have radically altered the acts of writing, reading, and distributing literature in ways that are still being realized.

The rise of digital publishing media has led to the restructuring of publishing-related industries as the ease, speed, and relative cheapness of digital publishing have significantly expanded the literary marketplace. Every existing major print periodical has of necessity developed an Internet counterpart, offering print content online and often publishing additional web-only content, and some former print publications have gone exclusively digital in their efforts to remain viable and competitive. The Internet has also made it possible for thousands of new web-primary or web-only publications to establish themselves and build reader-ships: online arts and culture magazines like *Guernica* and the *Los Angeles Review of Books*, poetry and fiction journals like *Blackbird* and *Fwriction*, feminist news and culture sites like *The Toast, Jezebel,* and *xoJane,* and numerous other ven-ues with every imaginable focus and concentration have sprung up, creating many more opportunities for writers to publish their works. Free blogging sites such as Wordpress, Blogger, and Tumblr have also made it possible for anyone with an Internet connection to make their writing available to a global pub-lic, building millions of interlinked mini-communities of readers and writers, and fan fiction sites offer devotees of various books, series, and characters the opportunity to share their own revisions and expansions of other writers' texts, creating an entirely new body of literature. And while the high cost of print publishing and the difficulties of predicting sales in rapidly changing markets has meant that many major publishers are less willing to take risks on unproven or out-of-the-mainstream writers, ebook technologies, self-publishing programs, social media networks, and online retail platforms have made it possible for writ-ers to produce, market, distribute, and sell their books without the imprimatur of a publishing house, or with the help of one of the many specialized small presses that have arisen as a result. While the availability of these technologies has meant a much greater variance in the quality of available books, it has also been especially beneficial for writers who tend to be marginalized by mainstream publishing houses—among whom women make up a significant number—and for writers who want greater artistic freedom or more control over the way their texts are marketed. The surging popularity of audiobooks and portable, digital audio technologies have also helped to make greater numbers of books accessible to people with visual impairments or reading difficulties. The reliance of these new media on various costly technologies, such as smartphones, ereaders, and tablets, not to mention Internet access, means that low-income writers and read-ers still face a disadvantage, although public libraries have been relatively quick to adapt and continue to be valuable community resources, loaning not only ebooks and audiobooks but also the technologies needed to access them. In general, the growth of digital media has had a democratizing effect, creating more options for both writers and readers.

These changes in the publishing world have also transformed the job of being a writer in the twenty-first century. Social media platforms and websites like Twitter, Tumblr, Facebook, Goodreads, and Reddit's Ask Me Anything forums have become spaces where readers can interact directly with even the most famous of writers and writers can interact with each other, a means of building reading and writing communities that also doubles as free or low-cost marketing for the writer and her work. The result is often a mix of the personal and professional as writers find their own ways of negotiating this highly visible new authorship. *New York Times*-bestselling author Roxane Gay is one of the more successful writers in this regard. Gay teaches creative writing at Purdue University, writes for a number of web and print publications, founded the online-print hybrid *Pank Magazine*, and ran *The Butter*, a vertical of *The Toast* that published original essays, fiction, and other content related to race, body image, popular culture, feminism, and a number of other subjects. Her debut novel *An Untamed State* and essay collection *Bad Feminist* were both released in 2014 to widespread acclaim. On Twitter and Tumblr, Gay mixes links to her articles, the websites she runs, and upcoming events with posts that are by turns silly, serious, funny, mundane, confessional, and deeply personal. She responds regularly to both fans and critics, answers questions about her work and the writing profession, offers advice, and even, if the mood strikes her, plays matchmaker for willing participants. But there are also subjects on which Gay maintains her privacy, like her current romantic relationship, and points beyond which she will not engage with aggressive, argumentative, and bigoted people. She is frank, too, about the challenges and hazards of the social media environment and its real-life emotional consequences, the joys, pains, and discomforts of talking to and being talked about so publicly by people who are effectively strangers. In these social media interactions Gay and her fellow women writers are modeling new and compelling ways for women to inhabit public social, creative, and intellectual spaces.

But this new kind of writer–reader relationship also can create an illusion of intimacy, blurring the boundaries between writers' public and private lives and sometimes posing a threat, especially for women writers. Writers must deal with the complicated mixtures of readers' expectations of availability and writers' sense of obligation to their readers that arises somewhat naturally from this situation, but there are also more pointed challenges. Public social media interactions can quickly spread beyond the initial participants and lead to disagreements that grow ugly, or a small but vociferous minority can become demanding, aggressive, and even violent if they are unhappy with a particular development. The result for many women writers, especially those who push back against criticism or take strong positions, is what young adult author Cassandra Clare has described as a "constant stream of hate, threats and insults" (Bell n. pag.), as well as stalking, the public revelation of personal information such as home addresses, and sometimes actual physical violence. In a recent interview with MTV News, Clare and fellow young adult author Maggie Stiefvater linked this hostility in part to the general public perception that women should be accommodating and pleasing, "always nice, always nurturing, never aggressive," and too modest to "[acknowledge their] hard work or success," and that any deviation from this model makes them inhuman "monsters" undeserving of kindness or decency (Bell n. pag.). The result is that many women writers, including Clare, have fled social media altogether, at least for a time, as they figure out how to maintain their safety and peace of mind while participating in these vital, passionate, and rapidly expanding online literary communities.

The technological and social changes of the last several years have also opened up new subject matters, new genres of literature, and new ways of thinking about the world and what constitutes literature. During a period in which the United States has been engaged in a series of wars against amorphous and sometimes difficult to define enemies, all grouped under what the Bush administration rather abstractly termed the "War on Terror," the subjects of war, combat, and military service have proven to be resonant ones. Many writers continue to explore the experiences of "the women who wait," those for whom "the war begins when the husbands, sons, lovers, and brothers return"—or do not (M. Ryan 43). Some frame their stories through the lenses of earlier wars, as Marian Palaia does in her examination of a woman haunted by her brother's disappearance in Vietnam in *The Given World* (2015), while others reference more current conflicts, as Siobhan Fallon does in her short story collection *You Know When the Men Are Gone* (2009). Countless other women link up in online networks made up entirely of military spouse bloggers who share their experiences, offer advice, and commiserate or celebrate in turn. As Jonathan Vincent points out, the combination of terrorism, new weapons and communications technologies, and the twenty-four hour news cycle have threatened to "subsume the entire human environment within a topography of potential war crisis" (48) so that even the most unsuspecting or private spaces may become war zones without a moment's notice, but these women reveal the ways in which for many women, war has always been and continues to be carried out on intimate ground.

But increased military activity around the world and shifts in U.S. military policy, including the removal of the restriction on women serving in combat positions in 2013, have also led to a marked rise in the number of military memoirs by women, and greater recognition for women's war writing.[2] The 2008 anthology *Powder: Writing by Women in the Ranks, from Vietnam to Iraq* collects poems and essays from women with active military service. In addition, as Kayla Williams has pointed out, many women have published fiction and nonfiction based on their war experiences in recent years, including Shoshana Johnson's memoir of her time as a prisoner of war, *I'm Still Standing* (2010), Jane Blair's account of her service as a Marine officer during the invasion of Iraq, *Hesitation Kills* (2011), Katey Schulz's collection of short stories, *Flashes of War* (2013), and Williams' own memoirs, *Love My Rifle More than You* (2005) and *Plenty of Time When We Get Home* (2015). There are also many self-published books, including transgender former Navy Seal Kristin Beck's account of her transition, *Warrior Princess* (2013), and legions of essays, poems, and other works published on less formal media such as blogs and websites. Women's increased access to military service raises important questions for many feminists who desire equality and yet oppose the military–industrial complex, or for whom U.S. military imperialism and its liberation of supposedly benighted peoples under regimes that are oppressive to women runs counter to their belief in the right of everyone to self-determination. These are questions for which there are no simple answers, and which offer new challenges to conceptualizations of feminism and progress.

The last several years have also seen increasing acceptance of a wider variety of literary forms and genres as worthy of scholarly and critical consideration. In what should by now be a familiar pattern to readers of this book, the popular works that are sometimes pejoratively called genre fiction—romance, chick lit, science fiction and fantasy, mystery/thriller, young adult, and other similar categories—have historically been dismissed by the literary establishment as formulaic, trite, and unserious; unsurprisingly, there is often a gender dimension to this criticism, in which the literature is either marginalized as exclusively feminine (as with romance, chick lit, and young adult literature) or perceived as predominantly and inherently masculine (as with science fiction and fantasy), categorizations that further diminish women's contributions to these genres.[3] But recent years have seen greater recognition that these literatures speak to their cultural moments and shape ongoing conversations about gender identity, race, the economy, cultural values and anxieties, and a host of other subjects in valid and important ways.[4] Romance novels have been reconsidered for their affirmations of female sexualities and desire, and writers such as Victoria Dahl and Feminista Jones are part of a growing group of what have been termed feminist romance writers. Young adult literature has also gone mainstream—and far beyond its original younger audiences—in the wake of J.K. Rowling's massive success with the Harry Potter series: the sparkly vampires and beefcakey werewolves of Stephenie Meyer's *Twilight Saga* have exploded the market for supernatural romance and fantasy; Suzanne Collins' *Hunger Games* trilogy and its teenaged heroine, Katniss Everdeen, have paved the way for a wave of female-centered dystopian fiction, including Marissa Meyer's beautifully imaginative reworkings of fairy tales in *The Lunar Chronicles*; many other women, including Malinda Lo, Jacqueline Woodson, Maureen Johnson, Christina Diaz Gonzalez, and Nnedi Okorafor, are also writing novels that explore the agonies and ecstasies of young adulthood through historical, supernatural, speculative, and realistic frameworks. And as Stephanie Foote has argued, mass-market mystery novels by and featuring women are the descendants of nineteenth-century regional fiction, documenting how women "become members of a place and help to regulate it and imagine its futures" and relying for their outcomes on women's local knowledge (306); notable examples are Chelsea Cain's Archie Sheridan and Gretchen Lowell series, set in Portland, Oregon, Judith Van Gieson's Claire Reynier series, set in New Mexico, and Dana Stabenow's Kate Shugak series, set in Alaska.

Perhaps most interestingly, visual formats such as comics and graphic novels have emerged as important new discursive spaces, both in terms of mainstream popularity and academic inquiry. Alison Bechdel's graphic memoir *Fun Home: A Family Tragicomic* (2006), which depicts Bechdel's young life in rural Pennsylvania, her process of self-discovery and lesbian coming out in college, and her complicated relationship with her closeted gay father, was a *New York Times* bestseller and is widely taught at colleges and universities. And in the midst of a comic book resurgence powered in part by Hollywood's recent commitment to blockbuster superhero movies, women writers, artists, and characters are steadily growing in numbers, thanks in large part to the hard work of many advocates pushing for greater inclusivity in a field that has been dominated by men since its inception. The Internet has made it possible for thousands of new webcomics by women to find readers; and mainstream comics publishers like Marvel have begun shifting their focuses to better reflect the diversity of their readerships, revamping the Ms. Marvel series to introduce the first Pakistani American and Muslim superhero, Kamala Khan, in 2014 (written by G. Willow Wilson and drawn by Adrian Alphona) and hiring more women writers, like Kelley Sue DeConnick, to develop projects like the new Captain Marvel series. The growing representation of women across these visual–textual genres opens up new dimensions in conversations about participation and representation, and the expansion of literary study to accommodate these new genres and formats is shifting scholarly conversations about what constitutes literature, how such frameworks are determined, and the terms of evaluation in provocative ways.

These changes have also made it more difficult to talk about literature in terms of national traditions as ideas, texts, and people move more freely and rapidly around the world than has ever before been possible. This transnational quality emerges clearly in literature from writers who explore the subjects of movement and connection between and among nations and peoples. Jhumpa Lahiri's stories and novels frequently feature cultural confrontations between Americans and people of Indian descent in both the United States and India. Her most recent novel, *The Lowland* (2014), tells the stories of two brothers who grow up in turbulent 1960s Calcutta before one, Subhash, moves to the United States for graduate school and the other, Udayan, becomes part of a radical political movement that eventually leads to his death. Lahiri's layered and echoing narrative suggests the resonances between New England and Calcutta landscapes, the brothers' life and career trajectories, and varying versions of the same events as it probes questions of kinship, difference, and destiny around the globe. Ruth Ozeki's *A Tale for the Time Being* (2014) blurs national and literary boundaries even further, imagining the central text with which it is preoccupied, the mysterious diary of Japanese teenager Nao, as an object that floats on the Pacific Ocean between nations and writers just as Ozeki's narrative floats between past and present, living and dead, and various potential and coexisting realities. These texts and the many others that deal with similar themes and subjects, as much as the ready availability of texts from writers around the world, suggest the ways that national boundaries are becoming less salient categories of literary discussion.

For all the ways that women's writing has changed in the last several years, there are still fundamental continuities. Many of the greatest writers of the last several decades have continued to produce work that responds to its social, political, and technological moment even as it reflects the arcs of their much longer careers, including Toni Morrison, Joan Didion, Maxine Hong Kingston, and Louise Erdrich. Poets continue to engage fruitfully with questions of subjectivity and the possibilities of self-expression through language, in many cases through experimentation with the often-challenged lyric form. Some, like Rae Armantrout, offer poems that initially seem like straightforward lyrics but which "upon on the slightest examination rapidly provoke a sort of vertigo effect as element after element begins to spin wildly toward more radical (and, often enough, sinister) possibilities" (Silliman ix), revealing the instability and inbuilt assumptions behind readers' interpretations of words, images, and other symbols. Others, like Claudia Rankine, have embraced the lyric title while carrying on a "quarrel within form about form," publishing volumes such as *Don't Let Me Be Lonely: An American Lyric* (2004) and *Citizen: An American Lyric* (2014) that fuse "documentary" with "lyric procedural" in detailed analyses of the role of race in contemporary life (Chiasson n. pag.). In their work, these writers extend ongoing literary and cultural conversations in new and challenging ways.

   Faith, spirituality, and doubt also continue to be subjects that inspire writers and readers, as they have done since the earliest days of European colonization in North America. While it is religious extremists who attract the most head-lines in the post-9/11 era, there are millions of women in the United States who find strength, spiritual nourishment, and moral and ethical grounding in religious faith, even as they experience doubt or question various doctrines and practices. Many writers have used their texts to reexamine or revise their own spiritual traditions. Marilynne Robinson has been one of the most prominent writers working in this vein. Her acclaimed *Gilead* novels, which she acknowl-edges she wrote as a corrective to misconceptions of American Calvinism, offer meditative explorations of faith, family, doubt, and the nature of joy in the lives of elderly Congregationalist pastor John Ames, his mysterious wife, Lila, and the neighboring Boughton family in mid-twentieth century Gilead, Iowa.[5] And Dara Horn has taken for the subjects of her four novels various points in Jewish history, not "romanticiz[ing] the Jewish past," as some of her Jewish American contemporaries do, but examining the "interlocking strands" of Jewish past and present in explorations of human agency and the working of the will of God in human lives (Austerlitz n. pag.). The Internet has also been a particularly fruitful area for religious discussion, offering formal and informal spaces for women to explore issues of faith, find likeminded believers, and build virtual faith com-munities around the world. The blog project *Feminism and Religion*, founded in 2011 by feminist theologians Xochitl Alvizo, Gina Messina Dysert, Caroline Kline, and Cynthie Garrity-Bond, publishes writing from women in a broad range of spiritual traditions who explore how faith and feminism can be mutu-ally affirming practices; but there are also countless individual blogs and websites with anywhere from a handful to hundreds of thousands of readers written by women recounting their own journeys through faith and doubt, the modern-day equivalent of the centuries-old tradition of spiritual autobiography being typed out day by day.

   The range of opportunities now available to women writers and the ostensible lack of restriction on their output have led some critics to suggest that women writers have effectively arrived at last. In the introduction to her hefty 2009 history of American women writers, *A Jury of Her Peers*, Elaine Showalter recalls the trajectory of women's writing she first described in *A Literature of Their Own* (1977), in which women's writing developed across history from a "feminine" period, involving the imitation of existing traditions, through a "feminist" period, during which it protested against these traditions, to a "female" mode, which involved "self-discovery" and aesthetic development; Showalter concluded by suggesting that women had finally reached the fourth stage, the "seamless participation in the literary mainstream" that she now termed "free" (xvii). But while women do have the freedom to choose what to write and how to write it, something unimaginable to Anne Bradstreet in 1650 or even to Anne Sexton in 1950, it's clear that in terms of power and equal opportunity, women still have a long way to go. VIDA: Women in Literary Arts is a research organization that tracks the presence of women as writers, reviewers, and the subjects of review in top-tier literary publications such as *The New Yorker*, the *New York Times Review of Books*, and the *Paris Review*, as well as smaller literary magazines, and calls these publications to accountability. Their annual VIDA Counts (beginning in 2009) have revealed the sometimes significant gender disparities that are the norm across literary publishing (in 2013, for example, the VIDA Count found that only 23 percent of *McSweeney's* content was produced by and/or was about women); the numbers for women of color and queer women are more difficult to measure, but evidence suggests they are more dismal still.[6] Studies in drama reveal similar disparities. In 2002, Susan Jonas and Suzanne Bennett found that only 17 percent of plays produced at not-for-profit theaters were written by women, and only 8 percent of the plays on Broadway, and in 2009, Emily Glassberg Sands found that only 18 percent of the plays produced by theaters with more than 99 seats were written by women (Murphy 365).

Successive years of VIDA Counts do demonstrate the progress that has resulted from count-related publicity and the efforts of some publications in response (to give *McSweeney's* their due, in 2014 their representation of women improved to 48 percent), but they also highlight the pervasive, often unconscious acceptance of literary hierarchies that privilege the work of men and the persistent, not insignificant effort required to overcome such internalized biases.[7] What's more, as Leslie Bow and others have pointed out, representation and visibility are important but are not in and of themselves indications of equality or justice (571). The struggle is well underway, but it is not over—and it too is likely to evolve as the terms of our conversations about gender evolve. In 2015, we can see that accepted categories of gender identity are opening up and becoming more fluid, and the concept of women's writing will likely itself become more fluid as a result or perhaps even grow obsolete, replaced by some more apt terminology. It is not only the trends and patterns of current literatures that continually shift around us in real time, but also the ways these literatures are connected to the movements of the wider world within which they are created. We can make observations and hazard some speculations about the course of twenty-first century literatures and women's participation in them, but it will be the challenge of the next generation of scholars to help us better see their paths.

By way of conclusion, we would like to offer an arresting image found during the course of research for this project: in the margins of the library's copy of *Loving in the War Years*, a reader had written back to Cherríe Moraga, scrawling a freeform poem into the blank space around Moraga's words. Moraga's collection is about the agonies of choosing between living openly as a lesbian and being accepted by her family and the broader Mexican American community. For Moraga, the book represents that choice, the releasing of something that must be expressed for her own survival, but which she acknowledges her family will never be able to read. Its publication is an assertion of identity that brings with it both freedom and great personal risk. We can only speculate about the intentions of the person who responded to Moraga's poem. It's not difficult to imagine that it was Moraga's courage which in turn created a space for someone to express what might likewise have been inexpressible elsewhere, but it's just as possible that this reader was irresistibly drawn to challenge or rebut something in the poem. This is the enduring legacy of the many women whose lives and words fill the pages of this book, that they have opened new spaces where their readers have been able either to locate themselves and build connections with others, finding coalition and camaraderie where they thought there had been none, or to discover intellectual, artistic, or spiritual provocations that spur debate and sharpen counterargument, leading in either case to the possibility of greater understanding. This, at last, is what American women writers have offered to their readers, and will continue to offer: the presentation, the challenge, and the invitation for their readers to join the conversation.

Notes

1 While police targeting of and violence against African Americans and other marginalized groups has been a problem for some time, a national conversation around the lawful use of lethal force by both police and civilians has arisen in the last several years, sparked by the shooting of seventeen-year-old Trayvon Martin in 2012 and the subsequent killings of several unarmed African American women, men, and children by police officers throughout the United States. *The Guardian* keeps a record of the number of people killed by U.S. law enforcement officers each year; in the end of July 2015, this number stood at 638 ("The Counted").

2 Women have been allowed to enlist in the U.S. military since the 1970s, when the draft ended. The numbers of women in all branches increased significantly throughout the 1980s and has not seen any significant increases or decreases since then (see the report prepared by the National Center for Veterans Affairs Analysis and Statistics 3).

3 See, for example, Monica M. Clark's account of a 2013 appearance by bestselling author Nicholas Sparks—a writer of romance by everyone's estimate but his own—at which he insisted that he does not write romance or chick lit but "love tragedies," a genre at which women just haven't happened to be as successful as men ("Nicholas Sparks").

4 See Jennifer Scanlon's "What's An Acquisitive Girl to Do?" for one examination of the ways the Great Recession manifests in recent chick lit novels.

5 See Robinson's lecture at the Lumen Cristi Institute, "The Freedom of a Christian," for more.
6 See VIDA's "The 2014 Larger Literary Landscape VIDA Count," which describes the methodology VIDA is developing and the inherent challenges of counting women of color, and "VIDA Announces Changes," where VIDA discusses the development of methods for counting contributions from LGBTQI writers and writers with disabilities.
7 This fact is only supported by the numbers of women who have reported significant difficulty getting agents' and publishers' attention when using their own names compared to when they adopt masculine pseudonyms (for a recent example, see Catherine Nichols' "Homme de Plume").

WORKS CITED

"The 2014 VIDA Count." *VIDA: Women in Literary Arts*. 4 Apr. 2015. Web. 21 Jul. 2015.

Adams, Abigail and John Adams. *The Letters of John and Abigail Adams*. Ed. Frank Shuffelton. New York: Penguin, 2004. Print.

Addams, Jane. *Newer Ideals of Peace*. Chautauqua, NY: Chautauqua, 1907. Print.

——. *Twenty Years at Hull-House*. Ed. Victoria Bissell Brown. Boston: Bedford/St. Martin's, 1999. Print.

Alcott, Louisa May. *Hospital Sketches and Camp and Fireside Stories*. Boston: Little, Brown, 1909. Print.

——. *The Journals of Louisa May Alcott*. Eds. Joel Myerson and Daniel Shealy. Boston: Little, Brown, 1989. Print.

——. *Little Women*. Oxford: Oxford UP, 2008. Print.

——. *Work, Eight Cousins, Rose in Bloom, Stories and Other Writings*. Ed. Susan Cheever. New York: Library of America, 2014. Print.

Allen, Paula Gunn. *The Sacred Hoop: Recovering the Feminine in American Indian Traditions*. Boston: Beacon, 1986. Print.

——. "Special Problems in Teaching Leslie Marmon Silko's *Ceremony*." *American Indian Quarterly* 14.4 (Autumn 1990): 379–86. Print.

Ammons, Elizabeth. *Conflicting Stories: American Women Writers at the Turn into the Twentieth Century*. New York: Oxford UP, 1991. Print.

——. *Edith Wharton's Argument with America*. Athens, GA: U of Georgia P, 1980. Print.

——. "Expanding the Canon of American Realism." *The Cambridge Companion to American Realism and Naturalism*. Ed. Donald Pizer. Cambridge: Cambridge UP, 1995. 95–116. Print.

Amory, Hugh and David D. Hall, eds. *A History of the Book in America, Volume 1: The Colonial Book in the Atlantic World*. Cambridge: Cambridge UP, 1999. Print.

Anderson, Benedict. *Imagined Communities: Reflections on the Origin and Spread of Nationalism*. Rev. ed. London: Verso, 2006. Print.

Anderson, Robert Charles. *The Great Migration Begins: Immigrants to New England 1620–1633*. Vol. 1. Boston: New England Historic Genealogical Society, 1995. Print.

Anderson, Sherwood. "Four American Impressions: Gertrude Stein, Paul Rosenfeld, Ring Lardner, Sinclair Lewis." *New Republic* 11 Oct. 1922: 171–3. PDF file.

———. "The Work of Gertrude Stein." *Geography and Plays*. By Gertrude Stein. Boston: Four Seas, 1922. 5–8. Print.

Angelo, Bonnie. "The Pain of Being Black: An Interview with Toni Morrison." 1989. *Conversations with Toni Morrison*. Ed. Danille Taylor-Guthrie. Jackson, MS: UP of Mississippi, 1994. 255–61. Print.

Angelou, Maya. "Still I Rise." *And Still I Rise*. New York: Random House, 1978. 41–2. Print.

Antin, Mary. *The Promised Land*. Boston: Houghton Mifflin, 1912. Print.

Anzaldúa, Gloria. *Borderlands / La Frontera: The New Mestiza*. 4e. San Francisco: Aunt Lute, 2012. Print.

Argersinger, Jana L. and Phyllis Cole, eds. *Toward a Female Genealogy of Transcendentalism*. Athens, GA: U of Georgia P, 2014. Print.

Armitage, David and Michael J. Braddick, eds. *The British–American World, 1500–1800*. New York: Palgrave Macmillan, 2002. Print.

Ashton, Jennifer. "Lyric, Gender, and Subjectivity in Modern and Contemporary Women's Poetry." Bauer 515–38.

———. "Periodizing Poetic Practice Since 1945." *The Cambridge Companion to American Poetry Since 1945*. Ed. Jennifer Ashton. Cambridge: Cambridge UP, 2013. 1–15. Print.

Auden, W.H. Foreword. *A Change of World*. By Adrienne Rich. New Haven, CT: Yale UP, 1951. 7–11. Print.

Austerlitz, Saul. "The Hidden One of N.J.: Why Dara Horn Is the Best of the New Breed of Jewish Novelists." *Tablet. Nextbook, Inc.* 9 Sep. 2013. Web. 17 Jul. 2015.

Austin, Mary. *Stories from the Country of Lost Borders*. Ed. Marjorie Pryse. New Brunswick, NJ: Rutgers UP, 1987. Print.

Bacon, Jon Lance. *Flannery O'Connor and Cold War Culture*. Cambridge: Cambridge UP, 1993. Print.

Bailey, Jennifer. "The Dangers of Femininity in Willa Cather's Fiction." *Journal of American Studies* 16.3 (1982): 391–406. Print.

Baker, Jennifer J. "Women's Writing of the Revolutionary Era." Bauer 91–118.

Balkun, Mary McAleer. "Sarah Kemble Knight and the Construction of the American Self." *Women's Studies: An Interdisciplinary Journal* 28.1 (1998): 7–27. Print.

Baraka, Amiri. "A Critical Reevaluation: *A Raisin in the Sun*'s Enduring Passion." *A Raisin in the Sun (Expanded Twenty-Fifth Anniversary Edition) and The Sign in Sidney Brustein's Window*. Ed. Robert Nemiroff. New York: New American Library, 1987. 9–20. Print.

Barbour, Hugh. "Quaker Prophetesses and Mothers in Israel." *The Influence of Quaker Women on American History: Biographical Studies*. Ed. Carol Stoneburner and John Stoneburner. Lewistown, NY: Mellen, 1986. 57–80. Print.

Barreca, Regina. Introduction. *Gentlemen Prefer Blondes: The Illuminating Diary of a Professional Lady and But Gentlemen Marry Brunettes*. By Anita Loos. New York: Penguin, 1998. vii–xxiv. Print.

Barringer, Felicity. "Journalism's Greatest Hits: Two Lists of a Century's Top Stories." *New York Times* 1 Mar. 1999. C1. Print.

Barry, Kathleen. "Reviewing Reviews: *Of Woman Born*." *Reading Adrienne Rich: Reviews and Re-Visions, 1951–81*. Ed. Jane Roberta Cooper. Ann Arbor, MI: U of Michigan P, 1984. 300–3. Print.

Bauer, Dale M., ed. *The Cambridge History of American Women Writers*. Cambridge: Cambridge UP, 2012. Print.

Baym, Nina. *American Women Writers and the Work of History, 1790–1860*. New Brunswick, NJ: Rutgers UP, 1995. Print.

———. "Reinventing Lydia Sigourney." *American Literature* 62.3 (Sep. 1990): 385–404. *JSTOR*. Web. 17 Jan. 2015.

——. *Woman's Fiction: A Guide to Novels by and about Women in America, 1820–1870.* 2e. Urbana, IL: U of Illinois P, 1993. Print.

Belasco, Susan. *Stowe in Her Own Time: A Biographical Chronicle of Her Life Drawn from Recollections, Interviews, and Memoirs of Family, Friends, and Associates.* Iowa City, IA: U of Iowa P, 2009. Print.

Bell, Crystal. "'Mortal Instruments' Creator Reveals How Female Authors Can Be 'Dehumanized' by Their Own Fandom." *MTV News.* 11 Jun. 2015. Web. 11 Jun. 2015.

Bendixen, Alfred and Judith Hamera, eds. and introduction. *The Cambridge Companion to American Travel Writing.* Cambridge: Cambridge UP, 2009. Print.

Bennett, Gwendolyn B. "Heritage." *American Negro Poetry.* Ed. Arna Bontemps. New York: Hill and Wang, 1963. 73–4. Print.

——. "To a Dark Girl." *Caroling Dusk: An Anthology of Verse by Negro Poets.* Ed. Countee Cullen. New York: Harper & Brothers, 1927. 157. Print.

Bennett, Paula Bernat. "'The Descent of the Angel': Interrogating Domestic Ideology in American Women's Poetry, 1858–1890." *American Literary History* 7.4 (1995): 591–610. Print.

——. *Poets in the Public Sphere: The Emancipatory Project of American Women's Poetry, 1800–1900.* Princeton, NJ: Princeton UP, 2003. Print.

Bercovitch, Sacvan. *American Jeremiad.* 2e. Madison, WI: U of Wisconsin P, 2012. Print.

——. *The Puritan Origins of the American Self.* 2e. New Haven, CT: Yale UP, 2011. Print.

Berlin, Ira. *Many Thousands Gone: The First Two Centuries of Slavery in North America.* Cambridge, MA: Harvard UP, 1998. Print.

Bernstein, Robin. "'Never Born': Angelina Weld Grimké's *Rachel* as Ironic Response to Topsy." *Journal of American Drama and Theatre* 19.2 (Spring 2007): 61–76. Print.

Bernstein, Susan David. "Transatlantic Sympathies and Nineteenth-Century Women's Writing." Bauer 256–72.

Bickman, Martin. "Le Guin's *The Left Hand of Darkness*: Form and Content." *Science Fiction Studies* 4.1 (Mar. 1977): 42–7. Print.

Biers, Katherine. "Stages of Thought: Emerson, Maeterlinck, Glaspell." *Modern Drama* 56.4 (2013): 457–77. Print.

Birchall, Diana. *Onoto Watanna: The Story of Winnifred Eaton.* Champaign, IL: U of Illinois P, 2001. Print.

Black, Alexander. "The Woman Who Saw It First." *Century* 107 (1923): 33–42. PDF file.

Blackmer, Corinne E. "Gertrude Stein." *The Gay and Lesbian Literary Heritage.* Ed. Claude J. Summers. New York: Henry Holt, 1995. 681–6. Print.

Blackstock, Carrie Galloway. "Anne Bradstreet and Performativity: Self-Cultivation, Self-Deployment." *Early American Literature* 32.3 (1997): 222–48. Print.

Blackwell, Maylei. *¡Chicana Power!: Contested Histories of Feminism in the Chicano Movement.* Austin, TX: U of Texas P, 2011. Print.

Bloom, Harold, ed. and introduction. *Ursula K. Le Guin.* New York: Chelsea House, 1986. Print.

Bodnar, John. *The Transplanted: A History of Immigrants in Urban America.* Bloomington, IN: Indiana UP, 1987. Print.

Boeckmann, Cathy. *A Question of Character: Scientific Racism and the Genres of American Fiction, 1892–1912.* Tuscaloosa, AL: U of Alabama P, 2000. Print.

Bona, Mary Jo and Irma Maini, eds. and introduction. *Multiethnic Literature and Canon Debates.* Albany, NY: State U of New York P, 2006. Print.

Bonner, Marita. "On Being Young—a Woman—and Colored." *The Crisis* 31 (Dec. 1925): 63–5. PDF file.

"Books of the Week." *New York Daily Times* 22 Apr. 1857: 2. *ProQuest Historical Newspapers: The New York Times.* Web. 12 Feb. 2015.

Bosman, Julie. "Professor Says He Has Solved a Mystery Over a Slave's Novel." *New York Times* 18 Sept. 2013: A1. Print.

Botshon, Lisa and Meredith Goldsmith, eds. *Middlebrow Moderns: Popular American Women Writers of the 1920s.* Boston: Northeastern UP, 2003. Print.

Bow, Leslie. "Asian American Women's Literature and the Promise of Committed Art." Bauer 557–75.

Bowers, Bathsheba. *An Alarm Sounded to Prepare the Inhabitants of the World to Meet the Lord in the Way of His Judgments.* New York: William Bradford, 1709. *Early American Imprints, Series I: Evans, 1639–1800.* Web. 22 Aug. 2014.

Boyle, Hal. "Grace Unfolds to Hal Boyle Hazard of Husband Losing Job." *Laconia (N.H.) Evening Citizen* 29 Aug. 1956: 1+. PDF file.

Bradshaw, Melissa. "Outselling the Modernism of Men: Amy Lowell and the Art of Self-Commodification." *Victorian Poetry* 38.1 (Spring 2000): 141–69. Print.

——. "Remembering Amy Lowell: Embodiment, Obesity, and the Construction of a Persona." *Amy Lowell, American Modern.* Eds. Adrienne Munich and Melissa Bradshaw. New Brunswick, NJ: Rutgers UP, 2004. 167–85. Print.

Bradstreet, Anne. *The Complete Works of Anne Bradstreet.* Eds. Joseph R. McElrath, Jr. and Allan P. Robb. Boston: Twayne, 1980. Print.

Brady, Kathleen. *Ida Tarbell: Portrait of a Muckraker.* New York: Seaview/Putnam, 1984. Print.

Branson, Susan. *These Fiery Frenchified Dames: Women and Political Culture in Early National Philadelphia.* Philadelphia: U of Pennsylvania P, 2001. Print.

Breitwieser, Mitchell Robert. *American Puritanism and the Defense of Mourning: Religion, Grief, and Ethnology in Mary White Rowlandson's Captivity Narrative.* Madison, WI: U of Wisconsin P, 1990. Print.

Brinkmeyer, Robert H. "Mexico, Memory, and Betrayal: Katherine Anne Porter's 'Flowering Judas.'" *'Flowering Judas': Katherine Anne Porter.* Ed. Virginia Spencer Carr. New Brunswick, NJ: Rutgers UP, 1993. 195–210. Print.

Britzolakis, Christina. *Sylvia Plath and the Theater of Mourning.* Oxford: Clarendon, 1999. Print.

Brodhead, Richard. *Cultures of Letters: Scenes of Reading and Writing in Nineteenth-Century America.* Chicago: U of Chicago P, 1993. Print.

——. "Sparing the Rod: Discipline and Fiction in Antebellum America." *Representations* 21 (Winter 1988): 67–77. Print.

Bronski, Michael. "Sylvia Rivera: 1951–2002." *Z Magazine.* 1 Apr. 2002. Web. 21 Jul. 2015.

Brooks, Gwendolyn. *Report from Part One.* Detroit, MI: Broadside Press, 1972. Print.

Brown, Gillian. *Domestic Individualism: Imagining Self in Nineteenth-Century America.* Berkeley, CA: U of California P, 1992. Print.

Brown, Kathleen M. *Good Wives, Nasty Wenches, and Anxious Patriarchs: Gender, Race, and Power in Colonial Virginia.* Chapel Hill, NC: U of North Carolina P, 1996. Print.

Brown, Sylvia. "The Eloquence of the Word and the Spirit: The Place of Puritan Women's Writing in Old and New England." *Women and Religion in Old and New Worlds.* Eds. Debra Meyers and Susan Dinan. London: Routledge, 2001. 187–212. Print.

Buell, Lawrence. *The Environmental Imagination: Thoreau, Nature Writing, and the Formation of American Culture.* Cambridge, MA: Belknap of Harvard UP, 1995. Print.

Bulson, Eric. "Little Magazine, World Form." *The Oxford Handbook of Global Modernisms.* Eds. Mark Wollaeger and Matt Eatough. Oxford: Oxford UP, 2012. 267–87. Print.

Burke, Virginia M. "Zora Neale Hurston and Fannie Hurst as They Saw Each Other." *CLA Journal* 20 (June 1977): 435–47. Print.

Bush, Sargent, Jr. "Sarah Kemble Knight (1666–1727)." *Legacy* 12.2 (1995): 112–20. Print.

Butler, Jon. *Becoming America: The Revolution Before 1776.* Cambridge: Harvard UP, 2000. Print.

Butler, Judith. *Bodies that Matter: On the Discursive Limits of "Sex."* New York: Routledge, 1993. Print.

——. *Gender Trouble: Feminism and the Subversion of Identity.* New York: Routledge, 1990. Print.

Byrd, Jodi. "The Stories We Tell: American Indian Women's Writing and the Persistence of Tradition." Bauer 11–29.

Byrd, Rudolph. "Create Your Own Fire: Audre Lorde and the Tradition of Black Radical Thought." *I Am Your Sister: Collected and Unpublished Writings of Audre Lorde.* Eds. Rudolph P. Byrd, Johnnetta Betsch Cole, and Beverly Guy-Sheftall. Oxford: Oxford UP, 2009. 3–36. Print.

Caldwell, Ellen M. "Ellen Glasgow and the Southern Agrarians." *American Literature* 56.2 (1984): 203–13. *JSTOR.* Web. 15 Apr. 2014.

Campbell, Donna. "'Where Are the Ladies?' Wharton, Glasgow, and American Women Naturalists." *Studies in American Naturalism* 1.1–2 (2006): 152–69. Print.

——. "Women Writers and Naturalism." *The Oxford Handbook of American Literary Naturalism.* Ed. Keith Newlin. New York: Oxford UP, 2011. 223–40. Print.

——. "'Written with a Hard and Ruthless Purpose': Rose Wilder Lane, Edna Ferber, and Middlebrow Regional Fiction." *Middlebrow Moderns: Popular American Women Writers of the 1920s.* Boston: Northeastern UP, 2003. 25–44. Print.

Cane, Aleta Feinsod. "'The Same Revulsion Against Them All': Ida Tarbell and Charlotte Perkins Gilman's Suffrage Dialogue." *Charlotte Perkins Gilman: New Texts, New Contexts.* Eds. Jennifer S. Tuttle and Carol Farley Kessler. Columbus, OH: Ohio State UP, 2011. 122–39. Print.

Cantú, Norma E. and Aída Hurtado. "Introduction to the Fourth Edition." *Borderlands / La Frontera: The New Mestiza.* 4e. By Gloria Anzaldúa. San Francisco: Aunt Lute, 2012. 3–13. Print.

Cappello, Mary. "'Looking About Me with All My Eyes': Censored Viewing, Carnival, and Louisa May Alcott's *Hospital Sketches.*" *Arizona Quarterly* 50.3 (Autumn 1994): 59–88. Print.

Capper, Charles. *Margaret Fuller: An American Romantic Life.* 2 vols. Oxford: Oxford UP, 1994–2002. Print.

Cappucci, Paul R. "Depicting the Oblique: Emily Dickinson's Poetic Response to the American Civil War." *War, Literature, and the Arts* 10.1 (Spring–Summer 1998): 260–73. Print.

Carby, Hazel V. Introduction. *The Magazine Novels of Pauline Hopkins.* Oxford: Oxford UP, 1988. xxix–l. Print.

——. *Reconstructing Womanhood: The Emergence of the Afro-American Woman Novelist.* Oxford: Oxford UP, 1987. Print.

Carmichael, Peter S. "The Classics: Diary Of A Southern Refugee During The War, By A Lady Of Virginia." *Civil War Times* 45.7 (2006): 68—9. *Academic Search Premier.* Web. 27 Jul. 2014.

Carpentier, Martha Celeste. "Apollonian Form and Dionysian Excess in Susan Glaspell's Drama and Fiction." *Disclosing Intertextualities: The Stories, Plays, and Novels of Susan Glaspell.* Eds. Martha C. Carpentier and Barbara Ozieblo. New York: Rodopi, 2006. 35–50. Print.

Carretta, Vince. Introduction. *Complete Writings.* By Phillis Wheatley. New York: Penguin, 2001. Print.

Carter-Sanborn, Kristin. "Restraining Order: The Imperialist Anti-Violence of Charlotte Perkins Gilman." *Arizona Quarterly: A Journal of American Literature, Culture, and Theory* 56.2 (2000): 1–36. Print.

Castiglia, Christopher. *Bound and Determined: Captivity, Culture-Crossing, and White Womanhood from Mary Rowlandson to Patty Hearst*. Chicago: U of Chicago P, 1996. Print.

Cather, Willa. "Books and Magazines." 1899. *The Awakening*. Ed. Margaret Culley. New York: Norton, 1976. 153–5. Print.

——. *The Kingdom of Art: Willa Cather's First Principles and Critical Statements 1893–1896*. Ed. Bernice Slote. Lincoln, NE: U of Nebraska P, 1966. Print.

——. *My Ántonia*. Ed. Charles Mignon with Kari Ronning. Lincoln, NE: U of Nebraska P, 1994. Print.

——. "The Novel Démeublé." *The New Republic* 12 Apr. 1922: 5–6. Print.

Chakkalakal, Tess. *Novel Bondage: Slavery, Marriage, and Freedom in Nineteenth-Century America*. Urbana, IL: U of Illinois P, 2011. Print.

Chaney, Michael A. "Gender Reversal and Cultural Critique in Frances Osgood's Poetry." *American Transcendental Quarterly* 14.1 (2000): 5–25. *MLA International Bibliography*. Web. 18 Sep. 2014.

Chang, Hsiao-hung. "Gender Crossing in Maxine Hong Kingston's *Tripmaster Monkey*." *MELUS* 22.1 (Spring 1997): 15–34. Print.

Chang, Juliana. "Introduction: On Recovering Asian American Poetry." *Quiet Fire: A Historical Anthology of Asian American Poetry 1892–1970*. New York: Asian American Writers Workshop, 1996. xv–xx. Print.

Chang-Rodriguez, Raquel. "Colonial Voices of the Hispanic Caribbean." *A History of Literature in the Caribbean*. Vol. 1. Eds. A. James Arnold, Julio Rodriquez, and J. Michael Dash. Amsterdam: John Benjamins, 1994. 111–37. Print.

Chaplin, Joyce E. "Race." Armitage and Braddick 155–72.

Chapman, Mary. "US Suffrage Literature." Bauer 326–51.

Charvat, William. *The Profession of Authorship in America, 1800–1870*. New York: Columbia UP, 1992. Print.

Chatelain, Marcia. *South Side Girls: Growing Up in the Great Migration*. Durham, NC: Duke UP, 2015. Print.

Chesnut, Mary. *Mary Chesnut's Civil War*. Ed. C. Vann Woodward. New Haven, CT: Yale UP, 1981. Print.

Cheung, King-Kok. *Articulate Silences: Hisaye Yamamoto, Maxine Hong Kingston, Joy Kogawa*. Ithaca, NY: Cornell UP, 1993. Print.

——. "Re-Viewing Asian American Literary Studies." *An Interethnic Companion to Asian American Literature*. Ed. King-Kok Cheung. Cambridge: Cambridge UP, 1997. 1–36. Print.

Chiang, Fay. "Looking Back: Basement Workshop, 1971–86." *Quiet Fire: A Historical Anthology of Asian American Poetry 1892–1970*. New York: Asian American Writers Workshop, 1996. 106–15. Print.

Chiasson, Dan. "Color Codes." *The New Yorker* 27 Oct. 2014. Web. 21 Jul. 2015.

Chin, Frank, Jeffery Paul Chan, Lawson Fusao Inada, and Shawn Wong, eds. and introduction. *Aiiieeeee! An Anthology of Asian-American Writings*. Washington, DC: Howard UP, 1974. Print.

Christian, Barbara. *Black Women Novelists: The Development of a Tradition, 1882–1976*. Westport, CT: Greenwood, 1980. Print.

Chu, Patricia P. *Assimilating Asians: Gendered Strategies of Authorship in Asian America*. Durham, NC: Duke UP, 2000. Print.

——. "Bildung and the Asian American Bildungsroman." *The Routledge Companion to Asian American and Pacific Islander Literature*. Ed. Rachel C. Lee. London: Routledge, 2014. 403–14. Print.

Churchill, Winston. *Winston S. Churchill: His Complete Speeches, 1897–1963*. Ed. Robert Rhodes James. Vol. 7. New York: Chelsea House, 1974. Print.

Churchwell, Sarah. "'Lost Among the Ads': *Gentlemen Prefer Blondes* and the Politics of Imitation." *Middlebrow Moderns: Popular American Women Writers of the 1920s.* Eds. Lisa Botshon and Meredith Goldsmith. Boston: Northeastern UP, 2003. 135–64. Print.

Ciardi, John. "Edna St. Vincent Millay: A Figure of Passionate Living." *Saturday Review of Literature* 11 Nov. 1950: 8+. Print.

Cima, Gay Gibson. "Black and Unmarked: Phillis Wheatley, Mercy Otis Warren, and the Limits of Strategic Anonymity." *Theatre Journal* 52.4 (Dec. 2000): 465–95. Print.

Cisneros, Sandra. *Caramelo.* New York: Knopf, 2002. Print.

Ciuba, Gary. "The Worm Against the Word: The Hermeneutical Challenge in Hurston's *Jonah's Gourd Vine.*" *African American Review* 34.1 (2000): 119–33. Print.

Clapp, Elizabeth J. and Julie Roy Jeffrey, eds. and introduction. *Women, Dissent, and Anti-Slavery in Britain and America, 1790–1865.* Oxford: Oxford UP, 2011. Print.

Clark, Keith. *The Radical Fiction of Ann Petry.* Baton Rouge, LA: Louisiana State UP, 2013. Print.

Clark, Monica M (Illegal Writing). "Nicholas Sparks Confirmed My Fears (Updated)." *Illegal Writing.* N.p. 10 Oct. 2013. Web. 17 Oct. 2013.

Clere, Sarah. "Thea's 'Indian Play' in *The Song of the Lark.*" *Willa Cather and Modern Cultures.* Eds. Melissa J. Homestead and Guy J. Reynolds. Lincoln, NE: U of Nebraska P, 2011. 21–44. Print.

Cohn, Ruby. *New American Dramatists: 1960–1980.* New York: Grove, 1982. Print.

Collins, Lucy. "'Our Lives Inseparable': The Contingent World of Adrienne Rich's *Twenty-One Love Poems.*" *Rebound: The American Poetry Book.* Eds. Michael Hinds and Stephen Matterson. Amsterdam: Rodopi, 2004. 141–54. Print.

Colman, Benjamin. *Reliquiae Turellae, et Lachrymae Paternae.* Boston: Kneeland and Green, 1735. *Early American Imprints, Series I: Evans, 1639–1800.* Web. 20 Aug. 2014.

Colum, Mary. "Edna Millay and Her Time." *New Republic* 12 Mar. 1951: 17–18. Print.

Congressional Record 2 Apr. 1917: 102–4. *ProQuest Congressional Publications.* Web. 5 Jun. 2015.

——. 3 Apr. 1924: 5459–78. *ProQuest Congressional Publications.* Web. 5 Jun. 2015.

Cooper, Anna Julia. *A Voice from the South.* Ed. and introduction Mary Helen Washington. Oxford: Oxford UP, 1988. Print.

Cott, Nancy F. "Young Women in the Great Awakening in New England." *Feminist Studies* 3.1 (1975): 15–29. Print.

"The Counted: People Killed by Police in the US." *The Guardian.* Guardian News and Media, n.d. Web. 16 Jul. 2015.

"The Courier's Double 'V' for a Double Victory Campaign Gets Country-Wide Support." *Pittsburgh Courier* 14 Feb. 1942: 1. *Center for Research Libraries Global Resource Network.* Web. 16 Jul. 2015.

Cowley, Malcolm. "What Books Survive from the 1930s?" *Journal of American Studies* 7.3 (1973): 293–300. Print.

Crenshaw, Kimberle. "Demarginalizing the Intersection of Race and Sex: A Black Feminist Critique of Antidiscrimination Doctrine, Feminist Theory and Antiracist Politics." *University of Chicago Law Forum* 4 (1989): 139–68. Print.

Cumberland, Debra. "A Struggle for Breath: Contemporary Vocal Theory in Cather's *The Song of the Lark.*" *American Literary Realism, 1870–1910* 28.2 (1996): 59–70. *JSTOR.* Web. 30 Apr. 2015.

Cushman, Clare, ed. *Supreme Court Decisions and Women's Rights.* Washington, DC: CQ Press, 2011. Print.

Damon, S. Foster. *Amy Lowell: A Chronicle.* Boston: Houghton Mifflin, 1935. Print.

Daut, Marlene. "Daring to Be Free / Dying to Be Free: Toward a Dialogic Haitian–U.S. Studies." *American Quarterly* 63.2 (2011): 375–89. Print.

Davidson, Adenike Marie. "Marginal Spaces, Marginal Texts: Alice Dunbar-Nelson and the African American Prose Poem." *Southern Quarterly* 44.1 (2006): 51–64. Print.

Davidson, Cathy N. *Revolution and the Word: The Rise of the Novel in America*. Oxford: Oxford UP, 1988. Print.

Davidson, Michael. "Pregnant Men: Modernism, Disability, and Biofuturity in Djuna Barnes." *Novel: A Forum on Fiction* 43.2 (2010): 207–26. Print.

——. "The San Francisco Renaissance." Ashton *Cambridge* 66–80.

Davis, Doris. "'De Talkin' Game': The Creation of Psychic Space in Selected Short Fiction of Zora Neale Hurston." *Tulsa Studies in Women's Literature* 26.2 (2007): 269–86. Print.

Davis, Gwen, and Beverly A. Joyce. Eds. *Poetry by Women to 1900: A Bibliography of American and British Women Writers*. Toronto: U of Toronto P, 1991. Print.

Davis, Rebecca Harding. *Margret Howth*. 1862. New York: Feminist Press, 1990. Print.

Davis, Simone W. "The 'Weak Race' and the Winchester: Political Voices in the Pamphlets of Ida B. Wells-Barnett." *Legacy* 12.2 (1995): 77–97. *Literature Resource Center*. Web. 28 Oct. 2014.

Davis, Thadious M. *Nella Larsen, Novelist of the Harlem Renaissance: A Woman's Life Unveiled*. Baton Rouge, LA: Louisiana State UP, 1994. Print.

——. *Southscapes: Geographies of Race, Region, and Literature*. Chapel Hill, NC: U of North Carolina P, 2011. Print.

Debo, Annette. "Signifying 'Afrika': Gwendolyn Brooks' Later Poetry." *Callaloo* 29.1 (2006): 168–81. Print.

Delaney, Lucy. *From the Darkness Cometh the Light or Struggles for Freedom. Six Women's Slave Narratives*. Ed. William L. Andrews. Oxford: Oxford UP, 1988. Print.

Deloria, Philip J. *Playing Indian*. New Haven, CT: Yale UP, 1998. Print.

Deloria, Philip J. and Neal Salisbury, eds. *A Companion to American Indian History*. Oxford: Blackwell, 2000. Print.

DeLyser, Dydia. *Ramona Memories: Tourism and the Shaping of Southern California*. Minneapolis, MN: U of Minnesota, 2005. Print.

DeMouy, Jane Krause. *Katherine Anne Porter's Women: The Eye of Her Fiction*. Austin, TX: U of Texas P, 1983. Print.

Denman, Kamilla. "Emily Dickinson's Volcanic Punctuation." *Emily Dickinson Journal* 2.1 (1993): 22–46. Print.

Derounian, Kathryn Zabelle. "The Publication, Promotion, and Distribution of Mary Rowlandson's Indian Captivity Narrative in the Seventeenth Century." *Early American Literature* 23.3 (1988): 239–61. *JSTOR*. Web. 5 Oct. 2013.

Deutsch, Sarah. *No Separate Refuge: Culture, Class and Gender on an Anglo-Hispanic Frontier in the American Southwest, 1880–1940*. New York: Oxford UP, 1989. Print.

Dickinson, Emily. *The Complete Poems of Emily Dickinson*. Ed. Thomas H. Johnson. Boston: Little, Brown, 1960. Print.

——. *The Letters of Emily Dickinson*. Ed. Thomas H. Johnson. Cambridge, MA: Harvard UP, 1986. Print.

Diffley, Kathleen. *Where My Heart Is Turning Ever: Civil War Stories and Constitutional Reform, 1861–1876*. Athen, GA: U of Georgia P, 1992. Print.

Dill, Elizabeth. "A Mob of Lusty Villagers: Operations of Domestic Desires in Hannah Webster Foster's *The Coquette*." *Eighteenth-Century Fiction* 15.2 (2003): 255–79. *Project Muse*. Web. 25 Feb. 2014.

Dobson, Joanne. "Sex, Wit, and Sentiment: Frances Osgood and the Poetry of Love." *American Literature* 65.4 (1993): 631–50. *JSTOR*. Web. 18 Sep. 2014.

Donaldson, Elizabeth J. "Amy Lowell and the Unknown Ladies: The Caryatides Talk Back." *Amy Lowell, American Modern*. Eds. Adrienne Munich and Melissa Bradshaw. New Brunswick, NJ: Rutgers UP, 2004. 27–42. Print.

Doolen, Andy. "Women Writers and the Early US Novel." Bauer 119–38.

Douglas, Christopher. "Reading Ethnography: The Cold War Social Science of Jade Snow Wong's *Fifth Chinese Daughter* and *Brown v. Board of Education.*" *Form and Transformation in Asian American Literature.* Eds. Zhou Xiaojing and Samina Najmi. Seattle, WA: U of Washington P, 2005. 101–24. Print.

Dowd, Gregory Evans. "Wag the Imperial Dog: Indians and Overseas Empires in North America, 1650–1776." Deloria and Salisbury 46–67.

Doyle, Laura. *Freedom's Empire: Race and the Rise of the Novel in Atlantic Modernity, 1640–1940.* Durham, NC: Duke University Press, 2008. Print.

Du Bois, W.E.B. *The Souls of Black Folk.* Eds. Henry Louis Gates, Jr. and Terri Hume Oliver. New York: Norton, 1999. Print.

Dubnick, Randa. *The Structure of Obscurity: Gertrude Stein, Language, and Cubism.* Urbana, IL: U of Illinois P, 1984. Print.

Dudden, Faye. *Fighting Chance: The Struggle Over Woman Suffrage and Black Suffrage in Reconstruction America.* Oxford: Oxford UP, 2011. Print.

Dunn, Maggie, and Ann Morris. *The Composite Novel: The Short Story Cycle in Transition.* New York: Twayne, 1995. Print.

DuPlessis, Rachel Blau. *The Pink Guitar: Writing as Feminist Practice.* New York: Routledge, 1990. Print.

Dymkowski, Christine. "On the Edge: The Plays of Susan Glaspell." *Modern Drama* 31.1 (1988): 91–105. Print.

Edmunds, R. David. "Native Americans and the United States, Canada, and Mexico." Deloria and Salisbury 397–421.

Ehlers, Sara. "Making It Old: The Victorian/Modern Divide in Twentieth-Century American Poetry." *Modern Language Quarterly: A Journal of Literary History* 73.1 (2012): 37–67. Print.

Eiselein, Gregory. "Emotion and the Jewish Historical Poems of Emma Lazarus." *Mosaic: A Journal for the Interdisciplinary Study of Literature* 37.1 (2004): n. pag. *ProQuest.* Web. 20 Jul. 2015.

Elbert, Monika M. *Separate Spheres No More: Gender Convergence in American Literature, 1830–1930.* Tuscaloosa, AL: U of Alabama P, 2000. Print.

Ellis, R.J. *Harriet Wilson's Our Nig: A Cultural Biography of a 'Two-Story' African American Novel.* Amsterdam: Rodopi, 2003. Print.

Emerson, Ralph Waldo. "The Over-Soul." *The Complete Essays and Other Writings of Ralph Waldo Emerson.* Ed. Brooks Atkinson. New York: Random House, 1940. 261–78. Print.

Ernest, John. "Nineteenth-Century African American Women Writers." Bauer 273–92.

Eustace, Nicole. *Passion is the Gale: Emotion, Power, and the Coming of the American Revolution.* Chapel Hill, NC: U of North Carolina P, 2008. Print.

Evans, Gareth. "Rakes, Coquettes and Republican Patriarchs: Class, Gender and Nation in Early American Sentimental Fiction." *Canadian Review of American Studies* 25.3 (1995): 41–62. *EBSCO Host.* Web. 12 Sep. 2014.

Evron, Nir. "Realism, Irony and Morality in Edith Wharton's *The Age of Innocence.*" *Journal of Modern Literature* 35.2 (2012): 37–51. Print.

Faderman, Lillian. *Odd Girls and Twilight Lovers: A History of Lesbian Life in Twentieth-Century America.* New York: Columbia UP, 1991. Print.

——. *Surpassing the Love of Men.* 1981. New York: HarperCollins, 2001. Print.

——. "'Which, Being Interpreted, Is as May Be, or Otherwise': Ada Dwyer Russell in Amy Lowell's Life and Work." *Amy Lowell: American Modern.* Eds. Melissa Bradshaw and Adrienne Munich. New Brunswick, NJ: Rutgers UP, 2004. 59–76. Print.

Faery, Rebecca Blevins. *Cartographies of Desire: Captivity, Race, and Sex in the Shaping of an American Nation.* Norman, OK: U of Oklahoma P, 1999. Print.

Fahs, Alice. "The Feminized Civil War: Gender, Northern Popular Literature, and the Memory of the War." *Journal of American History* 85.4 (March 1999): 1461–94. Print.

Fama, Katherine A. "Melancholic Remedies: Djuna Barnes' *Nightwood* as Narrative Theory." *Journal of Modern Literature* 37.2 (2014): 39–58. Print.

Faust, Drew Gilpin. ed. and introduction. *Macaria; or, Altars of Sacrifice.* By Augusta Jane Evans. Baton Rouge, LA: Louisiana State UP, 1992. Print.

Ferber, Edna. *A Kind of Magic.* Garden City, NY: Doubleday, 1963. Print.

——. *A Peculiar Treasure.* New York: Literary Guild of America, 1939. Print.

Ferguson, Robert. *The American Enlightenment: 1750–1820.* Cambridge, MA: Harvard UP, 1997. Print.

Fern, Fanny. "Male Criticism on Ladies' Books." *Ruth Hall and Other Writings by Fanny Fern.* Ed. Joyce W. Warren. New Brunswick, NJ: Rutgers UP, 1986. 285–6. Print.

Ferreira, Maria Aline. "Symbiotic Bodies and Evolutionary Tropes in the Work of Octavia Butler." *Science Fiction Studies* 37.3 (Nov. 2010): 401–15. Print.

Fetterley, Judith. "'My Sister! My Sister!': The Rhetoric of Catharine Sedgwick's *Hope Leslie.*" *No More Separate Spheres! A Next Wave American Studies Reader.* Eds. Cathy N. Davidson and Jessamyn Hatcher. Durham, NC: Duke UP, 2002. 67–92. Print.

——, ed. and introduction. *Provisions: A Reader from 19th-Century American Women.* Bloomington, IN: Indiana UP, 1985. Print.

Fields, Beverly. "The Poetry of Anne Sexton." *Poets in Progress.* 2e. Ed. Edward Hungerford. Evanston, IL: Northwestern UP, 1967. 251–85. Print.

Fiske, Sarah Symmes. *A Confession of Faith: or, a Summary of Divinity.* Boston: Benjamin Eliot, 1704. *Early American Imprints, Series I: Evans, 1639–1800.* Web. 14 Aug. 2014.

Fitzpatrick, Tara. "The Figure of Captivity: The Cultural Work of the Puritan Captivity Narrative." *American Literary History* 3.1 (Spring 1991): 1–26. Print.

Fleissner, Jennifer. *Women, Compulsion, Modernity: The Moment of American Naturalism.* Chicago: U of Chicago P, 2004. Print.

Fletcher, Caroline Violet. "'The Rules of the Institution': Susan Glaspell and Sisterhood." *Disclosing Intertextualities: The Stories, Plays, and Novels of Susan Glaspell.* Eds. Martha C. Carpentier and Barbara Ozieblo. New York: Rodopi, 2006. 239–56. Print.

Foote, Stephanie. "Local Knowledge and Women's Regional Writing." Bauer 293–308.

Foster, Frances Smith. "Reading *Incidents.*" *Harriet Jacobs and Incidents in the Life of a Slave Girl: New Critical Essays.* Eds. Deborah M. Garfield and Rafia Zafar. Cambridge: Cambridge UP, 1996. 57–75.

Franklin, R.W. "The Emily Dickinson Fascicles." *Studies in Bibliography: Papers of the Bibliographic Society of the University of Virginia* 36 (1983): 1–20. *MLA International Bibliography.* Web. 19 Jul. 2014.

Frederick, John T. "Hawthorne's 'Scribbling Women.'" *New England Quarterly* 48.2 (June 1975): 231–40. *JSTOR.* Web. 18 Sep. 2014.

Frederick, Richard G. "Ida Tarbell." *Great Lives from History: The 20th Century, 1901–2000.* Vol. 9. Ed. Robert F. Gorman. Pasadena, CA: Salem Press, 2008. 3947–9. Print.

Fredrickson, George M. "The Coming of the Lord: The Northern Protestant Clergy and the Civil War Crisis." *Religion and the American Civil War.* Eds. Randall M. Miller, Harry S. Stout, and Charles Reagan. Oxford: Oxford UP, 1998. 110–30. Print.

Freeman, Mary Wilkins. "A Poetess." *Atlantic Monthly* 81 (July 1890): 197–204. PDF file.

——. "The Revolt of Mother." *Atlantic Monthly* 81 (Sep. 1890): 553–61. PDF file.

Friedman, Susan. "Creating a Women's Mythology: H.D.'s *Helen in Egypt.*" *Women's Studies: An Interdisciplinary Journal* 5.2 (1977): 163–97. Print.

Fussell, Paul. *The Great War and Modern Memory.* New York: Oxford UP, 1975. Print.

Gainor, Ellen J. *Susan Glaspell in Context: American Theater, Culture, and Politics, 1915–48.* Ann Arbor, MI: U of Michigan P, 2001. Print.

Galewski, Elizabeth. "The Strange Case for Women's Capacity to Reason: Judith Sargent Murray's Use of Irony in 'On the Equality of the Sexes' (1790)." *Quarterly Journal of Speech* 93.1 (2007): 84–108. *Taylor and Francis Online.* Web. 3 Feb. 2014.

Games, Alison. "Migration." Armitage and Braddick 31–50.

Garber, Linda. *Identity Poetics: Race, Class, and the Lesbian Feminist Roots of Queer Theory.* New York: Columbia UP, 2001. Print.

García, Cristina. *Dreaming in Cuban.* New York: Knopf, 1992. Print.

Garcia, Velia. "La Chicana, Chicano Movement and Women's Liberation." 1977. *Chicana Feminist Thought: The Basic Historical Writings.* Ed. Alma M. García. London: Routledge, 1997. 199–201. Print.

Gates, Henry Louis, Jr. *The Signifying Monkey: A Theory of African American Literary Criticism.* 2e. Oxford: Oxford UP, 2014. Print.

——. *The Trials of Phillis Wheatley: America's First Black Poet and Her Encounters with the Founding Fathers.* New York: Basic Civitas, 2003. Print.

Gates, Henry Louis Jr. and Nellie McKay, eds. *The Norton Anthology of African American Literature.* 2e. New York: Norton, 2004. Print.

Gentry, Deborah S. *The Art of Dying: Suicide in the Works of Kate Chopin and Sylvia Plath.* New York: Peter Lang, 2006. Print.

Gerzina, Gretchen Holbrook. *Mr. and Mrs. Prince: How an Extraordinary Eighteenth-Century Family Moved Out of Slavery and into Legend.* New York: Amistad, 2008. Print.

Ghansah, Rachel Kaadzi. "The Radical Vision of Toni Morrison." *New York Times* 8 Apr. 2015. Web. 8 Apr. 2015.

Gibbons, William Conrad. *The U.S. Government and the Vietnam War.* 3 vols. Princeton, NJ: Princeton UP, 2014. Print.

Giddings, Paula. *When and Where I Enter: The Impact of Black Women on Race and Sex in America.* New York: Morrow, 1984. Print.

Gilbert, Julie Goldsmith. *Ferber: A Biography.* Garden City, NY: Doubleday, 1978. Print.

Gilbert, Sandra M. and Susan Gubar. "'Fecundate! Discriminate!' Charlotte Perkins Gilman and the Theologizing of Maternity." *Charlotte Perkins Gilman: Optimist Reformer.* Eds. Jill Rudd and Val Gough. Iowa City, IA: U of Iowa P, 1999. 200–16. Print.

——. *Masterpiece Theatre: An Academic Melodrama.* New Brunswick, NJ: Rutgers UP, 1995. Print.

Gilman, Charlotte Perkins. *Human Work.* New York: McClure, Philips, 1904. Print.

——. "Is America Too Hospitable?" *The Forum* 70 (1923): 1983–9. Reprinted in *Charlotte Perkins Gilman: A Nonfiction Reader,* ed. Larry Ceplair. New York: Columbia UP, 1991. 288–94. Print.

——. *Women and Economics.* Boston: Small, Maynard, 1898. Print.

Giovanni, Nikki. "For Saundra." *The Collected Poetry of Nikki Giovanni 1968–1998.* New York: William Morrow, 2003. 80. Print.

Glasgow, Ellen. *The Descendant.* New York: Harper and Brothers, 1897. Print.

Glazener, Nancy. "Women in Literary Culture During the Long Nineteenth Century." Bauer 139–64.

Glendening, John. "Evolution, Narcissism, and Maladaptation in Kate Chopin's *The Awakening.*" *American Literary Realism* 43.1 (2010): 41–73. Print.

González, Marcial. *Chicano Novels and the Politics of Form: Race, Class, and Reification.* Ann Arbor, MI: U of Michigan P, 2009. Print.

Goodman, Susan. *Ellen Glasgow: A Biography.* Baltimore, MD: Johns Hopkins UP, 1998. Print.

Greenberg, Amy. *Manifest Manhood and the Antebellum American Empire.* Cambridge: Cambridge UP, 2005. Print.

Griffitts, Hannah. "The Female Patriots." *Milcah Martha Moore's Book: A Commonplace Book from Revolutionary America.* Eds. Catherine La Courreye Blecki and Karin A Wulf. University Park, PA: Pennsylvania State UP, 1997. 172–3. Print.

Grimké, Angelina Emily. *Letters to Catherine E. Beecher.* 1838. Freeport, NY: Books for Libraries, 1971. Print.

Gross, Lawrence W. "The Trickster and World Maintenance: An Anishinaabe Reading of Louise Erdrich's *Tracks.*" *Studies in American Indian Literatures* 17.3 (Fall 2005): 48–66. Print.

Gruesser, John C. *Confluences: Postcolonialism, African American Literary Studies, and the Black Atlantic.* Athens, GA: U of Georgia P, 2005. Print.

Gubar, Susan. "Jewish American Women Writers and the Race Question." *The Cambridge Companion to Jewish American Literature.* Ed. Hana Wirth-Nesher and Michael Kramer. Cambridge: Cambridge UP, 2003. 231–49. Print.

Gunderson, Joan R. *To Be Useful to the World: Women in Revolutionary America, 1740–1790.* New York: Twayne, 1996. Print.

Gunew, Sneja. *Framing Marginality: Multicultural Literary Studies.* Melbourne: Melbourne UP, 1994. Print.

Gunning, Sandra. "Reading and Redemption in *Incidents in the Life of a Slave Girl.*" *Harriet Jacobs and Incidents in the Life of a Slave Girl: New Critical Essays.* Eds. Deborah M. Garfield and Rafia Zafar. Cambridge: Cambridge UP, 1996. 131–55. Print.

Gustafson, Sandra M. "Religion, Sensibility, and Sympathy." Bauer 74–90.

Hafen, P. Jane. "Native American Literatures." Deloria and Salisbury 234–47.

Hagedorn, Jessica. "Fillmore Street Poems: August 1967." Rexroth 27–8.

Hanson, Carter F. "Memory's Offspring and Utopian Ambiguity in Ursula K. Le Guin's 'The Day Before the Revolution' and *The Dispossessed.*" *Science Fiction Studies* 40.2 (July 2013): 246–62. Print.

Hapke, Laura. *Daughters of the Great Depression: Women, Work, and Fiction in the American 1930s.* Athens, GA: U of Georgia P, 1995. Print.

Harjo, Joy. "A Postcolonial Tale." *English Postcoloniality: Literatures from Around the World.* Eds. Radhika Mohanram and Gita Rajan. Westport, CT: Greenwood, 1996. 15. Print.

"Harlem in the 1920s." *Digital Harlem Blog. University of Sydney.* n.d. Web. 30 Apr. 2015.

Harper, Frances E.W. *Iola Leroy, or Shadows Uplifted.* Ed. Frances Smith Foster. Oxford: Oxford UP, 1988. Print.

Harriot, Thomas. *A Briefe and True Report of the New Found Land of Virginia and of the Commodities and of the Nature and Manner of the Naturall Inhabitants.* 1588. London: Theodor de Bry, 1590. *Early English Books Online.* Web. 16 Nov. 2015.

Harris, Jeane. "A Code of Her Own: Attitudes Toward Women in Willa Cather's Short Fiction." *Modern Fiction Studies* 36.1 (1990): 80–9. Print.

Harris, Jennifer. "Writing Vice: Hannah Webster Foster and *The Coquette.*" *Canadian Review of American Studies* 39.4 (2009): 363–81. *Project Muse.* Web. 24 Feb. 2014.

Harris, Sharon M. *Executing Race: Early American Women's Narratives of Race, Society, and the Law.* Columbus, OH: Ohio State UP, 2005. Print.

———. "Redefining the Feminine: Women and Work in Rebecca Harding Davis's 'In the Market.'" *Legacy* 8.2 (Fall 1991): 118–21. Print.

Harter, Odile. "Marianne Moore's Depression Collectives." *American Literature* 85.2 (2013): 333–61. Print.

Hartman, Saidiya V. *Scenes of Subjection: Terror, Slavery, and Self-Making in Nineteenth-Century America.* Oxford: Oxford UP, 1997. Print.

Harvey, Tamara. *Figuring Modesty in Feminist Discourse Across the Americas, 1633–1700.* Aldershot: Ashgate, 2008. Print.

Hattenhauer, Darryl. *Shirley Jackson's American Gothic.* Albany, NY: SUNY Press, 2003. Print.

Hawthorne, Nathaniel. *The French and Italian Notebooks.* Ed. Thomas Woodson. Columbus, OH: Ohio State UP, 1980. Print.

——. *Letters of Hawthorne to William Ticknor, 1851–1864.* Vol. 1. Newark, NJ: Carteret Book Club, 1910. Print.

Hayashi, Brian Masaru. *Democratizing the Enemy: The Japanese American Internment.* Princeton, NJ: Princeton UP, 2008. Print.

Healey, E. Claire and Keith Cushman, eds. *The Letters of D.H. Lawrence and Amy Lowell.* Santa Barbara, CA: Black Sparrow, 1985. Print.

Hejinian, Lyn. "The Rejection of Closure." *The Language of Inquiry.* Berkeley, CA: U of California P, 2000. 40–58. Print.

Helal, Kathleen M. "Celebrity, Femininity, Lingerie: Dorothy Parker's Autobiographical Monologues." *Women's Studies: An Interdisciplinary Journal* 33.1 (2004): 77–102. *Taylor and Francis Online.* Web. 15 May 2015.

Heller, Terry. "Living for the Other World: Sarah Orne Jewett as a Religious Writer." *Spectral America: Phantoms and the National Imagination.* Ed. Jeffrey Andrew Weinstock. Madison, WI: U of Wisconsin P, 2004. 78–100. Print.

Henton, Alice. "'Once Masculines … Now Feminines Awhile': Gendered Imagery and the Significance of Anne Bradstreet's 'The Tenth Muse.'" *New England Quarterly* 85.2 (June 2012): 302–25. Print.

"Heroic Women of America." *Godey's Magazine and Lady's Book* 31 (1845): 2. *ProQuest.* Web. 5 Nov. 2013.

Herring, Phillip. *Djuna: The Life and Work of Djuna Barnes.* New York: Viking, 1995. Print.

Hewitt, Elizabeth. "Dickinson's Lyrical Letters and Poetics of Correspondence." *The Arizona Quarterly* 52.1 (1996): 27–58. Print.

Higham, John. "Ideological Anti-Semitism in the Gilded Age." *The House of Mirth.* Ed. Elizabeth Ammons. New York: Norton, 1990. 296–303. Print.

Hoby, Hermione. "Toni Morrison: 'I'm Writing for Black People … I Don't Have to Apologise." *The Guardian* 25 Apr. 2015. Web. 26 Apr. 2015.

Holly, Carol. "Reading Resistance in Mary Wilkins Freeman's 'A Poetess.'" *American Literary Realism* 39.2 (2007): 95–108. Print.

Holm, Tom. "American Indian Warfare: The Cycles of Conflict and the Militarization of Native North America." Deloria and Salisbury 154–72.

Holstein, Suzy Clarkson. "Silent Justice in a Different Key: Glaspell's 'Trifles.'" *Midwest Quarterly: A Journal of Contemporary Thought* 44.3 (2003): 282–90. Print.

Homestead, Melissa J. "The Shape of Catharine Sedgwick's Career." Bauer 185–203.

Homestead, Melissa J. and Camryn Hansen. "Susanna Rowson's Transatlantic Career." *Early American Literature* 45.3 (2010): 619–54. *JSTOR.* Web. 27 Feb. 2014.

Hopkins, Pauline E. *Contending Forces: A Romance Illustrative of Negro Life North and South.* 1900. New York: AMS, 1971. Print.

Houston, Velina Hasu, ed. and introduction. *The Politics of Life: Four Plays by Asian American Women.* Philadelphia: Temple UP, 1993. Print.

Howard, June. "What Is Sentimentality?" *American Literary History* 11.1 (1999): 63–81. Print.

Howe, Craig. "Keep Your Thoughts Above the Trees: Ideas on Developing and Presenting Tribal Histories." *Clearing a Path: Theorizing the Past in Native American Studies.* Ed. Nancy Shoemaker. New York: Routledge, 2002. 161–80. Print.

Howe, Daniel Walker. *What Hath God Wrought: The Transformation of America, 1815–1848.* Oxford: Oxford UP, 2009. Print.

Howe, Susan. "Statement for the New Poetics Colloquium." *Jimmy and Lucy's House of K* 5 (1985): 13–17. PDF file.

Howells, William Dean. "The Editor's Study." *Harper's New Monthly* Sept. 1887: 638–42. PDF file.

Hudak, Leona M. *Early American Women Printers and Publishers 1639–1820.* Metuchen, NJ: Scarecrow Press, 1978. Print.

Hughes, Langston. *The Big Sea.* 1940. New York: Hill and Wang, 1968. Print.

——. "Harlem." *The Collected Works of Langston Hughes, Vol. 3: The Poems: 1951–1967.* Ed. Arnold Rampersad. Columbia, MO: U of Missouri P, 2001. 74. Print.

Hull, Gloria T. "Shaping Contradictions: Alice Dunbar-Nelson and the Black Creole Experience." *New Orleans Review* 15.1 (Spring 1988): 34–7. Print.

——. "'Two-Facing Life': The Duality of Alice Dunbar-Nelson." *Collections* 4 (1989): 19–35. Print.

Hulser, Kathleen. "Reading Uncle Tom's Image: From Anti-Slavery Hero to Insult." *New York Journal of American History* 65.1 (Spring 2003): 75–9. Print.

Hume, Beverly A. "'Inextricable Disordered Ranges': Mary Austin's Ecofeminist Explorations in *Lost Borders.*" *Studies in Short Fiction* 36.4 (1999): 183–97. *Academic Search Premier.* Web. 26 Sept. 2014.

Hutner, Gordon. "Modern Domestic Realism in America, 1950–1970." Bauer 501–14.

——. *What America Read: Taste, Class, and the Novel, 1920–1960.* Chapel Hill, NC: U of North Carolina P, 2009. Print.

Hyman, Stanley Edgar. Preface. *The Magic of Shirley Jackson.* New York: Farrar, Straus & Giroux, 1966. vii–ix. Print.

Innes, Stephen. *Creating the Commonwealth: The Economic Culture of Puritan New England.* New York: Norton, 1995. Print.

Jackson, Helen Hunt. *The Indian Reform Letters of Helen Hunt Jackson, 1879–1885.* Ed. Valerie Sherer Mathes. Norman, OK: U of Oklahoma P, 1998. Print.

Jackson, Mattie J. *The Story of Mattie J. Jackson. Speaking Lives, Authoring Texts: Three African American Women's Oral Slave Narratives.* Eds. DoVeanna S. Fulton Minor and Reginald Pitts. Albany, NY: State U of New York P, 2010. 99–130. Print.

Jacobs, Harriet A. *Incidents in the Life of a Slave Girl.* 1860. Ed. Jean Fagan Yellin. Cambridge, MA: Harvard UP, 2001. Print.

Jay, Karla. *Tales of the Lavender Menace: A Memoir of Liberation.* New York: Basic, 1999. Print.

Jewett, Sarah Orne. *The Country of the Pointed Firs. The Country of the Pointed Firs and Other Stories.* Ed. Sarah Way Sherman. Hanover, NH: U of New Hampshire P, 1997. 1–214. Print.

——. "The Foreigner." *The Country of the Pointed Firs and Other Stories.* Ed. Sarah Way Sherman. Hanover, NH: U of New Hampshire P, 1997. 233–57. Print.

——. "A White Heron." *A White Heron and Other Stories.* Boston: Houghton Mifflin, 1886. Print.

Johannessen, Lene M. *Threshold Time: Passage of Crisis in Chicano Literature.* Amsterdam: Rodopi, 2008. Print.

Johns, J. Adam. "Becoming Medusa: Octavia Butler's *Lilith's Brood* and Sociobiology." *Science Fiction Studies* 37.3 (Nov. 2010): 382–400. Print.

Johnson, Abby Arthur. "A Free Foot in the Wilderness: Harriet Monroe and *Poetry*, 1912–1936." *Illinois Quarterly* 37.4 (1975): 28–43. Print.

Johnson, James Weldon, ed. *The Book of American Negro Poetry.* New York: Harcourt, Brace, 1922. Print.

Jones, Sharon Lynette. *Rereading the Harlem Renaissance: Race, Class, and Gender in the Fiction of Jessie Fauset, Zora Neale Hurston, and Dorothy West.* Westport, CT: Greenwood Press, 2002. Print.

Jordan, June. "The Difficult Miracle of Black Poetry in America or Something Like a Sonnet for Phillis Wheatley." *Some of Us Did Not Die: New and Selected Essays*. New York: Basic, 2002. 174–86. Print.

——. "Getting Down to Get Over." *Things That I Do in the Dark*. New York: Random House, 1977. 27–37. Print.

Joudrey, Thomas J. "Maintaining Stability: Fancy and Passion in *The Coquette*." *The New England Quarterly* 86.1 (2013): 60–87. *MIT Press*. Web. 24 Feb. 2014.

Kaiser, Wilson. "The Micropolitics of Fascism in Carson McCullers's *The Heart Is a Lonely Hunter* and Sinclair Lewis's *It Can't Happen Here*." *Genre* 47.3 (Fall 2014): 285–307. Print.

Kam, Tanya K. "Velvet Coats and Manicured Nails: The Body Speaks Resistance in *Dust Tracks on a Road*." *Southern Literary Journal* 42.1 (2009): 73–87. Print.

Kassanoff, Jennie A. "Extinction, Taxidermy, Tableaux Vivants: Staging Race and Class in *The House of Mirth*." *PMLA* 115.1 (2000): 60–74. Print.

Katrak, Ketu H. "South Asian American Literature." *An Interethnic Companion to Asian American Literature*. Ed. King-Kok Cheung. Cambridge: Cambridge UP, 1997. 192–218. Print.

Katznelson, Ira. *When Affirmative Action Was White: An Untold History of Racial Inequality in Twentieth-Century America*. New York: Norton, 2005. Print.

Keeler, Emily M. "David Gilmour on Building Strong Stomachs." *Hazlitt*. Penguin Random House. 25 Sept. 2013. Web. 17 Oct. 2013.

Keetley, Dawn. "Unsettling the Frontier: Gender and Racial Identity in Caroline Kirkland's *A New Home, Who'll Follow?* and *Forest Life*." *Legacy* 12.1 (1995): 17–37. Print.

Kenner, Hugh. "The Making of the Modernist Canon." *Canons*. Ed. Robert von Hallberg. Chicago: U of Chicago P, 1984. 363–75. Print.

Kerber, Linda, Nancy F. Cott, Robert Gross, Lynn Hunt, Carroll Smith-Rosenberg, and Christine M. Stansell. "Beyond Roles, Beyond Spheres: Thinking about Gender in the Early Republic." *William and Mary Quarterly* 46 (1989): 565–85. Print.

Kerrison, Catherine. *Claiming the Pen: Women and Intellectual Life in the Early American South*. Ithaca, NY: Cornell UP, 2005. Print.

Kete, Mary Louise. *Sentimental Collaborations: Mourning and Middle-Class Identity in Nineteenth-Century America*. Durham, NC: Duke UP, 2000. Print.

Keyser, Catherine. "Edna St. Vincent Millay and the Very Clever Woman in Vanity Fair." *American Periodicals: A Journal of History, Criticism, and Bibliography* 17.1 (2007): 65–96. Print.

——. *Playing Smart: New York Women Writers and Modern Magazine Culture*. New Brunswick, NJ: Rutgers UP, 2010. Print.

Kicza, John E. "First Contacts." Deloria and Salisbury 27–45.

Kidwell, Clara Sue. "Native American Systems of Knowledge." Deloria and Salisbury 87–102.

Kim, Elaine H. "Defining Asian American Realities through Literature." *Cultural Critique* 6 (1987): 87–111. Print.

Kirkland, Caroline. *Forest Life*. 2 vols. 1844. Rpt. Ann Arbor, MI: University Microfilms, 1964. Print.

——. *A New Home—Who'll Follow? Or, Glimpses of Western Life*. 4e. New York: C.S. Francis, 1850. Print.

Klein, Stacey Jean. "Wielding the Pen: Margaret Preston, Confederate Nationalistic Literature and the Expansion of a Woman's Place in the South." *Civil War History* 49.3 (2003): 221–34. *Project MUSE*. Web. 29 Aug. 2014.

Knight, Sarah Kemble. *The Journal of Madam Knight*. Upper Saddle River, NJ: Gregg Press, 1970. Print.

Kohn, Denise, Sarah Meer, and Emily B. Todd. "Reading Stowe as a Transatlantic Writer." *Transatlantic Stowe: Harriet Beecher Stowe and European Culture*. Iowa City, IA: U of Iowa P, 2006. xi–xxxi. Print.

Korobkin, Laura L. "'Can Your Volatile Daughter Ever Acquire Your Wisdom?': Luxury and False Ideals in *The Coquette*." *Early American Literature* 41.1 (2006): 79–107. Print.

Kritzer, Amelia Howe. "Playing with Republican Motherhood: Self-Representation in Plays by Susanna Haswell Rowson and Judith Sargent Murray." *Early American Literature* 31.2 (1996): 150–66. *JSTOR*. Web. 3 Feb. 2014.

LaCroix, David. "To Touch Solid Evidence: The Implicity of Past and Present in Octavia E. Butler's *Kindred*." *The Journal of the Midwest Modern Language Association* 40.1 (Spring 2007): 109–19. Print.

Ladino, Jennifer K. *Reclaiming Nostalgia: Longing for Nature in American Literature*. Charlottesville, VA: U of Virginia P, 2012. Print.

Lambert, Constant. *Music Ho! A Study of Music in Decline*. New York: October House, 1967. Print.

Langley, April. "Lucy Terry Prince: The Cultural and Literary Legacy of Africana Womanism." *The Western Journal of Black Studies* 25.3 (2001): 153–62. *Academic Search Premier*. Web. 5 Nov. 2013.

Larsen, Nella. *The Complete Fiction of Nella Larsen*. Ed. Charles R. Larson. New York: Anchor, 1992. Print.

Lauter, Paul. "Melville Climbs the Canon." *American Literature* 66.1 (1994): 1–24. Print.

Lazarus, Emma. "1492." *Emma Lazarus: Selected Poems*. New York: Library of America, 2005. 87. Print.

———. "The New Colossus." *Emma Lazarus: Selected Poems*. New York: Library of America, 2005. 58. Print.

Le Sueur, Meridel. "Women on the Breadlines." 1932. *Ripening: Selected Works, 1927–1980*. By Meridel Le Sueur. Ed. Elaine Hedges. Old Westbury, NY: Feminist Press, 1982. 137–43. Print.

Lepore, Jill. *The Name of War: King Philip's War and the Origins of American Identity*. New York: Knopf, 1998. Print.

Lewis, R. W.B. *Edith Wharton: A Biography*. New York: Harper, 1975. Print.

Lichtenstein, Diane. "Words and Worlds: Emma Lazarus's Conflicting Citizenships." *Tulsa Studies in Women's Literature* 6.2 (1987). 247–63. Print.

Lim, Shirley Geok-lin. *Approaches to Teaching Kingston's The Woman Warrior*. New York: Modern Language Association, 1991. Print.

Lindemann, Marilee. *Willa Cather: Queering America*. New York: Columbia UP, 1999. Print.

Lindroth, Colette. "America Unmasked: Cultural Commentary in Susan Glaspell's Short Fiction." *Disclosing Intertextualities: The Stories, Plays, and Novels of Susan Glaspell*. Eds. Martha C. Carpentier and Barbara Ozieblo. New York: Rodopi, 2006. 257–74. Print.

Ling, Amy. *Between Worlds: Women Writers of Chinese Ancestry*. New York: Pergamon Press, 1990. Print.

———. "Edith Eaton: Pioneer Chinamerican Writer and Feminist." *American Literary Realism* 16 (Autumn 1983): 287–98. Print.

Locke, Alain. "The New Negro." *The New Negro*. Ed. Alain Locke. 1925. New York: Atheneum, 1977. 3–16. Print.

Loeffelholz, Mary. "What is a Fascicle?" *Harvard Library Bulletin* 10.1 (1999): 23–42. *MLA International Bibliography*. Web. 19 Nov. 2014.

Loos, Anita. *Gentlemen Prefer Blondes: The Illuminating Diary of a Professional Lady and But Gentlemen Marry Brunettes*. Ed. Regina Barreca. New York: Penguin, 1998. Print.

———. *Kiss Hollywood Good-by*. New York: Viking, 1974. Print.

Lorde, Audre. *The Cancer Journals*. San Francisco: Aunt Lute Books, 1980. Print.

——. "Equinox." *From a Land Where Other People Live*. Detroit, MI: Broadside, 1973. 11–12. Print.

——. "A Litany for Survival." *The Black Unicorn*. New York: Norton, 1978. 31–2. Print.

——. "The Master's Tools Will Never Dismantle the Master's House." *Sister Outsider: Essays and Speeches*. Trumansburg, NY: Crossing, 1984. 110–13. Print.

——. "Poetry Is Not a Luxury." 1977. *Sister Outsider: Essays and Speeches*. Trumansburg, NY: Crossing, 1984. 36–9. Print.

——. "The Transformation of Silence into Language and Action." *Sister Outsider: Essays and Speeches by Audre Lorde*. Trumansburg, NY: Crossing, 1984. 40–5. Print.

Lorde, Audre and Adrienne Rich. "An Interview: Audre Lorde and Adrienne Rich." 1981. *Sister Outsider: Essays and Speeches by Audre Lorde*. Trumansburg, NY: Crossing, 1984. 81–109. Print.

Love, Heather. *Feeling Backward: Loss and the Politics of Queer History*. Cambridge, MA: Harvard UP, 2007. Print.

Lowe, Lisa. *Immigrant Acts: On Asian American Cultural Politics*. Durham, NC: Duke UP, 1996. Print.

——. "Unfaithful to the Original: The Subject of *Dictée*." *Writing Self, Writing Nation*. Eds. Elaine H. Kim and Norma Alarcón. Berkeley, CA: Third Woman Press, 1994. 35–72. Print.

Lowell, Amy. "Emily Dickinson." *Poetry and Poets: Essays*. Boston: Houghton Mifflin, 1930. 88–108. Print.

——. "'H.D.' and John Gould Fletcher." *Tendencies in Modern Poetry*. Boston: Houghton Mifflin, 1917. 235–343. Print.

——. *Pictures of the Floating World*. New York: Macmillan, 1919. Print.

Lubin, Alex, ed. *Revising the Blueprint: Ann Petry and the Literary Left*. Jackson, MS: UP of Mississippi. 2007. Print.

Luis-Brown, David. *Waves of Decolonization: Discourses of Race and Hemispheric Citizenship in Cuba, Mexico, and the United States*. Durham, NC: Duke UP, 2008. Print.

Lupton, Mary Jane. "Zora Neale Hurston and the Survival of the Female." *Southern Literary Journal* 15.1 (1982): 45–54. Print.

Lutes, Jean M. "Self-Made Women: Novelists of the 1920s." Bauer 422–45.

Lyon, Janet. "Gender and Sexuality." *The Cambridge Companion to American Modernism*. Ed. Walter Kalaidjian. Cambridge: Cambridge UP, 2005. 221–41. Print.

Ma, Ming-Qian. "Poetry as History Revised: Susan Howe's 'Scattering as Behavior toward Risk.'" *American Literary History* 6.4 (Winter 1994): 716–37. Print.

Mackin, Jonna. "Split Infinitives: The Comedy of Performative Identity in Maxine Hong Kingston's *Tripmaster Monkey*." *Contemporary Literature* 46.3 (Autumn 2005): 511–34. Print.

MacPherson, Heidi Slettedahl. "Contemporary American Women's Writing: Women and Violence." Bauer 539–56.

Mader, Rodney. "Elizabeth Graeme Fergusson's 'The Deserted Wife.'" *The Pennsylvania Magazine of History and Biography* 135.2 (April 2011): 151–90. Print.

Marinetti, F.T. *Critical Writings*. Ed. Günter Berghaus. Trans. Doug Thompson. New York: Farrar, Straus and Giroux, 2006. Print.

Marom, Daniel. "Who Is the 'Mother of Exiles'? Jewish Aspects of Emma Lazarus's 'The New Colossus.'" *Prooftexts* 20 (2000): 231–61. Print.

Marsh, John. "Women on the Breadlines." Bauer 477–500.

Marshall, Megan. *Margaret Fuller: A New American Life*. Boston: Houghton Mifflin Harcourt, 2013. Print.

Martin, Wendy. *An American Triptych: Anne Bradstreet, Emily Dickinson, Adrienne Rich*. Chapel Hill, NC: U of North Carolina P, 1984. Print.

———. *The Cambridge Introduction to Emily Dickinson*. Cambridge: Cambridge UP, 2007. Print.

Mathur, Saloni. "Broadcasting Difference." *Samar* 1.2 (Winter 1992): 2–5. PDF file.

Matsumoto, Valerie J. *City Girls: The Nisei Social World in Los Angeles, 1920–1950*. Oxford: Oxford UP, 2014. Print.

May, Elaine Tyler. *Homeward Bound: American Families in the Cold War Era*. 2e. New York: Basic, 2008. Print.

Mays, Dorothy A. *Women in Early America: Struggle, Survival, and Freedom in a New World*. Santa Barbara, CA: ABC-CLIO, 2004. Print.

McCann, Sean. "'Bonds of Brotherhood': Pauline Hopkins and the Work of Melodrama." *ELH* 64.3 (Fall 1997): 789–822. Print.

McCarthy, Mary. *The Group*. New York: Harcourt, Brace & World, 1963. Print.

McCullers, Carson. *The Heart Is a Lonely Hunter*. 1940. New York: Houghton Mifflin, 1967. Print.

McCullough, Kate. *Regions of Identity: The Construction of America in Women's Fiction, 1885–1914*. Stanford, CA: Stanford UP, 1999. Print.

McDowell, Margaret B. *Edith Wharton*. 2e. Boston: Twayne, 1991. Print.

McGurl, Mark. *The Novel Art: Elevations of American Fiction After Henry James*. Princeton, NJ: Princeton UP, 2001. Print.

McHenry, Elizabeth. *Forgotten Readers: Recovering the Lost History of African-American Literary Societies*. Durham, NC: Duke UP, 2002. Print.

McQuade, Paula. "Household Religious Instruction in Seventeenth-Century England and America: The Case of Sarah Symmes Fiske's *A Confession of Faith* (Composed 1672)." *ANQ* 24.1–2 (2011): 108–17. Print.

Meer, Sarah. *Uncle Tom Mania: Slavery, Minstrelsy, and Transatlantic Culture in the 1850s*. Athens, GA: U of Georgia P, 2005. Print.

Menke, Pamela Glenn. "Behind the 'White Veil': Alice Dunbar-Nelson, Creole Color, and *The Goodness of St. Rocque*." *Songs of the Reconstructing South: Building Literary Louisiana, 1865–1945*. Eds. Suzanne Disheroon-Green and Lisa Abney. Westport, CT: Greenwood, 2002. 77–88. Print.

Merrim, Stephanie. *Early Modern Women's Writing and Sor Juana Ines de la Cruz*. Nashville, TN: Vanderbilt UP, 1999. Print.

Mersmann, James F. *Out of the Vietnam Vortex: A Study of Poets and Poetry Against the War*. Lawrence, KS: UP of Kansas, 1974. Print.

Michaelsen, Scott. "Narrative and Class in a Culture of Consumption: The Significance of Stories in Sarah Kemble Knight's 'Journal.'" *College Literature* 21.2 (1994): 33–46. *JSTOR*. Web. 2 Feb. 2014.

Mikolchak, Maria. "Kate Chopin's *The Awakening* as Part of the Nineteenth-Century American Literary Tradition." *Interdisciplinary Literary Studies: A Journal of Criticism and Theory* 5.2 (2004): 29–49. Print.

Millay, Edna St. Vincent. *Letters of Edna St. Vincent Millay*. Ed. Allan Ross Macdougall. New York: Harper & Brothers, 1952. Print.

Mills, Bruce. *Cultural Reformations: Lydia Maria Child and the Literature of Reform*. Athens, GA: U of Georgia P, 1994. Print.

Mirikitani, Janice. "Attack the Water." *Awake in the River*. San Francisco: Isthmus, 1978. n. pag. Print.

Moffet, Penelope. "West View: Denise Levertov: A Poet Heeds the Socio-Political Call." *Los Angeles Times Review of Books* 6 June 1982: 3. *ProQuest Historical Newspapers*. Web. 14 May 2015.

Moi, Toril. *Sexual/Textual Politics*. London: Methuen, 1985. Print.

Monda, Kimberly. "Self-Delusion and Self-Sacrifice in Nella Larsen's *Quicksand*." *African American Review* 31.1 (1997): 23–39. Print.

Monroe, Harriet. "Tradition." *Poetry, A Magazine of Verse*. Vol. 2. Chicago: printed by subscription. 1913. Print.

Moore, Lisa L. "Sister Arts: On Adrienne Rich, Audre Lorde, and Others." *Los Angeles Review of Books*. 28 Feb. 2013. Web. 15 June 2015.

Moore, Marianne. "Critics and Connoisseurs." *The Complete Poems of Marianne Moore*. New York: Macmillan/Viking, 1967. 38–9. Print.

Moraga, Cherríe. *Loving in the War Years: Lo Que Nunca Pasó por Sus Labios*. 2e. Cambridge, MA: South End, 2000. Print.

Moraga, Cherríe and Gloria Anzaldúa, eds. *This Bridge Called My Back: Writing by Radical Women of Color*. New York: Women of Color Press, 1983. Print.

Morales, Aurora Levins and Rosario Morales. "Ending Poem." *Getting Home Alive*. Ithaca, NY: Firebrand, 1986. 212–13. Print.

Morgan, Jo-Ann. *Uncle Tom's Cabin as Visual Culture*. Columbia, MO: U of Missouri P, 2007. Print.

Morgan, Thomas Lewis. "Criticizing Local Color: Innovative Conformity in Kate Chopin's Short Fiction." *Arizona Quarterly: A Journal of American Literature, Culture, and Theory* 70.1 (2014): 135–71. Print.

Mori, Chiye (Loretta). "Japanese-American." *Kashu Mainichi* 6 Nov. 1932: 2. Microfilm.

Morrison, Toni. *Beloved*. 1987. New York: Vintage, 2004. Print.

——. *The Bluest Eye*. 1970. New York: Vintage, 2007. Print.

——. "Rootedness: The Ancestor as Foundation." *Black Women Writers (1950–1980): A Critical Evaluation*. Ed. Mari Evans. New York: Anchor/Doubleday, 1984. 339–45. Print.

——. *Song of Solomon*. 1977. New York: Vintage, 2004. Print.

Morrisson, Mark. "Nationalism and the Modern American Canon." *The Cambridge Companion to American Modernism*. Ed. Walter Kalaidjian. Cambridge: Cambridge UP, 2005. 12–38. Print.

Mott, Frank Luther. *A History of American Magazines, 1741–1930*. Cambridge, MA: Belknap of Harvard UP, 1958. Print.

"Mrs. Lucy Prince." *Vermont Gazette* [Bennington, VT], Aug. 14, 1821: 3. *America's Historical Newspapers*. Web. 20 Aug. 2014.

Mulford, Carla, ed. and introduction. *Only for the Eyes of a Friend: The Poems of Annis Boudinot Stockton*. Charlottesville, VA: U of Virginia P, 1994. Print.

——. "Writing Women in Early American Studies: On Canons, Feminist Critique, and the Work of Writing Women into History." *Tulsa Studies in Women's Literature* 26.1 (Spring 2007): 107–18. Print.

Mullen, Bill. "Object Lessons: Fetishization and Class Consciousness in Ann Petry's *The Street*." *Revising the Blueprint: Ann Petry and the Literary Left*. Ed. Alex Lubin. Jackson, MS: UP of Mississippi, 2007. 35–48. Print.

Munich, Adrienne. "Family Matters: Genealogies and Intertexts in Amy Lowell's 'The Sisters.'" *Amy Lowell, American Modern*. Eds. Adrienne Munich and Melissa Bradshaw. New Brunswick, NJ: Rutgers UP, 2004. 9–26. Print.

Murphy, Brenda. "American Women Playwrights." Bauer 352–68.

Murray, Alice Yang. *Historical Memories of the Japanese American Internment and the Struggle for Redress*. Stanford, CA: Stanford UP, 2008. Print.

Murray, Judith Sargent. *The Gleaner: A Miscellaneous Production in Three Volumes*. 3 vols. Boston: Thomas and Andrews, 1798. *Eighteenth Century Collections Online*. Web. 21 Aug. 2014.

———. *Selected Writings of Judith Sargent Murray*. Ed. Sharon M. Harris. New York: Oxford UP, 1995. Print.

National Center for Veterans Affairs Analysis and Statistics. *America's Women Veterans: Military Service History and VA Benefit Utilization Statistics*. Washington, DC: U.S. Dept. of Veterans Affairs, 23 Nov. 2011. PDF file.

Naylor, Gloria. "Love and Sex in the Afro-American Novel." *Yale Review* 78.1 (Spring 1989): 19–31. Print.

Neal, Larry. "The Black Arts Movement." *The Drama Review* 12.4 (Summer 1968): 28–39. Print.

Nelson, Deborah. "Confessional Poetry." Ashton *Cambridge* 31–46.

Nicholls, David G. "Migrant Labor, Folklore, and Resistance in Hurston's Polk County: Reframing *Mules and Men*." *African American Review* 33.3 (1999): 467–79. Print.

Nichols, Catherine. "Homme de Plume: What I Learned Sending My Novel Out Under a Male Name." *Jezebel.com*. 4 Aug. 2015. Web. 5 Aug. 2015.

Noble, Marianne. *The Masochistic Pleasures of Sentimental Literature*. Princeton, NJ: Princeton UP, 2000. Print.

Norris, Frank. "Zola as a Romantic Writer." *The Wave* 27 June 1896: 3. PDF file.

North, Michael. *Novelty: A History of the New*. Chicago: U of Chicago P, 2013. Print.

Norton, Mary Beth. *Liberty's Daughters: The Revolutionary Experience of American Women, 1750–1800*. Ithaca, NY: Cornell UP, 1980. Print.

Nussbaum, Felicity. *"The Brink of All We Hate": English Satires on Women, 1760–1750*. Lexington, KY: UP of Kentucky, 1984. Print.

O'Connor, Flannery. "Good Country People." *A Good Man Is Hard to Find*. New York: Harcourt, Brace, 1955. 169–96. Print.

———. "The Life You Save May Be Your Own." *A Good Man Is Hard to Find*. New York: Harcourt, Brace, 1955. 53–68. Print.

O'Neill, Kimberly. "Latina Writers and the Usable Past." Bauer 590–607.

Oates, Joyce Carol. "Where Are You Going, Where Have You Been?" *Where Are You Going, Where Have You Been? Stories of Young America*. Greenwich, CT: Fawcett, 1974. 11–31. Print.

Obejas, Achy. *Days of Awe*. New York: Ballantine Books, 2001. Print.

———. *Memory Mambo: A Novel*. Pittsburgh, PA: Cleis Press, 1996. Print.

———. *We Came All the Way from Cuba So You Could Dress Like This?* Pittsburgh, PA: Cleis Press, 1994. Print.

Oktenberg, Adrian. "'Disloyal to Civilization': The *Twenty-One Love Poems* of Adrienne Rich." *Reading Adrienne Rich: Reviews and Re-Visions, 1951–81*. Ed. Jane Roberta Cooper. Ann Arbor, MI: U of Michigan P, 1984. 72–90. Print.

Olsen, Tillie (Tillie Lerner). "I Want You Women Up North to Know." 1934. *Feminist Studies* 7.3 (Autumn 1981): 367–70. Print.

Ong, Aiwah. *Flexible Citizenship: The Cultural Logics of Transnationality*. Durham, NC: Duke UP, 1999. Print.

Ortiz, Simon J. "Towards a National Indian Literature: Cultural Authenticity in Nationalism." 1981. *American Indian Literary Nationalism*. Eds. Jace Weaver, Craig S. Womack, and Robert Warrior. Albuquerque, NM: U of New Mexico P, 2006. 253–60. Print.

Ortolano, Scott. "Liberation, Degeneration, and Transcendence(?): The Promise and Paradox of the 'New Woman' in Edna Ferber's *Dawn O'Hara, the Girl Who Laughed* and Dorothy Parker's 'Big Blonde.'" Forthcoming from *Women's Studies: An Interdisciplinary Journal* 45.3 (Apr./May 2016).

Osgood, Frances Sargent Locke. "The Wraith of the Rose." *Nineteenth Century American Women Poets: An Anthology*. Ed. Paula Bernat Bennett. Oxford: Blackwell Publishers, 1998. 63–4. Print.

Ostriker, Alicia Suskin. *Stealing the Language: The Emergence of Women's Poetry in America.* Boston: Beacon, 1986, Print.

Ousterhout, Anne M. *The Most Learned Woman in America: A Life of Elizabeth Graeme Fergusson.* University Park, PA: Penn State UP, 2004. Print.

Owens, Louis. "Erdrich and Dorris's Mixed-Bloods and Multiple Narratives." *Louise Erdrich's Love Medicine: A Casebook.* Ed. Hertha Dawn Wong. Oxford: Oxford UP, 2000. 53–66. Print.

Painter, Nell Irvin. "Honest Abe and Uncle Tom." *Canadian Review of American Studies / Revue Canadienne d'Etudes Américaines* 30.3 (Jan. 2000): 245–72. Print.

Paley, Grace. "A Conversation with My Father." *Enormous Changes at the Last Minute.* New York: Farrar Straus Giroux, 1974. 159–67. Print.

Parker, Dorothy. "The Art of Fiction XIII: Dorothy Parker." *Paris Review* 13 (1956): 73–87. Print.

Parker, Robert Dale, ed. and introduction. *The Sound the Stars Make Rushing Through the Sky: The Writings of Jane Johnston Schoolcraft.* Philadelphia: U of Pennsylvania P, 2007. Print.

Parks, Edd Winfield. "Edna St. Vincent Millay." *Sewanee Review* 38 (1930): 42–9. Print.

Parry-Giles, Shawn J. and Diane M. Blair. "The Rise of the Rhetorical First Lady: Politics, Gender Ideology, and Women's Voice, 1789–2002." *Rhetoric & Public Affairs* 5.4 (Winter 2002): 565–99. Print.

Patterson, Martha H. *Beyond the Gibson Girl: Reimagining the American New Woman, 1895–1915.* Urbana, IL: U of Illinois P, 2005. Print.

Pearsall, Sarah M.S. "Gender." Armitage and Braddick 113–32.

Pegues, Dagmar. "Fear and Desire: Regional Aesthetics and Colonial Desire in Kate Chopin's Portrayals of the Tragic Mulatta Stereotype." *Southern Literary Journal* 43.1 (2010): 1–22. Print.

Perloff, Marjorie. "'Collision or Collusion with History': The Narrative Lyric of Susan Howe." *Contemporary Literature* 30.4 (1989): 518–33. Print.

Perry, Mark. *Lift Up Thy Voice: The Grimké Family's Journey from Slaveholders to Civil Rights Leaders.* New York: Viking, 2001. Print.

Pestana, Carla Gardina. "Religion." Armitage and Braddick 69–89.

Peterson, Mark A. "The Plymouth Church and the Evolution of New England Religious Culture." *New England Quarterly* 66.4 (Dec. 1993): 570–93. Print.

Peterson, Nancy J. "Introduction: Canonizing Toni Morrison." *Modern Fiction Studies* 39 (Fall/Winter 1993): 461–79. Print.

Peterson, Rachel. "Invisible Hands at Work: Domestic Service and Meritocracy in Ann Petry's Novels." *Revising the Blueprint: Ann Petry and the Literary Left.* Ed. Alex Lubin. Jackson, MS: UP of Mississippi, 2007. 72–96. Print.

Petrino, Elizabeth A. "'Silent Eloquence': The Social Codification of Floral Metaphors in the Poems of Frances Sargent Osgood and Emily Dickinson." *Legacy* 15.2 (1998): 139–57. JSTOR. Web. 19 Sep. 2014.

Pfeiffer, Kathleen. "*Summer* and Its Critics' Discomfort." *Women's Studies: An Interdisciplinary Journal* 20.2 (1991): 141–52. Print.

Phillips, Kate. *Helen Hunt Jackson: A Literary Life.* Berkeley, CA: U of California P, 2003. Print.

Phillips-Anderson, Michael. "Sojourner Truth, 'Address at the Woman's Rights Convention in Akron, Ohio,' (29 May 1851)." *Voices of Democracy* 7 (2012): 21–46. *Voices of Democracy: The U.S. Oratory Project.* Web. 7 Mar. 2012.

Pizer, Donald. *Realism and Naturalism in Nineteenth-Century American Literature.* Rev. ed. Carbondale, IL: Southern Illinois UP, 1984. Print.

Plant, Deborah. "The Folk Preacher and Folk Sermon in Zora Neale Hurston's *Dust Tracks on a Road.*" *Zora Neale Hurston.* Ed. Harold Bloom. New York: Chelsea House, 1986. 7–22. Print.

Plath, Sylvia. *The Bell Jar*. Foreword by Frances McCullough. New York: Harper Collins, 1996. Print.

——. "Lesbos." *Ariel: The Restored Edition*. Foreword by Frieda Hughes. New York: Harper Perennial, 2004. 38–40. Print.

Pollard, Cherise A. "Claiming Joy and Naming Sorrow: Exploring the Connections Between Womanly Truths and Feminist Practice in Lucille Clifton's Poetry." *Langston Hughes Review* 22 (2008): 19–26. Print.

Porter, Katherine Anne. *Flowering Judas and Other Stories*. New York: Harcourt Brace, 1935. Print.

——. "Gertrude Stein: A Self-Portrait." *Harper's* 1 Dec. 1947: 519–28. PDF file.

Potter, Tiffany. "Writing Indigenous Femininity: Mary Rowlandson's Narrative of Captivity." *Eighteenth-Century Studies* 36.2 (2003): 153–67. *Project Muse*. Web. 5 Oct. 2013.

Potts, William John. "Notes and Queries." *The Pennsylvania Magazine of History and Biography* 3.1 (1879): 109–20. *JSTOR*. Web. 5 Nov. 2013.

Pound, Ezra. "A Retrospect." *Literary Essays of Ezra Pound*. Ed. T.S. Eliot. London: Faber and Faber, 1958. 3–14. Print.

——. "Vorticism." *Fortnightly Review* 96 (1 Sept. 1914): 461–71. PDF file.

Proper, David R. "Lucy Terry Prince: Singer of History." *Reunion* 3.1 (1994): 6. *ProQuest*. Web. 8 Nov. 2013.

Pryse, Marjorie. "Linguistic Regionalism and the Emergence of Chinese American Literature in Sui Sin Far's 'Mrs. Spring Fragrance.'" *Legacy* 27.1 (2010): 83–108. Print.

Raab, Josef. "The Imagined Inter-American Community of María Amparo Ruiz de Burton." *Amerikastudien / American Studies* 53.1 (2008): 77–95. *JSTOR*. Web. 28 Feb. 2015.

Rayson, Ann L. "*Dust Tracks on a Road*: Zora Neale Hurston and the Form of Black Autobiography." *Negro American Literature Forum* 7.2 (1973): 39–45. Print.

"Recent Fiction." *Overland Monthly* 8.46 (Oct. 1886): 435–41. PDF file.

Renker, Elizabeth. "Nineteenth-Century American Women's Poetry: Past and Prospects." Bauer 232–55.

Rexroth, Kenneth, ed. *Four Young Women: Poems*. New York: McGraw-Hill, 1973. Print.

Rich, Adrienne. "Compulsory Heterosexuality and Lesbian Experience." *Blood, Bread, and Poetry: Selected Prose 1975–1985*. New York: Norton, 1986. 23–75. Print.

——. "Diving into the Wreck." *Diving into the Wreck: Poems 1971–1972*. New York: Norton, 1973. 22–4. Print.

——. "The Tensions of Anne Bradstreet." *Lies, Secrets and Silence: Selected Prose, 1966–1978*. New York: Norton, 1979. 21–32. Print.

——. "Transcendental Etude." *The Dream of a Common Language: Poems, 1974–1977*. New York: Norton, 1978. 72–7. Print.

——. "Twenty-One Love Poems." *The Dream of a Common Language: Poems, 1974–1977*. New York: Norton, 1978. 25–36. Print.

——. "When We Dead Awaken: Writing as Re-Vision (1971)." *On Lies, Secrets, and Silence: Selected Prose 1966–1978*. New York: Norton, 1978. 33–49. Print.

Rich, Charlotte J. "An 'Absent Mother': Charlotte Perkins Gilman, *Mag-Marjorie*, and the Politics of Maternal Responsibility." *Charlotte Perkins Gilman: New Texts, New Contexts*. Eds. Jennifer S. Tuttle and Carol Farley Kessler. Columbus, OH: Ohio State UP, 2011. 85–102.

Richards, Eliza. *Gender and the Poetics of Reception in Poe's Circle*. Cambridge: Cambridge UP, 2004. Print.

Richart, Bette. "Marianne Moore: In the Grand Tradition." *Commonweal* 65 (1956): 338–9. Print.

Riesman, David. "The Nylon War." *Abundance for What? And Other Essays*. New York: Doubleday. 1964. 67–79. Print.

Rifkin, Mark. "Romancing Kinship." *GLQ: A Journal of Lesbian and Gay Studies* 12.1 (2006): 27–59. *Academic Search Premier.* Web. 29 Sept. 2014.

Robinson, David M. "Margaret Fuller and the Transcendental Ethos: *Woman in the Nineteenth Century.*" *PMLA* 97.1 (Jan. 1982): 83–98. Print.

Robinson, Marilynne. "The Freedom of a Christian." The Lumen Cristi Institute, Chicago. 16 Feb. 2011. *Vimeo.* Web. 17 July 2015.

Rogin, Michael. *Blackface, White Noise: Jewish Immigrants in the Hollywood Melting Pot.* Berkeley, CA: U of California P, 1996. Print.

Rohy, Valerie. *Anachronism and Its Others: Sexuality, Race, Temporality.* Albany, NY: SUNY Press, 2009. Print.

Rojas, Maythee. "Shaking Up La Familia: Lesbian Motherhood and the Chican@ Nation in Sheila Ortiz Taylor's *Faultline.*" Forthcoming from *Women's Studies: An Interdisciplinary Journal.* 45.2 (Mar. 2016). PDF file.

Rosenmeier, Rosamond. *Anne Bradstreet Revisited.* Boston: Twayne, 1991. Print.

Rosenthal, M.L. "Poetry as Confession." *The Nation* 19 Sept. 1959: 154–5. Print.

Rowlandson, Mary. *The Sovereignty and Goodness of God, Together with the Faithfulness of His Promises Displayed.* Ed. Neal Salisbury. Boston: Bedford, 1997. Print.

Rubin, Joan Shelley. Foreword. Botshon and Goldsmith xi–xvii.

Ruiz, Julie. "Captive Identities: The Gendered Conquest of Mexico in *Who Would Have Thought It?*" *María Amparo Ruiz de Burton: Critical and Pedagogical Perspectives.* Eds. Amelia María de la Luz Montes and Anne Elizabeth Goldman. Lincoln, NE: U of Nebraska P, 2004. 112–32. Print.

Rust, Marion. "'Daughters of America,' *Slaves in Algiers*: Activism and Abnegation off Rowson's Barbary Coast." *Feminist Interventions in Early American Studies.* Ed. Mary C. Carruth. Tuscaloosa, AL: U of Alabama P, 2006. 227–39. Print.

Ryan, Maureen. "'The Other Side of Grief': American Women Writers and the Vietnam War." *Critique: Studies in Contemporary Fiction* 36.1 (1994): 41–58. Print.

Ryan, Susan M. "Moral Authority as Literary Property in Mid-Nineteenth-Century Print Culture." Bauer 165–84.

Sabine, Maureen. *Maxine Hong Kingston's Broken Book of Life: An Intertextual Study of The Woman Warrior and China Men.* Honolulu, HI: U of Hawai'i P, 2004. Print.

Salisbury, Neal, ed. and introduction. *The Sovereignty and Goodness of God, with Related Documents.* By Mary Rowlandson. Boston: Bedford, 1997. Print.

Salska, Agnieska. "Puritan Poetry: Its Public and Private Strain." *Early American Literature* 19 (1984): 107–21. Print.

San Juan, E., Jr. "Dialectics of Aesthetics and Politics in Maxine Hong Kingston's *The Fifth Book of Peace.*" *Criticism* 51.2 (Spring 2009): 181–209. Print.

Sánchez, María Carla. "'Prayers in the Market Place': Women and Low Culture in Catharine Sedgwick's 'Cacoethes Scribendi.'" *ATQ: American Transcendental Quarterly* 10 (Mar. 1996): 41–58. Print.

Sánchez-Eppler, Karen. *Touching Liberty: Abolition, Feminism, and the Politics of the Body.* Berkeley, CA: U of California P, 1993. Print.

Sarkela, Sandra J. "Freedom's Call: The Persuasive Power of Mercy Otis Warren's Dramatic Sketches, 1772–5." *Early American Literature* 44.3 (2009): 541–68. Print.

Scanlon, Jennifer. "What's an Acquisitive Girl to Do? Chick Lit and the Great Recession." *Women's Studies: An Interdisciplinary Journal* 42.8 (2013): 904–22. Print.

Schechter, Patricia A. *Ida B. Wells-Barnett and American Reform, 1880–1930.* Chapel Hill, NC: U of North Carolina P, 2001. Print.

Scheiber, Andrew. "Mastery and Majesty: Subject, Object, and the Power of Authorship in Catharine Sedgwick's 'Cacoethes Scribendi.'" *ATQ: American Transcendental Quarterly* 10 (March 1996): 41–58. Print.

Scheick, William J. "Dipolarity and Narration in Glasgow's *The Descendant.*" *Mississippi Quarterly* 49.2 (March 1996): 373–88. Print.

Schloesser, Pauline. *The Fair Sex: White Women and Racial Patriarchy in the Early American Republic.* New York: New York UP, 2002. Print.

Schneider, Bethany. "Not for Citation: Jane Johnston Schoolcraft's Synchronic Strategies." *ESQ: A Journal of the American Renaissance* 54.1–4 (2008): 111–44. Print.

Schoolcraft, Henry Rowe. *Personal Memoirs of a Residence of Thirty Years with the Indian Tribes on the American Frontiers.* Philadelphia: Lippincott, Grambo, 1851. Print.

Schoolcraft, Jane Johnston. *The Sound the Stars Make Rushing Through the Sky: The Writings of Jane Johnston Schoolcraft.* Ed. Robert Dale Parker. Philadelphia: U of Pennsylvania P, 2007. Print.

Schor, Esther. *Emma Lazarus.* New York: Schocken, 2006. Print.

Schrag, Peter. *Not Fit for Our Society: Nativism and Immigration.* Berkeley, CA: U of California P, 2010. Print.

Schrecker, Ellen. *Many Are the Crimes: McCarthyism in America.* Boston: Little, Brown, 1998. Print.

Schreiber, Evelyn Jaffe. *Race, Trauma, and Home in the Novels of Toni Morrison.* Baton Rouge, LA: Louisiana State UP, 2010. Print.

Schulze, Robin G. "Harriet Monroe's Pioneer Modernism: Nature, National Identity, and *Poetry, A Magazine of Verse.*" *Legacy* 21.1 (2004): 50–67. Print.

Schweik, Susan. *A Gulf So Deeply Cut: American Women Poets and the Second World War.* Madison, WI: U of Wisconsin P, 1991. Print.

Schweitzer, Ivy. "Anne Bradstreet Wrestles with the Renaissance." *Early American Literature* 23 (1988): 291–312. Print.

——. "My Body / Not to Either State Inclined: Early American Women Challenge Feminist Criticism." *Early American Literature* 44.2 (2009): 405–10. Print.

Sedgwick, Catharine Maria. "Cacoethes Scribendi." *The Vintage Book of American Women Writers.* Ed. Elaine Showalter. New York: Vintage, 2011. 64–76. Print.

——. *Hope Leslie; or, Early Times in the Massachusetts.* Ed. Mary Kelley. New Brunswick, NJ: Rutgers UP, 1987. Print.

——. *Redwood; A Tale.* New York: Bliss and White, 1824. Microfilm.

Sedgwick, Eve Kosofsky. *Epistemology of the Closet.* Berkeley, CA: U of California P, 1990. Print.

Senier, Siobhan. *Voices of American Indian Assimilation and Resistance: Helen Hunt Jackson, Sarah Winnemucca, and Victoria Howard.* Norman, OK: U of Oklahoma P, 2001. Print.

Sewell, Lisa. "Feminist Poetries." Ashton *Cambridge* 109–26.

Sexton, Anne. "For John, Who Begs Me Not to Enquire Further." *The Complete Poems.* Boston: Houghton Mifflin, 1981. 34–5. Print.

——. "Self in 1958." *Live or Die.* Boston: Houghton Mifflin, 1966. 73–4. Print.

Shafer, Yvonne. "O'Neill, Glaspell, and John Reed: Antiwar, Pro-American Reformers." *Eugene O'Neill Review* 32 (2010): 70–85. PDF file.

Shaffer, Jason. *Performing Patriotism: National Identity in the Colonial and Revolutionary American Theater.* Philadelphia: U of Penn P, 2007. Print.

Shange, Ntozake. *For Colored Girls Who Have Considered Suicide / When the Rainbow Is Enuf.* New York: Macmillan, 1975. Print.

Shea, Daniel. "Elizabeth Ashbridge and the Voice Within." *Journeys in New Worlds: Early American Women's Narratives.* Ed. William L. Andrews. Madison, WI: U of Wisconsin P, 1990. 119–46. Print.

Sherrard-Johnson, Cherene. "The Geography of Ladyhood: Racializing the Novel of Manners." Bauer 404–21.

Shields, David S. *Civil Tongues and Polite Letters in British America*. Chapel Hill, NC: U of North Carolina P, 1997. Print.

Shields, John C. *Phillis Wheatley's Poetics of Liberation: Backgrounds and Contexts*. Knoxville: U of Tennessee P, 2008. Print.

Showalter, Elaine, ed. and introduction. *Alternative Alcott*. By Louisa May Alcott. Brunswick, NJ: Rutgers UP, 1988. Print.

———. *A Jury of Her Peers: American Women Writers from Anne Bradstreet to Annie Proulx*. New York: Knopf, 2009. Print.

———. "Tradition and the Female Talent: *The Awakening* as a Solitary Book." *New Essays on The Awakening*. Ed. Wendy Martin. New York: Cambridge UP, 1988. 33–58. Print.

Sigourney, Lydia Huntley. "Death of an Infant." *Nineteenth Century American Women Poets: An Anthology*. Ed. Paula Bernat Bennett. Oxford: Blackwell Publishers, 1998. 6. Print.

———. "Indian Names." *Lydia Sigourney: Selected Poetry and Prose*. Ed. Gary Kelly. Toronto: Broadhead, 2008. 149–51. Print.

———. *Letters of Life*. New York: Appleton, 1867. Print.

Silber, Nina. *The Romance of Reunion: Northerners and the South, 1865–1900*. Chapel Hill, NC: U of North Carolina P, 1993. Print.

Silberman, Robert. "Opening the Text: *Love Medicine* and the Return of the Native American Woman." *Narrative Chance: Postmodern Discourse on Native American Literatures*. Ed. Gerald Vizenor. Norman, OK: U of Oklahoma P, 1993. 101–20. Print.

Silko, Leslie Marmon. *Conversations with Leslie Marmon Silko*. Ed. Ellen M. Arnold. Jackson, MS: U of Mississippi P, 2000. Print.

———. "Lullaby." *Storyteller*. New York: Arcade, 1981. 43–51. Print.

Silliman, Ron. Foreword. *Veil: New and Selected Poems*. By Rae Armantrout. Middletown, CT: Wesleyan UP, 2001. ix–xvi. Print.

Silverman, Debra B. "Nella Larsen's *Quicksand*: Untangling the Webs of Exoticism." *African American Review* 27.4 (1993): 599–614. Print.

Simpson, Audra. "From White into Red: Captivity Narratives as Alchemies of Race and Citizenship." *American Quarterly* 60.2 (June 2008): 251–7. Print.

Slotten, Martha C. "Elizabeth Graeme Fergusson: A Poet in 'The Athens of North America.'" *The Pennsylvania Magazine of History and Biography* 108.3 (Jul. 1984): 259–88. Print.

Smith, Dale. *Poets Beyond the Barricade: Rhetoric, Citizenship, and Dissent After 1960*. Tuscaloosa, AL: U of Alabama P, 2012. Print.

Smith, Stephanie. "Turn-of-the-Twentieth-Century Transitions: Women on the Edge of Tomorrow." Bauer 369–86.

Smith, Valerie. "*Song of Solomon*: Continuities of Community." *Toni Morrison: Critical Perspectives Past and Present*. Eds. Henry Louis Gates, Jr., and K.A. Appiah. New York: Amistad, 1993. 274–83. Print.

Smith-Rosenberg, Carroll. *Disorderly Conduct: Visions of Gender in Victorian America*. Oxford: Oxford UP, 1985. Print.

Smyth, J.E. *Edna Ferber's Hollywood*. Austin, TX: U of Texas P, 2010. Print.

Snader, Joe. *Caught Between Worlds: British Captivity Narratives in Fact and Fiction*. Lexington, KY: UP of Kentucky, 2000. Print.

Sofer, Andrew. "Maria Irene Fornes: Acts of Translation." *A Companion to Twentieth-Century American Drama*. Ed. David Krasner. Oxford: Blackwell, 2005. 440–55. Print.

Sollors, Werner. *Beyond Ethnicity: Consent and Descent in American Culture*. Oxford: Oxford UP, 1986. Print.

Somerville, Siobhan. "Passing through the Closet in Pauline E. Hopkins' *Contending Forces*." *American Literature* 69.1 (Mar. 1997): 138–66). Print.

Sorensen, Lise. "Susanna Rowson and the Transatlantic Captivity Narrative." *Transatlantic Literary Studies, 1660–1830*. Eds. Eve Tavor Bannet and Susan Manning. Cambridge: Cambridge UP, 2011. 169–85. Print.

Sorisio, Carolyn. "Sarah Winnemucca, Translation, and US Colonialism and Imperialism." *MELUS* 37.1 (2012): 35–60. *Academic Search Premier*. Web. 28 Sept. 2014.

——. "The Spectacle of the Body: Torture in the Antislavery Writing of Lydia Maria Child and Frances E.W. Harper." *Modern Language Studies* 30.1 (Spring 2000): 45–66. Print.

Southworth, E.D.E.N. *The Hidden Hand or, Capitola the Madcap*. Ed. Joanne Dobson. New Brunswick, NJ: Rutgers UP, 1988. Print.

Spigel, Lynn. *Make Room for TV: Television and the Family Ideal in Postwar America*. Chicago: U of Chicago P, 1992. Print.

Spillers, Hortense. "Afterword: Cross-Currents, Discontinuities: Black Women's Fiction." *Conjuring: Black Women, Fiction, and Literary Tradition*. Eds. Marjorie Pryse and Hortense J. Spillers. Bloomington, IN: Indiana UP, 1985. 249–61. Print.

Stabile, Susan M. *Memory's Daughters: The Material Culture of Remembrance in Eighteenth-Century America*. Ithaca, NY: Cornell UP, 2004. Print.

Stanford, Ann. *Anne Bradstreet, the Worldly Puritan: An Introduction to Her Poetry*. New York: B. Franklin, 1975. Print.

Stansell, Christine. *American Moderns: Bohemian New York and the New Century*. Princeton, NJ: Princeton UP, 2009. Print.

Steedman, Carolyn. "Poetical Maids and Cooks Who Wrote." *Eighteenth-Century Studies* 39.1 (Fall 2005), 1–27. Print.

Stein, Gertrude. *The Making of Americans*. 1925. Normal, IL: Dalkey Archive P, 1995. Print.

Stetson, Erlene, ed. *Black Sister: Poetry by Black American Women, 1746–1980*. Bloomington: Indiana UP, 1981. Print.

Stinson, Robert. "Ida M. Tarbell and the Ambiguities of Feminism." *Pennsylvania Magazine of History and Biography* 101.2 (Apr. 1977): 217–39. Print.

Stockton, Annis Boudinot. *Only for the Eye of a Friend: The Poems of Annis Boudinot Stockton*. Ed. Carla Mulford. Charlottesville, VA: U of Virginia P, 1995. Print.

Stover, Johnnie M. "Nineteenth-Century African American Women's Autobiography as Social Discourse: The Example of Harriet Ann Jacobs." *College English* 66.2 (2003): 133–54. Print.

Stowe, Harriet Beecher. *Uncle Tom's Cabin*. Ed. Elizabeth Ammons. New York: Norton, 1994. Print.

Strong, Pauline Turner. *American Indians and the American Imaginary: Cultural Representation Across the Centuries*. Boulder, CO: Paradigm, 2012. Print.

Sui Sin Far (Edith Maude Eaton). "The Inferior Woman." *Mrs. Spring Fragrance and Other Writings*. Eds. Amy Ling and Annette White-Parks. Urbana, IL: U of Illinois P, 1995. 28–41. Print.

Suyemoto, Toyo. "Gain." *I Call to Remembrance: Toyo Suyemoto's Years of Internment*. Ed. Susan B. Richardson. New Brunswick, NJ: Rutgers UP, 2007. 128. Print.

Sweet, Timothy. "Gender, Genre, and Subjectivity in Anne Bradstreet's Early Elegies." *Early American Literature* 23 (1988): 152–74. Print.

Takaki, Ronald. *Strangers from a Distant Shore: A History of Asian Americans*. Boston: Back Bay Books, 1998. Print.

Tarbell, Ida. *All in the Day's Work*. New York: Macmillan, 1939. Print.

Tate, Claudia. *Domestic Allegories of Political Desire: The Black Heroine's Text at the Turn of the Century*. Oxford: Oxford UP, 1988. Print.

——. "Maya Angelou: An Interview." 1983. *Maya Angelou's I Know Why the Caged Bird Sings: A Casebook*. Ed. Joanne Braxton. Oxford: Oxford UP, 1999. 149–58. Print.

Terry, Lucy. "Bars Fight." Gates and McKay 186–7.

Thornton, Russell. "Health, Disease, and Demography." Deloria and Salisbury 68–84.

Thurber, James. *Collecting Himself: James Thurber on Writing and Writers, Humor and Himself.* Ed. Michael J. Rosen. New York: Harper & Row, 1989. Print.

Tolentino, Cynthia. "Equatorial Archipelagoes." *The Routledge Companion to Asian American and Pacific Islander Literature.* Ed. Rachel C. Lee. London: Routledge, 2014. 268–78. Print.

Tomlinson, Susan. "'An Unwonted Coquetry': The Commercial Seductions of Jessie Fauset's *The Chinaberry Tree.*" *Middlebrow Moderns: Popular American Women Writers of the 1920s.* Eds. Lisa Botshon and Meredith Goldsmith. Boston: Northeastern UP, 2003. 227–43. Print.

Tompkins, Jane. *Sensational Designs: The Cultural Work of American Fiction 1790–1860.* New York: Oxford UP, 1985. Print.

Toulouse, Teresa. "The Sovereignty and Goodness of God in 1682: Royal Authority, Female Captivity, and 'Creole' Male Identity." *ELH* 67.4 (2000): 925–49. *Project Muse.* Web. 5 Oct. 2013.

Travis, Jennifer. "Accidents, Agency, and American Literary Naturalism." Bauer 387–403.

Tricomi, Albert. "Dialect and Identity in Harriet Jacobs' Autobiography and Other Slave Narratives." *Callaloo* 29.2 (2006): 619–33. Print.

——. "Harriet Jacobs' Autobiography and the Voice of Lydia Maria Child." *ESQ: A Journal of the American Renaissance* 53.3 (2007): 216–52. Print.

Trousdale, Rachel. "'Humor Saves Steps': Laughter and Humanity in Marianne Moore." *Journal of Modern Literature* 35.3 (2012): 121–38. Print.

Ullman, Leslie. "Review: Solitaries and Storytellers, Magicians and Pagans: Five Poets in the World." *The Kenyon Review* 13.2 (Spring 1991): 179–93. Print.

U.S. Bureau of the Census. *Historical Statistics of the United States 1789–1945.* Washington: U.S. Department of Commerce, 1949. Print.

Veblen, Thorstein. *The Theory of the Leisure Class: An Economic Study of Institutions.* 1899. Ed. Martha Banta. Oxford: Oxford UP, 2007. Print.

"VIDA Announces Changes to the VIDA Count and VIDA Count Team." *VIDA: Women in Literary Arts.* 23 May 2015. Web. 21 Jul. 2015.

Vietto, Angela. *Women and Authorship in Revolutionary America.* Aldershot: Ashgate, 2005. Print.

Vincent, Jonathan. "Women Writers and War." Bauer 30–54.

Walker, Alice. *In Search of Our Mothers' Gardens.* New York: Harcourt Brace Jovanovich, 1983. Print.

Walker, Cheryl. *The Nightingale's Burden: Women Poets and American Culture Before 1900.* Bloomington: Indiana UP, 1982. Print.

——. "Nineteenth-Century American Women Poets Revisited." *Nineteenth-Century American Women Writers: A Critical Reader.* Ed. Karen L. Kilcup. Malden, MA: Blackwell, 1998. 231–44. Print.

Walker, Margaret. "For Malcolm X." *Prophets for a New Day.* Detroit, MI: Broadside, 1970. 18. Print.

Wall, Cheryl A. "Mules and Men and Women: Zora Neale Hurston's Strategies of Narration and Visions of Female Empowerment." *Black American Literature Forum* 23.4 (1989): 661–80. Print.

Waller, Jennifer R. "'My Hand a Needle Better Fits': Anne Bradstreet and Women Poets in the Renaissance." *Dalhousie Review* 54 (1974): 436–50. Print.

Ward, Nathanael. "Mercury Shew'd Apollo." *The Tenth Muse (1650) and, from the Manuscripts, Meditations Divine and Morall Together with Letters and Occasional Pieces.* By Anne Bradstreet. Ed. Josephine K. Piercy. Gainesville, FL: Scholars' Facsimiles & Reprints. 1965. v. Print.

Warren, Mercy Otis. *History of the Rise, Progress, and Termination of the American Revolution, Interspersed with Biographical, Political and Moral Observations.* 2 vols. Ed. Lester H. Cohen. Indianapolis, IN: Liberty Fund, 1994. Print.

———. *Mercy Otis Warren: Selected Letters.* Eds. Sharon M. Harris and Jeffrey H. Richards. Athens, GA: U of Georgia P, 2009. Print.

Warrior, Robert. "A Marginal Voice." *Native Nations* 1.3 (1991): 29–30. Print.

Waterman, Arthur E. "Susan Glaspell and the Provincetown." *Modern Drama* 7.2 (1964): 174–84. Print.

Watts, Emily Stipes. *The Poetry of American Women from 1632 to 1945.* Austin, TX: U of Texas P, 1977. Print.

Weaver, Jace. "Splitting the Earth: First Utterances and Pluralist Separatism." *American Indian Literary Nationalism.* Eds. Jace Weaver, Craig S. Womack, and Robert Warrior. Albuquerque, NM: U of New Mexico P, 2005. 1–89. Print.

Weinbaum, Alys Eve. "Writing Feminist Genealogy: Charlotte Perkins Gilman, Racial Nationalism, and the Reproduction of Maternalist Feminism." *Feminist Studies* 27.2 (2001): 271–302. Print.

Weinberg, Steve. *Taking on the Trust: The Epic Battle of John D. Rockefeller.* New York: Norton, 2008. Print.

Welter, Barbara. "The Cult of True Womanhood: 1820–1860." *American Quarterly* 18 (1966): 151–74. Print.

Westbrook, Perry. *Mary Wilkins Freeman.* Rev. ed. Boston: Twayne, 1988. Print.

Wharton, Edith. *The Age of Innocence.* 1921. Ed. Cynthia Griffin Wolff. New York: Penguin, 1996. Print.

———. *Summer.* 1917. Ed. Elizabeth Ammons. New York: Penguin, 1993. Print.

Wheatley, Phillis. *Complete Writings.* Ed. and introduction Vince Carretta. New York: Penguin, 2001. Print.

White, Elizabeth. *Anne Bradstreet, "The Tenth Muse."* New York: Oxford UP, 1971. Print.

Whitehead, Karsonya Wise, ed. *Notes from a Colored Girl: The Civil War Pocket Diaries of Emilie Frances Davis.* By Emilie Frances Davis. Columbia, SC: U of South Carolina P, 2014. Print.

White-Parks, Annette. *Sui Sin Far/Edith Maude Eaton: A Literary Biography.* Urbana, IL: U of Illinois P, 1995. Print.

Wilcox, Kirstin R. "American Women's Writing in the Colonial Period." Bauer 55–73.

Wilentz, Gay. "Civilizations Underneath: African Heritage as Cultural Discourse in Toni Morrison's *Song of Solomon.*" *Toni Morrison's Song of Solomon: A Casebook.* Ed. Jan Furman. Oxford: Oxford UP, 2003. 137–64. Print.

Wilks, Jennifer M. "New Women and New Negroes: Archetypal Womanhood in *The Living Is Easy.*" *African American Review* 39.4 (Winter 2005): 569–79. Print.

Williams, Kayla. "Women Writing War: A List of Essential Contemporary War Literature by Women." *Los Angeles Review of Books.* 26 May 2014. Web. 16 Jul. 2015.

Williams, Susan S. "Writing, Authorship, and Genius: Literary Women and Modes of Literary Production." Bauer 204–31.

Williams, William Carlos. "Marianne Moore (1948)." *Selected Essays of William Carlos Williams.* New York: Random House, 1954. 292–4. Print.

Winetsky, Michael. "Historical and Performative Liberalism in Susan Glaspell's *Inheritors.*" *Journal of American Drama and Theatre* 23.1 (2011): 5–21. Print.

Wirth-Nesher, Hana. "Jewish American Women Writers." Bauer 458–76.

Wolfe, Andrea Powell. "Chasing the 'Coloured Phantom': Gender Performance as Revealing and Concealing Modernist Ideology in Millay's Sonnets." *Journal of American Culture* 32.2 (June 2009): 155–64. Print.

Wolfe, Tom. "The New Journalism." *The New Journalism.* Eds. Tom Wolfe and E.W. Johnson. New York: Harper & Row, 1973. 3–36. Print.

Wolosky, Shira. "An American-Jewish Typology: Emma Lazarus and the Figure of Christ." *Prooftexts* 16 (1996): 113–25. Print.

——. *Emily Dickinson: A Voice of War*. New Haven, CT: Yale UP, 1984. Print.

Womack, Craig S. "A Single Decade: Book-Length Native Literary Criticism Between 1986 and 1997." *Reasoning Together: The Native Critics Collective*. Eds. Craig S. Womack, Daniel Heath Justice, and Christopher B. Teuton. Norman, OK: U of Oklahoma P, 2008. 3–104. Print.

"Women's Rights Convention." *The Anti-Slavery Bugle* (New-Lisbon, OH) 21 Jun. 1851: 160. *Slavery and Anti-Slavery: A Transnational Archive*. Web. 18 Mar. 2015.

Wong, Sau-ling Cynthia. "Chinese American Literature." *An Interethnic Companion to Asian American Literature*. Ed. King-Kok Cheung. Cambridge: Cambridge UP, 1997. 39–61. Print.

——. "'Sugar Sisterhood': Situating the Amy Tan Phenomenon." *The Ethnic Canon: Histories, Institutions, and Interventions*. Ed. David Palumbo-Liu. Minneapolis, MN: U of Minnesota P, 1995. 174–210. Print.

Woollcott, Alexander. "Second Thoughts on First Nights: The Provincetown Plays." *New York Times* 9 Nov. 1919: XX2. *ProQuest Historical Newspapers*. Web. 14 Apr. 2015.

Worden, Daniel. "'I Like to Be Like a Man': Female Masculinity in Willa Cather's *O Pioneers!* and *My Ántonia*." *Violence, the Arts, and Willa Cather*. Eds. Joseph R. Urgo and Merrill Maguire Skaggs. Madison, NJ: Farleigh Dickinson UP, 2007. 273–81. Print.

Wright, Nancy E. "Epitaphic Conventions and the Reception of Anne Bradstreet's Public Voice." *Early American Literature*. 31.3 (1996): 243–63. Print.

Wyss, Hilary E. "Native Women Writing: Reading Between the Lines." *Tulsa Studies in Women's Literature* 26.1 (Spring 2007): 119–25. Print.

Yamada, Mitsuye. *Camp Notes and Other Poems*. Latham, NY: Women of Color P, 1992. Print.

Yellin, Jean Fagan, ed. and introduction. *Incidents in the Life of a Slave Girl*. By Harriet Jacobs. Cambridge, MA: Harvard UP, 2000. Print.

Yogi, Stan. "Japanese American Literature." *An Interethnic Companion to Asian American Literature*. Ed. King-Kok Cheung. Cambridge: Cambridge UP, 1997. 125–55. Print.

Young, Elizabeth. *Disarming the Nation: Women's Writing and the American Civil War*. Chicago: U of Chicago P, 1999. Print.

Zagarri, Rosemarie. "Mercy Otis Warren on Church and State." *The Forgotten Founders on Religion and Public Life*. Ed. Daniel L. Dreisbach, Mark D. Hall, and Jeffry H. Morrison. Notre Dame, IN: U of Notre Dame P, 2009. 278–94. Print.

Zahedieh, Nuala. "Economy." Armitage and Braddick 51–68.

Zamora, Lois Parkinson. *The Usable Past: The Imagination of History in Recent Fiction of the Americas*. Cambridge: Cambridge UP, 1997. Print.

Zauderer, Naomi B. "Consumption, Production, and Reproduction in the Work of Charlotte Perkins Gilman." *Charlotte Perkins Gilman: Optimist Reformer*. Eds. Jill Rudd and Val Gough. Iowa City, IA: U of Iowa P, 1999. 151–72. Print.

Zibrak, Arielle. "Writing Behind a Curtain: Rebecca Harding Davis and Celebrity Reform." *ESQ: A Journal of the American Renaissance* 60.4 (2014): 522–56. Print.

Zitkala Ša. *American Indian Stories*. Washington, DC: Hayworth, 1921. Print.

Zweizig, Suzanne M. "Bathsheba Bowers (c.1672–1718)." *Legacy* 11.1 (1994): 65–73. *JSTOR*. Web. 5 Nov. 2013.

INDEX

Taylor & Francis eBooks

·Helping you to choose the right eBooks for your Library

Add Routledge titles to your library's digital collection today. Taylor and Francis ebooks contains over 50,000 titles in the Humanities, Social Sciences, Behavioural Sciences, Built Environment and Law.

Choose from a range of subject packages or create your own!

Benefits for you

» Free MARC records
» COUNTER-compliant usage statistics
» Flexible purchase and pricing options
» All titles DRM-free.

Benefits for your user

» Off-site, anytime access via Athens or referring URL
» Print or copy pages or chapters
» Full content search
» Bookmark, highlight and annotate text
» Access to thousands of pages of quality research at the click of a button.

REQUEST YOUR **FREE** INSTITUTIONAL TRIAL TODAY

Free Trials Available
We offer free trials to qualifying academic, corporate and government customers.

eCollections – Choose from over 30 subject eCollections, including:

Archaeology	Language Learning
Architecture	Law
Asian Studies	Literature
Business & Management	Media & Communication
Classical Studies	Middle East Studies
Construction	Music
Creative & Media Arts	Philosophy
Criminology & Criminal Justice	Planning
Economics	Politics
Education	Psychology & Mental Health
Energy	Religion
Engineering	Security
English Language & Linguistics	Social Work
Environment & Sustainability	Sociology
Geography	Sport
Health Studies	Theatre & Performance
History	Tourism, Hospitality & Events

For more information, pricing enquiries or to order a free trial, please contact your local sales team:
www.tandfebooks.com/page/sales

 Routledge
Taylor & Francis Group

The home of
Routledge books

www.tandfebooks.com